MILL'S ETHICAL WRITINGS

COLLIER CLASSICS IN THE HISTORY OF THOUGHT

•

General Editors: Crane Brinton and Paul Edwards

(TITLES PUBLISHED)

BERKELEY: *Berkeley's Philosophical Writings.* Ed. by D. M. Armstrong

GIBBON: *Christianity and the Decline of Rome* (Vol. I of *The Decline and Fall of the Roman Empire*). Abridged and edited by Jacob Sloan, with an Introduction by C. D. Gordon

GIBBON: *Barbarism and the Fall of Rome* (Vol. II of *The Decline and Fall of the Roman Empire*). Abridged and edited by Jacob Sloan, with an Introduction by C. D. Gordon

HOBBES: *Body, Man, and Citizen.* Ed. by Richard S. Peters

HOBBES: *Leviathan.* Ed. by Richard S. Peters

HUME: *Hume's Ethical Writings.* Ed. by Alasdair MacIntyre

HUME: *On Human Nature and Understanding.* Ed. by Anthony Flew

JAMES: *Psychology: Briefer Course.* Foreword by Gardner Murphy

JAMES: *The Varieties of Religious Experience.* Introduction by Reinhold Niebuhr

LOCKE: *Locke's Essay Concerning Human Understanding.* Ed. by Maurice Cranston

LOCKE: *Locke on Politics, Religion, and Education.* Ed. by Maurice Cranston

MILL: *Mill's Essays on Literature and Society.* Ed. by J. B. Schneewind

MILL: *Mill's Ethical Writings.* Ed. by J. B. Schneewind

PRIESTLEY: *Priestley's Writings on Philosophy, Science, and Politics.* Ed. by John Passmore

American Thought before 1900: A Sourcebook from Puritanism to Darwinism. Ed. by Paul Kurtz

American Philosophy in the Twentieth Century: A Sourcebook from Pragmatism to Philosophical Analysis. Ed. by Paul Kurtz

JOHN STUART MILL

Mill's Ethical Writings

EDITED WITH AN INTRODUCTION
BY *J. B. SCHNEEWIND*

A Collier Books Original

COLLIER BOOKS, NEW YORK

COLLIER-MACMILLAN LTD., LONDON

Library of Congress Catalog Card Number: 65-17823

A Collier Books Original
First Edition 1965

ACKNOWLEDGMENT

The editor wishes to acknowledge the kindness
of Messrs. Longmans Green, and Co., for their
gracious permission to reprint lengthy extracts
from *The Letters of John Stuart Mill*, edited
by H. S. R. Elliot, 2 vols., London, 1910, of
which they are the publishers.

The Macmillan Company, New York
Collier-Macmillan Canada Ltd., Toronto, Ontario
Printed in the United States of America

Contents

Introduction

I DETEST as cordially as you can do the party of the 'Movement' "—so wrote Thomas Arnold, the great headmaster of Rugby School, in 1833—"both in France and in England. I detest Jacobinism in its root and in its branch, with all the godless Utilitarianism which is its favourite aspect at this moment in England. Nothing within my knowledge is more utterly wicked than the party of men who, fairly and literally, as I fear, blaspheme not the Son of Man, but the Spirit of God; they hate Christ, because he is of heaven and they are of evil."* This heated comment expresses an attitude which was by no means peculiar to Thomas Arnold. The term "Utilitarianism," which is used now simply as the name of a general type of moral philosophy, was generally taken in the early nineteenth century to refer to the set of doctrines invoked by a particular group of radical reformers to support their clamorous demands for fundamental legal and political changes. It was not only orthodox Christians and political opponents who rejected these doctrines utterly. Thomas Carlyle, for example, addressed the Utilitarian "Word-monger and Motive-grinder, who in thy Logic-mill hast an earthly mechanism for the Godlike itself, and wouldst fain grind out Virtue from the husks of Pleasure," exhorting him to realize that his "pig-philosophy" must be abandoned because, contrary to his belief, "Soul is *not* synonymous with Stomach."† And Macaulay stated his opinion of the political philosophy of the Utilitarians in a caustic review of a volume of essays by James Mill:‡

> The civilised part of the world has now nothing to fear from the hostility of savage nations. . . . But is it possible that in the bosom of civilization itself may be engendered

* From a letter to Bunsen, dated May 6, 1832, quoted in A. P. Stanley, *Life of Thomas Arnold.*
† Thomas Carlyle, *Sartor Resartus*, Bk. II, ch. 7.
‡ T. B. Macaulay, review of James Mill's "Essay on Government," first published in the *Edinburgh Review*, March, 1829.

7

the malady which shall destroy it? Is it possible that institutions may be established which, without the help of earthquake, of famine, of pestilence, or of the foreign sword, may undo the work of so many ages of wisdom and glory, and gradually sweep away everything but the rude arts necessary to the support of animal life? Is it possible that, in two or three hundred years, a few lean and half-naked fishermen may divide with owls and foxes the ruins of the greatest European cities—may wash their nets amidst the relics of her gigantic docks, and build their huts out of the capitals of her stately cathedrals? If the principles of Mr. Mill be sound, we say, without hesitation, that the form of government which he recommends will assuredly produce all this.

What, then, were the views that called forth such universal vituperation? They are views that can be traced back as far as the Epicureans, and that had been propounded in England, in various forms, by a line of thinkers from Hobbes to Priestley. As they were used by Jeremy Bentham and James Mill—the leaders of the radical reform movement—they center on two theories, one moral and one psychological. (i) The core of the moral theory is that man's ultimate good is happiness. "The greatest happiness of the greatest number" is the slogan in which Bentham sums up what he holds to be the final goal of all right action: as much happiness as possible for as many people as possible. And happiness consists simply in pleasure and the absence of pain, in a life in which on the whole there is a surplus of pleasure over pain. Our aim must therefore be to create a world in which this sort of life is lived by everyone. From this goal is derived the Benthamite rule for determining what we ought to do: make a scientific investigation of what pleases and what pains men, add up the pleasures resulting from any course of action for all those who are affected by it, subtract the sum of the pains that would result from the action, do the same for all the other alternatives open to the agent, and pick the act that yields the greatest positive surplus (or, if we must make a choice among evils, the least negative surplus). (ii) The major psychological thesis is that each man acts to obtain what he takes to be his *own* greatest good, that is, the greatest surplus of pleasure over pain *for himself*. Our motive in voluntary action is always the thought of some pleasure to be obtained or some pain to be avoided, and the only difference among motives is the difference in the sources of pleasure or pain.

Taken together, these two theories give rise to a problem: how *can* we do what we ought to do? We ought to act so as to bring about the greatest good of all, but we necessarily do act so as to try to bring about our own greatest good. The answer lies in what Bentham calls the "Duty-and-Interest-Juncture-Producing-Principle." Society must be arranged so that the two goals will coincide, so that in acting to obtain one's own good one will in fact be doing the best that can be done to bring about the general good. This can be managed, Bentham thinks, by artificially creating motives to do acts which are beneficial and to abstain from acts which are harmful. We can attach rewards to helpful acts and punishments to harmful ones, and these "sanctions," as Bentham calls them, may be made strong enough to overbalance men's propensities to act in undesirable ways. Some sanctions will be imposed formally by legislation, others informally by public opinion. Together, the two kinds of sanction will be sufficient to give men motives to act as they ought, and thus sufficient to make men good.

Clearly this is not a view that appeals primarily to nobility of character, to self-sacrifice, or to duty for duty's sake. It is, moreover, in Bentham's hands, a radically secular view. The moral theory does not depend on religious revelation or religious belief in any way, and religious motives find no special place in Bentham's scheme, for all motives, religious ones included, are pleasures and pains, and all work in exactly the same way. The view is secular also in rejecting any postponement of human satisfaction to some other world. It insists that men be made happy here and, if possible, now. Bentham puts his trust in legal and administrative arrangements. See to it that it is to the interest of each man and each group to do what will be for the interest of all, and you may hope for social improvement; otherwise not. The constant use of the "Duty-and-Interest-Juncture-Producing-Principle" gives point to Carlyle's pungent summary of Bentham's problem. It is a demand, he says, for an impossible alchemy: "Given a world of Knaves, to produce an Honesty from their united Action."*

* Thomas Carlyle, *Past and Present*, Bk. I, ch. 4.

Yet the men who held these views were as far from being "knaves" as men can be. They were disinterested and high-minded reformers—or, in Bentham's terminology, they were men who, by some fortunate quirk of their psychological make-up, just happened to take great pleasure in making the world better for others. Bentham was certainly such a man, and if James Mill was neither as amiable in character nor as sunny in disposition, he was no less devoted to the cause of the people. Not the least of what he intended to give them was a leader to carry on after the death of Bentham and himself: his first son.

MILL'S LIFE AND WRITINGS

John Stuart Mill was born in London on May 20, 1806. His father was a Scot who had come to England to make his career. Like Carlyle and many others, James Mill supported himself by his writings, and his writings brought him to the attention of Bentham, who had already published a number of important works on legal philosophy and legal reform. In a very short time Mill came to be Bentham's most important associate, not simply by accepting and propagating his theories but also by stimulating him to attack new problems and to take a more direct interest in the pressing issues of the day. Gradually a group of followers gathered around the two men. The all-absorbing concern that held them together was reform of institutions: of Parliament, first and foremost, and of the system whereby its members were chosen; of prisons; of the whole machinery of law; of educational institutions; of the place of the established church in the state; of economic practices—in short, of any organized aspect of the life of society which seemed to them to be either positively harmful or not as beneficial as it might be. And that included practically everything. John Stuart Mill was brought up in the midst of these men and their activities and was intended by his father and by Bentham, who took a great interest in him, to succeed them in leading the movement. James Mill taught his son personally, giving him one of the most famous educations ever recorded.* It included not only a formidable training in classics, history, economics, philosophy, and science, but a thorough indoctrination in Bentham-

* It is described at length in Mill's *Autobiography*, chs. I–III.

ism as well. The treatment seemed to work superbly. Mill absorbed his father's aims along with his father's information and at the age of fifteen decided that there was only one thing he wanted to be: "a reformer in the world."

This was a desire that never left him. He did, however, lose his early naïve confidence in the adequacy of the views of Bentham and his father. At the age of twenty, Mill passed through a period of intense depression. The achievement of all that he wanted for the reform of the world would leave him, he felt, cold, unmoved, and indifferent. For a while he feared that his intensively analytic training had destroyed all his capacity for emotion, and he was—typically—haunted by the awful thought that a similar state of ennui and despair might come to everyone, once the struggle for bare existence was lightened and physical comfort and security could be taken for granted. His depression began to disappear when he found that he could still weep (it was a passage from a sentimental French author, describing the death of a father, which moved him); he cultivated his feelings, he tells us, by reading Wordsworth and other poets, and gradually he recovered his interest in life and work. But as a result of this experience he began to reassess the theories that he had been taught, for he blamed the "crisis in [his] mental history" on his education, and his education on those theories. Still anxious to help mankind, he sought illumination and intellectual assistance from many writers whom the Benthamites had condemned as muddled, or reactionary, or sentimental; by the later part of 1831, he had reached something like a satisfactory arrangement of his new views and his old beliefs. In the autumn of that year, he explained his estimate of himself in a letter to a friend:*

The only thing which I can usefully do at present, and which I am doing more and more every day, is to work out *principles*, which are of use for all times, though to be applied cautiously and circumspectly to any; principles of morals, government, law, education, above all self-education. I am here much more in my element: the only thing that I believe I am really fit for is the investigation of abstract truth, and the more abstract the better.

* To John Stirling, in *Letters of John Stuart Mill*, ed. Elliot, Vol. I, p. 8.

Mill did not retire, as one in his position would tend to do today, to a university to teach and think. Instead he followed his father's precedent by becoming an executive of the East India Company, the private trading enterprise which for all practical purposes governed India for England. He there filled with great success an office involving an enormous amount of detailed administrative work and much serious political responsibility. All his writing, until his retirement in 1858, was done during vacations and in time left over from his India House work.

In 1830 Mill met Harriet Taylor, the woman he was eventually to marry. Although she was already the wife of a successful drug merchant and the mother of several children, the two of them rapidly formed an intimate friendship—"the most valuable friendship of my Life," Mill called it. He estimated her abilities so highly, thinking her intellectually equal to any man he knew and more sensitive and profound than Shelley, and attributed to her so great an influence on his work, that almost no one has been able to accept his picture of her. Her first husband died in 1849, and two years later Mill married her. She died—of tuberculosis, apparently caught from him—in 1858, leaving him in the care of her daughter. Thereafter the major episode in his life was a not altogether happy term spent in Parliament, from 1865 to 1868, as representative from Westminster. In his remaining years Mill spent much time in France, long his favorite country. Harriet had died at Avignon, and Mill too died there, on May 7, 1873, in the house he had bought so that he might always be near Harriet's grave.

Mill's life is primarily a life of thought, and its landmarks are his books. The *System of Logic* was published in 1843, the result of thirteen years of work. In it Mill's central concern is to find a useful methodology for the social (or, as he calls them, "moral") sciences by considering the methods used in the advanced and well-established physical sciences. The main results on this problem had been reached years before the book was published, and used in many of Mill's early essays. The classic *Principles of Political Economy* (1848) contains Mill's attempt to apply his methods to the one area of social life which he believed was ready for a thoroughgoing scientific treatment. Some of his later writings, such as *On Liberty* (1859), *Representative Government* (1861), and

The Subjection of Women (1869), are addressed to fairly specific issues which Mill thought crucial; others, such as *Utilitarianism* (1861) and *The Examination of Sir William Hamilton's Philosophy* (1865), are attempts to present and support fundamental philosophical principles. Mill wrote a great many essays, some philosophical, some on poets and poetry, some on history, many on current economic, social, and political problems. Those which he thought worth preserving he reprinted in a collection entitled *Dissertations and Discussions*, first published in 1859 and expanded in later editions. After his death there appeared two of his most important works, the *Autobiography* (1873) and *Three Essays on Religion* (1874).

MILL'S SITUATION AND HIS PURPOSE

Underlying Mill's manifold interests, shaping his aims, and influencing the ways in which he worked to achieve them, is a theory of historical change and of the conditions for stability in society. Mill was not the originator of the theory of history which he used—he learned it from the St. Simonian writers in France—but he accepted it early in his career, and some knowledge of it is important for an understanding of his writings on ethics.

According to this view, history proceeds in a series of alternating periods. Although the details of the events within each period are unique, there are nonetheless only two kinds of period: organic and critical. In an organic period, society is stable and well-organized; it is run by those who have ability and is united by a widely accepted set of opinions. Those who make and modify public opinion are a small and cohesive body—Mill is thinking here of the clergy in the Middle Ages—whose views, accepted by the mass of men as issuing from an authoritative source, provide a framework within which particular disputes can be carried on and particular problems solved. In a critical period, by contrast, the men in power are not the men with ability, and the men who form public opinion are not agreed among themselves. Consequently the old bonds of social cohesion slowly dissolve. Men begin to think for themselves and refuse to accept guidance from those wiser or more learned than themselves, the framework of beliefs is lost, and society splits with increasing rapidity into factions and parties not united by any common concern or shared viewpoint. Only with the gradual growth of a new framework of accepted beliefs can a stable society emerge again.

It is clear that, on this theory, opinion plays a major role in social change and social stability. Changes in opinion make for changes in society, agreement in opinion is necessary for stability in society. Mill explains this aspect of the theory in a number of places,* but nowhere with so clear an indication of its importance for moral philosophy as in an essay written in 1834. This essay is a reply to criticisms made by a Frenchman, one M. Chales, of a book by Edward Bulwer on England.† M. Chales praised England for its lack of moral philosophy: the absence of it shows, so he said, that the English are not decadent. Mill thinks his reasoning poor and his conclusion false.

The Greeks and Romans did not become immoral by theorizing on morals, though they did not (perhaps) begin to theorize on morals until they were becoming immoral. When ethical speculations come into vogue, it is generally symptomatic of a decay, or at least (in the medical sense) a *critical period* in a nation's morals. And why so? Because it is a proof that the people are no longer united by a common knowledge. But there never was, and never will be, a virtuous people, where there is not unanimity, or an agreement nearly approaching to it, in their notions of virtue. The most immoral periods in a nation's history are always the sceptical periods, when the old convictions are dying away, and no new ones having yet taken their place, each person "does what is right in his own eyes"; and as in those periods alone the doctrines of morals appear to *require* discussion, those are the only times when (except among casuists by profession) the discussion and the study of them comes into vogue. Such is now the case in Germany and France, but in England we are unfortunately in the predicament of having the will without the remedy. We *have* thrown off, or are rapidly getting rid of, our old convictions, and are not forming new. We *have* the diversities of opinion, the noisy conflicts; we do dispute on morality, but we do *not* philosophize on it, simply because we do not philosophize upon any thing—it is not our way, we set no

* Cf. *System of Logic*, Bk. VI, ch. X, and the early essays on *The Spirit of the Age*, ed. F. A. Hayek, Chicago, 1942.

† "Letter from an Englishman to a Frenchman," *Monthly Repository*, n.s. Vol. VIII, 1834, pp. 394–395.

value on systematic thought. This Mr. Bulwer blames us for, and surely with no little reason. I wish M. Chales would point out to us how, except by the inquiries and studies which he condemns, we can ever recover from the state which he laments, how except through moral philosophy we can ever hope to arrive again at unity in our moral convictions, the necessary preliminary to any elevation of the standard of our practice. Unless, indeed, we may permit ourselves to hope for a fresh revelation from heaven, which M. Chales, I presume, will hardly be bold enough to prophecy.

The importance of having a consensus on basic moral beliefs is clearly enormous, on Mill's view, and to obtain it sound moral philosophy is indispensable. The point is all the more vital because, with this analysis of the role of opinion in history, Mill couples the view that his own period is a critical period. His task, as he sees it, is to aid his times to make the transition to an organic period, not by attempting to go back to some supposedly golden past, but by absorbing the lessons of the period of criticism and progressing on to a new state of society based on a new set of beliefs. If the critical spirit were allowed to continue unchecked, it might well, Mill fears, lead to the sort of chaos and wanton destructiveness that characterized the last phases of the French Revolution. But though a renewal of agreement on these points is desirable, it will not be easy to bring it about. A thinker who lives during an organic period can propound his views directly and fully to the opinion-forming group. If they agree with him, he can be sure that the public will eventually come to agree as well, while disagreement will at least not cause fierce divisions in society. This is not true in a critical period. Public opinion being already splintered, new theories are apt to act as further sources of disunity and disagreement; they will at most serve as party slogans, not as comprehensive views. And there is in addition the problem of the peculiar temperament of the English people, who distrust general theories as such. It would be worse than useless to try to propagate a whole system among them. Mill tries to explain all this, in 1830, to the French friend who introduced him to St. Simonism:*

* Letter to Gustave d'Eichthal, published in *Cosmopolis*, May, 1897, pp. 353–354.

I think that mankind, and I am sure that my own country-men, are in a state of mind which renders them incapable of receiving a true *doctrine générale*, or of understanding it in a true sense if they did receive it. . . . The very idea of beginning a reformation in men's minds by preaching to them a comprehensive doctrine is a notion which would never enter into the head of any person who has lived long enough in England to know the people. Englishmen ha-bitually distrust the most obvious truths, if the person who advances them is suspected of having any general views. To produce any effect on their minds, you must carefully con-ceal the fact of your having any system or body of opin-ions, and must instruct them on isolated points, and endeavor to form their habits of thought by your mode of treating simple and practical questions. . . . Although we ought to arrive, if we can, at a general system of social philosophy, and to keep it always in our own view, we ought not to address it to the public, who are by no means ripe for its reception, but to avail ourselves of the good which is in them, to educate their minds, by accustoming them to think rightly on those subjects on which they al-ready think, to communicate to them all the truths which they are prepared for, and . . . to endeavor to alter those parts of our social institutions and policy which at present oppose improvement.

Mill's view of history, then, posed two problems for him. (i) Whatever theory he might construct, there would be the difficulty of gaining acceptance for it during a critical period. In solving this problem, Mill applied a lesson his father had taught him. James Mill had made him read, at an early age, the orations of Demosthenes, and had pointed out particu-larly "how everything important to his purpose was said at the exact moment when he had brought the minds of his audience into the state most fitted to receive it; how he made steal into their minds, gradually and by insinuation, thoughts which, if expressed in a more direct manner, would have aroused their opposition. Most of these reflections," Mill comments, "were beyond my capacity of full comprehension at the time; but they left seed behind, which germinated in due season."* Thus, in putting his moral views before the public, he did not at first publish a systematic treatise. Instead he suggested his opinions in numerous essays on a variety of

---

* *Autobiography*, Ch. I.

topics; he applied them constantly in his writings on current social and political issues; he outlined or defended an aspect or a part of them in a critical essay here and there, or he used them in the course of illustrating points in the *Logic*. It was not until quite late in his career that he presented, in *Utilitarianism*, anything like a complete exposition of his theory—and by then he had come to think that the state of the public mind was somewhat improved. (ii) The second problem Mill faced was, of course, that of formulating a moral theory that would be adequate for the purpose which, on his view, such a theory must serve. In working out a solution Mill never abandoned the basic Utilitarianism which he had been taught as a child. He did not go in search of a new first principle. His aim was rather to transform the old, narrow Utilitarianism from a party ideology into a comprehensive view, and to show that it need not be a divisive slogan but could serve as a unifying philosophy of life.

MILL'S REVISIONS OF UTILITARIANISM

Discussion of three main aspects of Mill's thought will suggest some of the ways in which he tries to make Utilitarianism more comprehensive and more widely acceptable than it was previously.

(A) Because the Benthamites accepted the view that all men necessarily seek their own pleasure in voluntary action, they were accused of teaching that men are brutish and selfish; because they held that pleasure and the absence of pain are the ultimate good, they were thought to be propagating a low, debasing view. Mill tries to eliminate these objections by (1) slightly modifying, and formulating more carefully, the Benthamite psychology of action, (2) emphasizing a point about its view of happiness which had not been made prominent before, and (3) revising its concept of pleasure.

(1) Mill holds that Bentham's formulation of the doctrine of psychological egoism is misleading. Granted that in some sense of "pleasure" and "pain" all voluntary actions are done for the sake of obtaining pleasure or avoiding pain for the agent, it is still erroneous to conclude from this that men are all selfish. Some men voluntarily do deeds which would normally be thought of as totally unselfish, and psychology has nothing to object to this view of them. The sense

in which the psychologist uses "pleasure" and "pain" is broad enough to allow him to include among his list of motives the pleasure of altruistic action and the pain of callousness which would be felt by a virtuous man. If Bentham speaks as though this were not so, it is because he confuses this broad sense of his key terms with the narrower, and more ordinary, sense in which it would be said, for instance, that the self-sacrificing crusader gives up a life of pleasure for a life of devotion to a cause. It is simply not true that in the narrow sense men seek their own pleasure in all their actions, nor, Mill insists, is it an implication of the psychology of Utilitarianism. A more serious mistake is made by Bentham, Mill thinks, in holding that men act for the sake of pleasures which they *foresee* will be consequences of their actions. Bentham overlooks the fact that the present thought of a particular act may be pleasant enough to lead to the doing of it without any further thought about the consequences that will result from it. Indeed the point of moral education— as we shall see later—is precisely to ensure that the thought of certain actions is so pleasant as to lead the agent to do them without worrying about their consequences, while the thought of others is painful enough to prevent them from being done. In this sort of situation no calculation at all, let alone "selfish" calculation, is involved.

(2) The fact that certain actions and states of mind may be felt to be pleasant in themselves is important for Mill's broadened understanding of the Utilitarian goal. It had seemed shocking to many people to make virtuous action simply a means to a goal beyond itself, and virtuous character not the highest good but only the best available tool for bringing into existence what is intrinsically good. The older Utilitarian vocabulary seemed to force this view upon its adherents, for it allowed only pleasure and the absence of pain to be ends in themselves and consequently made all else into mere means. But Mill points out that we can speak of certain activities and states of mind as being themselves *parts* of happiness, in the sense that they are actions or states in which we can directly take pleasure and which therefore are good for themselves and not for their consequences. Just as the miser finds his massed money pleasant in itself, and takes pleasure simply in having it, so the virtuous man takes pleasure simply in being and doing good, and virtue is for him part of the ultimate

good. Mill holds that the states of character and kinds of activity that are held to be intrinsically good by non-Utilitarians are capable of being made part of the ultimate good through education, and he argues that they ought to be made so when they are states or activities whose consequences are further contributory to the happiness of mankind. To take happiness as the ultimate good is not, then, to rule out the inherent goodness of virtue, nobility, and self-sacrifice, it is rather to give a more comprehensive account of man's goal, such as will be able to include these as well as all other states in which men can find satisfaction.

(3) A far more radical change in orthodox Benthamism is made by Mill in attempting to show why Utilitarianism is not an ignoble philosophy fit only for pigs. The Benthamites had recognized only one basic feature of pleasure and pain as relevant to moral choice: the *amount*. Bentham's famous "felicific calculus" was supposed to offer a means of calculating the quantity of pleasure and the quantity of pain that might reasonably be expected to result from any given action; once this was known, the Utilitarian principle dictated choice of the act that would produce the greatest surplus of pleasure over pain. The pleasures of artistic creation or of intelligent conversation were to be thrown into the balance along with the pleasures of scratching an itch or stuffing oneself at a banquet or drinking oneself into insensibility; the pains of grief at the loss of a child, or of despair at the betrayal of a noble cause, count equally, quantity for quantity, with the pains of toothache, hangover, or jealous rage at a successful rival. This proved offensive to many people, and Mill tries to alter the Utilitarian theory so as to remove the source of offense. He introduces a distinction between *kinds* of pleasures (or pains)—a qualitative distinction, a distinction between "higher" and "lower" pleasures, which, he thinks, will enable him to say that a large quantity of a lower pleasure may fail to be more valuable than even a small quantity of a higher pleasure. Though fewer people enjoy looking at paintings than at television, still, if the former is a higher pleasure, it may be more valuable; though the pleasures of drug addiction seem to be peculiarly intense, and the pleasures of intelligent conversation may not be so, still the latter may be more valuable than the former. The test here is *preference*: if those who have tried both prefer one

to the other, quite regardless of quantity, then the pleasure that is preferred must be the higher one. And since most people who enjoy art, talk, literature, etc., prefer them to carousing, brutality, etc., it seems clear that Mill will be able to allow that these are the higher and hence the more valuable pleasures. Utilitarianism is thus freed of the reproach of beastliness or of ignobility; it can compete for men's highest allegiances with the now outworn but undeniably noble moralities involved in Christian asceticism, medieval chivalry, and aristocratic codes of honor.

(B) The Benthamites were accused of being entirely too *a priori* in their ethics, of ignoring, despite their loud boast that they were the only remaining champions of the Philosophy of Experience, all that experience had to teach about morality. They denied the claims of the accepted morality of the people as contemptuously as they threw out the belief that the wisdom of the ages was embodied in the political institutions of the country, and they treated those who defended either of these as probably motivated by sinister self-interest. Against this, Mill argues that, in the traditions, customs, and commonsense morality of a people, as expressed in sayings and aphorisms handed down from generation to generation, there is to be found a source of guidance which is indispensable even to the reforming Utilitarian. We must (1) note briefly his reasons for holding this view and (2) indicate its importance for his philosophical position in ethics.

(1) Mill's attitude toward commonsense morality is supported by his analysis of the problems involved in obtaining sociological knowledge and the methods properly employed for this purpose. It is clear that, if we accept the fundamental Utilitarian imperative, we shall need much information about the consequences that actions will have on individuals and groups. Although the basic laws of psychology are known, Mill holds, they are by themselves too abstract to be useful for obtaining detailed answers to questions of the sort we shall have to answer, and indeed the number of factors involved in social interaction is too great even to permit the direct deduction of sociological laws from them. Experiment, which is the tool of the physical sciences for complex situations, is, for obvious reasons, also impossible. Our only resource is to gather as many generalizations as we can about

the tendencies of humans to act or respond in various ways under various circumstances, and then see whether we can arrange these systematically by connecting them with fundamental laws of human nature and human character. All of us have observed a certain amount of human life and formed from our experience and reading a number of generalizations, about friends, about groups we are members of, about our countrymen, perhaps about people in general. But personal observation has one formidable defect—and here we touch a basic theme in Mill's thought—in that it tends to be *one-sided*. Men tend to notice one aspect of what is before them and overlook the rest, and in forming theories to account for their observations they are all too apt to deny the existence of what they have failed to see. This is especially true when men's interests and passions are involved, and it is therefore all the more important, in such cases, to have reports—from all possible sorts of men, living under every variety of condition—concerning the benefits and harms that have resulted from various actions. Mill holds that, in the commonsense morality of a people, as in its proverbs and aphorisms, we have a vast fund of information of the sort needed by the social sciences, gathered from and passed through ages of experience and millions of lives, and therefore one of the best available correctives to the narrowness in theory that results from lack of factual knowledge. The wisdom of the ages, as so expressed, is of course unsystematic, but, Mill remarks, "to be unsystematic is of the essence of all truths which rest on specific experiment." The scientist or philosopher may try to organize these truths and connect them with the laws of psychology. "But we need not wait till this is done, before we record them, and act upon them. On the contrary, these detached truths are at once the materials and the tests of philosophy itself, since philosophy is not called in to prove them, but may very justly be required to account for them."*

Without being in the least inconsistent with his basic Utilitarianism, consequently, Mill is able to adopt a far more tolerant attitude toward the moral and political views of those who disagree with him than were the earlier Benthamites. Feeling that his opponents may be in possession of

* "Aphorisms" (1837), reprinted in *Dissertations and Discussions*, Vol. I, p. 207.

just that portion of the truth which he himself has overlooked, he need not quarrel with their way of putting their insight. Basic disagreements need not always be aired, and though you take as ultimate and inviolable a principle which I think is secondary and tentative, still we can agree to a course of action dictated by it without first having to settle our quarrel about fundamentals. In a transitional era, such settlement may be hard to reach; all the better, then, if we can do without it when it comes to the manifold questions of practice.

(2) While Mill's attitude toward commonsense morality has an important bearing on his tactics for aiding progress, it is at least as important for the way he handles the chief philosophical position opposed to Utilitarianism, the position he labels "Intuitionism." The Intuitionists interpret commonsense morality quite differently from the way Mill interprets it. They hold that each man is in some way able to "see" or "intuit" the absolute truth of a number of moral principles and rules, and that what one intuits in this way cannot be wrong. The propositions grasped by intuition are eternally true, as the axioms of geometry are eternally true; consequently, morality is immutable, not open to improvement and refinement as our sociological knowledge increases. Mill thinks that there are three main arguments in support of Intuitionism. First, the feeling accompanying moral judgments is unique, and therefore it must have a unique source, viz., the intuited moral truth. Second, moral judgments are not in fact generally arrived at by a process of reasoning; they come with the rapidity of sense perception, and Intuitionism alone accounts for this. Third, the moral principles and judgments even of the plain man have a degree of authority or weight which is inexplicable except on Intuitionist grounds, for the plain man's opinions on the consequences of actions are not usually as authoritative as his moral judgments. To each of these arguments Mill has a reply. By giving alternative psychological explanations of the peculiarity of moral feelings and the rapidity of moral judgment, explanations which remove the alleged need for the Intuitionist account of these features of moral thought, he undercuts the first two. And his reply to the third argument is, simply, that a Utilitarian account of the authority of commonsense morality and the moral opinions of the plain man is quite possible. We have already seen the grounds on which he holds that commonsense morality is to be respected: the plain man, heir to the whole

tradition of the people, is aided in judging by what he has learned from the past.

There is therefore, Mill thinks, no compelling reason to accept Intuitionism, and on general epistemological grounds he is opposed to it. He thinks, moreover, that Utilitarianism has one very considerable advantage over Intuitionism within the domain of morality. On the Intuitionist view moral disputes must come down, since intuition is supposed to be infallible, to a war of assertion and counter-assertion. A denial of an alleged intuition can be treated only in the way that a denial (say) that this page is white with lines of black on it can be treated: by charges either of blindness or of disingenuousness. And this is hardly a pleasant position for a moralist to be in, especially in an age when old opinions are changing rapidly, when there are many diverse groups with divergent interests within the community, and when old authority is being challenged. The Utilitarian, however, is not faced with this problem, for he holds that, while commonsense morality undoubtedly conveys much valuable knowledge, it is far from being infallible. Mixed with its insights there is faulty inference, mixed with its information there is superstition, mixed with sympathy and love there are prejudice and group interest, and all these sources of error must eventually be detected and eliminated. There is no easy or automatic way to do this, but at least it can be done rationally, by using the methods of the social sciences to help answer the question of what actions tend to make people happy. In his emphasis on the way in which Utilitarianism appeals to empirical science and rejects any claim to absolute infallibility or complete immunity to criticism, Mill is in agreement with one of the deepest and most important strains in Bentham's thought. No matter how far he may go in seeking to appreciate the wisdom of the ages and the good that lies in established institutions, he never abandons the belief that the Utilitarian principle provides a rational basis for their evaluation and points to the ways in which they may be improved.

(C) Nowhere is Mill's desire to learn from his opponents and to minimize points of disagreement more prominent than in his view of the importance of individual character and in his presentation of that view. The Benthamites were generally thought to have placed their hopes for progress wholly on impersonal economic, legal, and political arrangements, which

would improve the way men live and act without altering
what men are. Almost the whole range of vocal opinion during much of Mill's lifetime was united against this approach.
The reasons for such unanimity of sentiment are complex. In
large part, of course, the Christian emphasis on the individual
soul is responsible, even among those who had come to doubt
or disbelieve the Christian religious teaching, while the
strength and pride of the newly powerful middle class, self-
reliant and self-made, is another potent factor. Whatever the
reasons, the belief that the state of one's soul or the condition
of one's moral character was the most important thing in the
world could very easily have seemed to Mill to be one of
those truths that philosophy is not called on to prove but
may justly be required to account for. Mill presented this
view so forcefully that he has been frequently accused of the
radical inconsistency of teaching on the one hand that perfection of character is the only intrinsic good and, on the
other, that happiness is the only intrinsic good. There is,
however, no such contradiction in Mill's thought. He holds,
as might be expected, that the development and perfection
of character is "the highest utility." This belief is no mere
ad hoc reconciliation of contradictions: it rests on two basic
ideas of Mill's, one of which he thinks important for all times
and all social conditions, while the other is of special rele-
vance to his own times and his own country. Indications of
the former are to be found throughout his writings, not least
in those collected in the present volume, but the view is expressed most fully in the essay entitled "Nature," which Mill
had finished writing, in draft at least, early in 1854, but which
was published only posthumously as one of the *Three Essays
on Religion.* In that essay Mill considers whether there is any
sense in which we can take Nature as our guide for action.
He distinguishes two senses of the word "nature":

> In one sense, it means all the powers existing in either the
> outer or the inner world and everything which takes place
> by means of those powers. In another sense it means, not
> everything which happens, but only what takes place with-
> out the agency, or without the voluntary and intentional
> agency, of man.

Can we use the maxim "Follow Nature" if we take the term
"nature" in the first sense? Well, taking it in that sense, Mill
says, "There is no need of a recommendation to act according

to nature, since it is what nobody can possibly help doing. There is," he continues, "no mode of acting which is not conformable to nature in this sense of the term, and all modes of acting are so in exactly the same degree." Whether actions are good or bad, right or wrong, noble or ugly, they are happenings in the natural world, involving natural bodies moving in accordance with the natural laws which describe all such happenings. And since what is "natural" in this sense includes both what is good, right, and noble, and what is bad, wrong, and ugly, it cannot be a standard used to guide us in doing only what is good or right.

What then of the second sense of "nature," the sense in which it means "what happens without any human intervention?" Mill says that, if we take "nature" in this sense, the maxim "Follow Nature" is "palpably absurd and self-contradictory," since the whole point of human action is to "alter and improve nature." "All praise of civilization, or art, or contrivance, is so much dispraise of nature, and admission of imperfection which it is man's business and merit to be always endeavoring to correct or mitigate." Nature untouched by man, Mill goes on to argue, is violent, bloody, and reckless of life of any kind: "In sober truth, nearly all the things which men are hanged or imprisoned for doing to one another are nature's everyday performances." And this is not true simply of hurricanes, earthquakes, volcanoes, and landslides, not true only of animals; it holds of men as well. Human nature as simply natural—that is, in this sense of the term, as something which no one has tried to interfere with, to alter, improve, cultivate, or, in a word, to educate— man as merely natural is no more worthy of respect and awe than anything else that is merely natural. Our natural impulses or instincts are not given some superior right to be obeyed merely because they are natural.

Allowing everything to be an instinct which anybody has ever asserted to be one, it remains true that nearly every respectable attribute of humanity is the result, not of instinct, but of a victory over instinct, and that there is hardly anything valuable in the natural man except capacities—a whole world of possibilities, all of them dependent upon eminently artificial discipline for being realized.

The natural man is a sort of wild animal, cleverer than others but not as strong; to speak of the "natural goodness" of man is to sentimentalize in the fashion of Rousseau. "It is only," Mill says, "in a highly artificialized condition of human nature that the notion grew up, or, I believe, ever could have grown up, that goodness was natural, because only after a long course of artificial education did good sentiments become so habitual, and so predominant over bad, as to arise unprompted when occasion called for them." And he concludes with the remark that "the duty of man is the same in respect to his own nature as in respect to the nature of all other things, namely, not to follow but to amend it."

This quite general conclusion gives us the first reason for Mill's concern with the improvement of character. Man is civilized, virtuous, only as a result of education. Moral education is a necessity at all times and in all places, if society in any form is to exist. And moral education is not merely, is not even primarily, intellectual training. It is rather a matter of cultivating men's feelings, fostering their sympathy with others, and teaching them to control passions and desires. The task assumes a place of special importance in Mill's eyes for a reason which we have now briefly to indicate.

Mill's analysis of history has already been outlined, and to that outline need only be added the fact that Mill believes the advent of some form of mass rule or popular government to be inevitable in any country which has come to the stage reached, he holds, by the England of his times. The ruling group will never again be the small privileged elite that it was formerly, and there is no use trying to restore unity to the nation by setting up such a group. Increasingly, from now on, the rulers will be in reality the great mass of the people. The number and importance of their votes will swell their influence in politics, and the majority opinion is all too likely to gain an overwhelming and terrifying weight. It is consequently more important than ever before that the people be educated, both intellectually and morally. Society at this point may, as we have seen, move in either of two directions: it may become increasingly fragmented, filled with conflicting groups and detached individuals, devoid of any but the most limited loyalties, or it may begin to reorganize, to become increasingly cohesive, to develop into a society which attracts the loyalties of more and more of its members, finding them ever more willing to identify themselves with the society and to find their happiness in its well-being. Which way will it go? The answer, Mill thinks, depends on what we do. Those of us who have come to understand the situation and who are sympathetic enough to want to help others can, through educating feelings as well as minds—in other words, through building character—in the populace, help bring about a better society. If we succeed, we can hope to create a public which, when it finally gets the right to vote (which it did not have, to any very great extent in England, until 1867), will be able to select the best of the candidates, and willing to do so even at the expense of their own immediate interests, because their feelings and sympathies will have bound them to the welfare of society and made that more precious to them than their own material well-being. If we fail, we can only look forward to an increasingly tyrannical and un-enlightened mobocracy.

Thus a political forecast is the second reason behind Mill's belief in the importance of moral character. Unlike the Benthamites, he is not willing to trust an external "Duty-and-Interest-Juncture-Producing-Principle." It is rather within each man that he hopes to produce that identity of individual and social interest which is so essential for the greatest happiness of the greatest number.

SOME CRITICISMS

Having discussed some of the ways in which Mill tried to broaden the Benthamite theory of morality so that it might serve as a "Philosophy of Life" for a world struggling to make the transition from an old to a new order of society, we must now inquire as to the adequacy of Mill's ethical theory. With the purely psychological view that Mill accepted we need not be concerned. Although it was the most fully developed account available during Mill's lifetime, Associationism (as this theory is called) is now generally agreed to be inadequate as an explanation of psychological phenomena and unsuggestive as a guide to research; considered simply as a model of what a satisfactory psychological theory should be, it contains numerous flaws. The problems that are important for Mill's specifically ethical theory spring rather from the way he views the structure of morality. He sees it as having three levels. There is first the *highest principle*, which is of course the Utilitarian principle; it stands alone as the supreme arbiter of morality. Since it is too remote and abstract to be applied rapidly or accurately in most cases, we must usually rely on what Mill calls *secondary principles*, such as those exemplified in the rules and maxims of common-sense morality. Secondary principles are relevant to fewer cases than the highest principle (which is relevant to every case); they are authoritative only to the extent that they really embody the dictates of the highest principle for the kind of case to which they are relevant, and no further. Third, there are *particular moral judgments*, which will usually be derived by applying a secondary principle to a specific situation falling under it, and which are binding only in so far as they are correct applications of a valid secondary principle or, as will sometimes be the case, of the supreme principle. Mill's theory is thus similar to Plato's belief that Virtue is One. Just as Plato's Socrates argues that the many apparently independent virtues are really all manifestations, in different areas, of the one Good, so Mill holds that secondary principles, however absolute they may seem, simply spell out the requirements of the highest principle for different types of situation. It is this view of the general structure of morality that gives rise to the critical questions most often raised about Mill's ethics. (1) How can the highest principle be proven or at least be shown to be rationally justifiable? If all other moral rules and judgments depend on the supreme principle for their authoritativeness, from what can that principle itself derive its authority? (2) Are particular moral judgments as thoroughly subordinate to the supreme principle as Mill says they are? Are there no cases in which a secondary principle rightly dictates a particular judgment contravening the Utilitarian principle? (3) Is there really only *one* supreme principle of morality? Is a moral theory structured to show the dependence of the details of morality on a single principle adequate to account for all of our firmest moral convictions? We shall discuss these questions in order.

(1) In his *System of Logic*, Mill discusses two ways of proving a proposition: deduction and induction. He argues that these are the only types of reasoning, so that any proof of a first principle must use one or the other of them. Deductive reasoning, as exemplified in syllogisms and geometric systems, is rapidly ruled out. It is, according to Mill, a matter of merely verbal transformation of propositions, never giving new knowledge but only serving to make ex-

plicit what is contained in knowledge we already have. To prove a moral principle by deduction we would have to find a premise at least as general as the principle we wish to deduce. But in that case the premise and not the conclusion would be the first principle and, since the premise would still stand in need of proof, we would be no closer to giving support to a first principle than we were at the start. Induction, the only other mode of reasoning, seems a more promising alternative. It has as its function, according to Mill, to do what deduction cannot—namely, to provide us with propositions that are more than transformations of propositions already known; in other words, to supply us with new general knowledge. Induction depends on observation. The generalizations derived by the use of inductive procedures are essentially summaries of what has been observed and predictions that the same will be observed under the same circumstances in the future. All our scientific knowledge rests on inductively established generalizations, and so too, Mill thinks, does our mathematical knowledge. Can we not hope to establish the supreme principle of morality by the use of procedures that have been so successful elsewhere?

Induction can tell us at best what always in fact takes place—that one thing always precedes or follows another, or always coexists with another. Since science seeks laws of the succession and coexistence of phenomena, induction is its natural method. But morality is not concerned with what *does* or *will* happen. It is concerned with what *ought* to happen, or with the *goodness* of what happens. And this difference between science and morality makes it impossible, according to Mill, to obtain an inductive proof of a first principle of morality. Put most simply, it is a plainly logical matter. A premise about what *does* happen, taken by itself, does not entail any proposition about what *ought* to happen or about the *goodness* of what happens. Hence induction alone cannot establish any ethical propositions. One might try to remedy this logical gap between inductively established propositions and moral propositions by offering a definition of an ethical term, such as "ought" or "good," that would connect the term with facts. For example, one might define "good" as "what all men desire"; then, supposing that induction shows that all men do desire pleasure, one could argue as follows: All men desire pleasure (discovered by induction); What all men desire is good (by definition); therefore, pleasure is good. This seems to give us an ethical conclusion based primarily on a scientific truth. Mill has often been accused of arguing in this fashion, but the accusation is mistaken. He explicitly rejects the view that "definitions, as such, are the premises in any of our reasonings, except," he adds, "such as relate to words only"; and he holds that "the only kind of conclusion which can ever follow from a definition" is "a proposition relating to the meaning of words."* That is, Mill thinks that a conclusion depending on a definition—on a verbal premise rather than a substantive one—will itself be a merely verbal proposition, and no such proposition can serve as a first principle of any sort. "Can it be necessary to say," Mill asks scornfully, "that none, not even the most trivial knowledge with respect to things, ever was or could be originally got at by any conceivable manipulation of names, as such, and that what can be learned from names, is only what somebody who used the names knew before?"† Thus, even if one could get a definition of a moral term of the sort required to construct an argument, it would do no good, for the result would be an empty verbal proposition.

Now it is no accident that there is a logical gap between any inductively established generalization and a moral principle. It is due, Mill holds, to the crucial fact that science and morality have entirely different goals or functions. The difference is indicated clearly in an essay‡ written about 1831, in which Mill says that we must be careful not to confound

the essentially distinct, though closely connected, ideas of *science and art*. These two ideas differ from one another as the understanding differs from the will, or as the indicative mood in grammar differs from the imperative. The one deals in facts, the other in precepts. Science is a collection of *truths*; art is a body of *rules*, or directions for conduct. The language of science is, This is, or This is not; This does, or does not, happen. The language of art is, Do this; Avoid that. Science takes cognizance of a *phenomenon*, and endeavors to discover its laws; art proposes to itself an *end*,

* *System of Logic*, Bk. I, ch. VIII, sec. 5.
† *Ibid.*, Bk. II, ch. II, sec. 2.
‡ "On the Definition of Political Economy," in *Essays on Some Unsettled Questions of Political Economy* (1844), pp. 123–124, 135.

and looks out for *means* to effect it. . . . Morality itself is
not a science, but an art; not truths, but rules.

This view is reiterated in the last chapter of the *System of
Logic*; what it suggests (though Mill did not work out all its
implications) is that any attempt to deduce morality directly
from science is mistaken in principle because it involves
turning one kind of enterprise, the guiding and directing of
human action, into another, the predicting and explaining of
natural phenomena. And since morality is essentially a matter
of guiding action, to turn it into prediction and explanation
is really to abolish, not to establish, it. Induction, we are
forced to conclude, is of no more use than deduction for
giving support to a highest principle of morality.

Mill reached this conclusion early in his career and maintained it throughout his life. But it poses for him a very
serious question: how is his position superior to that of the
Intuitionists? Granted that Mill has only *one* unprovable
principle while the Intuitionists usually have several, is he not
in the same position with regard to his one that they are in
with regard to their several? He believes his to be the right
one but cannot prove it; must he not then resort to Intuition?
To avoid this criticism, Mill offers the famous arguments in
Chapter IV of *Utilitarianism*. A greater mare's nest has seldom
been constructed. It is now generally agreed that Mill is not,
in this chapter, betraying his own belief that proof of a first
moral principle is impossible, but there is no general agreement as to what he *is* doing. In the last fifteen years there
have been more essays dealing with the topic of "Mill's Proof"
than with any other single topic in the history of ethical
thought (some of these are listed in the bibliography to the
present volume); while the various explications and recon-
structions of what Mill said, however, are often ingenious
and interesting, they are frequently more informative about
the ethical and epistemological views of their authors than
they are about Mill's. Nevertheless, it is not surprising that
the topic should be so popular. Mill here struggles with, and
is alluringly suggestive about, one of the central problems of
ethical theory, and he poses the problem in precisely the form
in which it has perplexed recent philosophy. If he fails to
solve it, he is at least in no worse a position than most of his
critics.

(ii) Mill's view of the relation of the highest principle to particular moral judgments has recently come to be called "Act-Utilitarianism" because he holds that the Utilitarian principle determines, for each and every act, whether it is right or wrong. Secondary principles have no independent authority and cannot impose on us obligations that go counter to the highest principle. They merely result from generalizations which—like all generalizations, on Mill's view—are summaries of the teachings of experience about the consequences of a given type of action, and predictions that future instances of that type of action will have similar consequences. The mere fact that an act falls under a well-based secondary rule is never by itself a reason for doing the act. If, in a particular case in which (say) one has borrowed some money and is asked to return it, one calculates rightly that by keeping it one will cause more good to exist than by returning it, then one ought to keep it, and there is no reason at all to return it. For the rule "Return borrowed money!" rests on the fact that in most cases returning borrowed money does more good than keeping it, and it holds only for cases where this is true. Since each obligation springs from the good consequences to be expected from the particular act in question, there can be no obligation to follow the rule when the facts are unusual. The only reason for using secondary rules at all is to help us out if we cannot, for lack of time or information, predict the consequences of the specific alternatives open to us. Where, as in the present case, we know what the results will be, the secondary rule becomes quite irrelevant to deliberation, because we can use the Utilitarian principle itself.

Criticisms of Act-Utilitarianism take a number of forms, but generally center on one main point. They insist that there may be acts for the doing of which there are good reasons, and even right or obligatory acts, which would be condemned by the Utilitarian principle. In Mill's time, this point was frequently put by accusing Utilitarianism of substituting expediency for morality. More recently, critics have gone into greater detail. They have argued, for example, that Act-Utilitarianism gives an inadequate account of reasons for and against actions. By insisting that the obligation to perform an act always rests on the good consequences to be expected from that particular act, it overlooks those obligations that result from something that has happened in the past. We think, for instance, that, where we have made a promise, or received favors, or borrowed money, we are under an obligation because of what we said or did. Even if we can find a reason for not keeping a promise or not helping a benefactor in the future fact that the consequences in this case would be disastrous, we do not feel that this completely does away with the reason for doing the act that arises out of our having made a promise or accepted favors. The reason cited against doing the act may count as an excuse for not doing it, but no excuse would be necessary if there were not some obligation to do the act. Another way of bringing out the basic difficulty is to argue, against Mill, that the Utilitarian principle is not always relevant to the determination of whether particular acts are right or wrong. When we have accepted an official post with clearly defined duties, or when we have put ourselves into the sort of social position that carries definite responsibilities with it—as we do, for instance, when we marry—we are not required to consider the greatest good of the greatest number in each of our actions, but only whether we are carrying out our assigned duties properly or looking after the welfare of those for whom we have accepted responsibility. A still more forceful way of putting the objection to Act-Utilitarianism is to say that it leads to immoral conclusions. There is, for example, a generally accepted principle, which would count as a secondary rule for Mill, that criminals ought to be punished. If one asks why, the usual answer would be that it is for breaking the law, but (so runs the argument) the Act-Utilitarian must say that it is because of the beneficial consequences of punishment, e.g. in frightening off potential criminals so that they do not break the law, and in reforming the criminal who is being punished. The problem then seems to arise that some of these beneficial consequences might ensue even if the man being punished had not broken any law. If so, there would be good reason for inflicting punishment on an innocent man, according to Act-Utilitarianism, and this is plainly an immoral conclusion. What is useful in this case is wrong: the point made by each of the above arguments is always the same. Since the Act-Utilitarian cannot incorporate some of our deepest moral beliefs into his theory, his ethics must be rejected.

Two kinds of reply have been made to these criticisms. One admits the points they make but holds that these can be effectively met and absorbed by taking the view that the

Utilitarian principle is to apply primarily to rules rather than to particular acts, that its use comes not in determining the rights and wrongs of individual cases but in deciding for or against the adoption of secondary rules which, once adopted, will be the final determinant of specific obligations. On this view there may be instances in which it would be right to do what is not productive of the greatest good of the greatest number, if such an act is dictated by a rule that sets up a social practice or general way of behavior that is useful in most cases. It is, for example, useful on the whole to have the social practice of promise-making and promise-keeping. We are enabled by it to make sure that someone has a reason for doing an act, which otherwise we could not be sure he would have, and are thereby enabled to rely on his doing it, in a way in which otherwise we could not. In some cases, more harm than good may be done when someone keeps his promise, but not in most cases, so that the general rule "Keep your promises!" is justifiable on Utilitarian grounds. And once the rule has been established, the Utilitarian principle does not apply to the particular acts that fall under it: they are governed solely by the rule. This variety of ethical theory, sometimes called "Rule-Utilitarianism," has received much discussion and much important refinement recently, but it is not the view that Mill holds. It is more likely that he would reply to the criticisms discussed above in the way suggested by those who accuse the Rule-Utilitarians of "rule worship" and who argue that it is only if one is excessively rigid and conservative that one will insist on following rules even where human happiness is sacrificed in order to do so. The determined Act-Utilitarian may, that is, insist that, whatever the technicalities, the issue is fundamentally a moral one. He may argue that, even if Rule-Utilitarianism does provide a better description of commonsense morality than Act-Utilitarianism, still the latter presents a position that is morally superior, and consequently commonsense morality ought to be reformed in accordance with its dictates. The questions raised by the clash of these two versions of Utilitarianism have occupied an important place in recent discussions of ethics; the bibliography to this volume lists some of the relevant articles.

(3) The criticisms made of Mill's view of the relations among the highest principle, the secondary rules, and particular moral judgments, are indicative of a more general difficulty

with his position, which is due to his insistence that a *single*
moral principle is sufficient to determine all moral judgments.
It is not only Mill's critics who find this a problem. He himself
seems at times to think that the Utilitarian principle, taken
by itself, is inadequate, and the points at which he attempts
to remedy its failings are among the weakest, and the most
frequently attacked, in his ethical theory.

Perhaps the most notorious of these weaknesses is caused
by Mill's introduction of the idea that there are qualitative as
well as quantitative distinctions among pleasures. We have
seen that he does this in an attempt to show that Utilitarianism
can hold, with its critics, that self-sacrifice, nobility, strenuous
creative work, appreciation of art, etc., are more valuable than
the pleasures of eating, scratching, and carousing, even though
in some important sense they cause less pleasure. Mill seems to
be admitting at this point that there are fundamental values
other than sheer pleasure, and then, regretting the admission,
trying to rephrase it in Utilitarian language, by insisting that
these values are really pleasures, although they may be
different in kind from others. But even the rephrasing will not
save him: in allowing quality to count as well as quantity,
Mill is in fact admitting a second basic determinant of total
value and consequently of obligation. In so doing, he loses
what he claims to be one superiority of Utilitarianism over
Intuitionism—that, since the former has only one fundamental
principle, it can settle rationally all apparent conflicts among
secondary rules. A similar criticism applies to Mill's desperate
attempt to show that the Utilitarian view does not make virtue
into a mere means for the production of an external end:
happiness. Mill argues, it will be recalled, that being virtuous
may become part of a man's happiness, just as having money
has become part of a miser's happiness. But here a dilemma
faces him: if it is the pleasure associated with being virtuous
that gives the state of being virtuous its value, he has made no
headway against the objection, since pleasure, not virtue, is
still what is intrinsically valuable; while if it is the state of
being virtuous that is valuable, regardless of how pleasant or
unpleasant it may be, then he has introduced a source of
value fundamentally different from pleasure and, in so doing,
has again lost for Utilitarianism its superiority over Intuitionism.

If the view that pleasure is the only intrinsic value seems

to be in danger of breaking down, so does the thesis that the
only source of obligation is productiveness of value. Mill de-
fends that position in the somewhat neglected essay on justice
which forms the fifth chapter of *Utilitarianism*. He there
attempts to show that the weight attached to individual rights
can be explained on Utilitarian grounds, just as he earlier
argued that the authority allowed to commonsense morality
can be so explained. He gives a psychological analysis of the
special feelings, such as moral indignation, which we have
when rights are violated, and a Utilitarian interpretation of
rights as indicating those ways of *distributing* good that will
result in the greatest amount of good. This may be a tenable
account of some rights, but there is at least one crucial question it leaves unanswered: how are we to explain the moral
assumption that underlies our hatred of great inequality of
opportunities for the enjoyment of life, of vast privilege for
the few and dreadful deprivation for the many, of wealth and
luxury on one side, poverty and squalor on the other? How are
we, in short, to explain our moral belief that good ought to be
distributed equally and impartially?

Mill says that the duty of society to treat equally well all
who have deserved well of it and to be impartial in bestowing
its benefits is a "direct emanation" from the Greatest Happiness principle. He thinks that Bentham's dictum, "Everybody
to count for one, nobody for more than one" is not something
added to the principle of utility but is a mere "explanatory
commentary" on it, and that, consequently, no additional
account of the principle of impartiality is needed. But this
argument fails to meet the point. Bentham's dictum can be
taken in two senses. It may mean, "Count everybody's happiness according to amount and nobody's for more than its
actual amount, when you are calculating what will be the
right thing to do," and in this sense Mill is right in saying
that the dictum is not an addition to the Utilitarian principle,
but is merely another way of saying that equal amounts of
happiness are equally desirable. But Bentham's dictum may
also mean, "When you are distributing happiness, count everyone for one and no one for more than that"—in other words,
"Spread it around in equal shares." Now it is this stronger
sense of the dictum which is required to account for our
belief in the obligation to work for a fair division of the goods

of life, but this stronger sense is *not* a mere comment on the Utilitarian principle. The point can be clarified if we imagine distributing money to a group of people. In the first sense, Bentham's dictum would come to no more than the demand that the purchasing power of the dollar be constant, no matter who gets the money. In the second sense, it would amount to a demand that the money be divided equally among the people. We can adhere to the dictum in the first sense while grossly violating it in the second, although there is no doubt that a violation of it in the second sense would be as much a case of injustice as a violation of it in the first. Mill offers no other argument to show that the principle of justice is merely a gloss on the Utilitarian principle and not a separate fundamental principle. In view of the fact that a situation is conceivable in which a just distribution of good would cause the total amount of good to be lower than an unjust distribution, it seems likely that the principle of justice must be held to be a separate principle which may come into conflict with the Utilitarian principle.

CONCLUSION

It is a commonplace to say that Mill lived at a time when disaffection with Christianity was becoming more general and more widespread than it had ever been before. Affecting not only the cultivated upper classes but the middle and often illiterate working classes as well, it came not as a minor hesitation about this or that point of faith, but as a major change of view. Doubts about religion were no longer merely circulated clandestinely but publicly expressed by many of the most prominent leaders of thought; where there were no doubts about religion, it was often because there was no concern with it at all. With both these states of mind there came, among those who thought, much reflection about morality. In many cases, a rejection of Christianity meant primarily a denial or abandonment of the supernatural part of its doctrines, and left the moral part more or less untouched. But the official teaching had stressed the dependence of the moral code on religious revelation, and one of the most influential of religious groups, the Evangelicals, had insistently preached not only that without religion there could be no knowledge of morality, but that without religious motivation no one could be a really good man. What was one to think about these matters once one gave up one's religion?

Attempts to formulate a comprehensive alternative to the Christian view were made by many writers, but few if any of the results were as thoroughgoing and as carefully worked out as Mill's philosophy. He succeeded, moreover, to a considerable extent in his aim of constructing a view that would introduce new ideas without offending old habits of thought, for his broad Utilitarianism was a view that could be accepted by those who, having lost their religious beliefs, still adhered in large part to the morality that had been taught with it. At the same time, Utilitarianism would not leave the original religious morality untouched. It might not give its adherents a principle with which they could easily reach decisions on all disputed or difficult questions (nor, of course, did Mill think it would do so: "It is given to no human being," he wrote, "to stereotype a set of truths, and walk safely by their guidance with his mind's eye closed"*). But placing one's detailed moral beliefs in the Utilitarian framework would lead one to see them in a new light. Utilitarianism forces one to relate morality not to God's will, the soul's salvation, and blessedness in another life, but to man's desires, human happiness, and increasing satisfactoriness of life on earth. The feeling that moral principles and rules are awesome and imposing dictates from on high, to be neither challenged nor changed by reason but simply accepted and obeyed, is replaced by an attitude which takes them as one of the many devices that men construct, as they work together for the general welfare. Morality is felt to be an instrument in our hands, to be used by us and for us, to be changed or not as the facts demand and we see fit. This attitude toward morality is in essence the Benthamite attitude. It leads us to ask of every rule or prohibition, as Bentham asked of every law and institution, "What is the use of it?", and to conclude that what cannot be justified in terms of resultant happiness ought to be abandoned. And it is precisely because Utilitarianism fosters this liberal humanistic attitude that Mill hoped to see it become the replacement for what he took to be the rapidly decaying Christian framework.

Whatever the reasons—and they are complex—the human-

* "Aphorisms," *op. cit.*, pp. 2–8.

istic moral attitude has become increasingly widespread since Mill's time. Although it may take many different forms, it received its most influential philosophical articulation during the nineteenth century from Mill, and his ethical writings repay study now for the help they can give us in coming to a fuller understanding of its problems and its enduring strength.

Note on the Text

Detailed information regarding the dates and places of publication of the various essays and chapters reprinted in the present volume will be found in the Notes introducing each selection.

For some of the selections there is only one text available, that of the original publication. In the case of the essays which Mill himself collected in *Dissertations and Discussions*, I have given the text as Mill prepared it for republication: the changes he made in them are in general too slight to be of interest. The two chapters from the *System of Logic* are taken from the last edition revised by Mill, though it should be noted that no substantial changes were made at any point in either of them. The text of the chapter from the *Examination of Sir William Hamilton's Philosophy* is taken from the sixth edition (1889), which incorporates all the revisions made by Mill.

The text of *Utilitarianism* is that of the first publication, in 1861. It has been compared with the texts of the second (1864) and fourth (1871) editions, and the principal additions and changes made by Mill have been given in notes, printed at the end of the text.

Spelling and punctuation have been modernized.

MILL'S ETHICAL WRITINGS

Remarks on Bentham's Philosophy

["I wish," Mill wrote to Carlyle in April, 1833, "I wish you could see something I have written lately about Bentham and Benthamism—but you can't." The mystery was cleared up when Mill wrote again in August. Mentioning Edward Lytton Bulwer's *England and the English*, and offering to send a copy of it to Carlyle, Mill said, "I told you in one of my letters that I had been writing something about Bentham and his philosophy; it was for Bulwer, at his request, for the purposes of this book. Contrary to my expectations at that time, he has printed part of this paper *ipsissimis verbis* as an appendix to his book, so you will see it; but I do not acknowledge it, nor mean to do so." Mill had also written some comments on his father's views, but Bulwer had so badly mangled them that Mill refused to claim them as his own. The essay on Bentham, however, he included in his private bibliography of his works. It is reprinted here in its entirety.

Mill later wrote a much longer essay on Bentham, and followed it with a long appreciation of Coleridge. There is no short essay giving Mill's view of Coleridge, but the following excerpt from a letter to J. P. Nichol, a Scottish friend, dated April 15, 1834, will give the reader some idea of what it was. (This letter and a number of others may be found in the *Fortnightly Review*, n.s. LXI, January–June 1897, pp. 660–678.)

. . . For instance, I was wondering whether you were a reader of Coleridge, and should certainly have asked you the question very soon, when you unexpectedly wrote to me about him exactly what I think of him myself—except, by the way, when you say, 'as a politician he seems unprincipled.' I think he is not *un*principled but *principled*—his views on politics are, I have reason to believe, systematic. Did you ever read his little work on Church and State? If not, read it; if you have, tell me whether you agree with it in the main (I mean the Church part of it) as I do. Few persons have exercised more influence over my thoughts and character than Coleridge has; not much by personal knowledge of him, though I have seen and conversed with him several times, but by his works, and by the fact that several persons with whom I have been very intimate were completely trained in his school. Through them, too, I have had opportunities of reading various unpublished manuscripts of his; and, on the whole, I can trace through what I know of his works, pieced together by what I have otherwise learned of his opinions, a most distinct thread of connection. I consider him the most systematic thinker of our time, without excepting even Bentham, whose edifice is as well bound together, but is constructed on so much simpler a plan, and covers so much less ground. On the whole, there is more food for thought—and the best kind of thought—in Coleridge than in all other contemporary writers; and it is in many respects a great good that almost all the most accomplished and zealous of the rising defenders of the Church of England are pupils of his. They are mischievous only in this, that they will be effectual in keeping up, for a time, what they will not be effectual in shaping to their ideal of what it ought to be.]

IT IS NO LIGHT TASK to give an abridged view of the philosophical opinions of one, who attempted to place the vast subjects of morals and legislation upon a scientific basis: a mere outline is all that can be attempted.

The first principles of Mr. Bentham's philosophy are these —that happiness, meaning by that term pleasure and exemption from pain, is the only thing desirable in itself; that all other things are desirable solely as means to that end; that the production, therefore, of the greatest possible happiness is the only fit purpose of all human thought and action, and consequently of all morality and government; and moreover, that pleasure and pain are the sole agencies by which the conduct of mankind is in fact governed, whatever circumstances the individual may be placed in, and whether he is aware of it or not.

Mr. Bentham does not appear to have entered very deeply into the metaphysical grounds of these doctrines; he seems to have taken those grounds very much upon the showing of the metaphysicians who preceded him. The principle of utility, or as he afterward called it, "the greatest-happiness principle," stands no otherwise demonstrated in his writings than by an enumeration of the phrases of a different description which have been commonly employed to denote the rule of life, and the rejection of them all, as having no intelligible meaning, further than as they may involve a tacit reference to considerations of utility. Such are the phrases "law of nature," "right reason," "natural rights," "moral sense." All these Mr. Bentham regarded as mere covers for dogmatism, excuses for setting up one's own *ipse dixit* as a rule to bind other people. "They consist, all of them," says he, "in so many contrivances for avoiding the obligation of appealing to any external standard, and for prevailing upon the reader to accept the author's sentiment or opinion as a reason for itself."

This, however, is not fair treatment of the believers in other moral principles than that of utility. All modes of speech are employed in an ignorant manner, by ignorant people; but no one who had thought deeply and systematically enough to be entitled to the name of a philosopher, ever supposed that his *own* private sentiments of approbation and disapprobation must necessarily be well-founded, and needed not to be compared with any external standard. The answer of such persons to Mr. Bentham would be, that by an inductive and analytical examination of the human mind, they had satisfied themselves that what we call our moral sentiments (that is, the feelings of complacency and aversion we experience when we compare actions of our own or of other people with our standard of right and wrong), are as much part of the original constitution of man's nature as the desire of happiness and the fear of suffering; that those sentiments do not indeed attach themselves to the same actions under all circumstances, but neither do they, in attaching themselves to actions, follow the law of utility; but certain other general laws, which are the same in all mankind, naturally, though education or external circumstances may counteract them, by creating artificial associations stronger than they. No *proof* indeed can be given that we ought to abide by these laws, but neither can any *proof* be given that we ought to regulate our conduct by utility. All that can be said is that the pursuit of happiness is natural to us; and so, it is contended, is the reverence for, and the inclination to square our actions by, certain general laws of morality.

Any one who is acquainted with the ethical doctrines either of the Reid and Stewart school, or of the German metaphysicians (not to go further back), knows that such would be the answer of those philosophers to Mr. Bentham; and it is an answer of which Mr. Bentham's writings furnish no sufficient refutation. For it is evident, that these views of the origin of moral distinctions are *not* what he says all such views are, destitute of any precise and tangible meaning; nor chargeable with setting up as a standard the feelings of the particular person. They set up as a standard what are assumed (on grounds which are considered sufficient) to be the instincts of the species, or principles of our common nature as universal and inexplicable as instincts.

To pass judgment on these doctrines belongs to a profounder and subtler metaphysics than Mr. Bentham possessed. I apprehend it will be the judgment of posterity that in his views of what in the felicitous expression of Hobbes may be called the *philosophia prima*, it has for the most part, even when he was most completely in the right, been reserved for others to *prove* him so. The greatest of Mr. Bentham's defects, his insufficient knowledge and appreciation of the thoughts of other men, shows itself constantly in his grappling with some delusive shadow of an adversary's opinions, and leaving the actual substance unharmed.

After laying down the principle of utility, Mr. Bentham is occupied, through the most voluminous and the most permanently valuable part of his works, in constructing the outlines of practical ethics and legislation, and filling up some portions of the latter science (or rather art) in great detail; by the uniform and unflinching application of his own greatest-happiness principle, from which the eminently consistent and systematic character of his intellect prevented him from ever swerving. In the writings of no philosopher, probably, are to be detected so few contradictions—so few instances of even momentary deviation from the principles he himself has laid down.

It is perhaps fortunate that Mr. Bentham devoted a much larger share of his time and labor to the subject of legislation, than to that of morals; for the mode in which he understood and applied the principle of utility appears to me far more conducive to the attainment of true and valuable results in the former, than in the latter of these two branches of inquiry. The recognition of happiness as the only thing desirable in itself, and of the production of the state of things most favorable to happiness as the only rational end both of morals and policy, by no means necessarily leads to the doctrine of expediency as professed by Paley: the ethical canon which judges of the morality of an act or a class of actions, solely by the probable *consequences* of that particular kind of act, supposing it to be generally practised. This is a very small part indeed of what a more enlarged understanding of the "greatest-happiness principle" would require us to take into the account. A certain kind of action, as for example, theft, or lying, would, if commonly practised, occasion certain evil consequences to society, but those evil consequences are far from constituting the entire moral bearings of the vices of theft or lying. We shall have a very imperfect view of the relation of those practises to the general happiness, if we suppose them to exist singly, and insulated. All acts suppose certain dispositions, and habits of mind and heart, which may be in themselves states of enjoyment or of wretchedness, and which must be fruitful in *other* consequences besides those particular acts. No person can be a thief or a liar without being much else, and if our moral judgments and feelings with respect to a person convicted of either vice were grounded solely upon the pernicious tendency of thieving and of lying, they would be partial and incomplete; many considerations would be omitted, which are at least equally "germane to the matter"; many which, by leaving them out of our general views, we may indeed teach ourselves a habit of overlooking, but which it is impossible for any of us not to be influenced by, in particular cases, in proportion as they are forced upon our attention.

Now, the great fault I have to find with Mr. Bentham as a moral philosopher, and the source of the chief part of the temporary mischief which, in that character, along with a vastly greater amount of permanent good, he must be allowed to have produced, is this: that he has practically, to a very great extent, confounded the principle of utility with the principle of specific consequences, and has habitually made up his estimate of the approbation or blame due to a particular kind of action, from a calculation solely of the consequences to which that very action, if practised generally, would itself lead. He has largely exemplified, and contributed very widely to diffuse, a tone of thinking, according to which any kind of action or any habit, which in its own specific consequences cannot be proved to be necessarily or probably productive of unhappiness to the agent himself or to others, is supposed to be fully justified; and any disapprobation or aversion entertained towards the individual by reason of it, is set down from that time forward as prejudice and superstition. It is not considered (at least not habitually considered) whether the act or habit in question, though not in itself necessarily pernicious, may not form part of a *character* essentially pernicious, or at least essentially deficient in some quality eminently conducive to the "greatest happiness." To apply such a standard as this would indeed often require a much deeper insight into the formation of character, and knowledge of the internal workings of human nature, than Mr. Bentham possessed. But, in a greater or less degree, he, and every one else, judges by this standard: even those who are warped, by some partial view, into the omission of all such elements from their general speculations.

When the moralist thus overlooks the relation of an act to a certain state of mind as its cause, and its connexion through that common cause with large classes and groups of actions apparently very little resembling itself, his estimation even of the consequences of the very act itself is rendered imperfect. For it may be affirmed with few exceptions, that any act whatever has a tendency to fix and perpetuate the state or character of mind in which itself has originated. And if that important element in the moral relations of the action, be not taken into account by the moralist as a cause, neither probably will it be taken into account as a consequence.

Mr. Bentham is far from having altogether overlooked this side of the subject. Indeed, those most original and instructive, though, as I conceive, in their spirit, partially erroneous chapters, on *motives* and on *dispositions*, in his first great work, the Introduction to the Principles of Morals and Legislation, open up a direct and broad path to these most important topics. It is not the less true that Mr. Bentham, and many others following his example, when they came to discuss particular questions of ethics, have commonly, in the superior stress which they laid upon the specific consequences of a class of acts, rejected all contemplation of the action in its general bearings upon the entire moral being of the agent, or have, to say the least, thrown those considerations so far into the background as to be almost out of sight. And by so doing they have not only marred the value of many of their speculations, considered as mere philosophical inquiries, but have always run the risk of incurring, and in many cases have in my opinion actually incurred, serious practical errors.

This incompleteness, however, in Mr. Bentham's general views, was not of a nature materially to diminish the value of his speculations through the greater part of the field of legislation. Those of the bearings of an action, upon which Mr.

Bentham bestowed almost exclusive attention, were also those with which almost alone legislation is conversant. The legislator enjoins or prohibits an action, with very little regard to the general moral excellence or turpitude which it implies; he looks to the consequences to society of the particular kind of action; his object is not to render people incapable of *desiring* a crime, but to deter them from actually *committing* it. Taking human beings as he finds them, he endeavors to supply such inducements as will constrain even persons of the dispositions the most at variance with the general happiness, to practise as great a degree of regard to it in their actual conduct, as can be obtained from them by such means without preponderant inconvenience. A theory, therefore, which considers little in an action besides that action's *own* consequences, will generally be sufficient to serve the purposes of a philosophy of legislation. Such a philosophy will be most apt to fail in the consideration of the greater social question: the theory of organic institutions and general forms of policy; for those (unlike the details of legislation) to be duly estimated, must be viewed as the great instruments of forming the national character, of carrying forward the members of the community toward perfection, or preserving them from degeneracy. This, as might in some measure be expected, is a point of view in which, except for some partial or limited purpose, Mr. Bentham seldom contemplates these questions. And this signal omission is one of the greatest of the deficiencies by which his speculations on the theory of government, though full of valuable ideas, are rendered, in my judgment, altogether inconclusive in their general results.

To these we shall advert more fully hereafter. As yet I have not acquitted myself of the more agreeable task of setting forth some part of the services which the philosophy of legislation owes to Mr. Bentham.

The greatest service of all, that for which posterity will award most honor to his name, is one that is his exclusively, and can be shared by no man present or to come; it is the service which can be performed only once for any science, that of pointing out by what method of investigation it may be *made* a science. What Bacon did for physical knowledge, Mr. Bentham has done for philosophical legislation. Before Bacon's time, many physical facts had been ascertained, and previously to Mr. Bentham, mankind were in possession of many just and valuable detached observations on the making of laws. But he was the first who attempted regularly to deduce all the secondary and intermediate principles of law, by direct and systematic inference from the one great axiom or principle of general utility. In all existing systems of law, those secondary principles or dicta in which the essence of the systems resided, had grown up in detail, and even when founded in views of utility, were not the result of any scientific and comprehensive course of inquiry, but more frequently were purely technical; that is, they had grown out of circumstances purely *historical*, and not having been altered when those circumstances changed, had nothing left to rest upon but fictions, and unmeaning forms. Take for instance the law of real property, the whole of which continues to this very day to be founded on the doctrine of feudal tenures, when those tenures have long ceased to exist except in the phraseology of Westminster Hall. Nor was the *theory* of law in a better state than the practical systems; speculative jurists having dared little more than to refine somewhat upon the technical maxims of the particular body of jurisprudence which they happened to have studied. Mr. Bentham was the first who had the genius and courage to conceive the idea of bringing back the science to first principles. This could not be done, could scarcely even be attempted, without, as a necessary consequence, making obvious the utter worthlessness of many, and the crudity and want of precision of almost all, the maxims which had previously passed everywhere for principles of law.

Mr. Bentham, moreover, has warred against the errors of existing systems of jurisprudence, in a more direct manner than by merely presenting the contrary truths. The force of argument with which he rent asunder the fantastic and illogical maxims on which the various technical systems are founded, and exposed the flagrant evils which they practically produce, is only equaled by the pungent sarcasm and exquisite humor with which he has derided their absurdities, and the eloquent declamation which he continually pours forth against them, sometimes in the form of lamentation, and sometimes of invective.

This then was the first, and perhaps the grandest achievement of Mr. Bentham: the entire discrediting of all technical systems, and the example which he set of treating law as no peculiar mystery, but a simple piece of practical business, wherein means were to be adapted to ends, as in any of the other arts of life. To have accomplished this, supposing him to have done nothing else, is to have equaled the glory of the greatest scientific benefactors of the human race.

But Mr. Bentham, unlike Bacon, did not merely prophesy a science; he made large strides towards the creation of one. He was the first who conceived, with anything approaching to precision, the idea of a Code or complete body of law, and the distinctive characters of its essential parts—the Civil Law, the Penal Law, and the Law of Procedure. On the first two of these three departments he rendered valuable service; the third he actually created. Conformably to the habits of his mind, he set about investigating, *ab initio*, a philosophy or science for each of the three branches. He did with the received principles of each, what a good code would do with the laws themselves —extirpated the bad, substituting others; reenacted the good, but in so much clearer and more methodical a form that those who were most familiar with them before scarcely recognized them as the same. Even upon old truths, when they pass through his hands, he leaves so many of his marks, that often he almost seems to claim the discovery of what he has only systematized.

In creating the philosophy of Civil Law, he proceeded not much beyond establishing on the proper basis some of its most general principles, and cursorily discussing some of the most interesting of its details. Nearly the whole of what he has published on this branch of law is contained in the *Traités de Législation*, edited by M. Dumont. To the most difficult part, and that which most needed a master-hand to clear away its difficulties, the nomenclature and arrangement of the Civil Code, he contributed little, except detached observations and criticisms upon the errors of his predecessors. The *"Vue Générale d'un Corps Complet de Législation,"* included in the work just cited, contains almost all which he has given to us on this subject.

In the department of Penal Law, he is the author of the best attempt yet made toward a philosophical classification of offenses. The theory of punishments (for which however more had been done by his predecessors than for any other part of the science of law) he left nearly complete.

The theory of Procedure (including that of the constitution

of the courts of justice) he found in a more utterly barbarous state than even either of the other branches, and he left it incomparably the most perfect. There is scarcely a question of practical importance in this most important department, which he has not settled. He has left next to nothing for his successors.

He has shown with the force of demonstration, and has enforced and illustrated the truth in a hundred ways, that by sweeping away the greater part of the artificial rules and forms which obtain in all the countries called civilized, and adopting the simple and direct modes of investigation which all men employ in endeavoring to ascertain facts for their own private knowledge, it is possible to get rid of at least nine tenths of the expense, and ninety-nine hundredths of the delay, of law proceedings, not only with no increase, but with an almost incredible diminution of the chances of erroneous decision. He has also established irrefragably the principles of a good judicial establishment: a division of the country into districts, with *one* judge in each, appointed only for a limited period, and deciding all sorts of cases, with a deputy under him, appointed and removable by himself; an appeal lying in all cases whatever, but by the transmission of papers only, to a supreme court or courts, consisting each of only *one* judge, and stationed in the metropolis.

It is impossible within the compass of this sketch, to attempt any further statement of Mr. Bentham's principles and views on the great science which first became a science in his hands.

As an analyst of human nature (the faculty in which above all it is necessary that an ethical philosopher should excel) I cannot rank Mr. Bentham very high. He has done little in this department, beyond introducing what appears to me a very deceptive phraseology, and furnishing a catalog of the "springs of action," from which some of the most important are left out.

That the actions of sentient beings are wholly determined by pleasure and pain, is the fundamental principle from which he starts; and thereupon Mr. Bentham creates a *motive*, and an *interest*, corresponding to each pleasure or pain, and affirms that our actions are determined by our *interests*, by the *preponderant* interest, by the *balance* of motives. Now if this only means what was before asserted, that our actions are determined by pleasure and pain, that simple and unambiguous mode of stating the proposition is preferable. But under cover of the obscurer phrase a meaning creeps in, both to the author's mind and the reader's, which goes much further, and is entirely false: that all our acts are determined by pains and pleasures *in prospect*, pains and pleasures to which we look forward as the *consequences* of our acts. This, as a universal truth, can in no way be maintained. The pain or pleasure which determines our conduct is as frequently one which *precedes* the moment of action as one which follows it. A man *may*, it is true, be deterred in circumstances of temptation, from perpetrating a crime, by his dread of the punishment, or of the remorse, which he fears he may have to endure *after* the guilty act; and in that case we may say, with some kind of propriety, that his conduct is swayed by the balance of motives, or if you will, of interests. But the case *may* be, and is to the full as likely to be, that he recoils from the very thought of committing the act; the idea of placing himself in such a situation is so painful, that he cannot dwell upon it long enough to have even the physical power of perpetrating the crime. His conduct is determined by pain; but by a pain which precedes the act, not by one which is expected to follow it. Not only *may* this be so, but unless it be so, the man is not really virtuous. The fear of pain *consequent* upon the act, cannot arise, unless there be *deliberation*; and the man as well as "the woman who deliberates" is in imminent danger of being lost. With what propriety shrinking from an action without deliberation can be called yielding to an *interest*, I cannot see. *Interest* surely conveys, and is intended to convey, the idea of an *end*, to which the conduct (whether it be act or forbearance) is designed as the *means*. Nothing of this sort takes place in the above example. It would be more correct to say that conduct is *sometimes* determined by an *interest*, that is, by a deliberate and conscious aim; and sometimes by an *impulse*, that is, by a feeling (call it an association if you think fit) which has no ulterior end, the act or forbearance becoming an end in itself.

The attempt, again, to *enumerate* motives, that is, human desires and aversions, seems to me to be in its very conception an error. Motives are innumerable: there is nothing whatever which may not become an object of desire or of dislike by association. It may be desirable to distinguish by peculiar notice the motives which are strongest and of most frequent operation; but Mr. Bentham has not even done this. In his list of motives, though he includes sympathy, he omits conscience, or the feeling of duty: one would never imagine from reading him that any human being ever did an act merely because it is right, or abstained from it merely because it is wrong. In this Mr. Bentham differs widely from Hartley, who, although he considers the moral sentiments to be wholly the result of association, does not therefore deny them a place in his system, but includes the feelings of "the moral sense" as one of the six classes into which he divides pleasures and pains. In Mr. Bentham's own mind, deeply imbued as it was with the "greatest-happiness principle," this motive was probably so blended with that of sympathy as to be undistinguishable from it; but he should have recollected that those who acknowledge another standard of right and wrong than happiness, or who have never reflected on the subject at all, have often very strong feelings of moral obligation; and whether a person's standard be happiness or any thing else, his attachment to his standard is not necessarily in proportion to his benevolence. Persons of weak sympathies have often a strong feeling of justice; and others, again, with the feelings of benevolence in considerable strength, have scarcely any consciousness of moral obligation at all.

It is scarcely necessary to point out that the habitual omission of so important a spring of action, in an enumeration professing to be complete, must tend to create a habit of overlooking the same phenomenon, and, consequently, making no allowance for it, in other moral speculations. It is difficult to imagine any more fruitful source of gross error; though one would be apt to suppose the oversight an impossible one, without this evidence of its having been committed by one of the greatest thinkers our species has produced. How can we suppose him to be alive to the existence and force of the motive in particular cases, who omits it in a deliberate and comprehensive enumeration of all the influences by which human conduct is governed?

In laying down as a philosophical axiom, that men's actions are always obedient to their interests, Mr. Bentham did no more than dress up the very trivial proposition, that all persons do what they feel themselves most disposed to do, in terms which appeared to him more precise, and better suited to the purposes of philosophy than those more familiar expressions.

He by no means intended by this assertion to impute universal selfishness to mankind, for he reckoned the motive of sympathy as an *interest*, and would have included conscience under the same appellation, if that motive had found any place in his philosophy, as a distinct principle from benevolence. He distinguished two kinds of interests, the self-regarding and the social; in vulgar discourse the name is restricted to the former kind alone.

But there cannot be a greater mistake than to suppose that, because we may ourselves be perfectly *conscious* of an ambiguity in our language, that ambiguity therefore has no effect in perverting our modes of thought. I am persuaded, from experience, that this habit of speaking of all the feelings which govern mankind under the name of *interests*, is almost always in point of fact connected with a tendency to consider *interest* in the vulgar sense, that is, purely self-regarding interest, as exercising, by the very constitution of human nature, a far more exclusive and paramount control over human actions than it really does exercise. Such, certainly, was the tendency of Mr. Bentham's own opinions. Habitually, and throughout his works, the moment he has shown that a man's *selfish* interest would prompt him to a particular course of action, he lays it down without further parley that the man's interest lies that way; and, by sliding insensibly from the vulgar sense of the word into the philosophical, and from the philosophical back into the vulgar, the conclusion which is always brought out is that the man will act as the selfish interest prompts. The extent to which Mr. Bentham was a believer in the predominance of the selfish principle in human nature, may be seen from the sweeping terms in which, in his Book of Fallacies, he expressly lays down that predominance as a philosophical axiom.

"In *every* human breast (rare and short-lived ebullitions, the result of some extraordinarily strong stimulus or excitement, excepted) self-regarding interest is predominant over social interest; each person's own individual interest over the interests of all other persons taken together."Pp. 392–3.

In another passage of the same work (p. 363) he says, "Taking the whole of life together, there exists not, *nor ever can exist*, that human being in whose instance any public interest he can have had will not, in so far as depends upon himself, have been sacrificed to his own personal interest.

Towards the advancement of the public interest, all that the most public-spirited (which is as much as to say the most virtuous) of men can do, is to do what depends upon himself toward bringing the public interest, that is, his own personal share in the public interest, to a state as nearly approaching to coincidence, and on as few occasions amounting to a state of repugnance, as possible, with his private interests."

By the promulgation of such views of human nature, and by a general tone of thought and expression perfectly in harmony with them, I conceive Mr. Bentham's writings to have done and to be doing very serious evil. It is by such things that the more enthusiastic and generous minds are prejudiced against all his other speculations, and against the very attempt to make ethics and politics a subject of precise and philosophical thinking—which attempt, indeed, if it were necessarily connected with such views, would be still more pernicious than the vague and flashy declamation for which it is proposed as a substitute. The effect is still worse on the minds of those who are not shocked and repelled by this tone of thinking, for on them it must be perverting to their whole moral nature. It is difficult to form the conception of a tendency more inconsistent with all rational hope of good for the human species, than that which must be impressed by such doctrines upon any mind in which they find acceptance.

There are, there have been, many human beings in whom the motives of patriotism or of benevolence have been permanent steady principles of action, superior to any ordinary, and in not a few instances, to any possible, temptations of personal interest. There are, and have been, multitudes in whom the motive of conscience or moral obligation has been thus paramount. There is nothing in the constitution of human nature to forbid its being so in all mankind. Until it is so, the race will never enjoy one-tenth part of the happiness which our nature is susceptible of. I regard any considerable increase of human happiness, through mere changes in outward circumstances, unaccompanied by changes in the state of the desires, as hopeless; not to mention that, while the desires are circumscribed in self, there can be no adequate motive for exertions tending to modify to good ends even those external circumstances. No man's individual share of any public good which he can hope to realize by his efforts, is an equivalent for the sacrifice of his ease, and of the personal objects which he might attain by another course of conduct. The balance can be turned in favor of virtuous exertion, only by the interest of *feeling* or by that of *conscience*, those "social interests," the necessary subordination of which to "self-regarding" is so lightly assumed.

But the power of any one to realize in himself the state of mind without which his own enjoyment of life can be but poor and scanty, and on which all our hopes of happiness or moral perfection to the species must rest, depends entirely upon his having faith in the actual existence of such feelings and dispositions in others, and in their possibility for himself. It is for those in whom the feelings of virtue are weak, that ethical writing is chiefly needful, and its proper office is to strengthen those feelings. But to be qualified for this task, it is necessary, first to have, and next to show, in every sentence and in every line, a firm unwavering confidence in man's capability of virtue. It is by a sort of sympathetic contagion, or inspiration, that a noble mind assimilates other minds to itself, and no one was ever inspired by one whose own inspiration was not sufficient to give him faith in the possibility of making others feel what *he* feels.

Upon those who *need* to be strengthened and upheld by a really inspired moralist—such a moralist as Socrates, as Plato, or (speaking humanly and not theologically) as Christ, the effect of such writings as Mr. Bentham's, if they be read and believed and their spirit imbibed, must either be hopeless despondency and gloom, or a reckless giving themselves up to a life of that miserable self-seeking, which they are there taught to regard as inherent in their original and unalterable nature.

Mr. Bentham's speculations on politics in the narrow sense, that is, on the theory of government, are distinguished by his usual characteristic, that of beginning at the beginning. He places before himself man in society without a government, and considering what sort of government it would be advisable to construct, finds that the most expedient would be a representative democracy. Whatever may be the value of this conclusion, the mode in which it is arrived at appears to me to be fallacious; for it assumes that mankind are alike in all times and all places, that they have the same wants and are exposed to the same evils, and that if the same institutions do not suit them, it is only because in the more backward stages of improvement, they have not wisdom to see what institutions are most for their good. How to invest certain servants of the people with the power necessary for the protection of person and property, with the greatest possible facility to the people of changing the depositories of that power, when they think it is abused—such is the only problem in social organization which Mr. Bentham has proposed to himself. Yet this is but a part of the real problem. It never seems to have occurred to him to regard political institutions in a higher light, as the principal means of the social education of a people. Had he done so, he would have seen that the same institutions will no more suit two nations in different stages of civilization, than the same lessons will suit children of different ages. As the degree of civilization already attained varies, so does the kind of social influence necessary for carrying the community forward to the next stage of its progress. For a tribe of North American Indians, improvement means taming down their proud and solitary self-dependence; for a body of emancipated Negroes, it means accustoming them to be self-dependent, instead of being merely obedient to orders; for our semibarbarous ancestors, it would have meant, softening them; for a race of enervated Asiatics, it would mean hardening them. How can the same social organization be fitted for producing so many contrary effects?

The prevailing error of Mr. Bentham's views of human nature appears to me to be this: he supposes mankind to be swayed by only a part of the inducements which really actuate them, but of that part he imagines them to be much cooler and more thoughtful calculators than they really are. He has, I think, been, to a certain extent, misled in the theory of politics by supposing that the submission of the mass of mankind to an established government is mainly owing to a reasoning perception of the necessity of legal protection, and of the common interest of all in a prompt and zealous obedience to the law. He was not, I am persuaded, aware, how very much of the really wonderful acquiescence of mankind in any government which they find established, is the effect of mere habit and imagination, and therefore depends upon the preservation of something like continuity of existence in the institutions, and identity in their outward forms; cannot transfer itself easily to new institutions, even though in themselves preferable, and is greatly shaken when there occurs any thing like a break in the line of historical duration, any thing which can be termed the end of the old constitution and the beginning of a new one.

The constitutional writers of our own country, anterior to Mr. Bentham, had carried feelings of this kind to the height of a superstition; they never considered what was best adapted to their own times, but only what had existed in former times, even in times that had long gone by. It is not very many years since such were the principal grounds on which parliamentary reform itself was defended. Mr. Bentham has done much service in discrediting, as he has done completely, this school of politicians, and exposing the absurd sacrifice of present ends to antiquated means; but he has, I think, himself fallen into a contrary error. The very fact that a certain set of political institutions already exist, have long existed, and have become associated with all the historical recollections of a people, is in itself, as far as it goes, a property which adapts them to that people, and gives them a great advantage over any new institutions in obtaining that ready and willing resignation to what has once been decided by lawful authority, which alone renders possible those innumerable compromises between adverse interests and expectations, without which no government could be carried on for a year, and with difficulty even for a week. Of the perception of this important truth, scarcely a trace is visible in Mr. Bentham's writings.

It is impossible, however, to contest to Mr. Bentham, on this subject or on any other which he has touched, the merit, and it is very great, of having brought forward into notice one of the faces of the truth, and a highly important one. Whether on government, on morals, or on any of the other topics on which his speculations are comparatively imperfect, they are still highly instructive and valuable to any one who is capable of supplying the remainder of the truth; they are calculated to mislead only by the pretension which they invariably set up of being the whole truth, a complete theory and philosophy of the subject. Mr. Bentham was more a thinker than a reader; he seldom compared his ideas with those of other philosophers, and was by no means aware how many thoughts had existed in other minds which his doctrines did not afford the means either to refute or to appreciate.

Two Letters

[The first of the following selections is an excerpt from a letter to Mill's friend, John Stirling, dated May 24, 1832, and the second a complete letter to Thomas Carlyle, written over a year and a half later. Both of them are taken from the *Letters of John Stuart Mill*, ed. H. S. R. Elliot, vol. I.]

I

. . . I HAVE LONG SINCE renounced any hankering for being happier than I am, and only since then have I enjoyed anything which can be called well-being. How few are they who have discovered the wisdom of the precept—"Take no thought of the morrow" when considered as all the sayings of Christ should be, not as laws laid down with strict logical precision for regulating the details of our conduct—since such must be, like all other maxims of prudence, *variable*—but as the bodying forth in words of the *spirit* of all morality, right self-culture, the principles of which cannot change, as man's nature changes not, though surrounding circumstances do. I do not mean, by using the word self-culture, to prejudge anything whether such culture can come from man himself or must come directly from God; all I mean is that it is culture of the man's self, of his feelings and will, fitting him to look abroad and see how he is to act, not imposing on him by express definition a prescribed mode of action, which it is clear to me that many of the precepts of the Gospel were never intended to do, being manifestly unsuited to that end; witness that which I have just cited, or the great one of doing to all men as you desire that they should do to you, or of turning the left cheek, &c., which last the Quakers have made themselves ridiculous by attempting to act upon a very little more literally than other people. All these would be vicious as moral statutes, binding the tribunal, but they are excellent as instruction to the judge in the *forum conscientiae*, in what spirit he is to look at the evidence, what posture he must assume in order that he may see clearly the moral bearings of the thing which he is looking at.

I I

KENSINGTON, 12th January 1834.

My Dear Carlyle—Your little note dated the 24th was evidently written before you received my letter written I forget when, but which I fear lost the first week's post. I am therefore still expecting an answer to that letter, but shall not wait for it, mindful that I still owe you an answer to your last long letter, and a fuller answer, too, than can be given in any moderate space. I feel that letter a kind of call upon me to a more complete unfolding to you of my opinions and ways of thinking than I have ever yet made; which, however, cannot be all accomplished at once, but must be gradual. In the very fact that there has not been that full explanation, and that I feel *moved* to it now, you may see that there has taken place a great change in my character, and one of which you will wholly approve, a change, not from any kind of insincerity, but *to* a far higher kind of sincerity than belonged to me before. This change has been progressive, and had barely begun to take place when you were in London two years ago. I was then, and had been for one year, in an intermediate state, a state of *reaction* from logical-utilitarian narrowness of the very narrowest kind, out of which after much unhappiness and inward struggling I had emerged, and had taken temporary refuge in its extreme opposite. My first state had been one of intense philosophic intolerance, not arising from the scornfulness of the heart but from the onesidedness of the understanding, seeing nothing myself but the distorted image, thrown back from many most oblique and twisted reflectors, of *one* side only of the truth. I felt towards all who saw any other side, not indeed a feeling of disdain, for that never was in my character, but the very utmost excess of intellectual *vilipending*. At that time I was thought to *outrer* the doctrines of utilitarianism even by those who now consider me a lost sheep who has strayed from the flock and been laid hold of by the wolves. That was not wonderful, because even in the narrowest of my then associates, they being older men, their ratiocinative and nicely concatenated dreams were at some point or other, and in some degree or other, corrected and limited by their experience of actual realities, while I, a schoolboy fresh from the logic school, had never conversed with a reality, never seen one, knew not what manner of thing it was, had only spun, first other people's and then my own deductions from assumed premises. Now when I had got out of this state, and saw that my premises were mere generalisations of some of the innumerable aspects of Reality, and that far from being the most important ones; and when I had tried to go *all round* every object which I surveyed, and to place myself at all points of view, so as to have the best chance of seeing all sides, I think it is scarcely surprising that for a time I became catholic and tolerant in an extreme degree, and thought onesidedness almost the one great evil in human affairs, seeing it was the evil which had been the bane of my own teachers, and was also that of those who were warring against my teachers. I never indeed was tolerant of aught but earnest belief; but I saw, or seemed to see, so much of good and of truth in the positive part of the most opposite opinions and practices, could they but be divested of their exclusive pretensions, that I scarcely felt myself called upon to *deny* anything but denial itself. I never made strongly prominent my differences with any sincere, truth-loving person, but held communion with him through our points of agreement, endeavored in the first place to appropriate to myself whatever was positive in him, and, if he gave me any encouragement, brought before *him* also whatever of positive might be in *me*, which he till then had not. A character most unlike yours, of a quite lower kind, and which if I had not outgrown, and speedily too, there could have been little worth in me. Do you remember a paper I wrote in an early number of *Tait*, reviewing a book by a Mr. Lewes (a man of considerable worth, of whom I shall have something more to say yet). That paper paints exactly the state of my mind and feelings at that time. It was the truest paper I had ever written, for it was the most completely an outgrowth of my own mind and character; not that what is there taught was the best I even then had to teach, nor perhaps did I even think it so, but it contained what was *uppermost* in me at that time, and differed from most also that I knew in having *emanated* from me, not, with more or less perfect assimilation, merely *worked* itself *into* me. Now, from this my intellectual history, in relating which I have faith that I have not presumed too much upon your interest in me, you will easily see why it is that we two have so rarely canvassed together, or even mentioned to each other, our differences. I never, or rarely, felt myself called upon to come into *collision* with any one, except those to whom I felt myself altogether superior, and with whom, if I had any intellectual communion, it was not for the sake of *learning* but of *teaching*. I have not till lately, and very gradually, found out that this is not honest; that although I have not positively, I have negatively, done much to give to you and to others a false opinion of me, though the deliberation with which you form your opinions, always waiting for sufficient grounds, has, I think, protected *you* from forming an actually false opinion of me, and I have only to accuse myself of not having afforded you sufficient means of forming the true. Whether if you knew me thoroughly I should stand higher, or lower, either in your esteem or in your affection, L know not; in some things you seem to think me *further* from you than I am, in others perhaps I am further from you than you know. On the whole I think if all were told I should stand lower; but there cannot fail, anyway, to be much which we shall mutually not only respect but greatly prize in each other, and after all, this, as you and I both know, is altogether of secondary importance, the first being, that we, and all persons and all things, should be seen truly, and as they are.

Our differences are indeed of the first importance, and to you must appear of infinite importance, though for reasons which you will feel the force of, they do not, in my feeling, throw me to so great a distance from you as they perhaps will in yours. The first and principal of these differences is that I have only what appears to you much the same thing as, or even worse than, no God at all, namely, a merely probable God. By *probable* I do not mean as you sometimes do, in the sense of the Jesuits, that which has weighty authorities in its favor. I mean that the existence of a Creator is not to me a matter of faith or of intuition, and as a proposition to be proved by evidence, it is but a hypothesis, the proofs of which, as you I know agree with me, do not amount to absolute certainty. As this is my condition in spite of the strongest wish to believe, I fear it is hopeless; the unspeakable good it would be to me to have a *faith* like yours, I mean as firm as yours, on that, to you, fundamental point, I am as strongly conscious of when life is a happiness to me, as when it is, what it has been for long periods now past by, a burthen. But I know that neither you nor any one else can be of any use to me in this, and I content myself with doing no ill by never propagating my uncertainties. The reason why I think I shall never alter in this matter is that none of the ordinary *difficulties*, as they are called, as the origin of evil, and such like, are any serious obstacles to me; it is not that the logical understanding invading the province of another faculty will not let that other higher faculty do its office—there is wanting something positive in me which exists in others, whether that something be, as skeptics say, an acquired association, or as you say, a natural faculty; so you see I am nearly as proper an object of your pity as Cavaignac; nevertheless I do not feel myself so, having, as I have, other supports, which the want of that one cannot take away. With respect to the immortality of the soul I see no reason to believe that it perishes, nor sufficient ground for complete assurance that it survives; but if it does there is every reason to think that it continues in another state such as it has made itself here, and no further affected by the change than it would be by any equally great event during its sojourn on earth, were such possible; consequently in all we do here we are working in our hereafter as well as our "now." Now, were you aware that I was in such a state of uncertainty on these main points? I am almost sure that you were not much mistaken in the matter, but yet were not quite certain that you knew.

Another of our differences is that I am still, and am likely to remain, a utilitarian, though not one of "the people called utilitarians," indeed, having scarcely one of my secondary premises in common with them; nor a utilitarian at all, unless in quite another sense from what perhaps any one except myself understands by the word. It would take a whole letter to make it quite clear to you what I mean, and I feel perfectly that I have stated the difference between us in a manner and in terms which give no just idea of what it really is, and that every explanation I shall hereafter make will show that difference to be less than the words I have used seem to import. One of the explanations I have to give, I partly indicate by saying, as I do most fully, that I entirely recognize with you the "infinite nature of Deity." Yet, by this too, if unexplained, I should convey an idea of as much *greater* an agreement with you than the truth warrants, as I do in the *other case* of a *less* agreement. This also must wait till another time for a fuller development. You will see, partly, with what an immense number and variety of explanations my utilitarianism must be taken, and that those explanations affect its essence, not merely its accidental forms, when I tell you that on the very point on which you express your belief so kindly and with so much *ménagement*, and appeal to my future self, and promise not to be angry if I differ from you "even with vehemence," I agree and have long agreed with you, even in the most decided and vehement manner. I have never, at least since I had any convictions of my own, belonged to the benevolentiary, soup-kitchen school. Though I hold the good of the species (or rather of its separate units) to be the ultimate end (which is the alpha and omega of my utilitarianism), I believe with the fullest belief that this end can in no other way be forwarded but by the means you speak of, namely, by each taking for his exclusive aim the development of what is best in *himself*. I qualify or explain this doctrine no otherwise than as you yourself do, since you hold that every human creature has an appointed task to perform, which task he is to know and find out for himself; this can only be by discovering in what manner such faculties as he possesses or can acquire may produce most good in the world, meaning by the world a larger or a smaller part of it, as may happen. Thus *you* think it a part of your *duty*, of your *work*, to address yourself, through the press, to the "species" at large. Further than that I do not go, perhaps even less far, and when once I have written down my belief and sent it forth in such manner as happens or seems to be the most effectual within my reach, I harass myself as little as you do with any thought about the consequences, being like yourself perfectly satisfied that what I have done, if done in the spirit of my own creed, will "prove in reality all and the utmost that I was capable of doing" for mankind.

And now do not "take it ill" if I say how much it surprised me that you should think it necessary to say you would not "take it ill" if I differed from you. I never for an instant suspected that you would take ill any difference of opinion while you continue fully assured that the dissentient is sincere, earnest, and truth-loving, and you never allow me to be under a moment's fear that you are unassured of that in my case. Grieved you might be at what you might deem my errors, but *that* feeling you could not mean to disavow, nor would it be any pleasure to me, but the contrary, if you could. In your recent letters you have several times expressed *surprise* at opinions and feelings of mine which you did not expect, and which you have said proved to you how little you yet know me; and which in truth *did* show how small a part of my character I had yet shown to you, so much smaller a part than I was aware of: truly I begin to think that instead of being, as you thought I was, the most self-conscious person living, I am much less self-conscious *now* (whatever I was once) than almost anybody. But what most shows how little I had afforded you an insight into me, is that the fact of *my* having recently read the New Testament, and what I wrote to you of the impressions it had made upon me, should have formed, as it seems to have done, an era in your opinion and feeling concerning me. In my own history it is no era; it has made no new impression, only strengthened the best of the old; I have for years had the very same idea of Christ, and the same unbounded reverence for him as now; it was because of this reverence that I sought a more perfect acquaintance with the records of his life, that indeed gave new life to the reverence, which in any case was becoming or was closely allied with all that was becoming a living principle in my character.

Here is a very long letter, yet how little it says of all that is to be said! However, you see that you are likely to know much more of me hereafter than you have known hitherto. Make my kind remembrances to Mrs. Carlyle, and believe me faithfully yours,   J. S. MILL.

THREE

Blakey's *History of Moral Science*

[Robert Blakey's undistinguished *History of Moral Science*, in two volumes, appeared early in 1833, and in October of that year Mill reviewed it in the *Monthly Repository*, a magazine edited by a friend of his, in which many of his early essays were published. The first part of the review summarizes and criticizes Blakey's historical views. The second part, which is here reprinted, deals directly with some issues of moral philosophy.]

AT THE CONCLUSION of his abstract of the opinions of previous authors, which, it is but justice to say, is in general much fairer, and even more intelligent, than might be supposed from the specimens which we have given, Mr. Blakey sums up the result of the examination in the following words:

> All the systems we have examined may, I conceive, be referred to six distinct heads. 1st. The eternal and immutable nature of all moral distinctions. 2nd. That utility, public or private, is the foundation of moral obligation. 3rd. That all morality is founded upon the will of God. 4th. That a moral sense, feeling, or emotion, is the ground of virtue. 5th. That it is by supposing ourselves in the situation of others, or by a species of sympathetic mechanism, that we derive our notions of good and evil. And 6th, the doctrine of vibrations,* and the association of ideas. (p. 317)

After declaring that "there are none of these different systems that are not in some degree founded on truth," and that "we cannot resolve all the moral feelings and habits of our nature into one general principle," he assigns, nevertheless, his reasons for preferring to all the other theories the doctrine

---

* The doctrine of *vibrations*, a mere physiological hypothesis, which has no connection at all with Hartley's theory of association, ought not to have been included in an enumeration of theories of morals.

"that virtue depends upon the will of God," as made known by revelation.

Mr. Blakey's enumeration is illogical; it confounds two distinct, though nearly connected, questions: the *standard* or *test* of moral obligation, and the *origin* of our moral *sentiments*. It is one question what rule we *ought* to obey, and why; another question how our feelings of approbation and disapprobation *actually* originate. The former is the fundamental question of practical morals; the latter is a problem in mental philosophy. Adam Smith's doctrine of *sympathy* which stands fifth, and the doctrine of *association* which stands sixth in Mr. Blakey's list, are theories respecting the nature and origin of our *feelings* of morality. His second and third are theories respecting the *rule* or *law* by which we ought to guide our *conduct*. His first and fourth involve, or may be so understood as to involve, *both* considerations.

These several theories, therefore, are not exclusive of one another. It is possible, for instance, to hold with Hartley, that our *feelings* of morality originate in association, and with Bentham that our *conduct*, in all things which depend on our will, and among the rest, in the cultivation of those very feelings, should be guided by *utility*; or with our author, that the will of God is itself the foundation of the obligations of virtue. David Hume seems to have combined the recognition of utility as the standard or test of morality, with the belief in a moral sense, independent of association. Paley has no theory respecting the nature of moral *feelings*, but his notion of the moral *law* is compounded of the second and third of the theories enumerated by our author.

But of all those theories, whether ethical or metaphysical, whether declaring what our *conduct should* be, or what our *feelings are*, none surely is so utterly destitute of plausibility as Mr. Blakey's own doctrine, that virtue is *constituted* by the will of God.

If we believe this, we believe that God does not *declare* what is good, and *command* us to do it, but that God actually *makes* it good. Good is whatever God makes it. What we call evil, is only evil because he has arbitrarily prohibited it. The countless myriads to whom he has never signified his will are under no moral obligations. This doctrine takes away all motives to yield obedience to God, except those which induce a slave to obey his master. He must be obeyed because he is the stronger. He is not to be obeyed because he is good, for *that* implies a good which he could not have made bad by his mere will. If we had the misfortune to believe that the world is ruled by an evil principle, that there is no God but only a devil, or that the devil has more power over us than God, we ought by this rule to obey the devil. Mr. Blakey is evidently quite unconscious of these consequences of his theory. But, that they are legitimate consequences who can doubt?

And this theory Mr. Blakey believes to rest upon the authority of scripture.

> "I venture to affirm," says he, "that from Genesis to Revelation inclusive, there is not a single passage, which, when fairly examined, claims the attention and homage of mankind upon any other ground than what is implied in the command which accompanies it." (p. 326)

The scriptures, as Mr. Blakey himself says elsewhere, do not enter into speculative questions; they tell us *what* to do, not *why*. But do they not say perpetually, God is good, God is just, God is righteous, God is holy? And are we to understand by these affirmations nothing at all, but the identical and unmeaning proposition God is himself, or a proposition which has so little to do with morality as this, God is powerful? Has God in short no moral attributes? no attributes but those which the devil is conceived to possess in a smaller degree? and no title to our obedience but such as the devil would have, if there were a devil, and the universe were without God?

Mr. Blakey insists much upon the sublimity of the scriptures, and the perfection of scripture morality, considerations which tell strongly against his own doctrine; for if we are capable of recognizing excellence in the commands of the Omnipotent, they must possess excellence independently of his command, and excellence discoverable by us even without revelation; for whatever reason can recognize when found, reason can find. If the morality of the scriptures is admirable because it conduces to happiness, this implies that the production of happiness is a legitimate purpose of morals; if because it accords with our sympathies, *that* implies that morality may be founded on sympathy. If the precepts of scripture have nothing intrinsically good, but are good solely by reason of the power from which they emanate, their character ought to

be as mysterious and incomprehensible to us as the cere-
monies of magic; nor could there on that supposition be any
reason apparent to us why we are not commanded to hate our
neighbor instead of to love him.

Not being of opinion, with Mr. Blakey, that our reception
of a philosophic doctrine ought to be determined, not solely
by its truth, but by what we imagine respecting the arguments
it may afford for or against our religious belief, we ought not,
perhaps, to notice the claim which Mr. Blakey sets up for his
doctrine, of being peculiarly favorable to the interests of revealed religion. But though such arguments go for nothing
with those who can trust themselves to judge of the true and
the false, who are resolved to believe the truth, *whatever* may
be its consequences, and are not afraid of finding one truth
irreconcilable with another, those who are diffident of their
own intellectual powers naturally dread any doctrine which
they can be led to think tends to shake from under their feet
the foundation on which they have built all their hopes and
purposes. Mr. Blakey, therefore, shall not be allowed the exclusive use of this argument. We tell him that *his* doctrine is
more destructive to the foundations of Christianity than any
of the theories of moral obligation which he has enumerated,
by taking away altogether its internal evidences, the only ones
which are not common to it with a thousand superstitions. In
Judea itself, both before and after Christ appeared, numbers
of false Christs and charlatans of all descriptions had pretended to work miracles, and had been believed, believed not
only by their proselytes, but by those who rejected them, and
who ascribed their miraculous powers to the agency of evil
spirits. If these impostors sunk, and were heard of no more,
while Christianity spread itself over the earth, it was not that
greater credence was given to the Christian miracles than to
theirs; it was that the simple-hearted men who gathered themselves round the founder of Christianity, far from believing
the doctrines to be excellent because they came from God,
believed them to come from God because they felt them to be
excellent. The fervor of their love and admiration could not
find fit utterance but in the phrase, "he spake as never man
spake." Christianity had perished with its founder if Mr.
Blakey's theory had been true. The world has acknowledged
him as sent of God, has believed him to *be* God, because
there *was* a standard of morality by which man could test not

the word of man merely, but what was vouched for as the word of God, because of that *internal* evidence, which according to the repeated declarations of Christ himself, ought to have been sufficient. It was out of the hardness of their hearts that they needed signs. Had all been right within, the precepts themselves would have sufficed to prove their own origin.

We have expended more words than were perhaps necessary upon so preposterous a doctrine. Our excuse must be the infinitely mischievous tendency of a theory of moral duty, according to which God is to be obeyed, not because God is good, nor because it is good to obey him, but from some motive or principle which might have dictated equally implicit obedience to the powers of darkness. Such a philosophy, in proportion as it is realized in men's lives and characters, must extirpate from their minds all reverence, all admiration, and all conscience, and leave them only the abject feelings of a slave.

Such a theory cannot be combated too often; it should be warred against wherever it rears its head. But with regard to most of the other conflicting opinions respecting the primary grounds of moral obligation, it appears to us that a degree of importance is often attached to them, more than commensurate to the influence they really exercise for good or for evil. Doubtless they are important, as all questions in morals are important: a clear conception of the ultimate foundation of morality is essential to a systematic and scientific treatment of the subject, and to the decision of some of its disputed practical problems. But the most momentous of the differences of opinion on the details of morality have quite another origin. The real character of any man's ethical system depends not on his first and fundamental principle, which is of necessity so general as to be rarely susceptible of an immediate application to practice, but upon the nature of those secondary and intermediate maxims, *vera illa et media axiomata*, in which, as Bacon observes, real wisdom resides. The grand consideration is not what any person regards as the ultimate end of human conduct, but through what intermediate ends he holds that his ultimate end is attainable and should be pursued, and in these there is a nearer agreement between some who differ, than between some who agree, in their conception of the ultimate end. When disputes arise as to any of the secondary maxims, they can be decided, it is true, only by an appeal to first principles; but the necessity of this appeal may be avoided far oftener than is commonly believed; it is surprising how few, in comparison, of the disputed questions of practical morals, require for their determination any premises but such as are common to all philosophic sects.

Comment on Plato's *Gorgias*

[Mill had studied Plato from his earliest childhood. In 1834 and 1835 he published, in the *Monthly Repository*, a series of detailed copious abstracts of several Platonic dialogues. For the most part he simply presented Plato, as nearly as possible in direct translation and with no comment, but he concluded his abstract of the *Gorgias* with the interesting comment which is here reprinted.]

THE READER HAS NOW SEEN the substance of what the greatest moralist of antiquity finds to say in recommendation of a virtuous life. His arguments, like those of moralists in general, are not of a nature to convince many, except those who do not need conviction; there are few of them which Polus and Callicles, had the author endowed them with dialectical skill equal to his own, might not easily have parried. But is not this an inconvenience necessarily attending the attempt to prove the eligibility of virtue by argument? Argument may show what general regulation of the desires, or what particular course of conduct, virtue requires: *how* to live virtuously, is a question the solution of which belongs to the understanding; but the understanding has no inducements which it can bring to the aid of one who has not yet determined whether he will endeavor to live virtuously or no. It is impossible, by any arguments, to prove that a life of obedience to duty is preferable, so far as respects the agent himself, to a life of circumspect and cautious selfishness. It will be answered, perhaps, that virtue is the road to happiness, and that "honesty is the best policy." Of this celebrated maxim, may we not venture to say, once for all, without hesitation or reserve, that it is not true? The whole experience of mankind runs counter to it. The life of a good man or woman is full of unpraised and unrequited sacrifices. In the present dialogue, which, though scanty in conclusive arguments, is rich in profound reflections, there is one remark of which the truth is quite universal: that the world loves its like, and refuses its favor to its unlike. To be more honest than the many is nearly as prejudicial, in a worldly sense, as to be a greater rogue. They, indeed, who have no conception of any higher honesty than is practised by the majority of the society in which they live, are right in considering such honesty as accordant with policy. But how is he indemnified, who scruples to do that which his neighbors do without scruple? Where is the reward, in any worldly sense, for heroism? Civilization, with its *laissez-aller* and its *laissez-faire* which it calls tolerance, has, in two thousand years, done thus much for the moral hero, that he now runs little risk of drinking hemlock like Socrates, or, like Christ, of dying on the cross. The worst that can well happen to him is to be everywhere ill spoken of, and to fail in all his worldly concerns; and if he be unusually fortunate, he may, perhaps, be so well treated by the rest of mankind, as to be allowed to be honest in peace.

The old monk in Rabelais had a far truer notion of worldly wisdom: "To perform your appointed task indifferently well; never to speak ill of your superiors; and to let the mad world go its own way, for it *will* go its own way."

All valid arguments in favor of virtue, presuppose that we already desire virtue, or desire some of its ends and objects. You may prove to us that virtue tends to the happiness of mankind, or of our country; but that supposes that we already care for mankind, or for our country. You may tell us that virtue will gain us the approbation of the wise and the good; but this supposes that the wise and good are already more to us than other people are. Those only will go along with Socrates in the preceding dialogue, who already feel that the accordance of their lives and inclinations with some scheme of duty is necessary to their comfort; whose feelings of virtue are already so strong, that if they allow any other consideration to prevail over those feelings, they are really conscious that the health of their souls is gone, and that they are, as Plato affirms, in a state of disease. But no arguments which Plato urges have power to make those love or desire virtue, who do not already; nor is this ever to be effected through the intellect, but through the imagination and the affections.

The love of virtue, and every other noble feeling, is not communicated by reasoning, but caught by inspiration or sympathy from those who already have it; and its nurse and foster-mother is Admiration. We acquire it from those we love and reverence, especially from those whom we earliest love and reverence; from our ideal of those, whether in past or in present times, whose lives and characters have been the mirrors of all noble qualities; and lastly, from those who, as poets or artists, can clothe those feelings in the most beautiful forms, and breathe them into us through our imagination and our sensations. It is thus that Plato has deserved the title of a great moral writer. Christ did not argue about virtue, but commanded it; Plato, when he argues about it, argues for the most part inconclusively, but he resembles Christ in the love which he inspires for it, and in the stern resolution never to swerve from it, which those who can relish his writings naturally feel when perusing them. And the present writer regrets that his imperfect abstract is so ill fitted to convey any idea of the degree in which this dialogue makes the feelings and course of life which it inculcates commend themselves to our inmost nature, by associating them with our most impressive conceptions of beauty and power.

Professor Sedgwick's Discourse on the Studies of the University of Cambridge

[Adam Sedgwick, geologist, minister of the Church of England, and prominent teacher at Cambridge University, attacked Utilitarianism as he understood it, in a Discourse primarily concerned with evaluating the education offered at his University. Mill replied at length in an article which appeared in the *London Review* in April, 1835. Writing to J. P. Nichol a few months earlier, he said:

> The article on Sedgwick will, I am sure, interest you. I have said a number of things in it which I have never put into print before, and have represented the "utilitarian theory of morals," as he calls it, I think for the first time in its true colors. At all events, I have incidentally represented my own mode of looking at ethical questions, having never yet seen in print any statement of the principles on the subject to which I could subscribe.

Mill reprinted the article in *Dissertations and Discussions*, the collection he made of those of his periodical writings which he wished preserved. In the selection here reprinted, the first section, dealing with Sedgwick's remarks on education at Cambridge, has been omitted. The text is that of the *Dissertations and Discussions*.]

IT IS A FACT in human nature that we have moral judgments and moral feelings. We judge certain actions and dispositions to be right, others wrong; this we call approving and disapproving them. We have also feelings of pleasure in the contemplation of the former class of actions and dispositions —feelings of dislike and aversion—to the latter; which feelings, as everybody must be conscious, do not exactly resemble any other of our feelings of pain or pleasure.

Such are the phenomena. Concerning their reality there is no dispute. But there are two theories respecting the origin of these phenomena, which have divided philosophers from the earliest ages of philosophy. One is that the distinction between right and wrong is an ultimate and inexplicable fact, that we perceive this distinction, as we perceive the distinction of colors, by a peculiar faculty, and that the pleasures and pains, the desires and aversions, consequent upon this perception are all ultimate facts in our nature, as much so as the pleasures and pains, or the desires and aversions, of which sweet or bitter tastes, pleasing or grating sounds, are the object. This is called the theory of the moral sense—or of moral instincts—or of eternal and immutable morality—or of intuitive principles of morality—or by many other names; to the differences between which, those who adopt the theory often attach great importance, but which, for our present purpose, may all be considered as equivalent.

The other theory is that the ideas of right and wrong, and the feelings which attach themselves to those ideas, are not ultimate facts but may be explained and accounted for, are not the result of any peculiar law of our nature, but of the same laws on which all our other complex ideas and feelings depend; that the distinction between moral and immoral acts is not a peculiar and inscrutable property in the acts themselves, which we perceive by a sense, as we perceive colors by our sense of sight, but flows from the ordinary properties of those actions, for the recognition of which we need no other faculty than our intellects and our bodily senses. And the particular property in actions, which constitutes them moral or immoral, in the opinion of those who hold this theory (all of them, at least, who need here be noticed), is the influence of those actions, and of the dispositions from which they emanate, upon human happiness.

This theory is sometimes called the theory of Utility, and is what Mr. Sedgwick means by "the utilitarian theory of morals."

Maintaining this second theory, Mr. Sedgwick calls "denying the existence of moral feelings" (p. 32). This is, in the first place, misstating the question. Nobody denies the existence of moral feelings. The feelings exist, manifestly exist, and cannot be denied. The questions on which there is a difference are—first, whether they are simple or complex feelings, and if complex, of what elementary feelings they are composed, which is a question of metaphysics; and secondly, what kind of acts and dispositions are the proper objects of those feelings, in other words, what is the principle of morals. These questions, and more peculiarly the last, the theory which has been termed utilitarian professes to solve.

Paley adopted this theory. Mr. Sedgwick, who professes the other theory, treats Paley, and all who take Paley's side of the question, with extreme contumely.

We shall show that Mr. Sedgwick has no right to represent Paley as a type of the theory of utility, that he has failed in refuting even Paley, and that the tone of high moral reprobation which he has assumed towards all who adopt that theory is altogether unmerited on their part, and on his, from his extreme ignorance of the subject, peculiarly unbecoming.

Those who maintain that human happiness is the end and test of morality are bound to prove that the principle is true, but not that Paley understood it. No one is entitled to found an argument against a principle, upon the faults or blunders of a particular writer who professed to build his system upon it, without taking notice that the principle may be understood differently, and has in fact been understood differently by other writers. What would be thought of an assailant of Christianity, who should judge of its truth or beneficial tendency from the view taken of it by the Jesuits, or by the Shakers? A doctrine is not judged at all until it is judged in its best form. The principle of utility may be viewed in as many different lights as every other rule or principle may. If it be liable to mischievous misinterpretations, this is true of all very general, and therefore of all first, principles. Whether the ethical creed of a follower of utility will lead him to moral or immoral consequences, depends on what he thinks useful, just as, with a partisan of the opposite doctrine—that of innate conscience—it depends on what he thinks his conscience enjoins. But either the one theory or the other must be true. Instead, therefore, of caviling about the abuses and perversions of either, real manliness would consist in accepting the true, with all its liabilities to abuse and perversion, and then bending the whole force of our intellects to the establishment of such secondary and intermediate maxims, as may be guides to the *bona fide* inquirer in the application of the principle, and salutary checks to the sophist and the dishonest casuist.

There are faults in Paley's conception of the philosophy of morals, both in its foundations and in its subsequent stages, which prevent his book from being an example of the conclusions justly deducible from the doctrine of utility, or of the influences of that doctrine, when properly understood, upon the intellect and character.

In the first place, he does not consider utility as itself the source of moral obligation, but as a mere index to the will of God, which he regards as the ultimate groundwork of all morality, and the origin of its binding force. This doctrine (not that utility is an index to the will of God, but that it is an index and nothing else) we consider as highly exceptionable, and having really many of those bad effects on the mind, erroneously ascribed to the principle of utility.

The only view of the connection between religion and morality which does not annihilate the very idea of the latter, is that which considers the Deity as not making, but recognizing and sanctioning, moral obligation. In the minds of most English thinkers down to the middle of the last century, the idea of duty, and that of obedience to God, were so indissolubly united, as to be inseparable even in thought; and when we consider how in those days religious motives and ideas stood in the front of all speculations, it is not wonderful that religion should have been thought to constitute the essence of all obligations to which it annexed its sanction. To have inquired, Why am I bound to obey God's will? would, to a Christian of that age, have appeared irreverent. It is a question, however, which, as much as any other, requires an answer from a Christian philosopher. "Because he is my Maker" is no answer. Why should I obey my Maker? From gratitude? Then gratitude is in itself obligatory, independently of my Maker's will. From reverence and love? But why is he a proper object of love and reverence? Not because he is my Maker. If I had been made by an evil spirit, for evil purposes, my love and reverence (supposing me to be capable of such feelings) would have been due, not to the evil, but to the good Being. Is it because he is just, righteous, merciful? Then these attributes are in themselves good, independently of his pleasure. If any person has the misfortune to believe that his Creator commands wickedness, more respect is due to him for disobeying such imaginary commands, than for obeying them. If virtue would not be virtue unless the Creator commanded it—if it derive all its obligatory force from his will—there remains no ground for obeying him except his power, no motive for morality except the selfish one of the hope of heaven, or the selfish and slavish one of the fear of hell.

Accordingly, in strict consistency with this view of the nature of morality, Paley not only represents the proposition that we ought to do good and not harm to mankind, as a mere corollary from the proposition that God wills their good, and not their harm—but represents the motive to virtue, and the motive which constitutes it virtue, as consisting solely in the hope of heaven and the fear of hell.

It does not, however, follow that Paley believed mankind to have no feelings except selfish ones. He doubtless would have admitted that they are acted upon by other motives, or, in the language of Bentham and Helvetius, that they have other interests than merely self-regarding ones. But he chose to say that actions done from those other motives are not virtuous. The happiness of mankind, according to him, was the end for which morality was enjoined; yet he would not admit anything to be morality, when the happiness of mankind, or of any of mankind except ourselves, is the inducement of it. He annexed an arbitrary meaning to the word virtue. How he came to think this arbitrary meaning the right one may be a question. Partly, perhaps, by the habit of thinking and talking of morality under the metaphor of a *law*. In the notion of a law, the idea of the command of a superior, enforced by penalties, is of course the main element.

If Paley's ethical system is thus unsound in its foundations, the spirit which runs through the details is no less exceptionable. It is, indeed, such as to prove that neither the character nor the objects of the writer were those of a philosopher. There is none of the single-minded earnestness for truth, whatever it may be, the intrepid defiance of prejudice, the firm resolve to look all consequences in the face, which the word philosopher supposes, and without which nothing worthy of note was ever accomplished in moral or political philosophy. One sees throughout that he has a particular set of conclusions to come to, and will not, perhaps cannot, allow himself to let in any premises which would interfere with them. His book is one of a class which has since become very numerous, and is likely to become still more so—an apology for commonplace. Not to lay a solid foundation, and erect an edifice over it suited to the professed ends, but to construct pillars, and insert them under the existing structure, was Paley's object.

He took the doctrines of practical morals which he found current. Mankind were, about that time, ceasing to consider mere use and wont, or even the ordinary special pleading from texts of scripture, as sufficient warrants for those common opinions, and were demanding something like a philosophic basis for them. This philosophic basis Paley, consciously or unconsciously, made it his endeavor to supply. The skill with which his book was adapted to satisfy this want of the time accounts for the popularity which attended it, notwithstanding the absence of that generous and inspiring tone which gives so much of their usefulness as well as of their charm to the writings of Plato and Locke and Fenelon, and which mankind are accustomed to pretend to admire, whether they really respond to it or not.

When an author starts with such an object, it is of little consequence what premises he sets out from. In adopting the principle of utility, Paley, there is no doubt, followed the convictions of his intellect, but if he had started from any other principle, we have as little doubt that he would have arrived at the very same conclusions. These conclusions, namely, the received maxims of his time, were (it would have been strange if they were not) accordant in many points with those which philosophy would have dictated. But had they been accordant on all points, that was not the way in which a philosopher would have dealt with them.

The only deviation from commonplace which has been made an accusation (for all departures from commonplace are made accusations) against Paley's moral system, is that of too readily allowing exceptions to important rules; and this Mr. Sedgwick does not fail to lay hold of, and endeavor, as others have done before him, to fix it upon the principle of utility as an immoral consequence. It is, however, imputable to the very same cause which we have already pointed out. Along with the prevailing maxims, Paley borrowed the prevailing laxity in their application. He had not only to maintain existing doctrines, but to save the credit of existing practices also. He found in his country's morality (especially its political morality), modes of conduct universally prevalent, and applauded by all persons of station and consideration, but which, being acknowledged violations of great moral principles, could only be defended as cases of exception, resting on special grounds of expediency; and the only expediency which it was possible to ascribe to them was political expediency—that is, conduciveness to the interest of the ruling powers. To this, and not to the tendencies of the principle of utility, is to be ascribed the lax morality taught by Paley, and justly objected to by Mr. Sedgwick, on the subject of lies, of subscription to articles, of the abuses of influence in the British constitution, and various other topics. The principle of utility leads to no such conclusions. Let us be permitted to add that, if it did, we should not of late years have heard so much in reprobation of it from all manner of persons, and from none more than from the sworn defenders of those very malpractices.

When an inquirer knows beforehand the conclusions which he is to come to, he is not likely to seek far for grounds to rest them upon. Accordingly, the considerations of expediency upon which Paley founds his moral rules, are almost all of the most obvious and vulgar kind. In estimating the consequences of actions, in order to obtain a measure of their morality, there are always two sets of considerations involved: the consequences to the outward interests of the parties concerned (including the agent himself), and the consequences to the characters of the same persons, and to their outward interests so far as dependent on their characters. In the estimation of the first of these two classes of considerations, there is in general not much difficulty, nor much room for difference of opinion. The actions which are directly hurtful, or directly useful, to the outward interests of oneself or of other people, are easily distinguished, sufficiently at least for the guidance of a private individual. The rights of individuals, which other individuals ought to respect, over external things, are in general sufficiently pointed out by a few plain rules, and by the laws of one's country. But it often happens that an essential part of the morality or immorality of an action or a rule of action consists in its influence upon the agent's own mind: upon his susceptibilities of pleasure or pain, upon the general direction of his thoughts, feelings, and imagination, or upon some particular association. Many actions, moreover, produce effects upon the character of other persons besides the agent. In all these cases there will naturally be as much difference in the moral judgments of different persons, as there is in their views of human nature, and of the formation of character. Clear and comprehensive views of education and human culture must therefore precede, and form the basis of, a philosophy of morals; nor can the latter subject ever be understood, but in proportion as the former is so. For this, much yet remains to be done. Even the materials, though abundant, are not complete. Of those which exist, a large proportion have never yet found their way into the writings of philosophers, but are to be gathered, on the one hand, from actual observers of mankind, on the other, from those autobiographers, and from those poets or novelists, who have spoken out unreservedly, from their own experience, any true human feeling. To collect together these materials, and to add to them, will be a labor for successive generations. But Paley, instead of having brought from the philosophy of education and character any new light to illuminate the subject of morals, has not even availed himself of the lights which had already been thrown upon it from that source. He, in fact, had meditated little on this branch of the subject, and had no ideas in relation to it but the commonest and most superficial.

Thus much we have been induced to say, rather from the importance of the subject, than for the sake of a just estimate of Paley, which is a matter of inferior consequence; still less for the sake of repelling Mr. Sedgwick's onslaught, which, as we shall soon see, might have been more summarily disposed of.

Mr. Sedgwick's objections to the principle of utility are of two kinds: first, that it is not true; secondly, that it is dangerous, degrading, and so forth. What he says against its truth, when picked out from a hundred different places, and brought together, would fill about three pages, leaving about twenty consisting of attacks upon its tendency. This already looks ill; for, after all, the truth or falsehood of the principle is the main point. When, of a dissertation on any controverted question, a small part only is employed in proving the author's own opinion, a large part in ascribing odious consequences to the opposite opinion, we are apt to think either that, on the former point, there was not very much to be said, or, if there was, that the author is not very well qualified to say it. One thing is certain: that if an opinion have ever such mischievous consequences, that cannot prevent any thinking person from believing it, if the evidence is in its favor. Un-

thinking persons, indeed, if they are very solemnly assured
that an opinion has mischievous consequences, may be fright-
ened from examining the evidence. When, therefore, we find
that this mode of dealing with an opinion is the favorite one—
is resorted to in preference to the other, and with greater
vehemence, and at greater length—we conclude that it is
upon unthinking rather than upon thinking persons that the
author calculates upon making an impression; or else, that he
himself is one of the former class of persons—that his own
judgment is determined, less by evidence presented to his understanding, than by the repugnancy of the opposite opinion
to his partialities and affections; and that, perceiving clearly
the opinion to be one which it would be painful to him to
adopt, he has been easily satisfied with reasons for rejecting it.

All that the Professor says to disprove the principle of
utility, and to prove the existence of a moral sense, is found
in the following paragraph:

Let it not be said that our moral sentiments are super-
induced by seeing and tracing the consequences of crime.
The assertion is not true. The early sense of shame comes
before such trains of thought, and is not, therefore, caused
by them; and millions, in all ages of the world, have grown
up as social beings and moral agents, amenable to the laws
of God and man, who never traced or thought of tracing
the consequences of their actions, nor ever referred them to
any standard of utility. Nor let it be said that the moral
sense comes of mere teaching—that right and wrong pass
as mere words, first from the lips of the mother to the
child, and then from man to man; and that we grow up
with moral judgments gradually ingrafted in us from without, by the long-heard lessons of praise and blame, by the
experience of fitness, or the sanction of the law. I repeat
that the statement is not true—that our moral perceptions
show themselves not in any such order as this. The question
is one of feeling; and the moral feelings are often strongest
in very early life, before moral rules or legal sanctions have
once been thought of. Again, what are we to understand by
teaching? Teaching implies capacity: one can be of no use
without the other. A faculty of the soul may be called
forth, brought to light, and matured; but cannot be created,
any more than we can create a new particle of matter, or
invent a new law of nature. (pp. 52–53)

The substance of the last three sentences is repeated at somewhat greater length shortly after (pp. 54–55), in a passage

from which we need only quote the following words: "No training (however greatly it may change an individual mind) can create a new faculty, any more than it can give a new organ of sense." In many other parts of the Discourse, the same arguments are alluded to, but no new ones are introduced.

Let us, then, examine these arguments.

First, the Professor says, or seems to say, that our moral sentiments cannot be generated by experience of consequences, because a child feels the sense of shame before he has any experience of consequences; and likewise because millions of persons grow up, have moral feelings, and live morally, "who never traced, or thought of tracing, the consequences of their actions," but who yet, it seems, are suffered to go at large, which we thought was not usually the case with persons who never think of the consequences of their actions. The Professor continues, "who never traced, or thought of tracing, the consequences of their actions, nor ever referred them to any standard of utility."

Secondly, that our moral feelings cannot arise from teaching, because those feelings are often strongest in very early life.

Thirdly, that our moral feelings cannot arise from teaching, because teaching can only call forth a faculty, but cannot create one.

Let us first consider the singular allegation that the sense of shame in a child precedes all experience of the consequences of actions. Is it not astounding that such an assertion should be ventured upon by any person of sane mind? At what period in a child's life, after it is capable of forming the idea of an action at all, can it be without experience of the consequences of actions? As soon as it has the idea of one person striking another, is it not aware that striking produces pain? As soon as it has the idea of being commanded by its parent, has it not the notion that, by not doing what is commanded, it will excite the parent's displeasure? A child's knowledge of the simple fact (one of the earliest he becomes acquainted with), that some acts produce pain and others pleasure, is called by pompous names, "seeing and tracing the consequences of crime," "trains of thought," "referring actions to a standard," terms which imply continued reflection and large abstractions; and because these terms are absurd when used of a child or an uneducated person, we are to conclude that a child or an uneducated person has no notion that one thing is caused by another. As well might it be said that a child requires an instinct to tell him that he has ten fingers, because he knows it before he has ever thought of "carrying on arithmetical computations." Though a child is not a jurist or a moral philosopher (to whom alone the Professor's phrases would be properly applicable), he has the idea of himself hurting or offending some one, or of some one hurting or annoying him. These are ideas which precede any sense of shame in doing wrong; and it is out of these elements, and not out of abstractions, that the supporters of the theory of utility contend that the idea of wrong, and our feelings of disapprobation of it, are originally formed. Mr. Sedgwick's argument resembles one we often hear, that the principle of utility must be false, because it supposes morality to be founded on the good of society, an idea too complex for the majority of mankind, who look only to the particular persons concerned. Why, none but those who mingle in public transactions, or whose example is likely to have extensive influence, have any occasion to look beyond the particular persons concerned. Morality, for all other people, consists in doing good and refraining from harm, to themselves and to those who immediately surround them. As soon as a child has the idea of voluntarily producing pleasure or pain to any one person, he has an accurate notion of utility. When he afterwards gradually rises to the very complex idea of "society," and learns in what manner his actions may affect the interests of other persons than those who are present to his sight, his conceptions of utility, and of right and wrong founded on utility, undergo a corresponding enlargement, but receive no new element.

Again, if it were ever so true that the sense of shame in a child precedes all knowledge of consequences, what is that to the question respecting a moral sense? Is the sense of shame the same thing with a moral sense? A child is ashamed of doing what he is told is wrong; but so is he also ashamed of doing what he knows is right, if he expects to be laughed at for doing it; he is ashamed of being duller than another child, of being ugly, of being poor, of not having fine clothes, of not being able to run, or wrestle, or box so well as another. He is ashamed of whatever causes him to be thought less of by the persons who surround him. This feeling of shame is accounted for by obvious associations; but suppose it to be innate, what would that prove in favor of a moral sense? If all that Mr. Sedgwick can show for a moral sense is the sense of shame, it might well be supposed that all our moral sentiments are the result of opinions which come to us from without, since the sense of shame so obviously follows the opinion of others, and, at least in early years, is wholly determined by it.

On the Professor's first argument no more needs here be said. His second is the following: that moral feelings cannot "come of mere teaching," because they do not grow up gradually, but are often strongest in very early life.

Now, this is, in the first place, a mistaking of the matter in dispute. The Professor is not arguing with Mandeville, or with the rhetoricians in Plato. Nobody, with whom he is concerned, says that moral feelings "come of mere teaching." It is not pretended that they are factitious and artificial associations, inculcated by parents and teachers purposely to further certain social ends, and no more congenial to our natural feelings than the contrary associations. The idea of the pain of another is naturally painful; the idea of the pleasure of another is naturally pleasurable. From this fact in our natural constitution, all our affections both of love and aversion towards human beings, in so far as they are different from those we entertain toward mere inanimate objects which are pleasant or disagreeable to us, are held, by the best teachers of the theory of utility, to originate. In this, the unselfish part of our nature, lies a foundation, even independently of inculcation from without, for the generation of moral feelings.

But if, because it is not inconsistent with the constitution of our nature that moral feelings should grow up independently of teaching, Mr. Sedgwick would infer that they generally do so, or that teaching is not the source of almost all the moral feeling which exists in the world, his assertion is a piece of sentimentality completely at variance with the facts. If by saying that "moral feelings are often strongest in very early life," Mr. Sedgwick means that they are strongest in children, he only proves his ignorance of children. Young children have affections, but not moral feelings; and children whose will is never resisted, never acquire them. There is no selfishness equal to that of children, as every one who is acquainted with children well knows. It is not the hard, cold selfishness of a grown person, for the most affectionate children have it, where their affection is not supplying a counter-impulse; but the most selfish of grown persons does not come up to a child in the reckless seizing of any pleasure to himself, regardless of the consequences to others. The pains of others, though naturally painful to us, are not so until we have realized them by an act of imagination, implying voluntary attention; and that no very young child ever pays, while under the impulse of a present desire. If a child restrains the indulgence of any wish, it is either from affection or sympathy, which are quite other feelings than those of morality, or else (whatever Mr. Sedgwick may think) because he has been taught to do so. And he only learns the habit gradually, and in proportion to the assiduity and skill of the teaching.

The assertion that "moral feelings are often strongest in very early life" is true in no sense but one which confirms what it is brought to refute. The time of life at which moral feelings are apt to be strongest, is the age when we cease to be merely members of our own families, and begin to have intercourse with the world; that is, when the teaching has continued longest in one direction, and has not commenced in any other direction. When we go forth into the world, and meet with teaching, both by precept and example, of an opposite tendency to that which we have been used to, the feeling begins to weaken. Is this a sign of its being wholly independent of teaching? Has a boy quietly educated in a well-regulated home, or one who has been at a public school, the strongest moral feelings?

Enough has probably been said on the Professor's second argument. His third is that teaching may strengthen our natural faculties, and call forth those which are powerless because untried, but cannot create a faculty which does not exist—cannot, therefore, have created the moral faculty.

It is surprising that Mr. Sedgwick should not see that his argument begs the question in dispute. To prove that our moral judgments are innate, he assumes that they proceed from a distinct faculty. But this is precisely what the adherents of the principle of utility deny. They contend that the morality of actions is perceived by the same faculties by which we perceive any other of the qualities of actions, namely, our intellects and our senses. They hold the capacity of perceiving moral distinctions to be no more a distinct faculty than the capacity of trying causes, or of making a speech to a jury. This last is a very peculiar power, yet no one says that it must have preexisted in Sir James Scarlett before he was called to the bar, because teaching and practice cannot create a new faculty. They can create a new power; and a faculty is but a finer name for a power. Mr. Sedgwick loses sight of the very meaning of the word faculty—*facultas*. He talks of a faculty "powerless because untried." A power powerless!*

The only color for representing our moral judgments as the result of a peculiar part of our nature, is that our feelings of moral approbation and disapprobation are really peculiar feelings. But is it not notorious that peculiar feelings, unlike any others which we have experience of, are created by association every day? What does the Professor think of the feelings of ambition, the desire of power over our fellow-creatures, and the pleasure of its possession and exercise? These are peculiar feelings. But they are obviously generated by the law of association, from the connection between power over our fellow-creatures and the gratification of almost all our other inclinations. What will the Professor say of the chivalrous point of honor? What of the feelings of envy and jealousy? What of the feelings of the miser to his gold? Who ever looked upon these last as the subject of a distinct natural faculty? Their origin in association is obvious to all the world. Yet they are feelings as peculiar, as unlike any other part of our nature, as the feelings of conscience.

It will hardly be believed that what we have now answered is all that Mr. Sedgwick advances to prove the principle of utility untrue; yet such is the fact. Let us now see whether he is more successful in proving the pernicious consequences of the principle, and the "degrading effect" which it produces "on the temper and conduct of those who adopt it."

The Professor's talk is more indefinite, and the few ideas he has are more overlaid with declamatory phrases, on this point, than even on the preceding one. We can, however, descry through the mist some faint semblance of two tangible objections: one, that the principle of utility is not suited to man's capacity—that if we were ever so desirous of applying it correctly, we should not be capable; the other, that it debases the moral practice of those who adopt it—which

* We cannot help referring the Professor back to Locke, and to that very chapter "On Power" which he singles out for peculiar objurgation. We recommend to his special attention the admirable remarks in that chapter on the abuse of the word "faculty."

seems to imply (strange as the assertion is) that the adoption of it as a principle is not consistent with an attempt to apply it correctly.

We must quote Mr. Sedgwick's very words, or it would hardly be believed that we quote him fairly:

> Independently of the bad effects produced on the moral character of man, by a system which makes expediency (in whatever sense the word be used) the test of right and wrong, we may affirm, on a more general view, that the rule itself is utterly unfitted to his capacity. Feeble as man may be, he forms a link in a chain of moral causes, ascending to the throne of God; and trifling as his individual acts may seem, he tries in vain to follow out their consequences as they go down into the countless ages of coming time. Viewed in this light, every act of man is woven into a moral system, ascending through the past—descending to the future—and preconceived in the mind of the Almighty. Nor does this notion, as far as regards ourselves, end in mere quietism and necessity. For we know right from wrong, and have that liberty of action which implies responsibility; and, as far as we are allowed to look into the ways of Providence, it seems compatible with his attributes to use the voluntary acts of created beings as second causes in working out the ends of his own will. Leaving, however, out of question that stumbling-block which the prescience of God has often thrown in the way of feeble and doubting minds, we are at least certain that man has not foreknowledge to trace the consequences of a single action of his own; and hence that utility (in the highest sense of which the word is capable) is, as a test of right and wrong, unfitted to his understanding, and therefore worthless in its application. (pp. 63–64)

Mr. Sedgwick appears to be one of that numerous class who never take the trouble to set before themselves fairly an opinion which they have an aversion to. Who ever said it was necessary to foresee all the consequences of each individual action, "as they go down into the countless ages of coming time?" Some of the consequences of an action are accidental; others are its natural result, according to the known laws of the universe. The former, for the most part, cannot be foreseen; but the whole course of human life is founded upon the fact that the latter can. In what reliance do we ply our several trades—in what reliance do we buy or sell, eat or drink, write books or read them, walk, ride, speak, think—except on our foresight of the consequences of those actions? The commonest person lives according to maxims of prudence wholly founded on foresight of consequences; and we are told by a wise man from Cambridge that the foresight of consequences, as a rule to guide ourselves by, is impossible! Our foresight of consequences is not perfect. Is anything else in our constitution perfect? *Est quodam prodire tenus, si non datur ultra: Non possis oculo quantum contendere Lynceus; Non tamen idcirco contemnas lippus inungi.* If the Professor quarrels with such means of guiding our conduct as we are gifted with, it is incumbent on him to show that, in point of fact, we have been provided with better. Does the moral sense, allowing its existence, point out any surer practical rules? If so, let us have them in black and white. If nature has given us rules which suffice for our conduct, without any consideration of the probable consequences of our actions, produce them. But no; for two thousand years, nature's moral code has been a topic for declamation, and no one has yet produced a single chapter of it: nothing but a few elementary generalities, which are the mere alphabet of a morality founded upon utility. Hear Bishop Butler, the oracle of the moral-sense school, and whom our author quotes:

> However much men may have disputed about the nature of virtue, and whatever ground for doubt there may be about particulars, yet in general there is an universally acknowledged standard of it. It is that which all ages and all countries have made a profession of in public; it is that which every man you meet puts on the show of; it is that which the primary and fundamental laws of all civil constitutions over the face of the earth make it their business and endeavor to enforce the practice of upon mankind: namely, justice, veracity, and regard to the common good. (p. 130)

Mr. Sedgwick praises Butler for not being more explanatory.* Did Butler, then, or does Mr. Sedgwick, seriously believe that mankind have not sufficient foresight of conse-

---

* "Here everything," says he, "remains indefinite: yet all the successive propositions have their meaning. The author knew well that the things he had to deal with were indefinite, and that he could not fetter them in the language of a formal definition, without violating their nature. But how small has been the number of moral writers who have understood the real value of this forbearance!"

quences to perceive the advantage of "justice, veracity, and regard to the common good?" That, without a peculiar faculty, they would not be able to see that these qualities are useful to them?

When, indeed, the question arises, *what is* justice?—that is, what are those claims of others which we are bound to respect? and *what is* the conduct required by "regard to the common good?"—the solutions which we can deduce from our foresight of consequences are not infallible. But let any one try those which he can deduce from the moral sense. Can he deduce any? Show us, written in the human heart, any answer to *these* questions. Bishop Butler gives up the point, and Mr. Sedgwick praises him for doing so. When Mr. Sedgwick wants something definite to oppose to the indefiniteness of a morality founded on utility, he has recourse not to the moral sense, but to Christianity. With such fairness as this does he hold the balance between the two principles: he supposes his moral-sense man provided with all the guidance which can be derived from a revelation from heaven, and his utilitarian destitute of any such help. When one sees the question so stated, one cannot wonder at any conclusion. Need we say that Revelation, as a means of supplying the uncertainty of human judgment, is as open to one of the two parties as to the other? Need we say that Paley, the very author who, in this Discourse, is treated as the representative of the utilitarian system, appeals to Revelation throughout? and obtains no credit from Mr. Sedgwick for it, but the contrary; for Revelation, it seems, may be referred to in aid of the moral sense, but not to assist or rectify our judgments of utility.

The truth, however, is, that Revelation (if by Revelation be meant the New Testament), as Paley justly observed, enters little into the details of ethics. Christianity does not deliver a code of morals, any more than a code of laws. Its practical morality is altogether indefinite, and was meant to be so. This indefiniteness has been considered by some of the ablest defenders of Christianity as one of its most signal merits, and among the strongest proofs of its divine origin: being the quality which fits it to be an universal religion, and distinguishes it both from the Jewish dispensation, and from all other religions, which as they invariably enjoin, under their most awful sanctions, acts which are only locally or temporarily useful, are in their own nature local and temporary. Christianity, on the contrary, influences the conduct by shaping the character itself; it aims at so elevating and purifying the desires, that there shall be no hindrance to the fulfilment of our duties when recognized; but of what our duties are, at least in regard to outward acts, it says very little but what moralists in general have said. If, therefore, we would have any definite morality at all, we must perforce resort to that "foresight of consequences," of the difficulties of which the Professor has so formidable an idea.

But this talk about uncertainty is mere exaggeration. There would be great uncertainty if each individual had all to do for himself, and only his own experience to guide him. But we are not so situated. Every one directs himself in morality, as in all his conduct, not by his own unaided foresight, but by the accumulated wisdom of all former ages, embodied in traditional aphorisms. So strong is the disposition to submit to the authority of such traditions, and so little danger is there, in most conditions of mankind, of erring on the other side, that the absurdest customs are perpetuated through a lapse of ages from no other cause. A hundred millions of human beings think it the most exalted virtue to swing by a hook before an idol, and the most dreadful pollution to drink cow-broth—only because their forefathers thought so. A Turk thinks it the height of indecency for women to be seen in the streets unveiled; and when he is told that in some countries this happens without any evil result, he shakes his head and says, "If you hold butter to the fire it will melt." Did not many generations of the most educated men in Europe believe every line of Aristotle to be infallible? So difficult is it to break loose from a received opinion. The progress of experience, and the growth of the human intellect, succeed but too slowly in correcting and improving traditional opinions. There is little fear, truly, that the mass of mankind should insist upon "tracing the consequences of actions" by their own unaided lights; they are but too ready to let it be done for them once for all, and to think they have nothing to do with rules of morality (as Tory writers say they have with the laws) but to obey them.

Mr. Sedgwick is master of the stock phrases of those who know nothing of the principle of utility but the name. To act upon rules of conduct, of which utility is recognized as the basis, he calls "waiting for the calculations of utility"—a thing, according to him, in itself immoral, since "to hesitate is to rebel." On the same principle, navigating by rule instead of by instinct might be called waiting for the calculations of astronomy. There seems no absolute necessity for putting off the calculations until the ship is in the middle of the South Sea. Because a sailor has not verified all the computations in the Nautical Almanac, does he therefore "hesitate" to use it?

Thus far Mr. Sedgwick on the difficulties of the principle of utility, when we mean to apply it honestly. But he further charges the principle with having a "debasing" and "degrading" effect.

A word like "debasing," applied to anything which acts upon the mind, may mean several things. It may mean, making us unprincipled, regardless of the rights and feelings of other people. It may mean, making us slavish: spiritless, submissive to injury or insult, incapable of asserting our own rights and vindicating the just independence of our minds and actions. It may mean, making us cowardly, slothful, incapable of bearing pain or nerving ourselves to exertion for a worthy object. It may mean, making us narrow-minded, pusillanimous, in Hobbes's sense of the word: too intent upon little things to feel rightly about great ones, incapable of having our imagination fired by a grand object of contemplation, incapable of thinking, feeling, aspiring, or acting, on any but a small scale. An opinion which produced any of these effects upon the mind would be rightly called debasing. But when, without proving, or even in plain terms asserting, that it produces these effects, or any effects which he can make distinctly understood, a man merely says of an opinion that it is debasing—all he really says is that he has a feeling, which he cannot exactly describe, but upon which he values himself, and to which the opinion is in some way or other offensive. What definite proposition concerning the effect of any doctrine on the mind can be extracted from such a passage as this?

> If expediency be the measure of right, and every one claim the liberty of judgment, virtue and vice have no longer any fixed relations to the moral condition of man, but change with the fluctuations of opinion. Not only are his actions tainted by prejudice and passion, but his rule of life, under this system, must be tainted in like degree—must be brought down to its own level; for he will no longer be able, com-

patibly with his principles, to separate the rule from its application. No high and unvarying standard of morality, which his heart approves, however infirm his practice, will be offered to his thoughts. But his bad passions will continue to do their work in bending him to the earth; and unless he be held upright by the strong power of religion (an extrinsic power which I am not now considering), he will inevitably be carried down, by a degrading standard of action, to a sordid and groveling life. It may perhaps be said that we are arguing against a rule, only from its misapprehension and abuse. But we reply that every precept is practically bad when its abuse is natural and inevitable— that the system of utility brings down virtue from a heavenly throne, and places her on an earthly tribunal, where her decisions, no longer supported by any holy sanction, are distorted by judicial ignorance, and tainted by base passion. (p. 63)

What does this tell us? First, that if utility be the standard, different persons may have different opinions on morality. This is the talk about uncertainty, which has been already disposed of. Next, that where there is uncertainty, men's passions will bias their judgment. Granted; this is one of the evils of our condition, and must be borne with. We do not diminish it by pretending that nature tells us what is right, when nobody ever ventures to set down what nature tells us, nor affects to expound her laws in any way but by an appeal to utility. All that the remainder of the passage does is to repeat, in various phrases, that Mr. Sedgwick feels such a "standard of action" to be "degrading"; that Mr. Sedgwick feels it to be "sordid" and "groveling." If so, nobody can compel Mr. Sedgwick to adopt it. If he feels it debasing, no doubt it would be so to him. But until he is able to show some reason why it must be so to others, may we be permitted to suggest that perhaps the cause of its being so to himself is only that he does not understand it?
Read this:

Christianity considers every act grounded on mere worldly consequences as built on a false foundation. The mainspring of every virtue is placed by it in the affections, called into renewed strength by a feeling of self-abasement—by gratitude for an immortal benefit—by communion with God—and by the hopes of everlasting life. Humility is the foundation of the Christian's honor—distrust of self is the ground of his strength—and his religion tells him that every work of man is counted worthless in the sight of heaven, as the means of his pardon or the price of his redemption. Yet it gives him a pure and perfect rule of life, and does not for an instant exempt him from the duty of obedience to his rule; for it ever aims at a purgation of the moral faculties, and a renewal of the defaced image of God, and its moral precepts have an everlasting sanction. And thus does Christian love become an efficient and abiding principle—not tested by the world, but above the world, yet reaching the life-spring of every virtuous deed, and producing in its season a harvest of good and noble works incomparably more abundant than ever rose from any other soil.

The utilitarian scheme starts, on the contrary, with an abrogation of the authority of conscience—a rejection of the moral feelings as the test of right and wrong. From first to last, it is in bondage to the world, measuring every act by a worldly standard, and estimating its value by worldly consequences. Virtue becomes a question of calculation—a matter of profit or loss; and if man gain heaven at all on such a system, it must be by arithmetical details—the computation of his daily work—the balance of his moral ledger. A conclusion such as this offends against the spirit breathing in every page of the book of life, yet is it fairly drawn from the principle of utility. It appears, indeed, not only to have been foreseen by Paley, but to have been accepted by him—a striking instance of the tenacity with which man ever clings to system, and is ready to embrace even its monstrous consequences rather than believe that he has himself been building on a wrong foundation. (pp. 66–67)

In a note, he adds:

The following are the passages here referred to:
"The Christian religion hath not ascertained *the precise quantity of virtue* necessary to salvation.

"It has been said that it can never be a just economy of Providence to admit one part of mankind into heaven, and condemn the other to hell, since there must be very little to choose between the worst man who is received into heaven, and the best who is excluded. And how know we, it might be answered, but that there may be as little to choose in their conditions?"—*Moral Philosophy*, Book i. Ch. 7.

In the latter years of his life, Paley would, I believe, have been incapable of uttering or conceiving sentiments such as these.

So that a "purgation of the moral faculties" is necessary; the moral feelings require to be corrected. Yet the moral feelings are "the test of right and wrong"; and whoever "rejects" them as a test, must be called hard names. But we do not want to convict Mr. Sedgwick of inconsistency; we want to get at his meaning. Have we come to it at last? The gravamen of the charge against the principle of utility seems to lie in a word. Utility is a *worldly* standard, and estimates every act by *worldly* consequences.

Like most persons who are speaking from their feelings only, on a subject on which they have never seriously thought, the Professor is imposed upon by words. He is carried away by an ambiguity. To make his assertion about the *worldliness* of the standard of utility true, it must be understood in one sense; to make it have the invidious effect which is intended, it must be understood in another. By "worldly," does he mean to imply what is commonly meant when the word is used as a reproach—an undue regard to interest in the vulgar sense, our wealth, power, social position, and the like, our command over agreeable outward objects, and over the opinion and good offices of other people? If so, to call utility a worldly standard is to misrepresent the doctrine. It is not true that utility estimates actions by this sort of consequences; it estimates them by all their consequences. If he means that the principle of utility regards only (to use a scholastic distinction) the *objective* consequences of actions, and omits the *subjective*, attends to the effects on our outward condition, and that of other people, too much—to those on our internal sources of happiness or unhappiness, too little; this criticism is, as we have already remarked, in some degree applicable to Paley, but to charge this blunder upon the principle of utility, would be to say, that if it is your rule to judge of a thing by its consequences, you will judge only by a portion of them. Again, if Mr. Sedgwick meant to speak of a "worldly standard" in contradiction to a religious standard, and to say that if we adopt the principle of utility, we cannot admit religion as a sanction for it, or cannot attach importance to religious motives or feelings, the assertion would be simply false, and a gross injustice even to Paley. What, therefore, can Mr. Sedgwick mean? Merely this: that our actions take place in the world, that their consequences are produced in the world, that we have been placed in the world, and that there, if anywhere, we must earn a place in heaven. The morality founded on utility allows this, certainly; does Mr. Sedgwick's system of morality deny it?

Mark the confusion of ideas involved in this sentence: "Christianity considers every act grounded on merely worldly consequences as built on a false foundation." What is saving a father from death, but saving him from a worldly consequence? What are healing the sick, clothing the naked, sheltering the houseless, but acts which wholly consist in producing a worldly consequence? Confine Mr. Sedgwick to unambiguous words, and he is already answered. What is really true is, that Christianity considers no act as meritorious which is done from mere worldly *motives*, that is, which is in no degree prompted by the desire of our own moral perfection, or of the approbation of a perfect being. These motives, we need scarcely observe, may be equally powerful, whatever be our standard of morality, provided we believe that the Deity approves it.

Mr. Sedgwick is scandalized at the supposition that the place awarded to each of us in the next world will depend on the balance of the good and evil of our lives. According to his notions of justice, we presume, it ought to depend wholly upon one of the two. As usual, Mr. Sedgwick begins by a misapprehension: he neither understands Paley, nor the conclusion which, he says, is "fairly drawn from the principles of utility." Paley held, with other Christians, that our place hereafter would be determied by our degree of moral perfection—that is, by the balance, not of our good and evil deeds, which depend upon opportunity and temptation, but of our good and evil dispositions, by the intensity and continuity of our *will* to do good, by the strength with which we have *struggled* to be virtuous, not by our accidental lapses, or by the unintended good or evil which has followed from our actions. When Paley said that Christianity has not ascertained "the precise quantity of virtue necessary to salvation," he did not mean the number or kind of beneficial actions; he meant that Christianity has not decided what positive strength of virtuous inclinations, and what capacity of resisting temptations, will procure acquittal at the tribunal of God. And most wisely is this left undecided. Nor can there be a solution more consistent with the attributes which Christianity ascribes to the Deity, than Paley's own—that every step of advance in the direction of moral perfection will be something gained towards everlasting welfare.

The remainder of Mr. Sedgwick's argument—if argument it can be called—is a perpetual *ignoratio elenchi*. He lumps up the principle of utility—which is a theory of right and wrong—with the theory, if there be such a theory, of the universal selfishness of mankind. We never know, for many sentences together, which of the two he is arguing against; he never seems to know it himself. He begins a sentence on the one, and ends it on the other. In his mind they seem to be one and the same. Read this:

> Utilitarian philosophy and Christian ethics have in their principles and motives no common bond of union, and ought never to have been linked together in one system; for, palliate and disguise the difference as we may, we shall find at last that they rest on separate foundations, one deriving all its strength from the moral feelings, and the other from the selfish passions of our nature. (p. 67)

Or this:

> If we suppress the authority of conscience, reject the moral feelings, rid ourselves of the sentiments of honor, and sink (as men too often do) below the influence of religion, and if, at the same time, we are taught to think that utility is the universal test of right and wrong, what is there left within us as an antagonist power to the craving of passion, or the base appetite of worldly gain? In such a condition of the soul, all motive not terminating in mere passion becomes utterly devoid of meaning. On this system, the sinner is no longer abhorred as a rebel against his better nature—as one who profanely mutilates the image of God; he acts only on the principles of other men, but he blunders in calculating the chances of his personal advantage; and thus we deprive virtue of its holiness, and vice of its deformity, humanity of its honor, and language of its meaning; we shut out, as no better than madness or folly, the loftiest sentiments of the heathen as well as of the Christian world; and all that is great or generous in our nature droops under the influence of a cold and withering selfishness. (pp. 76–77)

Every line of this passage convicts Mr. Sedgwick of never having taken the trouble to know the meaning of the terms in which the doctrine he so eagerly vilifies is conveyed. What has "calculating the chances of personal advantage" to do with the principle of utility? The object of Mr. Sedgwick is to represent that principle as leading to the conclusion that a vicious man is no more a subject of disapprobation than a person who blunders in a question of prudence. If Mr. Sedgwick did but know what the principle of utility is, he would see that it leads to no such conclusion. Some people have been led to that conclusion, not by the principle of utility, but either by the doctrine of philosophical necessity, incorrectly understood, or by a theory of motives which has been called the selfish theory; and even from that it does not justly follow.

The finery about shutting out "lofty sentiments" scarcely deserves notice. It resembles what is said in the next page about "suppressing all the kindly emotions which minister to virtue." We are far from charging Mr. Sedgwick with wilful misrepresentation, but this is the very next thing to it—misrepresentation in voluntary ignorance. Who proposes to suppress any "kindly emotion?" Human beings, the Professor may be assured, will always love and honor every sentiment, whether "lofty" or otherwise, which is either directly pointed to their good, or tends to raise the mind above the influence of the petty objects for the sake of which mankind injure one another. The Professor is afraid that the sinner will be "no longer abhorred." We imagined that it was not the sinner who should be abhorred, but sin. Mankind, however, are sufficiently ready to abhor whatever is obviously noxious to them. A human being filled with malevolent dispositions, or coldly indifferent to the feelings of his fellow-creatures, will never, the Professor may assure himself, be amiable in their eyes. Whether they will speak of him as "a rebel against his better nature," "one who profanely mutilates the image of God," and so on, will depend upon whether they are proficient in commonplace rhetoric. But whatever words they use, rely on it that, while men dread and abhor a wolf or a serpent, which have no better nature, and no image of God to mutilate, they will abhor with infinitely greater intensity a human being who, outwardly resembling themselves, is inwardly their enemy, and, being far more powerful than "toad or asp," voluntarily cherishes the same disposition to mischief.

If utility be the standard, "the end," in the Professor's opinion, "will be made to sanctify the means" (p. 78). We answer—just so far as in any other system, and no farther. In every system of morality, the end, when good, justifies all means which do not conflict with some more important good. On Mr. Sedgwick's own scheme, are there not ends which sanctify actions, in other cases deserving the utmost abhorrence —such, for instance, as taking the life of a fellow-creature in cold blood, in the face of the whole people? According to the principle of utility, the end justifies all means necessary to its attainment, except those which are more mischievous than the end is useful—an exception amply sufficient.

We have now concluded our examination of Mr. Sedgwick: first, as a commentator on the studies which form part of a liberal education; and next, as an assailant of the "utilitarian theory of morals." We have shown that, on the former subject, he has omitted almost everything which ought to have been said, that almost all which he has said is trivial, and much of it erroneous. With regard to the other part of his design, we have shown that he has not only failed to refute the doctrine that human happiness is the foundation of morality, but has, in the attempt, proved himself not to understand what the doctrine is, and to be capable of bringing the most serious charges against other men's opinions, and themselves, which even a smattering of the knowledge appropriate to the subject would have shown to be groundless.

We by no means affect to consider Mr. Sedgwick as (what he would not himself claim to be) a sufficient advocate of the cause he has espoused, nor pretend that his pages contain the best that can be said, or even the best that has been said, against the theory of utility. That theory numbers among its enemies, minds of almost every degree of power and intellectual accomplishments, among whom many are capable of making out a much better apparent case for their opinion. But Mr. Sedgwick's is a fair enough sample of the popular arguments against the theory; his book has had more readers and more applauders than a better book would have had, because it is level with a lower class of capacities, and though, by pointing out its imperfections, we do little to establish our own opinion, it is something to have shown on how light grounds, in some cases, men of gravity and reputation arraign the opinion, and are admired and applauded for so arraigning it.

The question is not one of pure speculation. Not to mention

the importance, to those who are entrusted with the education of the moral sentiments, of just views respecting their origin and nature, we may remark that, upon the truth or falseness of the doctrine of a moral sense, it depends whether morality is a fixed or a progressive body of doctrine. If it be true that man has a sense given him to determine what is right and wrong, it follows that his moral judgments and feelings cannot be susceptible of any improvement; such as they are they ought to remain. The question, what mankind in general ought to think and feel on the subject of their duty, must be determined by observing what, when no interest or passion can be seen to bias them, they think and feel already. According to the theory of utility, on the contrary, the question, what is our duty, is as open to discussion as any other question. Moral doctrines are no more to be received without evidence, nor to be sifted less carefully, than any other doctrines. An appeal lies, as on all other subjects, from a received opinion, however generally entertained, to the decisions of cultivated reason. The weakness of human intellect, and all the other infirmities of our nature, are considered to interfere as much with the rectitude of our judgments on morality, as on any other of our concerns; and changes as great are anticipated in our opinions on that subject, as on every other, both from the progress of intelligence, from more authentic and enlarged experience, and from alterations in the condition of the human race, requiring altered rules of conduct.

It deeply concerns the greatest interests of our race, that the only mode of treating ethical questions which aims at correcting existing maxims, and rectifying any of the perversions of existing feeling, should not be borne down by clamor. The contemners of analysis have long enough had all the pretension to themselves. They have had the monopoly of the claim to pure, and lofty, and sublime principles; and those who gave reasons to justify their feelings have submitted to be cried down as low, and cold, and degraded. We hope they will submit no longer; and not content with meeting the metaphysics of their more powerful adversaries by profounder metaphysics, will join battle in the field of popular controversy with every antagonist of name and reputation, even when, as in the present case, his name and reputation are his only claims to be heard on such a subject.

SIX

M. de Tocqueville on Democracy in America

[Mill was a student of French thought and French politics all his life, and Alexis de Tocqueville (1805–1859) was the French thinker in whom Mill found most to admire and least to criticize. He reviewed de Tocqueville's masterpiece, *Democracy in America,* twice: once in 1835, when the first volume appeared, and again in 1840, on the publication of the second volume. The later essay, which appeared in the *Edinburgh Review*, provides an excellent introduction to de Tocqueville's work. It also provides illuminating examples and discussions of Mill's own views on the methods of the social sciences and on the crucial importance of sociological knowledge for reform of society. In addition, it shows Mill working out a number of themes which are more fully developed in the famous essay *On Liberty* (1859).

The text given here is that of the *Dissertations and Discussions.*]

IT HAS BEEN the rare fortune of M. de Tocqueville's book to have achieved an easy triumph, both over the indifference of our at once busy and indolent public to profound speculation, and over the particular obstacles which oppose the reception of speculations from a foreign, and above all from a French, source. There is some ground for the remark often made upon us by foreigners, that the character of our national intellect is insular. The general movement of the European mind sweeps past us, without our being drawn into it, or even looking sufficiently at it to discover in what direction it is tending; and, if we had not a tolerably rapid original movement of our own, we should long since have been left in the distance. The French language is almost universally cultivated on this side of the Channel; a flood of human beings perpetually ebbs and flows between London and Paris; national prejudices and animosities are becoming numbered among the things that were; yet the revolution which has taken place in the tendencies of French thought, which has changed the character of the higher literature of France, and almost that of the French language, seems hitherto, as far as the English public are concerned, to have taken place in vain. At a time when the prevailing tone of French speculation is one of exaggerated reaction against the doctrines of the eighteenth century, French philosophy, with us, is still synonymous with Encyclopedism. The Englishmen may almost be numbered who are aware that France has produced any great names in prose literature since Voltaire and Rousseau; and while modern history has been receiving a new aspect from the labors of men who are not only among the profoundest thinkers, but the clearest and most popular writers, of their age, even those of their works which are expressly dedicated to the history of our own country remain mostly untranslated, and in almost all cases unread.

To this general neglect, M. de Tocqueville's book forms, however, as we have already said, a brilliant exception. Its reputation was as sudden, and is as extensive, in this country as in France, and in that large part of Europe which receives its opinions from France. The progress of political dissatisfaction, and the comparisons made between the fruits of a popular constitution on one side of the Atlantic, and of a mixed government with a preponderating aristocratic element on the other, had made the working of American institutions a party question. For many years, every book of travels in America had been a party pamphlet, or had at least fallen among partisans, and been pressed into the service of one party or of the other. When, therefore, a new book, of a grave and imposing character, on Democracy in America, made its appearance even on the other side of the British Channel, it was not likely to be overlooked, or to escape an attempt to convert it to party purposes. If ever political writer had reason to believe that he had labored successfully to render his book incapable of such a use, M. de Tocqueville was entitled to think so. But though his theories are of an impartiality without example, and his practical conclusions lean towards Radicalism, some of his phrases are susceptible of a Tory application. One of these is "the tyranny of the majority." This phrase was forthwith adopted into the Conservative dialect, and trumpeted by Sir Robert Peel in his Tamworth oration, when, as booksellers' advertisements have since frequently reminded us, he "earnestly requested the perusal" of the book by all and each of his audience. And we believe it has since been the opinion of the country gentlemen, that M. de Tocqueville is one of the pillars of Conservatism, and his book a definitive demolition of America and of Democracy. The error has done more good than the truth would perhaps have done, since the result is that the English public now know and read the first philosophical book ever written on Democracy, as it manifests itself in modern society, a book the essential doctrines of which it is not likely that any future speculations will subvert, to whatever degree they may modify them, while its spirit, and the general mode in which it treats its subject, constitute it the beginning of a new era in the scientific study of politics.

The importance of M. de Tocqueville's speculations is not to be estimated by the opinions which he has adopted, be these true or false. The value of his work is less in the conclusions than in the mode of arriving at them. He has applied, to the greatest question in the art and science of government, those principles and methods of philosophizing to which mankind are indebted for all the advances made by modern times in the other branches of the study of nature. It is not risking too much to affirm of these volumes that they contain the first analytical inquiry into the influence of Democracy. For the first time, that phenomenon is treated of as something which, being a reality in nature, and no mere mathematical or metaphysical abstraction, manifests itself by innumerable properties, not by some one only, and must be looked at in many aspects before it can be made the subject even of that modest and conjectural judgment which is alone attainable respecting a fact at once so great and so new. Its consequences are by no means to be comprehended in one single description, nor in one summary verdict of approval or condemnation. So complicated and endless are their ramifications, that he who sees furthest into them will longest hesitate before finally pronouncing whether the good or the evil of its influence, on the whole, preponderates.

M. de Tocqueville has endeavored to ascertain and discriminate the various properties and tendencies of Democracy, the separate relations in which it stands towards the different interests of society, and the different moral and social requisites of human nature. In the investigation, he has of necessity left much undone, and much which will be better done by those who come after him and build upon his foundations. But he has earned the double honor of being the first to make the attempt, and of having done more towards the success of it than probably will ever again be done by any one individual. His method is, as that of a philosopher on such a subject must be, a combination of deduction with induction: his evidences are, laws of human nature, on the one hand; the example of America and France, and other modern nations, so far as applicable, on the other. His conclusions never rest on either species of evidence alone; whatever he classes as an effect of Democracy he has both ascertained to exist in those countries in which the state of society is democratic, and has also succeeded in connecting with Democracy by deductions *a priori*, tending to show that such would naturally be its influences upon beings constituted as mankind are, and placed in a world such as we know ours to be. If this be not the true Baconian and Newtonian method applied to society and government, if any better, or even any other, be possible—M. de Tocqueville would be the first to say, *candidus imperti*; if not, he is entitled to say to political theorists, whether calling themselves philosophers or practical men, *His utere mecum*.

That part of *Democracy in America* which was first published professes to treat of the political effects of Democracy; the second is devoted to its influence on society in the widest sense, on the relations of private life, on intellect, morals, and the habits and modes of feeling which constitute national character. The last is both a newer and a more difficult subject of inquiry than the first; there are fewer who are competent, or who will even think themselves competent, to judge M. de Tocqueville's conclusions. But, we believe, no one in the least entitled to an opinion will refuse to him the praise of having probed the subject to a depth which had never before been sounded, of having carried forward the controversy into a wider and a loftier region of thought, and pointed out many questions essential to the subject, which had not been before attended to—questions which he may or may not have solved, but of which, in any case, he has greatly facilitated the solution.

The comprehensiveness of M. de Tocqueville's views, and the impartiality of his feelings, have not led him into the common infirmity of those who see too many sides to a question —that of thinking them all equally important; he is able to arrive at a decided opinion. Nor has the more extensive range

of considerations embraced in his Second Part affected practically the general conclusions which resulted from his First.
They may be stated as follows: That Democracy, in the modern world, is inevitable, and that it is, on the whole, desirable,
but desirable only under certain conditions, and those conditions capable, by human care and foresight, of being realized,
but capable also of being missed. The progress and ultimate
ascendancy of the democratic principle has, in his eyes, the
character of a law of nature. He thinks it an inevitable result
of the tendencies of a progressive civilization; by which expressions he by no means intends to imply either praise or
censure. No human effort, no accident even, unless one which
should throw back civilization itself, can avail, in his opinion,
to defeat, or even very considerably to retard, this progress.
But, though the fact itself appears to him removed from human control, its salutary or baneful consequences do not. Like
other great powers of nature, the tendency, though it cannot
be counteracted, may be guided to good. Man cannot turn
back the rivers to their source, but it rests with himself
whether they shall fertilize or lay waste his fields. Left to its
spontaneous course, with nothing done to prepare before it
that set of circumstances under which it can exist with safety,
and to fight against its worse by an apt employment of its
better peculiarities, the probable effects of Democracy upon
human well-being, and upon whatever is best and noblest in
human character, appear to M. de Tocqueville extremely formidable. But with as much of wise effort devoted to the purpose as it is not irrational to hope for, most of what is mischievous in its tendencies may, in his opinion, be corrected,
and its natural capacities of good so far strengthened and
made use of as to leave no cause for regret in the old state of
society, and enable the new one to be contemplated with calm
contentment, if without exultation.

It is necessary to observe, that by Democracy M. de Tocqueville does not, in general, mean any particular form of
government. He can conceive a Democracy under an absolute
monarch. Nay, he entertains no small dread lest in some
countries it should actually appear in that form. By Democracy, M. de Tocqueville understands equality of conditions,
the absence of all aristocracy, whether constituted by political
privileges or by superiority in individual importance and social power. It is toward Democracy in this sense, toward
equality between man and man, that he conceives society to

be irresistibly tending. Toward Democracy in the other and more common sense, it may or may not be traveling. Equality of conditions tends naturally to produce a popular government, but not necessarily. Equality may be equal freedom or equal servitude. America is the type of the first; France, he thinks, is in danger of falling into the second. The latter country is in the condition which, of all that civilized societies are liable to, he regards with the greatest alarm—a democratic state of society without democratic institutions. For in democratic institutions M. de Tocqueville sees, not an aggravation, but a corrective of the most serious evils incident to a democratic state of society. No one is more opposed than he is to that species of democratic radicalism which would admit at once to the highest of political franchises untaught masses who have not yet been experimentally proved fit even for the lowest. But the ever-increasing intervention of the people, and of all classes of the people, in their own affairs, he regards as a cardinal maxim in the modern art of government; and he believes that the nations of civilized Europe, though not all equally advanced, are all advancing, toward a condition in which there will be no distinctions of political rights, no great or very permanent distinctions of hereditary wealth, when, as there will remain no classes nor individuals capable of making head against the government, unless all are and are fit to be alike citizens, all will ere long be equally slaves.

The opinion that there is this irresistible tendency to equality of conditions is perhaps, of all the leading doctrines of the book, that which most stands in need of confirmation to English readers. M. de Tocqueville devotes but little space to the elucidation of it. To French readers, the historical retrospect upon which it rests is familiar, and facts known to every one establish its truth so far as relates to that country. But the English public, who have less faith in irresistible tendencies, and who, while they require for every political theory an historical basis, are far less accustomed to link together the events of history in a connected chain, the proposition will hardly seem to be sufficiently made out. Our author's historical argument is, however, deserving of their attention.

Let us recollect the situation of France seven hundred years ago, when the territory was divided amongst a small number of families, who were the owners of the soil and the rulers of the inhabitants: the right of governing descended with the family inheritance from generation to generation; force was the only means by which man could act on man; and landed property was the sole source of power.

Soon, however, the political power of the clergy was founded, and began to extend itself; the clergy opened its ranks to all classes—to the poor and the rich, the villein and the lord; equality penetrated into the government through the church; and the being who as a serf must have vegetated in pereptual bondage, took his place as a priest in the midst of nobles, and not unfrequently above the heads of kings.

The different relations of men became more complicated and more numerous as society gradually became more stable and more civilized. Thence the want of civil laws was felt; and the order of legal functionaries soon rose from the obscurity of their tribunals and their dusty chambers, to appear at the court of the monarch, by the side of the feudal barons in their ermine and their mail.

Whilst the kings were ruining themselves by their great enterprises, and the nobles exhausting their resources by private wars, the lower orders were enriching themselves by commerce. The influence of money began to be perceptible in state affairs. The transactions of business opened a new road to power, and the financier rose to a station of political influence in which he was at once flattered and despised.

Gradually the spread of mental acquirements, and the increasing taste for literature and the arts, opened chances of success to talent; knowledge became a means of government, intelligence became a social power, and the man of letters took a part in the affairs of the state.

The value attached to the privileges of birth decreased in the exact proportion in which new paths were struck out to advancement. In the eleventh century, nobility was beyond all price; in the thirteenth, it might be purchased: it was conferred for the first time in 1270; and equality was thus introduced into the government through aristocracy itself.

In the course of these seven hundred years, it sometimes happened, that in order to resist the authority of the crown, or to diminish the power of their rivals, the nobles granted a certain share of political rights to the people; or, more frequently, the king permitted the inferior orders to enjoy a degree of power, with the intention of lowering the aristocracy.

As soon as land was held on any other than a feudal tenure, and personal property began in its turn to confer influence and power, every improvement which was introduced in commerce or manufactures was a fresh element of the equality of conditions. Henceforward every new discovery, every new want which grew up, and every new desire which craved satisfaction, was a step towards the universal level. The taste for luxury, the love of war, the sway of fashion, the most superficial as well as the deepest passions of the human heart, cooperated to enrich the poor and to impoverish the rich.

From the time when the exercise of the intellect became a source of power and of wealth, it is impossible not to consider every addition to science, every fresh truth, every new idea, as a germ of power placed within the reach of the people. Poetry, eloquence, and memory, the grace of wit, the glow of imagination, the depth of thought, and all the gifts which are bestowed by Providence without respect of persons, turned to the advantage of Democracy; and, even when they were in the possession of its adversaries, they still served its cause by bringing into relief the natural greatness of man; its conquests spread, therefore, with those of civilization and knowledge, and literature became an arsenal, where the poorest and the weakest could always find weapons to their hand.

In perusing the pages of our history, we shall scarcely meet with a single great event, in the lapse of seven hundred years, which has not turned to the advantage of equality.

The Crusades, and the wars with the English, decimated the nobles, and divided their possessions; the erection of corporate towns introduced an element of democratic liberty into the bosom of feudal monarchy; the invention of firearms equalized the villein and the noble on the field of battle; printing opened the same resources to the minds of all classes; the post was established, so as to bring the same information to the door of the poor man's cottage and to the gate of the palace; and Protestantism proclaimed that all men are alike able to find the road to heaven. The discovery of America offered a thousand new paths to fortune, and placed riches and power within the reach of the adventurous and the obscure.

If we examine what was happening in France at intervals of fifty years, beginning with the eleventh century, we shall invariably perceive that a twofold revolution has taken place in the state of society. The noble has gone down on the social ladder, and the *roturier* has gone up; the one descends as the other rises. Every half-century brings them nearer to each other.

Nor is this phenomenon at all peculiar to France. Whithersoever we turn our eyes, we witness the same continual revolution throughout the whole of Christendom.

Everywhere the various occurrences of national existence have turned to the advantage of Democracy; all men have aided it by their exertions. Those who have intentionally labored in its cause and those who have served it unwittingly, those who have fought for it and those who have declared themselves its opponents—have all been driven along in the same track, have all labored to one end, some ignorantly, and some unwillingly; all have been blind instruments in the hands of God.

The gradual development of the equality of conditions is therefore a providential fact, and possesses all the characteristics of a divine decree; it is universal, it is durable, it constantly eludes all human interference, and all events as well as all men contribute to its progress.

Would it be wise to imagine that a social impulse which dates from so far back can be checked by the efforts of a generation? Is it credible that the democracy which has annihilated the feudal system, and vanquished kings, will respect the *bourgeois* and the capitalist? Will it stop now that it is grown so strong, and its adversaries so weak?

It is not necessary that God himself should speak in order to disclose to us the unquestionable signs of his will. We can discern them in the habitual course of nature, and in the invariable tendency of events.

The Christian nations of our age seem to me to present a most alarming spectacle. The impulse which is bearing them along is so strong that it cannot be stopped, but it is not yet so rapid that it cannot be guided. Their fate is in their hands; yet a little while, and it may be so no longer. (*Introduction to the First Part.*)

That such has been the actual course of events in modern history, nobody can doubt; and as truly in England as in France. Of old, every proprietor of land was sovereign over its inhabitants, while the cultivators could not call even their bodily powers their own. It was by degrees only, and in a succession of ages, that their personal emancipation was effected, and their labor became theirs to sell for whatever they could obtain for it. They became the rich men's equals in the eye of the law; but the rich had still the making of the law, and the administering of it, and the equality was at first little more than nominal. The poor, however, could now acquire property; the path was open to them to quit their own class for a higher; their rise, even to a considerable station, gradually became a common occurrence, and, to those who acquired a large fortune, the other powers and privileges of aristocracy were successively opened, until hereditary honors have become less a power in themselves than a symbol and ornament of great riches. While individuals thus continually rose from the mass, the mass itself multiplied and strengthened, the towns obtained a voice in public affairs, the many, in the aggregate, became, even in property, more and more a match for the few, and the nation became a power distinct from the small number of individuals who once disposed even of the crown, and determined all public affairs at their pleasure. The Reformation was the dawn of the government of public opinion. Even at that early period, opinion was not formed by the higher classes exclusively; and while the publicity of all State transactions, the liberty of petition and public discussion, the press—and of late, above all, the periodical press—have rendered public opinion more and more the supreme power, the same causes have rendered the formation of it less and less dependent upon the initiative of the higher ranks. Even the direct participation of the people at large in the government, had, in various ways, been greatly extended before the political events of the last few years, when Democracy has given so signal a proof of its progress in society by the inroads it has been able to make into the political constitution; and in spite of the alarm which has been taken by the possessors of large property, who are far more generally opposed than they had been within the present generation to any additional strengthening of the popular element in the House of Commons, there is at this moment a much stronger party for a further parliamentary reform, than many good observers thought there was, twelve years ago, for that which has already taken place.

But there is a surer mode of deciding the point than any historical retrospect. Let us look at the powers which are even now at work in society itself.

To a superficial glance at the condition of our own country, nothing can seem more unlike any tendency to equality of condition. The inequalities of property are apparently greater than in any former period of history. Nearly all the land is parceled out, in great estates, among comparatively few families; and it is not the large but the small properties which are in process of extinction. A hereditary and titled nobility, more potent by their vast possessions than by their social precedency, are constitutionally and really one of the great powers in the State. To form part of their order is that which every ambitious man aspires to, as the crowning glory of a successful career. The passion for equality, of which M. de Tocqueville speaks almost as if it were the great moral lever of modern times, is hardly known in this country, even by name. On the contrary, all ranks seem to have a passion for inequality. The hopes of every person are directed to rising in the world, not to pulling the world down to him. The greatest enemy of the political conduct of the House of Lords submits to their superiority of rank as he would to the ordinances of nature, and often thinks any amount of toil and watching repaid by a nod of recognition from one of their number.

We have put the case as strongly as it could be put by an adversary, and have stated as facts some things which, if they have been facts, are giving visible signs that they will not always be so. If we look back even twenty years, we shall find that the popular respect for the higher classes is by no means the thing it was; and, though all who are rising wish for the continuance of advantages which they themselves hope to share, there are, among those who do not expect to rise, increasing indications that a leveling spirit is abroad; and political discontents, in whatever manner originating, show an increasing tendency to take that shape. But it is the less necessary to dwell upon these things, as we shall be satisfied with making out, in respect to the tendency to equality in England, much less than M. de Tocqueville contends for. We do not maintain that the time is drawing near when there will be no distinction of classes; but we do contend that the power of the higher classes, both in government and in society, is diminishing, while that of the middle and even the lower classes is increasing, and likely to increase.

The constituent elements of political importance are property, intelligence, and the power of combination. In every one of these elements, is it the higher classes, or the other portion of society, that have lately made, and are continuing to make, the most rapid advances?

Even with regard to the element of property, there cannot

be room for more than a momentary doubt. The class who are rich by inheritance are so far from augmenting their fortunes, that it is much if they can be said to keep them up. A territorial aristocracy always live up to their means—generally beyond them. Our own is no exception to the rule; and as their control over the taxes becomes every day more restricted, and the liberal professions more overcrowded, they are condemned more and more to bear the burden of their own large families, which it is not easy to do, compatibly with leaving to the heir the means of keeping up, without becoming embarrassed, the old family establishments. It is a matter of notoriety how severely the difficulty of providing for younger sons is felt, even in the highest rank, and that, as a provision for daughters, alliances are now courted which would not have been endured a generation ago. The additions to the "money power" of the higher ranks consist of the riches of the *novi homines*, who are continually aggregated to that class from among the merchants and manufacturers, and occasionally from the professions. But many of these are merely successors to the impoverished owners of the land they buy, and the fortunes of others are taken, in the way of marriage, to pay off the mortgages of older families. Even with these allowances, no doubt the number of wealthy persons is steadily on the increase; but what is this to the accumulation of capitals, and growth of incomes, in the hands of the middle class? It is that class which furnishes all the accessions to the aristocracy of wealth; and, for one who makes a large fortune, fifty acquire, without exceeding, a moderate competency, and leave their children to work, like themselves, at the laboring oar.

In point of intelligence, it can still less be affirmed that the higher classes maintain the same proportional ascendancy as of old. They have shared with the rest of the world in the diffusion of information. They have improved, like all other classes, in the decorous virtues. Their humane feelings and refined tastes form, in general, a striking contrast to the coarse habits of the same class a few generations ago. But it would be difficult to point out what new idea in speculation, what invention or discovery in the practical arts, what useful institution, or what permanently valuable book, Great Britain has owed, for the last hundred years, to her hereditary aristocracy, titled or untitled;* what great public enterprise, what important national movement in religion or politics, those classes have originated, or have so much as taken in it the principal share. Considered in respect to active energies and laborious habits, to the stirring qualities which fit men for playing a considerable part in the affairs of mankind, few will say that our aristocracy have not deteriorated. It is, on the other hand, one of the commonplaces of the age, that knowledge and intelligence are spreading, in a degree which was formerly thought impossible, to the lower, and down even to the lowest rank. And this is a fact, not accomplished, but in the mere dawn of its accomplishment, and which has shown hitherto but a slight promise of its future fruits. It is easy to scoff at the kind of intelligence which is thus diffusing itself, but it is intelligence still. The knowledge which is power is not the highest description of knowledge only; any knowledge which gives the habit of forming an opinion, and the capacity of expressing that opinion, constitutes a political power, and, if combined with the capacity and habit of acting in concert, a formidable one.

It is in this last element, the power of combined action, that the progress of the Democracy has been the most gigantic. What combination can do has been shown by an experiment, of now many years' duration, among a people the most backward in civilization (thanks to English misgovernment), between the Vistula and the Pyrenees. Even on this side of the Irish Channel we have seen something of what could be done by political unions, antislavery societies, and the like; to say nothing of the less advanced, but already powerful, organization of the working classes, the progress of which has been suspended only by the temporary failure arising from the manifest impracticability of its present objects. And these various associations are not the machinery of democratic combination, but the occasional weapons which that spirit forges as it needs them. The real political unions of England are the newspapers. It is these which tell every person what all other persons are feeling, and in what manner they are ready to act: it is by these that the people learn, it may truly be said, their own wishes, and through these that

* The chief exceptions, since the accession of the house of Hanover, are the chemist Cavendish in the last century, and the Earl of Rosse in the present.

they declare them. The newspapers and the railroads are solving the problem of bringing the Democracy of England to vote, like that of Athens, simultaneously in one *agora*; and the same agencies are rapidly effacing those local distinctions which rendered one part of our population strangers to another, and are making us more than ever (what is the first condition of a powerful public opinion) a homogeneous people. If America has been said to prove that, in an extensive country, a popular government may exist, England seems destined to afford the proof that, after a certain stage in civilization, it must; for as soon as the numerically stronger have the same advantages, in means of combination and celerity of movement, as the smaller number, they are the masters, and, except by their permission, no government can any longer exist.

It may be said, doubtless, that, though the aristocratic class may be no longer in the ascendant, the power by which it is succeeded is not that of the numerical majority; that the middle class in this country is as little in danger of being outstripped by the democracy below, as of being kept down by the aristocracy above; and that there can be no difficulty for that class, aided as it would be by the rich, in making head, by its property, intelligence, and power of combination, against any possible growth of those elements of importance in the inferior classes, and in excluding the mass of mere manual laborers from any share in political rights, unless such a restricted and subordinate one as may be found compatible with the complete ascendancy of property.

We are disposed partially to agree in this opinion. Universal suffrage is never likely to exist and maintain itself where the majority are *prolétaires*; and we are not unwilling to believe that a laboring class in abject poverty, like a great part of our rural population, or which expends its surplus earnings in gin or in waste, like so much of the better-paid population of the towns, may be kept politically in subjection, and that the middle classes are safe from the permanent rule of such a body, though perhaps not from its Swing outrages or Wat Tyler insurrections. But this admission leaves the fact of a tendency towards Democracy practically untouched. There is a Democracy short of pauper suffrage; the working classes themselves contain a middle as well as a lowest class. Not to meddle with the *vexata quæstio*, whether the lowest class is or is not improving in condition, it is certain that a larger and larger body of manual laborers are rising above that class, and acquiring at once decent wages and decent habits of conduct. A rapidly increasing multitude of our working people are becoming, in point of condition and habits, what the American working people are; and, if our boasted improvements are of any worth, there must be a growing tendency in society and government to make this condition of the laboring classes the general one. The nation must be most slenderly supplied with wisdom and virtue, if it cannot do something to improve its own physical condition, to say nothing of its moral. It is something gained, that well-meaning persons of all parties now at length profess to have this end in view. But in proportion as it is approached to, in proportion as the working class becomes what all proclaim their desire that it should be, well paid, well taught, and well conducted—in the same proportion will the opinions of that class tell, according to its numbers, upon the affairs of the country. Whatever portion of the class succeeds in thus raising itself becomes a part of the ruling body; and, if the suffrage be necessary to make it so, it will not be long without the suffrage.

Meanwhile, we are satisfied if it be admitted that the government of England is progressively changing from the government of a few, to the government, not indeed of *the* many, but of many—from an aristocracy with a popular infusion, to the *régime* of the middle class. To most purposes, in the constitution of modern society, the government of a numerous middle class is Democracy. Nay, it not merely *is* Democracy, but the only Democracy of which there is yet any example; what is called universal suffrage in America arising from the fact that America is *all* middle class, the whole people being in a condition, both as to education and pecuniary means, corresponding to the middle class here. The consequences which we would deduce from this fact will appear presently, when we examine M. de Tocqueville's view of the moral, social, and intellectual influences of Democracy. This cannot be done until we have briefly stated his opinions on the purely political branch of the question. To this part of our task we shall now proceed, with as much conciseness as is permitted by the number and importance of the ideas which, holding an essential place among the grounds of his general conclusions, have a claim not to be omitted even from the most rapid summary.

We have already intimated that M. de Tocqueville recognizes such a thing as a democratic state of society without a democratic government—a state in which the people are all equal, and subjected to one common master, who selects indiscriminately from all of them the instruments of his government. In this sense, as he remarks, the government of the Pasha of Egypt is a specimen of Democracy, and to this type (with allowance for difference of civilization and manners) he thinks that all nations are in danger of approximating, in which the equalization of conditions has made greater progress than the spirit of liberty. Now, this he holds to be the condition of France. The kings of France have always been the greatest of levelers: Louis XI, Richelieu, Louis XIV, alike labored to break the power of the *noblesse*, and reduce all intermediate classes and bodies to the general level. After them came the Revolution, bringing with it the abolition of hereditary privileges, the emigration and dispossession of half the great landed proprietors, and the subdivision of large fortunes by the revolutionary law of inheritance. While the equalization of conditions was thus rapidly reaching its extreme limits, no corresponding progress of public spirit was taking place in the people at large. No institutions capable of fostering an interest in the details of public affairs were created by the Revolution: it swept away even those which despotism had spared; and, if it admitted a portion of the population to a voice in the government, gave it them only on the greatest but rarest occasion—the election of the great council of the State. A political act, to be done only once in a few years, and for which nothing in the daily habits of the citizen has prepared him, leaves his intellect and moral dispositions very much as it found them; and, the citizens not being encouraged to take upon themselves collectively that portion of the business of society which had been performed by the privileged classes, the central government easily drew to itself, not only the whole local administration, but much of what, in countries like ours, is performed by associations of individuals. Whether the government was revolutionary or counter-revolutionary, made no difference; under one and the other, every thing was done *for* the people, and nothing *by* the people. In France, consequently, the arbitrary power of the magistrate in detail is almost without limit. And when, of late, some attempts have been made to associate a portion of the citizens in the management of local affairs, comparatively few have been found, even among those in good circumstances (anywhere but in the large towns), who could be induced willingly to take any part in that management, who, when they had no personal object to gain, felt the public interest sufficiently their own interest not to grudge every moment which they withdrew from their occupations or pleasures to bestow upon it. With all the eagerness and violence of party contests in France, a nation more passive in the hands of any one who is uppermost does not exist. M. de Tocqueville has no faith in the virtues, nor even in the prolonged existence, of a superficial love of freedom, in the face of a practical habit of slavery; and the question, whether the French are to be a free people, depends, in his opinion, upon the possibility of creating a spirit and a habit of local self-government.

M. de Tocqueville sees the principal source and security of American freedom, not so much in the election of the President and Congress by popular suffrage, as in the administration of nearly all the business of society by the people themselves. This it is, which, according to him, keeps up the habit of attending to the public interest, not in the gross merely, or on a few momentous occasions, but in its dry and troublesome details. This, too, it is which enlightens the people, which teaches them by experience how public affairs must be carried on. The dissemination of public business as widely as possible among the people, is, in his opinion, the only means by which they can be fitted for the exercise of any share of power over the legislature, and generally also the only means by which they can be led to desire it.

For the particulars of this education of the American people by means of political institutions, we must refer to the work itself, of which it is one of the minor recommendations, that it has never been equaled even as a mere statement and explanation of the institutions of the United States. The general principle to which M. de Tocqueville has given the sanction of his authority merits more consideration than it has yet received from the professed laborers in the cause of national education. It has often been said, and requires to be repeated still oftener, that books and discourses alone are not education, that life is a problem, not a theorem, that action can only be learnt in action. A child learns to write its name only by a succession of trials, and is a man to be taught to use his mind and guide his conduct by mere precept? What can be learnt in schools is important, but not all-important. The main branch of the education of human beings is their habitual employment, which must be either their individual vocation, or some matter of general concern, in which they are called to take a part. The private money-getting operation of almost every one is more or less a mechanical routine; it brings but few of his faculties into action, while its exclusive pursuit tends to fasten his attention and interest exclusively upon himself, and upon his family as an appendage of himself, making him indifferent to the public, to the more generous objects and the nobler interests, and, in his inordinate regard for his personal comforts, selfish and cowardly. Balance these tendencies by contrary ones; give him something to do for the public, whether as a vestryman, a juryman, or an elector—and, in that degree, his ideas and feelings are taken out of this narrow circle. He becomes acquainted with more varied business, and a larger range of considerations. He is made to feel that, besides the interests which separate him from his fellow-citizens, he has interests which connect him with them, that not only the common weal is his weal, but that it partly depends upon his exertions. Whatever might be the case in some other constitutions of society, the spirit of a commercial people will be, we are persuaded, essentially mean and slavish, wherever public spirit is not cultivated by an extensive participation of the people in the business of government in detail, nor will the desideratum of a general diffusion of intelligence among either the middle or lower classes be realized but by a corresponding dissemination of public functions, and a voice in public affairs.

Nor is this inconsistent with obtaining a considerable share of the benefits (and they are great) of what is called centralization. The principle of local self-government has been undeservedly discredited by being associated with the agitation against the new poor law. The most active agency of a central authority in collecting and communicating information, giving advice to the local bodies, and even framing general rules for their observance, is no hindrance, but an aid, to making the local liberties an instrument of educating the people. The existence of such a central agency allows of intrusting to the people themselves, or to local bodies representative of them, many things of too great national importance to be committed unreservedly to the localities, and completes the efficacy of local self-government as a means of instruction, by accustoming the people not only to judge of particular facts, but to understand and apply, and feel practically the value of, principles. The mode of administration provided for the English poor laws by the late act seems to us to be, in its general conception, almost theoretically perfect; and the extension of a similar mixture of central and local management to several other branches of administration, thereby combining the best fruits of popular intervention with much of the advantage of skilled supervision and traditional experience, would, we believe, be entitled to no mean rank in M. de Tocqueville's list of correctives to the inconveniences of Democracy.

In estimating the effects of democratic government as distinguished from a democratic condition of society, M. de Tocqueville assumes the state of circumstances which exists in America—a popular government in the State, combined with popular local institutions. In such a government he sees great advantages, balanced by no inconsiderable evils.

Among the advantages, one which figures in the foremost rank is that of which we have just spoken—the diffusion of intelligence, the remarkable impulse given by democratic institutions to the active faculties of that portion of the community who in other circumstances are the most ignorant, passive, and apathetic. These are characteristics of America which strike all travelers. Activity, enterprise, and a respectable amount of information, are not the qualities of a few among the American citizens, nor even of many, but of all. There is no class of persons who are the slaves of habit and routine. Every American will carry on his manufacture, or cultivate his farm, by the newest and best methods applicable to the circumstances of the case. The poorest American understands and can explain the most intricate parts of his country's institutions, can discuss her interests, internal and foreign. Much of this may justly be attributed to the universality of easy circumstances, and to the education and habits which the first settlers in America brought with them, but our author is certainly not wrong in ascribing a certain portion of it to the perpetual exercise of the faculties of every man among the people, through the universal practice of submitting all public questions to his judgment.

It is incontestable that the people frequently conduct public business very ill, but it is impossible that the people should take a part in public business without extending the circle of their ideas, and without quitting the ordinary routine of their mental occupations. The humblest individual who is called upon to cooperate in the government of society acquires a certain degree of self-respect, and, as he possesses power, minds more enlightened than his own offer him their services. He is canvassed by a multitude of claimants who need his support, and who, seeking to deceive him in a thousand different ways, instruct him during the process. He takes a part in political undertakings which did not originate in his own conception, but which give him a general taste for such undertakings. New ameliorations are daily suggested to him in the property which he holds in common with others, and this gives him the desire of improving that property which is peculiarly his own. He is, perhaps, neither happier nor better than those who came before him, but he is better informed, and more active. I have no doubt that the democratic institutions of the United States, joined to the physical constitution of the country, are the cause (not the direct, as is so often asserted, but the indirect cause) of the prodigious commercial activity of the inhabitants. It is not engendered by the laws, but it proceeds from habits acquired through participation in making the laws.

When the opponents of Democracy assert that a single individual performs the functions which he undertakes better than the government of the people at large, it appears to me that they are perfectly right. The government of an individual, supposing an equal degree of instruction on either side, has more constancy, more perseverance, than that of a multitude; more combination in its plans, and more perfection in its details; and is better qualified judiciously to discriminate the characters of the men it employs. If any deny this, they have never seen a democratic government, or have formed their opinion only upon a few instances. It must be conceded, that, even when local circumstances and the disposition of the people allow democratic institutions to subsist, they never display a regular and methodical system of government. Democratic liberty is far from accomplishing all the projects it undertakes with the skill of an intelligent despotism. It frequently abandons them before they have borne their fruits, or risks them when the consequences may prove dangerous, but, in the end, it produces greater results than any absolute government. It does fewer things well, but it does a greater number of things. Not what is done by a democratic government, but what is done under a democratic government by private agency, is really great. Democracy does not confer the most skilful kind of government upon the people, but it produces that which the most skilful governments are frequently unable to awaken —namely, an all-pervading and restless activity, a super-abundant force, an energy which is never seen elsewhere, and which may, under favorable circumstances, beget the most amazing benefits. These are the true advantages of Democracy.—Vol. ii., chap. 6.

The other great political advantage which our author ascribes to Democracy requires less illustration, because it is more obvious, and has been oftener treated of—that the course of legislation and administration tends always in the direction of the interest of the greatest number. Although M. de Tocqueville is far from considering this quality of Democracy as the panacea in politics which it has sometimes been supposed to be, he expresses his sense of its importance, if in measured, in no undecided terms. America does not exhibit to us what we see in the best mixed constitutions—the class interests of small minorities wielding the powers of legislation, in opposition both to the general interest and to the general opinion of the community: still less does she exhibit what has been characteristic of most representative governments, and is only gradually ceasing to characterize our own —a standing league of class interests, a tacit compact, among the various knots of men who profit by abuses, to stand by one another in resisting reform. Nothing can subsist in America that is not recommended by arguments, which, in appearance at least, address themselves to the interest of the many. However frequently, therefore, that interest may be mistaken, the direction of legislation toward it is maintained in the midst of the mistakes; and if a community is so situated or so ordered that it can "support the transitory action of bad laws, and can await without destruction the result of the *general tendency* of the laws," that country, in the opinion of M. de Tocqueville, will prosper more under a democratic government than under any other. But, in aristocratic governments, the interest, or at best the honor and glory, of the ruling class, is considered as the public interest; and all that is most valuable to the individuals composing the subordinate classes is apt to be immolated to that public interest with all the rigor of antique patriotism.

The men who are intrusted with the direction of public affairs in the United States are frequently inferior, both in point of capacity and of morality, to those whom aristocratic institutions would raise to power, but their interest is identified and confounded with that of the majority of their fellow-citizens. They may frequently be faithless, and frequently mistaken; but they will never systematically adopt a line of conduct hostile to the majority, and it is impossible that they should give a dangerous or an exclusive character to the government.

The maladministration of a democratic magistrate is, moreover, a mere isolated fact, the effects of which do not last beyond the short period for which he is elected. Corruption and incapacity do not act as common interests which connect men permanently with one another. A corrupt or an incapable magistrate will not concert his measures with another magistrate, simply because that individual is corrupt and incapable like himself, and these two men will never unite their endeavors to promote or screen the corruption or inaptitude of their remote posterity. The ambition and the maneuvers of the one will serve, on the contrary, to unmask the other. The vices of the magistrate in democratic States are usually those of his individual character.

But, under aristocratic governments, public men are swayed by the interest of their order, which, if it is sometimes blended with the interests of the majority, is frequently distinct from them. This interest is a common and lasting bond which unites them together. It induces them to coalesce, and combine their efforts towards attaining an end which is not always the happiness of the greatest number; and it not only connects the persons in authority with each other, but links them also to a considerable portion of the governed, since a numerous body of citizens belongs to the aristocracy, without being invested with official functions. The aristocratic magistrate, therefore, finds himself supported in his own natural tendencies by a portion of society itself, as well as by the government of which he is a member.

The common object which connects the interest of the magistrates in aristocracies with that of a portion of their contemporaries identifies it also with future generations of their order. They labor for ages to come, as well as for their own time. The aristocratic magistrate is thus urged towards the same point by the passions of those who surround him, by his own, and, I might almost say, by those of his posterity. Is it wonderful that he should not resist? And hence it is that the class spirit often hurries along with it those whom it does not corrupt, and makes them unintentionally fashion society to their own particular ends, and prefashion it for their descendants.—*Ibid.*

These, then, are the advantages ascribed by our author to a democratic government. We are now to speak of its disadvantages.

According to the opinion which is prevalent among the more cultivated advocates of Democracy, one of its greatest recommendations is that, by means of it, the wisest and worthiest are brought to the head of affairs. The people, it is said, have the strongest interest in selecting the right men. It is presumed that they will be sensible of that interest, and, subject to more or less liability of error, will in the main succeed in placing a high, if not the highest, degree of worth and talent in the highest situations.

M. de Tocqueville is of another opinion. He was forcibly struck with the general want of merit in the members of the American legislatures and other public functionaries. He accounts for this, not solely by the people's incapacity to discriminate merit, but partly also by their indifference to it. He thinks there is little preference for men of superior intellect, little desire to obtain their services for the public, occasionally even a jealousy of them, especially if they be also rich. They, on their part, have still less inclination to seek any such employment. Public offices are little lucrative, confer little power, and offer no guarantee of permanency. Almost any other career holds out better pecuniary prospects to a man of ability and enterprise, nor will instructed men stoop to those mean arts, and those compromises of their private opinions, to which their less distinguished competitors willingly resort. The depositaries of power, after being chosen with little regard to merit, are, partly perhaps for that very reason, frequently changed. The rapid return of elections, and even a taste for variety, M. de Tocqueville thinks, on the part of electors (a taste not unnatural wherever little regard is paid to qualifications), produces a rapid succession of new men in the legislature and in all public posts. Hence, on the one hand, great instability in the laws—every newcomer desiring to do something in the short time he has before him, while, on the other hand, there is no political *carrière*; statesmanship is not a profession. There is no body of persons educated for public business, pursuing it as their occupation, and who transmit from one to another the results of their experience. There are no traditions, no science or art of public affairs. A functionary knows little, and cares less, about the principles on which his predecessor has acted, and his successor thinks as little about his. Public transactions are therefore conducted with a reasonable share, indeed, of the common sense and common information which are general in a democratic community, but with little benefit from specific study and experience, without consistent system, long-sighted views, or persevering pursuit of distant objects.

This is likely enough to be a true picture of the American Government, but can scarcely be said to be peculiar to it. There are now few governments remaining, whether representative or absolute, of which something of the same sort might not be said. In no country where the real government resides in the minister, and where there are frequent changes of ministry, are far-sighted views of policy likely to be acted upon, whether the country be England or France, in the eighteenth century or in the nineteenth.* Crude and ill-considered legislation is the character of all governments whose laws are made, and acts of administration performed, *impromptu*—not in pursuance of a general design, but from the pressure of some present occasion; of all governments in which the ruling power is to any great extent exercised by persons not trained to government as a business. It is true, that the governments which have been celebrated for their profound policy have generally been aristocracies; but they have been very narrow aristocracies, consisting of so few members, that every member could personally participate in the business of administration. These are the governments which have a natural tendency to be administered steadily, that is, according to fixed principles. Every member of the governing body being trained to government as a profession, like other professions they respect precedent, transmit their experience from genera-

* A few sentences are here inserted from another paper by the author.

tion to generation, acquire and preserve a set of traditions; and, all being competent judges of each other's merits, the ablest easily rises to his proper level. The governments of ancient Rome and modern Venice were of this character; and, as all know, for ages conducted the affairs of those States with admirable constancy and skill, on fixed principles—often unworthy enough, but always eminently adapted to the ends of those governments. When the governing body, whether it consists of the many or of a privileged class, is so numerous, that the large majority of it do not and cannot make the practice of government the main occupation of their lives, it is impossible that there should be wisdom, foresight, and caution in the governing body itself. These qualities must be found, if found at all, not in the body, but in those whom the body trust. The opinion of a numerous ruling class is as fluctuating, as liable to be wholly given up to immediate impulses, as the opinion of the people. Witness the whole course of English history. All our laws have been made on temporary impulses. In no country has the course of legislation been less directed to any steady and consistent purpose.

In so far as it is true that there is a deficiency of remarkable merit in American public men (and our author allows that there is a large number of exceptions), the fact may perhaps admit of a less discreditable explanation. America needs very little government. She has no wars, no neighbors, no complicated international relations, no old society with its thousand abuses to reform, no half-fed and untaught millions in want of food and guidance. Society in America requires little but to be let alone. The current affairs which her government has to transact can seldom demand much more than average capacity; and it may be in the Americans a wise economy, not to pay the price of great talents when common ones will serve their purpose. We make these remarks by way of caution, not of controversy. Like many other parts of our author's doctrines, that of which we are now speaking affords work for a succession of thinkers and of accurate observers, and must, in the main, depend on future experience to confirm or refute it.

We now come to that one among the dangers of Democracy respecting which so much has been said, and which our author designates as "the despotism of the majority."

It is perhaps the greatest defect of M. de Tocqueville's

book, that, from the scarcity of examples, his propositions, even when derived from observation, have the air of mere abstract speculations. He speaks of the tyranny of the majority, in general phrases, but gives hardly any instances of it, nor much information as to the mode in which it is practically exemplified. The omission was in the present instance the more excusable, as the despotism complained of was at that time, politically at least, an evil in apprehension more than in sufferance, and he was uneasy rather at the total absence of security against the tyranny of the majority, than at the frequency of its actual exertion.

Events, however, which have occurred since the publication of the first part of M. de Tocqueville's work, give indication of the shape which tyranny is most likely to assume when exercised by a majority.

It is not easy to surmise any inducements of interest, by which, in a country like America, the greater number could be led to oppress the smaller. When the majority and the minority are spoken of as conflicting interests, the rich and the poor are generally meant; but where the rich are content with being rich, and do not claim as such any political privileges, their interest and that of the poor are generally the same: complete protection to property, and freedom in the disposal of it, are alike important to both. When, indeed, the poor are so poor that they can scarcely be worse off, respect on their part for rights of property which they cannot hope to share is never safely to be calculated upon. But where all have property, either in enjoyment or in reasonable hope, and an appreciable chance of acquiring a large fortune, and where every man's way of life proceeds on the confident assurance that, by superior exertion, he will obtain a superior reward—the importance of inviolability of property is not likely to be lost sight of. It is not affirmed of the Americans, that they make laws against the rich, or unduly press upon them in the imposition of taxes. If a laboring class, less happily circumstanced, could prematurely force themselves into influence over our own legislature, there might then be danger, not so much of violations of property, as of undue interference with contracts, unenlightened legislation for the supposed interest of the many, laws founded on mistakes in political economy. A minimum of wages, or a tax on machinery, might be attempted; as silly and as inefficacious attempts might be made to keep up wages by law as were so long made by the British Legislature to keep them down by the same means. We have no wish to see the experiment tried; but we are fully convinced that experience would correct the one error as it has corrected the other, and in the same way; namely, by complete practical failure.

It is not from the separate interests, real or imaginary, of the majority, that minorities are in danger, but from its antipathies of religion, political party, or race; and experience in America seems to confirm, what theory rendered probable, that the tyranny of the majority would not take the shape of tyrannical laws, but that of a dispensing power over all laws. The people of Massachusetts passed no law prohibiting Roman Catholic schools, or exempting Protestants from the penalties of incendiarism; they contented themselves with burning the Ursuline convent to the ground, aware that no jury would be found to redress the injury. In the same reliance, the people of New York and Philadelphia sacked and destroyed the houses of the Abolitionists, and the schools and churches of their black fellow citizens, while numbers who took no share in the outrage amused themselves with the sight. The laws of Maryland still prohibit murder and burglary; but, in 1812, a Baltimore mob, after destroying the printing office of a newspaper which had opposed the war with England, broke into the prison to which the editors had been conveyed for safety, murdered one of them, left the others for dead; and the criminals were tried and acquitted. In the same city, in 1835, a riot which lasted four days, and the foolish history of which is related in M. Chevalier's *Letters*, was occasioned by the fraudulent bankruptcy of the Maryland Bank. It is not so much the riots, in such instances, that are deplorable; these might have occurred in any country; it is the impossibility of obtaining aid from an executive dependent on the mob, or justice from juries which formed part of it; it is the apathetic cowardly truckling of disapproving lookers-on, almost a parallel to the passive imbecility of the people of Paris, when a handful of hired assassins perpetrated the massacres of September. For where the majority is the sole power, and a power issuing its mandates in the form of riots, it inspires a terror which the most arbitrary monarch often fails to excite. The silent sympathy of the majority may support on the scaffold the martyr of one man's tyranny, but, if we would imagine the situation of a victim of the majority itself, we must look to the annals of religious persecution for a parallel.

Yet neither ought we to forget, that even this lawless violence is not so great, because not so lasting, an evil, as tyranny through the medium of the law. A tyrannical law remains because, so long as it is submitted to, its existence does not weaken the general authority of the laws. But in America, tyranny will seldom use the instrument of law, because there is, in general, no permanent class to be tyrannized over. The subjects of oppression are casual objects of popular resentment, who cannot be reached by law, but only by occasional acts of lawless power, and to tolerate these, if they ever became frequent, would be consenting to live without law. Already, in the United States, the spirit of outrage has raised a spirit of resistance to outrage: of moral resistance first, as was to be wished and expected; if that fail, physical resistance will follow. The majority, like other despotic powers, will be taught, by experience, that it cannot enjoy both the advantages of civilized society, and the barbarian liberty of taking men's lives and property at its discretion. Let it once be generally understood that minorities will fight, and majorities will be shy of provoking them. The bad government of which there is any permanent danger under modern civilization is in the form of bad laws and bad tribunals; government by the *sic volo*, either of a king or a mob, belongs to past ages, and can no more exist, for long together, out of the pale of Asiatic barbarism.

The despotism, therefore, of the majority within the limits of civil life, though a real evil, does not appear to us to be a formidable one. The tyranny which we fear, and which M. de Tocqueville principally dreads, is of another kind—a tyranny not over the body, but over the mind.

It is the complaint of M. de Tocqueville, as well as of other travelers in America, that in no country does there exist less independence of thought. In religion, indeed, the varieties of opinion which fortunately prevailed among those by whom the colonies were settled have produced a toleration in law and in fact extending to the limits of Christianity. If by ill fortune there had happened to be a religion of the majority, the case would probably have been different. On every other subject, when the opinion of the majority is made up, hardly any one, it is affirmed, dares to be of any other opinion, or at least to profess it. The statements are not clear as to the nature or amount of the inconvenience that would be suffered by any one who presumed to question a received opinion. It seems certain, however, that scarcely any person has that courage; that, when public opinion considers a question as settled, no further discussion of it takes place; and that not only nobody dares (what everybody may venture upon in Europe) to say any thing disrespectful to the public, or derogatory to its opinions, but that its wisdom and virtue are perpetually celebrated with the most servile adulation and sycophancy.

These considerations, which were much dwelt on in the author's First Part, are intimately connected with the views promulgated in his Second, respecting the influence of Democracy on intellect.

The Americans, according to M. de Tocqueville, not only profess, but carry into practice, on all subjects except the fundamental doctrines of Christianity and Christian ethics, the habit of mind which has been so often inculcated as the one sufficient security against mental slavery—the rejection of authority, and the assertion of the right of private judgment. They regard the traditions of the past merely in the light of materials, and as "a useful study for doing otherwise and better." They are not accustomed to look for guidance either to the wisdom of ancestors, or to eminent contemporary wisdom, but require that the grounds on which they act shall be made level to their own comprehension. And, as is natural to those who govern themselves by common sense rather than by science, their cast of mind is altogether unpedantic and practical: they go straight to the end, without favor or prejudice towards any set of means, and aim at the substance of things, with something like a contempt for form.

From such habits and ways of thinking, the consequence which would be apprehended by some would be a most licentious abuse of individual independence of thought. The fact is the reverse. It is impossible, as our author truly remarks, that mankind in general should form all their opinions for themselves; an authority from which they mostly derive them may be rejected in theory; but it always exists in fact. That law above them, which older societies have found in the traditions of antiquity, or in the dogmas of priests or philosophers, the Americans find in the opinions of one another. All being nearly equal in circumstances, and all nearly alike in intelligence and knowledge, the only authority which commands an involuntary deference is that of numbers. The more perfectly each knows himself the equal of every single individual, the more insignificant and helpless he feels against the aggregate mass, and the more incredible it appears to him that the opinion of all the world can possibly be erroneous. "Faith in public opinion," says M. de Tocqueville, "becomes in such countries a species of religion, and the majority its prophet." The idea that the things which the multitude believe are still disputable is no longer kept alive by dissentient voices; the right of private judgment, by being extended to the incompetent, ceases to be exercised even by the competent; and speculation becomes possible only within the limits traced, not, as of old, by the infallibility of Aristotle, but by that of "our free and enlightened citizens," or "our free and enlightened age."

On the influence of Democracy upon the cultivation of science and art, the opinions of M. de Tocqueville are highly worthy of attention. There are many who, partly from theoretic considerations, and partly from the marked absence in America of original efforts in literature, philosophy, or the fine arts, incline to believe that modern Democracy is fatal to them, and that, wherever its spirit spreads, they will take flight. M. de Tocqueville is not of this opinion. The example of America, as he observes, is not to the purpose, because America is, intellectually speaking, a province of England— a province in which the great occupation of the inhabitants is making money, because for that they have peculiar facilities, and are therefore, like the people of Manchester or Birmingham, for the most part contented to receive the higher branches of knowledge ready-made from the capital. In a democratic nation, which is also free, and generally educated, our author is far from thinking that there will be no public to relish or remunerate the works of science and genius. Although there will be great shifting of fortunes, and no hereditary body of wealthy persons sufficient to form a class, there will be, he thinks, from the general activity, and the absence of artificial barriers, combined with the inequality of human intelligence, a far greater number of rich individuals (*infiniment plus nombreux*) than in an aristocratic society. There will be, therefore, though not so complete a leisure, yet a leisure extending perhaps to more persons, while, from the closer contact and greater mutual intercourse between classes, the love of intellectual pleasures and occupations will spread downward very widely among those who have not the same advantages of leisure. Moreover, talents and knowledge being in a democratic society the only means of rapid improvement in fortune, they will be, in the abstract at least, by no means undervalued; whatever measure of them any person is capable of appreciating, he will also be desirous of possessing. Instead, therefore, of any neglect of science and literature, the eager ambition which is universal in such a state of society takes that direction as well as others, and the number of those who cultivate these pursuits becomes "immense."

It is from this fact—from the more active competition in the products of intellect, and the more numerous public to which they are addressed—that M. de Tocqueville deduces the defects with which the products themselves will be chargeable. In the multiplication of their quantity he sees the deterioration of their quality. Distracted by so great a multitude, the public can bestow but a moment's attention on each; they will be adapted, therefore, chiefly for striking at the moment. Deliberate approval, and a duration beyond the hour, become more and more difficult of attainment. What is written for the judgment of a highly instructed few, amidst the abundance of writings may very probably never reach them; and their suffrage, which never gave riches, does not now confer even glory. But the multitude of buyers affords the possibility of great pecuniary success and momentary notoriety for the work which is made up to please at once, and to please the many. Literature thus becomes not only a trade, but is carried on by the maxims usually adopted by other trades which live by the number, rather than by the quality, of their customers: that much pains need not be bestowed on commodities intended for the general market, and that what is saved in the workmanship may be more profitably expended in self-advertisement. There will thus be an immense mass of third- and fourth-rate productions, and very few first-rate. Even the turmoil and bustle of a society in which every one is striving to get on, is in itself, our author observes, not favorable to meditation. "*Il règne dans le sein de ces nations un petit mouvement incommode, une sorte de roulement incessant des hommes les uns sur les autres, qui trouble et distrait l'esprit sans l'animer et l'élever.*" Not to mention that the universal tendency to action, and to rapid action, directs the taste to applications rather than principles, and hasty approximations to truth rather than scientific accuracy in it.

Passing now from the province of intellect to that of sentiments and morals, M. de Tocqueville is of opinion that the general softening of manners, and the remarkable growth in modern times of humanity and philanthropy, are in great part the effect of the gradual progress of social equality. Where the different classes of mankind are divided by impassable barriers, each may have intense sympathies with his own class— more intense than it is almost possible to have with mankind in general; but those who are far below him in condition are so unlike himself, that he hardly considers them as human beings, and, if they are refractory and troublesome, will be unable to feel for them even that kindly interest which he experiences for his more unresisting domestic cattle. Our author cites a well-known passage of Madame de Sévigné's *Letters* in exemplification of the want of feeling exhibited even by good sort of persons towards those with whom they have no *fellow*-feeling. In America, except towards the slaves (an exception which proves the rule), he finds the sentiments of philanthropy and compassion almost universal, accompanied by a general kindness of manner, and obligingness of disposition, without much of ceremony and punctilio. As all feel that they are not above the possible need of the good-will and good offices of others, every one is ready to afford his own. The general equality penetrates also into the family relations. There is more intimacy, he thinks, than in Europe, between parents and children, but less, except in the earliest years, of paternal authority, and the filial respect which is founded on it. These, however, are among the topics which we must omit, as well as the connection which our author attempts to trace between equality of conditions and strictness of domestic morals, and some other remarks on domestic society in America, which do not appear to us to be of any considerable value.

M. de Tocqueville is of opinion, that one of the tendencies of a democratic state of society is to make every one, in a manner, retire within himself, and concentrate his interests, wishes, and pursuits within his own business and household.

The members of a democratic community are like the sands of the seashore, each very minute, and no one adhering to any other. There are no permanent classes, and therefore no *esprit de corps*; few hereditary fortunes, and therefore few local attachments, or outward objects consecrated by family feeling. A man feels little connection with his neighbors, little with his ancestors, little with his posterity. There are scarcely any ties to connect any two men together, except the common one of country. Now, the love of country is not, in large communities, a passion of spontaneous growth. When a man's country is his town, where his ancestors have lived for generations, of which he knows every inhabitant, and has recollections associated with every street and building; in which alone, of all places on the earth, he is not a stranger; which he is perpetually called upon to defend in the field, and in whose glory or shame he has an appreciable share, made sensible by the constant presence and rivalry of foreigners—in such a state of things, patriotism is easy. It was easy in the ancient republics, or in modern Switzerland. But, in great communities, an intense interest in public affairs is scarcely natural, except to a member of an aristocracy, who alone has so conspicuous a position, and is so personally identified with the conduct of the government, that his credit and consequence are essentially connected with the glory and power of the nation he belongs to—its glory and power (observe), not the well-being of the bulk of its inhabitants. It is difficult for an obscure person, like the citizen of a Democracy, who is in no way involved in the responsibility of public affairs, and cannot hope to exercise more than the minutest influence over them, to have the sentiment of patriotism as a living and earnest feeling. There being no intermediate objects for his attachments to fix upon, they fasten themselves on his own private affairs; and, according to national character and circumstances, it becomes his ruling passion either to improve his condition in life, or to take his ease and pleasure by the means which it already affords him.

As, therefore, the state of society becomes more democratic, it is more and more necessary to nourish patriotism by artificial means, and of these none are so efficacious as free institutions—a large and frequent intervention of the citizens in the management of public business. Nor does the love of country alone require this encouragement, but every feeling which connects men either by interest of sympathy with their neighbors and fellow citizens. Popular institutions are the great means of rendering general in a people, and especially among the richer classes, the desire of being useful in their generation—useful to the public or to their neighbors, without distinction of rank—as well as courteous and unassuming in their habitual intercourse.

When the public is supreme, there is no man who does not feel the value of public good-will, or who does not endeavor to court it by drawing to himself the esteem and affection of those amongst whom he is to live. Many of the passions which congeal and keep asunder human hearts are then obliged to retire, and hide below the surface. Pride must be dissembled; disdain does not break out; selfishness is afraid of itself. Under a free government, as most public offices are elective, the men whose elevated minds or aspiring hopes are too closely circumscribed in private life constantly feel that they cannot do without the population which surrounds them. Men learn at such times to think of their fellow-men from ambitious motives; and they frequently find it, in a manner, their interest to be forgetful of self.

I may here be met by an objection, derived from electioneering intrigues—the meannesses of candidates, and the calumnies of their opponents. These are opportunities of animosity which occur oftener, the more frequent elections become. Such evils are doubtless great, but they are transient, whereas the benefits which attend them remain. The desire of being elected may lead some men for a time to mutual hostility, but this same desire leads all men, in the long run, mutually to support each other; and, if it happens that an election accidentally severs two friends, the electoral system brings a multitude of citizens permanently together who would always have remained unknown to each other. Freedom engenders private animosities, but despotism gives birth to general indifference. . . .

A brilliant achievement may win for you the favor of a people at one stroke, but to earn the love and respect of the population which surrounds you requires a long succession of little services and obscure good offices, a constant habit of kindness, and an established reputation for disinterestedness. Local freedom, then, which leads a great number of citizens to value the affections of their neighbors, and of those with whom they are in contact, perpetually draws men back to one another, in spite of the propensities which sever them, and forces them to render each other mutual assistance.

In the United States, the more opulent citizens take great care not to stand aloof from the people; on the contrary, they constantly keep on easy terms with them, they listen to them, they speak to them every day. They know that the rich, in democracies, always stand in need of the poor, and that, in democratic times, a poor man's attachment depends more on manner than on benefits conferred. The very magnitude of such benefits, by setting the difference of conditions in a strong light, causes a secret irritation to those who reap advantage from them, but the charm of simplicity of manners is almost irresistible. . . . This truth does not penetrate at once into the minds of the rich. They generally resist it as long as the democratic revolution lasts, and they do not acknowledge it immediately after that revolution is accomplished. They are very ready to do good to the people, but they still choose to keep them at arm's length. They think that is sufficient, but they are mistaken. They might spend fortunes thus, without warming the hearts of the population around them; that population does not ask them for the sacrifice of their money, but of their pride.

It would seem as if every imagination in the United States were on the stretch to invent means of increasing the wealth and satisfying the wants of the public. The best informed inhabitants of each district are incessantly using their information to discover new means of augmenting the general prosperity, and, when they have made any such discoveries, they eagerly surrender them to the mass of the people. . . .

I have often seen Americans make great and real sacrifices to the public welfare, and I have a hundred times remarked, that, in case of need, they hardly ever fail to lend faithful support to each other. The free institutions which the inhabitants of the United States possess, and the political rights of which they make so much use, remind every citizen, and in a thousand ways, that he is a member of society. They at every instant impress upon his mind the notion that it is the duty as well as the interest of men to make themselves useful to their fellow creatures, and as he sees no particular reason for disliking them, since he is never either their master or their slave, his heart readily leans to the side of kindness. Men attend to the interests of the public, first by necessity, afterwards by choice; what was calculation becomes an instinct, and, by dint of working for the good of one's fellow citizens, the habit and the taste for serving them is at length acquired.

Many people in France consider equality of conditions

as one evil, and political freedom as a second. When they are obliged to yield to the former, they strive at least to escape from the latter. But I contend that, in order to combat the evils which equality may produce, there is only one effectual remedy: namely, political freedom.—Vol. iii., part ii., chap. 4.

With regard to the tone of moral sentiment characteristic of Democracy, M. de Tocqueville holds an opinion which we think deserves the attention of moralists. Among a class composed of persons who have been born into a distinguished position, the habitual springs of action will be very different from those of a democratic community. Speaking generally (and making abstraction both of individual peculiarities and of the influence of moral culture), it may be said of the first that their feelings and actions will be mainly under the influence of pride, of the latter, under that of interest. Now, as, in an aristocratic society, the elevated class, though small in number, sets the fashion in opinion and feeling, even virtue will, in that state of society, seem to be most strongly recommended by arguments addressing themselves to pride, in a Democracy, by those which address themselves to self-interest. In the one, we hear chiefly of the beauty and dignity of virtue, the grandeur of self-sacrifice; in the other, of honesty the best policy, the value of character, and the common interest of every individual in the good of the whole.

Neither the one nor the other of these modes of feeling, our author is well aware, constitutes moral excellence, which must have a deeper foundation than either the calculations of self-interest, or the emotions of self-flattery. But as an auxiliary to that higher principle, and as far as possible a substitute for it when it is absent, the latter of the two, in his opinion, though the least sentimental, will stand the most wear.

The principle of enlightened self-interest is not a lofty one, but it is clear and sure. It does not aim at mighty objects, but it attains, without impracticable efforts, all those at which it aims. As it lies within the reach of all capacities, every one can without difficulty apprehend and retain it. By its adaptation to human weaknessess, it easily obtains great dominion; nor is its dominion precarious, since it employs self-interest itself to correct self-interest, and uses, to direct the passions, the very instrument which excites them.

The doctrine of enlightened self-interest produces no

great acts of self-sacrifice, but it suggests daily small acts of self-denial. By itself it cannot suffice to make a virtuous man, but it disciplines a multitude of citizens in habits of regularity, temperance, moderation, foresight, self-command; and, if it does not at once lead men to virtue by their will, it draws them gradually in that direction by their habits. If the principle of "interest rightly understood" were to sway the whole moral world, extraordinary virtues would doubtless be more rare, but I think that gross depravity would then also be less common. That principle, perhaps, prevents some men from rising far above the level of mankind, but a great number of others, who were falling below that level, are caught and upheld by it. Observe some few individuals, they are lowered by it; survey mankind, it is raised.

I am not afraid to say that the principle of enlightened self-interest appears to me the best suited of all philosophical theories to the wants of the men of our time, and that I regard it as their chief remaining security against themselves. Towards it, therefore, the minds of the moralists of our age should turn. Even should they judge it incomplete, it must nevertheless be adopted as necessary.

No power upon earth can prevent the increasing equality of conditions from impelling the human mind to seek out what is useful, or from inclining every member of the community to concentrate his affections on himself. It must therefore be expected that personal interest will become more than ever the principal if not the sole spring of men's actions, but it remains to be seen how each man will understand his personal interest.

I do not think that the doctrine of self-interest, as it is professed in America, is self-evident in all its parts, but it contains a great number of truths so evident that men, if they are but instructed, cannot fail to see them. Instruct them, then, at all hazards: for the age of implicit self-sacrifice and instinctive virtues is already flying far away from us, and the time is fast approaching, when freedom, public peace, and social order itself, will not be able to exist without instruction.—Vol. iii., part ii., chap. 8.

M. de Tocqueville considers a democratic state of society as eminently tending to give the strongest impulse to the desire of physical well-being. He ascribes this not so much to the equality of conditions as to their mobility. In a country like America, every one may acquire riches; no one, at least, is artificially impeded in acquiring them, and hardly any one is born to them. Now, these are the conditions under which the passions which attach themselves to wealth, and to what wealth can purchase, are the strongest. Those who are born in the midst of affluence are generally more or less *blasés* to its enjoyments. They take the comfort or luxury to which they have always been accustomed, as they do the air they breathe. It is not *le but de la vie*, but *une manière de vivre*. An aristocracy, when put to the proof, has in general shown wonderful facility in enduring the loss of riches and of physical comforts. The very pride, nourished by the elevation which they owed to wealth, supports them under the privation of it. But to those who have chased riches laboriously for half their lives, to lose it is the loss of all, *une vie manquée*, a disappointment greater than can be endured. In a democracy, again, there is no contented poverty. No one being forced to remain poor, many who were poor daily becoming rich, and the comforts of life being apparently within the reach of all, the desire to appropriate them descends to the very lowest rank. Thus—

The desire of acquiring the comforts of the world haunts the imagination of the poor, and the dread of losing them, that of the rich. Many scanty fortunes spring up. Those who possess them have a sufficient share of physical gratifications to conceive a taste for those pleasures—not enough to satisfy it. They never procure them without exertion, and they never indulge in them without apprehension. They are, therefore, always straining to pursue or to retain gratifications so precious, so incomplete, and so fugitive.

If I inquire what passion is most natural to men who are at once stimulated and circumscribed by the obscurity of their birth or the mediocrity of their fortune, I can discover none more peculiarly appropriate to them than this love of physical prosperity. The passion for physical comforts is essentially a passion of the middle classes; with those classes it grows and spreads, and along with them it becomes preponderant. From them it mounts into the higher orders of society, and descends into the mass of the people.

I never met, in America, with any citizen so poor as not to cast a glance of hope and longing towards the enjoyments of the rich, or whose imagination did not indulge itself by anticipation in those good things which fate still obstinately withheld from him.

On the other hand, I never perceived, amongst the

wealthier inhabitants of the United States, that proud contempt of the indulgences of riches which is sometimes to be met with even in the most opulent and dissolute aristocracies. Most of these wealthy persons were once poor. They have felt the stimulus of privation, they have long struggled with adverse fortune, and, now that the victory is won, the passions which accompanied the contest have survived it; their minds are, as it were, intoxicated by the petty enjoyments which they have pursued for forty years.

Not but that in the United States, as elsewhere, there are a certain number of wealthy persons, who, having come into their property by inheritance possess, without exertion, an opulence they have not earned. But even these are not less devotedly attached to the pleasures of material life. The love of physical comfort is become the predominant taste of the nation; the great current of man's passion runs in that channel, and sweeps every thing along in its course.—Vol. iii., part ii., chap. 10.

A regulated sensuality thus establishes itself—the parent of effeminacy rather than of debauchery; paying respect to the social rights of other people, and to the opinion of the world; not "leading men away in search of forbidden enjoyments, but absorbing them in the pursuit of permitted ones. This spirit is frequently combined with a species of religious morality; men wish to be as well off as they can in this world, without foregoing their chance of another."

From the preternatural stimulus given to the desire of acquiring and of enjoying wealth, by the intense competition which necessarily exists where an entire population are the competitors, arises the restlessness so characteristic of American life.

It is strange to see with what feverish ardor the Americans pursue their own welfare, and to watch the vague dread that constantly torments them, lest they should not have chosen the shortest path which may lead to it. A native of the United States clings to this world's goods as if he were certain never to die, and is so hasty in grasping at all within his reach, that one would suppose he was constantly afraid of not living long enough to enjoy them. He clutches every thing; he holds nothing fast, but soon loosens his grasp to pursue fresh gratifications. . . .

At first sight, there is something surprising in this strange unrest of so many happy men, uneasy in the midst of abundance. The spectacle is, however, as old as the world: the novelty is to see a whole people furnish an example of it. . . .

When all the privileges of birth and fortune are abolished, when all professions are accessible to all, and a man's own energies may place him at the top of any one of them —an easy and unbounded career seems open to his ambition, and he will readily persuade himself that he is born to no vulgar destinies. But this is an erroneous notion, which is corrected by daily experience. The same equality which allows every citizen to conceive these lofty hopes renders all the citizens individually feeble. It circumscribes their powers on every side, while it gives freer scope to their desires. Not only are they restrained by their own weakness, but they are met at every step by immense obstacles, which they did not at first perceive. They have swept away the privileges of some of their fellow-creatures which stood in their way, but they have now to encounter the competition of all. The barrier has changed its shape rather than its place. When men are nearly alike, and all follow the same track, it is very difficult for any one individual to get on fast, and cleave a way through the homogeneous throng which surrounds and presses upon him. This constant strife between the wishes springing from the equality of conditions, and the means it supplies to satisfy them, harasses and wearies the mind.—Vol. iii., part ii., chap. 13.

And hence, according to M. de Tocqueville, while every one is devoured by ambition, hardly any one is ambitious on a large scale. Among so many competitors for but a few great prizes, none of the candidates starting from the vantage-ground of an elevated social position, very few can hope to gain those prizes, and they not until late in life. Men in general, therefore, do not look so high. A vast energy of passion in a whole community is developed and squandered in the petty pursuit of petty advancements in fortune, and the hurried snatching of petty pleasures.

To sum up our author's opinion of the dangers to which mankind are liable as they advance towards equality of condition: his fear, both in government and in intellect and morals, is not of too great liberty but of too ready submission, not of anarchy but of servility, not of too rapid change but of Chinese stationariness. As Democracy advances, the opinions of mankind on most subjects of general interest will become, he believes, as compared with any former period, more rooted and more difficult to change, and mankind are more and more in danger of losing the moral courage and pride of independence which make them deviate from the beaten path, either in speculation or in conduct. Even in politics, it is to be apprehended lest, feeling their personal insignificance, and conceiving a proportionally vast idea of the importance of society at large; being jealous, moreover, of one another but not jealous of the central power, which derives its origin from the majority, or which at least is the faithful representative of its desire to annihilate every intermediate power—they should allow that central government to assume more and more control, engross more and more of the business of society, and, on condition of making itself the organ of the general mode of feeling and thinking, should suffer it to relieve mankind from the care of their own interests, and keep them under a kind of tutelage, trampling, meanwhile, with considerable recklessness, as often as convenient, upon the rights of individuals, in the name of society and the public good.

Against these political evils, the corrective to which our author looks is popular education and, above all, the spirit of liberty, fostered by the extension and dissemination of political rights. Democratic institutions, therefore, are his remedy for the worst mischiefs to which a democratic state of society is exposed. As for those to which democratic institutions are themselves liable, these, he holds, society must struggle with, and bear with so much of them as it cannot find the means of conquering. For M. de Tocqueville is no believer in the reality of mixed governments. There is, he says, always and everywhere, a strongest power; in every government, either the king, the aristocracy, or the people, have an effective predominance, and can carry any point on which they set their heart. "When a community really comes to have a mixed government, that is, to be equally divided between two adverse principles, it is either falling into a revolutionary state or into dissolution." M. de Tocqueville believes that the preponderant power which must exist everywhere is most rightly placed in the body of the people, but he thinks it most pernicious, that this power, whether residing in the people or elsewhere, should be "checked by no obstacles which may retard its course, and force it to moderate its own vehemence." The difference, in his eyes, is great between one sort of democratic institutions and another. That form of Democracy should be sought out and devised, and in every way endeavored to be carried into practice, which, on the one hand, most exercises and cultivates the intelligence and mental activity of the majority, and, on the other, breaks the headlong impulses of popular opinion by delay, rigor of forms, and adverse discussion. "The organization and the establishment of Democracy" on these principles "is the great political problem of our time."

And, when this problem is solved, there remains an equally serious one—to make head against the tendency of Democracy towards bearing down individuality, and circumscribing the exercise of the human faculties within narrow limits. To sustain the higher pursuits of philosophy and art, to vindicate and protect the unfettered exercise of reason, and the moral freedom of the individual—these are purposes to which, under a Democracy, the superior spirits, and the government so far as it is permitted, should devote their utmost energies.

I shall conclude by one general idea, which comprises not only all the particular ideas which have been expressed in the present chapter, but also most of those which it is the object of this book to treat of.

In the ages of aristocracy which preceded our own, there were private persons of great power, and a social authority of extreme weakness. The principal efforts of the men of those times were required to strengthen, aggrandize, and secure the supreme power, and, on the other hand, to circumscribe individual independence within narrower limits, and to subject private interests to public. Other perils and other cares await the men of our age. Amongst the greater part of modern nations, the government, whatever may be its origin, its constitution, or its name, has become almost omnipotent, and private persons are falling, more and more, into the lowest stage of weakness and dependence.

The general character of old society was diversity; unity and uniformity were nowhere to be met with. In modern society, all things threaten to become so much alike, that the peculiar characteristics of each individual will be entirely lost in the uniformity of the general aspect. Our forefathers were ever prone to make an improper use of the notion that private rights ought to be respected, and we are naturally prone, on the other hand, to exaggerate the idea, that the interest of an individual ought to bend to the interest of the many.

The political world is metamorphosed; new remedies

must henceforth be sought for new disorders. To lay down extensive, but distinct and immovable, limits to the action of the ruling power; to confer certain rights on private persons, and secure to them the undisputed enjoyment of their rights; to enable individual man to maintain whatever independence, strength, and originality he still possesses; to raise him by the side of society at large and uphold him in that position—these appear to me the main objects for the legislator in the age upon which we are now entering.

It would seem as if the rulers of our time sought only to use men in order to effect great things. I wish that they would try a little more to make great men; that they would set less value upon the work, and more upon the workmen; that they would never forget that a nation cannot long remain strong, when every man belonging to it is individually weak; and that no form or combination of social polity has yet been devised to make an energetic people out of a community of citizens personally feeble and pusillanimous.— Vol. iv., part iv., chap. 7.

If we were here to close this article, and leave these noble speculations to produce their effect without further comment, the reader, probably, would not blame us. Our recommendation is not needed in their behalf. That nothing on the whole comparable in profundity to them had yet been written on Democracy, will scarcely be disputed by any one who has read even our hasty abridgment of them. We must guard, at the same time, against attaching to these conclusions, or to any others that can result from such inquiries, a character of scientific certainty that can never belong to them. Democracy is too recent a phenomenon, and of too great magnitude, for any one who now lives to comprehend its consequences. A few of its more immediate tendencies may be perceived or surmised; what other tendencies, destined to overrule or to combine with these, lie behind, there are not grounds even to conjecture. If we revert to any similar fact in past history, any change in human affairs approaching in greatness to what is passing before our eyes, we shall find that no prediction which could have been made at the time, or for many generations afterwards, would have borne any resemblance to what has actually been the course of events. When the Greek commonwealths were crushed, and liberty in the civilized world apparently extinguished by the Macedonian invaders; when a rude, unlettered people of Italy stretched their conquests and their dominion from one end to the other of the known world; when that people in turn lost its freedom and its old institutions, and fell under the military despotism of one of its own citizens—what similarity is there between the effects we now know to have been produced by these causes, and any thing which the wisest person could then have anticipated from them? When the Roman Empire, containing all the art, science, literature, and industry of the world, was overrun, ravaged, and dismembered by hordes of barbarians, everybody lamented the destruction of civilization, in an event which is now admitted to have been the necessary condition of its renovation. When the Christian religion had existed but for two centuries; when the pope was only beginning to assert his ascendancy—what philosopher or statesman could have foreseen the destinies of Christianity, or the part which has been acted in history by the Catholic Church? It is thus with other really great historical facts—the invention of gunpowder for instance, or of the printing press. Even when their direct operation is as exactly measurable, because as strictly mechanical, as these were, the mere scale on which they operate gives birth to endless consequences, of a kind which would have appeared visionary to the most far-seeing contemporary wisdom.

It is not, therefore, without a deep sense of the uncertainty attaching to such predictions, that the wise would hazard an opinion as to the fate of mankind under the new democratic dispensation. But without pretending to judge confidently of remote tendencies, those immediate ones which are already developing themselves require to be dealt with as we treat any of the other circumstances in which we are placed—by encouraging those which are salutary, and working out the means by which such as are hurtful may be counteracted. To exhort men to this, and to aid them in doing it, is the end for which M. de Tocqueville has written, and in the same spirit we will now venture to make one criticism upon him—to point out one correction, of which we think his views stand in need, and for want of which they have occasionally an air of oversubtlety and false refinement, exciting the distrust of common readers, and making the opinions themselves appear less true, and less practically important, than, it seems to us, they really are.

M. de Tocqueville, then, has, at least apparently, confounded the effects of Democracy with the effects of Civilization. He has bound up in one abstract idea the whole of the tendencies of modern commercial society, and given them one name—Democracy, thereby letting it be supposed that he ascribes to equality of conditions several of the effects naturally arising from the mere progress of national prosperity, in the form in which that progress manifests itself in modern times.

It is no doubt true, that, among the tendencies of commercial civilization, a tendency to the equalization of conditions is one, and not the least conspicuous. When a nation is advancing in prosperity, when its industry is expanding, and its capital rapidly augmenting—the number also of those who possess capital increases in at least as great a proportion; and, though the distance between the two extremes of society may not be much diminished, there is a rapid multiplication of those who occupy the intermediate positions. There may be princes at one end of the scale, and paupers at the other, but between them there will be a respectable and well-paid class of artisans, and a middle class who combine property and industry. This may be called, and is, a tendency to equalization. But this growing equality is only one of the features of progressive civilization, one of the incidental effects of the progress of industry and wealth—a most important effect, and one which, as our author shows, reacts in a hundred ways upon the other effects, but not, therefore, to be confounded with the cause.

So far is it, indeed, from being admissible, that *mere* equality of conditions is the mainspring of those moral and social phenomena which M. de Tocqueville has characterized, that when some unusual chance exhibits to us equality of conditions by itself, severed from that commercial state of society and that progress of industry of which it is the natural concomitant, it produces few or none of the moral effects ascribed to it. Consider, for instance, the French of Lower Canada. Equality of conditions is more universal there than in the United States; for the whole people, without exception, are in easy circumstances, and there are not even that considerable number of rich individuals who are to be found in all the great towns of the American Republic. Yet do we find in Canada that go-ahead spirit, that restless, impatient eagerness for improvement in circumstances, that mobility, that shifting and fluctuating—now up, now down, now here, now there, that absence of classes and class spirit, that jealousy of

superior attainments, that want of deference for authority and
leadership, that habit of bringing things to the rule and square
of each man's own understanding—which M. de Tocqueville
imputes to the same cause in the United States? In all these
respects, the very contrary qualities prevail. We by no means
deny, that, where the other circumstances which determine
these effects exist, equality of conditions has a very perceptible effect in corroborating them. We think M. de Tocqueville has shown that it has, but that it is the exclusive, or even
the principal cause, we think the example of Canada goes far
to disprove.

For the reverse of this experiment, we have only to look at
home. Of all countries in a state of progressive commercial
civilization, Great Britain is that in which the equalization of
conditions has made least progress. The extremes of wealth
and poverty are wider apart, and there is a more numerous
body of persons, at each extreme, than in any other commercial community. From the habits of the population in regard
to marriage, the poor have remained poor; from the laws
which tend to keep large masses of property together, the rich
have remained rich, and often, when they have lost the substance of riches, have retained its social advantages and outward trappings. Great fortunes are continually accumulated,
and seldom redistributed. In this respect, therefore, England is
the most complete contrast to the United States. But in commercial prosperity, in the rapid growth of industry and wealth,
she is the next after America, and not very much inferior to
her. Accordingly, we appeal to all competent observers,
whether, in nearly all the moral and intellectual features of
American society, as represented by M. de Tocqueville, this
country does not stand next to America; whether, with the
single difference of our remaining respect for aristocracy, the
American people, both in their good qualities and in their defects, resemble any thing so much as an exaggeration of our
own middle class; whether the spirit which is gaining more
and more the ascendant with us, is not in a very great degree
American; and whether all the moral elements of an American state of society are not most rapidly growing up.

For example, that entire unfixedness in the social position
of individuals, that treading upon the heels of one another,
that habitual dissatisfaction of each with the position he oc-
cupies, and eager desire to push himself into the next above

it—has not this become, and is it not becoming more and more, an English characteristic? In England, as well as in America, it appears to foreigners, and even to Englishmen recently returned from a foreign country, as if everybody had but one wish—to improve his condition, never to enjoy it; as if no Englishman cared to cultivate either the pleasures or the virtues corresponding to his station in society, but solely to get out of it as quickly as possible, or if that cannot be done, and until it is done, to seem to have got out of it. "The hypocrisy of luxury," as M. de Tocqueville calls the maintaining an appearance beyond one's real expenditure, he considers as a democratic peculiarity. It is surely an English one. The highest class of all, indeed, is, as might be expected, comparatively exempt from these bad peculiarities. But the very existence of such a class, whose immunities and political privileges are attainable by wealth, tends to aggravate the struggle of the other classes for the possession of that passport to all other importance, and it perhaps required the example of America to prove that the "sabbathless pursuit of wealth" could be as intensely prevalent, where there were no aristocratic distinctions to tempt to it.

Again: the mobility and fluctuating nature of individual relations, the absence of permanent ties, local or personal—how often has this been commented on as one of the organic changes by which the ancient structure of English society is becoming dissolved? Without reverting to the days of clanship, or to those in which the gentry led a patriarchal life among their tenantry and neighbors, the memory of man extends to a time when the same tenants remained attached to the same landlords, the same servants to the same household. But this, with other old customs, after progressively retiring to the remote corners of our island, has nearly taken flight altogether, and it may now be said that, in all the relations of life, except those to which law and religion have given permanence, change has become the general rule, and constancy the exception.

The remainder of the tendencies which M. de Tocqueville has delineated may mostly be brought under one general agency as their immediate cause—the growing insignificance of individuals in comparison with the mass. Now, it would be difficult to show any country in which this insignificance is more marked and conspicuous than in England, or any incompatibility between that tendency and aristocratic institutions. It is not because the individuals composing the mass are all equal, but because the mass itself has grown to so immense a size, that individuals are powerless in the face of it, and because the mass, having by mechanical improvements become capable of acting simultaneously, can compel, not merely any individual, but any number of individuals, to bend before it. The House of Lords is the richest and most powerful collection of persons in Europe, yet they not only could not prevent, but were themselves compelled to pass, the Reform Bill. The daily actions of every peer and peeress are falling more and more under the yoke of *bourgeois* opinion; they feel every day a stronger necessity of showing an immaculate front to the world. When they do venture to disregard common opinion, it is in a body, and when supported by one another, whereas formerly every nobleman acted on his own notions, and dared be as eccentric as he pleased. No rank in society is now exempt from the fear of being peculiar, the unwillingness to be, or to be thought, in any respect original. Hardly anything now depends upon individuals, but all upon classes, and, among classes, mainly upon the middle class. That class is now the power in society, the arbiter of fortune and success. Ten times more money is made by supplying the wants, even the superfluous wants, of the middle, nay of the lower classes, than those of the higher. It is the middle class that now rewards even literature and art: the books by which most money is made are the cheap books; the greatest part of the profit of a picture is the profit of the engraving from it. Accordingly, all the intellectual effects which M. de Tocqueville ascribes to Democracy are taking place under the Democracy of the middle class. There is a greatly augmented number of moderate successes, fewer great literary and scientific reputations. Elementary and popular treatises are immensely multiplied, superficial information far more widely diffused; but there are fewer who devote themselves to thought for its own sake, and pursue in retirement those profounder researches, the results of which can only be appreciated by a few. Literary productions are seldom highly finished; they are got up to be read by many, and to be read but once. If the work sells for a day, the author's time and pains will be better laid out in writing a second than in improving the first. And this is not because books are no longer written for the aristocracy; they never were so. The aristocracy (saving individual exceptions) never were a reading class. It is because books are now written for a numerous, and therefore an unlearned public, no longer principally for scholars, and men of science, who have knowledge of their own, and are not imposed upon by half-knowledge, who have studied the great works of genius, and can make comparisons.*

As for the decay of authority, and diminution of respect for traditional opinions, this could not well be so far advanced among an ancient people—all whose political notions rest on an historical basis, and whose institutions themselves are built on prescription, and not on ideas of expediency, as in America, where the whole edifice of government was constructed, within the memory of man, upon abstract principles. But surely this change also is taking place as fast as could be expected under the circumstances. And even this effect, though it has a more direct connection with Democracy, has not an exclusive one. Respect for old opinions must diminish wherever science and knowledge are rapidly progressive. As the people in general become aware of the recent date of the most important physical discoveries, they are liable to form a rather contemptuous opinion of their ancestors. The mere visible fruits of scientific progress in a wealthy society, the mechanical improvements, the steam engines, the railroads, carry the feeling of admiration for modern, and disrespect for ancient times, down even to the wholly uneducated classes. For that

* On this account, among others, we think M. de Tocqueville right in the great importance he attaches to the study of Greek and Roman literature, not as being without faults, but as having the contrary faults to those of our own day. Not only do those literatures furnish examples of high finish and perfection in workmanship, to correct the slovenly habits of modern hasty writing, but they exhibit, in the military and agricultural commonwealths of antiquity, precisely that order of virtues in which a commercial society is apt to be deficient; and they altogether show human nature on a grander scale—with less benevolence but more patriotism, less sentiment but more self-control; if a lower average of virtue, more striking individual examples of it; fewer small goodnesses but more greatness and appreciation of greatness; more which tends to exalt the imagination, and inspire high conceptions of the capabilities of human nature. If, as every one may see, the want of affinity of these studies to the modern mind is gradually lowering them in popular estimation, this is but a confirmation of the need of them, and renders it more incumbent upon those who have the power to do their utmost towards preventing their decline.

other mental characteristic which M. de Tocqueville finds in America—a positive, matter-of-fact spirit, a demand that all things shall be made clear to each man's understanding, an indifference to the subtler proofs which address themselves to more cultivated and systematically exercised intellects, for what may be called, in short, the dogmatism of common sense —we need not look beyond our own country. There needs no Democracy to account for this; there needs only the habit of energetic action, without a proportional development of the taste for speculation. Bonaparte was one of the most remarkable examples of it, and the diffusion of half-instruction, without any sufficient provision made by society for sustaining the higher cultivation, tends greatly to encourage its excess.

Nearly all those moral and social influences, therefore, which are the subject of M. de Tocqueville's Second Part, are shown to be in full operation in aristocratic England. What connection they have with equality is with the growth of the middle class, not with the annihilation of the extremes. They are quite compatible with the existence of peers and *prolétaires*, nay, with the most abundant provision of both those varieties of human nature. If we were sure of retaining for ever our aristocratic institutions, society would no less have to struggle against all these tendencies, and perhaps even the loss of those institutions would not have so much effect as is supposed in accelerating their triumph.

The evil is not in the preponderance of a democratic class, but of any class. The defects which M. de Tocqueville points out in the American, and which we see in the modern English mind, are the ordinary ones of a commercial class. The portion of society which is predominant in America, and that which is attaining predominance here, the American many and our middle class, agree in being commercial classes. The one country is affording a complete, and the other a progressive, exemplification that, whenever any variety of human nature becomes preponderant in a community, it imposes upon all the rest of society its own type, forcing all either to submit to it or to imitate it.

It is not in China only that a homogeneous community is naturally a stationary community. The unlikeness of one person to another is not only a principle of improvement, but would seem almost to be the only principle. It is profoundly remarked by M. Guizot that the short duration or stunted growth of the earlier civilizations arose from this—that, in each of them, some one element of human improvement existed exclusively, or so preponderatingly as to overpower all the others, whereby the community, after accomplishing rapidly all which that one element could do, either perished for want of what it could not do, or came to a halt, and became immovable. It would be an error to suppose that such could not possibly be our fate. In the generalization which pronounces the "law of progress" to be an inherent attribute of human nature, it is forgotten that, among the inhabitants of our earth, the European family of nations is the only one which has ever yet shown any capability of spontaneous improvement, beyond a certain low level. Let us beware of supposing that we owe this peculiarity to any superiority of nature, and not rather to combinations of circumstances, which have existed nowhere else, and may not exist for ever among ourselves. The spirit of commerce and industry is one of the greatest instruments, not only of civilization in the narrowest, but of improvement and culture in the widest sense; to it, or to its consequences, we owe nearly all that advantageously distinguishes the present period from the middle ages. So long as other coordinate elements of improvement existed beside it, doing what it left undone, and keeping its exclusive tendencies in equipoise by an opposite order of sentiments, principles of action, and modes of thought—so long the benefits which it conferred on humanity were unqualified. But example and theory alike justify the expectation that with its complete preponderance would commence an era either of stationariness or of decline.

If, to avert this consummation, it were necessary that the class which wields the strongest power in society should be prevented from exercising its strength, or that those who are powerful enough to overthrow the government should not claim a paramount control over it, the case of civilized nations would be almost hopeless. But human affairs are not entirely governed by mechanical laws, nor men's characters wholly and irrevocably formed by their situation in life. Economical and social changes, though among the greatest, are not the only forces which shape the course of our species. Ideas are not always the mere signs and effects of social circumstances; they are themselves a power in history. Let the idea take hold of the more generous and cultivated minds that the most serious danger to the future prospects of mankind is in the unbalanced influence of the commercial spirit; let the wiser and better-hearted politicians and public teachers look upon it as their most pressing duty to protect and strengthen whatever, in the heart of man or in his outward life, can form a salutary check to the exclusive tendencies of that spirit— and we should not only have individual testimonies against it, in all the forms of genius, from those who have the privilege of speaking, not to their own age merely, but to all time; there would also gradually shape itself forth a national education which, without overlooking any other of the requisites of human well-being, would be adapted to this purpose in particular.

What is requisite in politics for the same end is not that public opinion should not be what it is and must be, the ruling power, but that, in order to the formation of the best public opinion, there should exist somewhere a great social support for opinions and sentiments different from those of the mass. The shape which that support may best assume is a question of time, place, and circumstance, but (in a commercial country, and an age, when, happily for mankind, the military spirit is gone by) there can be no doubt about the elements which must compose it: they are, an agricultural class, a leisured class, and a learned class.

The natural tendencies of an agricultural class are in many respects the reverse of those of a manufacturing and commercial. In the first place, from their more scattered position and less exercised activity of mind, they have usually a greater willingness to look up to, and accept of, guidance. In the next place, they are the class who have local attachments, and it is astonishing how much of character depends upon this one circumstance. If the agricultural spirit is not felt in America as a counterpoise to the commercial, it is because American agriculturists have no local attachments; they range from place to place, and are, to all intents and purposes, a commercial class. But in an old country, where the same family has long occupied the same land, the case will naturally be different. From attachment to places, follows attachment to persons who are associated with those places. Though no longer the permanent tie which it once was, the connection between tenants and landlords is one not lightly broken off— one which both parties, when they enter into it, desire and hope will be permanent. Again: with attachment to the place comes generally attachment to the occupation; a farmer seldom becomes any thing but a farmer. The rage of money-getting can scarcely, in agricultural occupations, reach any dangerous height; except where bad laws have aggravated the natural fluctuations of price, there is little room for gambling. The rewards of industry and skill are sure, but moderate; an agriculturist can rarely make a large fortune. A manufacturer or merchant, unless he can outstrip others, knows that others will outstrip him, and ruin him, while, in the irksome drudgery to which he subjects himself as a means, there is nothing agreeable to dwell on except the ultimate end. But agriculture is in itself an interesting occupation, which few wish to retire from, and which men of property and education often pursue merely for their amusement. Men so occupied are satisfied with less gain, and are less impatient to realize it. Our town population, it has long been remarked, is becoming almost as mobile and uneasy as the American. It ought not to be so with our agriculturists; they ought to be the counterbalancing element in our national character; they should represent the type opposite to the commercial—that of moderate wishes, tranquil tastes, cultivation of the excitements and enjoyments near at hand, and compatible with their existing position.

To attain this object, how much alteration may be requisite in the system of rackrenting and tenancy at will, we cannot undertake to show in this place. It is sufficiently obvious, also, that the corn laws must disappear; there must be no feud raging between the commercial class and that by whose influence and example its excesses are to be tempered; men are not prone to adopt the characteristics of their enemies. Nor is this all. In order that the agricultural population should count for any thing in politics, or contribute its part to the formation of the national character, it is absolutely necessary that it should be educated. And let it be remembered that, in an agricultural people, the diffusion of information and intelligence must necessarily be artificial—the work of government, or of the superior classes. In populous towns, the mere collision of man with man, the keenness of competition, the habits of society and discussion, the easy access to reading—even the dulness of the ordinary occupations, which drives men to other excitements—produce of themselves a certain development of intelligence. The least favored class of a town population are seldom actually stupid, and have often, in some directions, a morbid keenness and acuteness. It is otherwise with the peasantry. Whatever it is desired that they should know, they must be taught; whatever intelligence is expected to grow up among them must first be implanted, and sedulously nursed.

It is not needful to go into a similar analysis of the tendencies of the other two classes—a leisured and a learned class. The capabilities which they possess for controlling the excess of the commercial spirit by a contrary spirit are at once apparent. We regard it as one of the greatest advantages of this country over America, that it possesses both these classes; and we believe that the interests of the time to come are greatly dependent upon preserving them, and upon their being rendered, as they much require to be, better and better qualified for their important functions.

If we believed that the national character of England, instead of reacting upon the American character and raising it, was gradually assimilating itself to those points of it which the best and wisest Americans see with most uneasiness, it would be no consolation to us to think that we might possibly avoid the institutions of America, for we should have all the effects of her institutions, except those which are beneficial. The American many are not essentially a different class from our ten-pound householders, and, if the middle class are left to the mere habits and instincts of a commercial community, we shall have a "tyranny of the majority," not the less irksome because most of the tyrants may not be manual laborers. For it is a chimerical hope to overbear or outnumber the middle class; whatever modes of voting, whatever redistribution of the constituencies, are really necessary for placing the government in their hands, those, whether we like it or not, they will assuredly obtain.

The ascendancy of the commercial class in modern society and politics is inevitable, and under due limitations, ought not to be regarded as an evil. That class is the most powerful, but it needs not therefore be all-powerful. Now, as ever, the great problem in government is to prevent the strongest from becoming the only power, and repress the natural tendency of the instincts and passions of the ruling body to sweep away all barriers which are capable of resisting, even for a moment, their own tendencies. Any counterbalancing power can henceforth exist only by the sufferance of the commercial class, but that it should tolerate some such limitation, we deem as important as that it should not itself be held in vassalage.

Of the Logic of Practice, or Art; Including Morality and Policy

[Aside from the essay on Sedgwick, Mill wrote little that bears directly on the problems of moral philosophy in his earlier years. His major concern was the writing of the *System of Logic*, which appeared in 1843. In that work, his aim was to construct a methodology for the social sciences by examining the methods used in the successful physical sciences. The basis for Mill's estimate of the importance of having methods which would enable the social sciences to be equally successful is brought out in the final chapter of the *System*, which also contains some interesting suggestions about moral rules and ultimate ends. The chapter (Book VI, Ch. xii) is here given complete; the text is that of the eighth (and final) edition (1872).]

I

IN THE PRECEDING CHAPTERS we have endeavored to characterize the present state of those among the branches of knowledge called Moral, which are sciences in the only proper sense of the term, that is, inquiries into the course of nature. It is customary, however, to include under the term Moral Knowledge, and even (though improperly) under that of Moral Science, an inquiry the results of which do not express themselves in the indicative, but in the imperative mood, or in periphrases equivalent to it; what is called the knowledge of duties, practical ethics, or morality.

Now, the imperative mood is the characteristic of art, as distinguished from science. Whatever speaks in rules or precepts, not in assertions respecting matters of fact, is art; and ethics or morality is properly a portion of the art corresponding to the sciences of human nature and society.*

* It is almost superfluous to observe, that there is another meaning of the word Art, in which it may be said to denote the poetical department or aspect of things in general, in contradistinction to the scientific. In the text, the word is used in its older, and I hope, not yet obsolete, sense.

The Method, therefore, of Ethics, can be no other than that of Art, or Practice, in general; and the portion yet uncompleted, of the task which we proposed to ourselves in the concluding Book, is to characterize the general Method of Art, as distinguished from Science.

I I

In all branches of practical business, there are cases in which individuals are bound to conform their practice to a pre-established rule, while there are others in which it is part of their task to find or construct the rule by which they are to govern their conduct. The first, for example, is the case of a judge under a definite written code. The judge is not called upon to determine what course would be intrinsically the most advisable in the particular case in hand, but only within what rule of law it falls, what the legislator has ordained to be done in the kind of case, and must therefore be presumed to have intended in the individual case. The method must here be wholly and exclusively one of ratiocination, or syllogism; and the process is obviously what, in our analysis of the syllogism, we showed that all ratiocination is, namely the interpretation of a formula.

In order that our illustration of the opposite case may be taken from the same class of subjects as the former, we will suppose, in contrast with the situation of the judge, the position of a legislator. As the judge has laws for his guidance, so the legislator has rules and maxims of policy; but it would be a manifest error to suppose that the legislator is bound by these maxims in the same manner as the judge is bound by the laws, and that all he has to do is to argue down from them to the particular case, as the judge does from the laws. The legislator is bound to take into consideration the reasons or grounds of the maxim; the judge has nothing to do with those of the law, except so far as a consideration of them may throw light upon the intention of the lawmaker, where his words have left it doubtful. To the judge, the rule, once positively ascertained, is final; but the legislator, or other practitioner, who goes by rules rather than by their reasons, like the old-fashioned German tacticians who were vanquished by Napoleon, or the physician who preferred that his patients should die by rule rather than recover contrary to it, is rightly judged to be a mere pedant and the slave of his formulas.

Now the reasons of a maxim of policy, or of any other rule of art, can be no other than the theorems of the corresponding science.

The relation in which rules of art stand to doctrines of science may be thus characterized. The art proposes to itself an end to be attained, defines the end, and hands it over to the science. The science receives it, considers it as a phenomenon or effect to be studied and, having investigated its causes and conditions, sends it back to art with a theorem of the combinations of circumstances by which it could be produced. Art then examines these combinations of circumstances and, according as any of them are or are not in human power, pronounces the end attainable or not. The only one of the premises, therefore, which Art supplies, is the original major premise, which asserts that the attainment of the given end is desirable. Science then lends to Art the proposition (obtained by a series of inductions or of deductions) that the performance of certain actions will attain the end. From these premises Art concludes that the performance of these actions is desirable and, finding it also practicable, converts the theorem into a rule or precept.

I I I

It deserves particular notice that the theorem or speculative truth is not ripe for being turned into a precept, until the whole, and not a part merely, of the operation which belongs to science has been performed. Suppose that we have completed the scientific process only up to a certain point, have discovered that a particular cause will produce the desired effect, but have not ascertained all the negative conditions which are necessary, that is, all the circumstances which, if present, would prevent its production. If, in this imperfect state of the scientific theory, we attempt to frame a rule of art, we perform that operation prematurely. Whenever any counteracting cause, overlooked by the theorem, takes place, the rule will be at fault; we shall employ the means and the end will not follow. No arguing from or about the rule itself will then help us through the difficulty; there is nothing for it but to turn back and finish the scientific process which should have preceded the formation of the rule. We must reopen the investigation, to inquire into the remainder of the conditions on which the effect depends, and only after we have ascertained the whole of these, are we prepared to transform the completed law of the effect into a precept, in which those circumstances or combinations of circumstances which the science exhibits as conditions are prescribed as means.

It is true that, for the sake of convenience, rules must be formed from something less than this ideally perfect theory; in the first place, because the theory can seldom be made ideally perfect; the next because, if all the counteracting contingencies, whether of frequent or of rare occurrence, were included, the rules would be too cumbrous to be apprehended and remembered by ordinary capacities, on the common occasions of life. The rules of art do not attempt to comprise more conditions than require to be attended to in ordinary cases, and are therefore always imperfect. In the manual arts, where the requisite conditions are not numerous, and where those which the rules do not specify are generally either plain to common observation or speedily learnt from practice, rules may often be safely acted on by persons who know nothing more than the rule. But in the complicated affairs of life, and still more in those of states and societies, rules cannot be relied on, without constantly referring back to the scientific laws on which they are founded. To know what are the practical contingencies which require a modification of the rule, or which are altogether exceptions to it, is to know what combinations of circumstances would interfere with, or entirely counteract, the consequences of those laws; and this can only be learnt by a reference to the theoretic grounds of the rule.

By a wise practitioner, therefore, rules of conduct will only be considered as provisional. Being made for the most numerous cases, or for those of most ordinary occurrence, they point out the manner in which it will be least perilous to act, where time or means do not exist for analyzing the actual circumstances of the case, or where we cannot trust our judgment in estimating them. But they do not at all supersede the propriety of going through (when circumstances permit) the scientific process requisite for framing a rule from the data of the particular case before us. At the same time, the common rule may very properly serve as an admonition that a certain mode of action has been found by ourselves and others to be well adapted to the cases of most common occurrence, so that, if it be unsuitable to the case in hand, the reason of its being so will be likely to arise from some unusual circumstance.

I V

The error is therefore apparent of those who would deduce the line of conduct proper to particular cases from supposed universal practical maxims: overlooking the necessity of constantly referring back to the principles of the speculative science, in order to be sure of attaining even the specific end which the rules have in view. How much greater still, then, must the error be of setting up such unbending principles, not merely as universal rules for attaining a given end, but as rules of conduct generally, without regard to the possibility, not only that some modifying cause may prevent the attainment of the given end by the means which the rule prescribes, but that success itself may conflict with some other end, which may possibly chance to be more desirable.

This is the habitual error of many of the political speculators whom I have characterized as the geometrical school, especially in France, where ratiocination from rules of practice forms the staple commodity of journalism and political oratory; a misapprehension of the functions of Deduction which has brought much discredit, in the estimation of other countries, upon the spirit of generalization so honorably characteristic of the French mind. The commonplaces of politics, in France, are large and sweeping practical maxims, from which, as ultimate premises, men reason downwards to particular applications, and this they call being logical and consistent. For instance, they are perpetually arguing that such and such a measure ought to be adopted, because it is a consequence of the principle on which the form of government is founded, of the principle of legitimacy, or the principle of the sovereignty of the people. To which it may be answered, that if these be really practical principles, they must rest on speculative grounds; the sovereignty of the people (for example) must be a right foundation for government, because a government thus constituted tends to produce certain beneficial effects. Inasmuch, however, as no government produces all possible beneficial effects, but all are attended with more or fewer inconveniences, and since these cannot usually be combated by means drawn from the very causes which produce them, it would be often a much stronger recommendation of some practical arrangement that it does not follow from what is called the general principle of the government, than that it does. Under a government of legitimacy, the presumption is far rather in favor of institutions of popular origin, and in a democracy, in favor of arrangements tending to check the impetus of popular will. The line of argumentation so commonly mistaken in France for political philosophy tends to the practical conclusion that we should exert our utmost efforts to aggravate, instead of alleviating, whatever are the characteristic imperfections of the system of institutions which we prefer, or under which we happen to live.

V

The grounds, then, of every rule of art are to be found in the theorems of science. An art, or a body of art, consists of the rules, together with as much of the speculative propositions as comprises the justification of those rules. The complete art of any matter includes a selection of such a portion from the science as is necessary to show on what conditions the effects which the art aims at producing depend. And Art in general consists of the truths of Science, arranged in the most convenient order for practice, instead of the order which is the most convenient for thought. Science groups and arranges its truths so as to enable us to take in at one view as much as possible of the general order of the universe. Art, though it must assume the same general laws, follows them only into such of their detailed consequences as have led to the formation of rules of conduct, and brings together from parts of the field of science most remote from one another the truths relating to the production of the different and heterogeneous conditions necessary to each effect which the exigencies of practical life require to be produced.*

Science, therefore, following one cause to its various effects,

---

* Professor Bain and others call the selection from the truths of science made for the purpose of an art, a Practical Science, and confine the name Art to the actual rules.

while art traces one effect to its multiplied and diversified causes and conditions, there is need of a set of intermediate scientific truths, derived from the higher generalities of science, and destined to serve as the generalia or first principles of the various arts. The scientific operation of framing these intermediate principles, M. Comte characterizes as one of those results of philosophy which are reserved for futurity. The only complete example which he points out as actually realized, and which can be held up as a type to be imitated in more important matters, is the general theory of the art of Descriptive Geometry, as conceived by M. Monge. It is not, however, difficult to understand what the nature of these intermediate principles must generally be. After framing the most comprehensive possible conception of the end to be aimed at, that is, of the effect to be produced, and determining in the same comprehensive manner the set of conditions on which that effect depends, there remains to be taken a general survey of the resources which can be commanded for realizing this set of conditions; and when the result of this survey has been embodied in the fewest and most extensive propositions possible, those propositions will express the general relation between the available means and the end, and will constitute the general scientific theory of the art, from which its practical methods will follow as corollaries.

VI

But though the reasonings which connect the end or purpose of every art with its means belong to the domain of Science, the definition of the end itself belongs exclusively to Art, and forms its peculiar province. Every art has one first principle, or general major premise, not borrowed from science: that which enunciates the object aimed at, and affirms it to be a desirable object. The builder's art assumes that it is desirable to have buildings; architecture (as one of the fine arts), that it is desirable to have them beautiful or imposing. The hygienic and medical arts assume, the one that the preservation of health, the other that the cure of disease, are fitting and desirable ends. These are not propositions of science. Propositions of science assert a matter of fact: an existence, a coexistence, a succession, or a resemblance. The propositions now spoken of do not assert that anything is, but enjoin or recommend that something should be. They are a class by themselves. A proposition of which the predicate is expressed by the words *ought* or *should be*, is generically different from one which is expressed by *is*, or *will be*. It is true that, in the largest sense of the words, even these propositions assert something as a matter of fact. The fact affirmed in them is that the conduct recommended excites in the speaker's mind the feeling of approbation. This, however, does not go to the bottom of the matter, for the speaker's approbation is no sufficient reason why other people should approve, nor ought it to be a conclusive reason even with himself. For the purposes of practice, every one must be required to justify his approbation; and for this there is need of general premises, determining what are the proper objects of approbation, and what the proper order of precedence among those objects.

These general premises, together with the principal conclusions which may be deduced from them, form (or rather might form) a body of doctrine, which is properly the Art of Life, in its three departments: Morality, Prudence or Policy, and Æsthetics, the Right, the Expedient, and the Beautiful or Noble, in human conduct and works. To this art (which, in the main, is unfortunately still to be created), all other arts are subordinate, since its principles are those which must determine whether the special aim of any particular art is worthy and desirable, and what is its place in the scale of desirable things. Every art is thus a joint result of laws of nature disclosed by science, and of the general principles of what has been called Teleology, or the Doctrine of Ends,* which, borrowing the language of the German metaphysicians, may also be termed, not improperly, the Principles of Practical Reason.

A scientific observer or reasoner, merely as such, is not an adviser for practice. His part is only to show that certain consequences follow from certain causes and that, to obtain certain ends, certain means are the most effectual. Whether the ends themselves are such as ought to be pursued, and if so, in what cases and to how great a length, it is no part of his business as a cultivator of science to decide, and science

* The word Teleology is also, but inconveniently and improperly, employed by some writers as a name for the attempt to explain the phenomena of the universe from final causes.

alone will never qualify him for the decision. In purely physical science, there is not much temptation to assume this ulterior office, but those who treat of human nature and society invariably claim it; they always undertake to say, not merely what is, but what ought to be. To entitle them to do this, a complete doctrine of Teleology is indispensable. A scientific theory, however perfect, of the subject matter, considered merely as part of the order of nature, can in no degree serve as a substitute. In this respect the various subordinate arts afford a misleading analogy. In them there is seldom any visible necessity for justifying the end, since in general its desirableness is denied by nobody, and it is only when the question of precedence is to be decided between that end and some other, that the general principles of Teleology have to be called in; but a writer on Morals and Politics requires those principles at every step. The most elaborate and well-digested exposition of the laws of succession and coexistence among mental or social phenomena, and of their relation to one another as causes and effects, will be of no avail towards the art of Life or of Society, if the ends to be aimed at by that art are left to the vague suggestions of the *intellectus sibi permissus*, or are taken for granted without analysis or questioning.

V I I

There is, then, a *Philosophia Prima* peculiar to Art, as there is one which belongs to Science. There are not only first principles of Knowledge, but first principles of Conduct. There must be some standard by which to determine the goodness or badness, absolute and comparative, of ends, or objects of desire. And whatever that standard is, there can be but one; for if there were several ultimate principles of conduct, the same conduct might be approved by one of those principles and condemned by another, and there would be needed some more general principle, as umpire between them.

Accordingly, writers on moral philosophy have mostly felt the necessity not only of referring all rules of conduct, and all judgments of praise and blame, to principles, but of referring them to some one principle, some rule, or standard, with which all other rules of conduct were required to be consistent, and from which by ultimate consequence they could all be deduced. Those who have dispensed with the assumption of such an universal standard have only been enabled to do so by supposing that a moral sense or instinct, inherent in our constitution, informs us both what principles of conduct we are bound to observe and also in what order these should be subordinated to one another.

The theory of the foundations of morality is a subject which it would be out of place, in a work like this, to discuss at large, and which could not to any useful purpose be treated incidentally. I shall content myself therefore with saying that the doctrine of intuitive moral principles, even if true, would provide only for that portion of the field of conduct which is properly called moral. For the remainder of the practice of life some general principle, or standard, must still be sought; and if that principle be rightly chosen, it will be found, I apprehend, to serve quite as well for the ultimate principle of Morality, as for that of Prudence, Policy, or Taste.

Without attempting in this place to justify my opinion, or even to define the kind of justification which it admits of, I merely declare my conviction that the general principle to which all rules of practice ought to conform, and the test by which they should be tried, is that of conduciveness to the happiness of mankind or rather of all sentient beings; in other words, that the promotion of happiness is the ultimate principle of Teleology.*

I do not mean to assert that the promotion of happiness should be itself the end of all actions, or even of all rules of action. It is the justification, and ought to be the controller, of all ends, but is not itself the sole end. There are many virtuous actions and even virtuous modes of action (though the cases are, I think, less frequent than is often supposed), by which happiness in the particular instance is sacrificed, more pain being produced than pleasure. But conduct of which this can be truly asserted admits of justification only because it can be shown that, on the whole, more happiness will exist in the world if feelings are cultivated which will make people, in certain cases, regardless of happiness. I fully admit that this is true: that the cultivation of an ideal noble-

---

* For an express discussion and vindication of this principle, see the little volume entitled "Utilitarianism."

ness of will and conduct should be to individual human beings an end, to which the specific pursuit either of their own happiness or of that of others (except so far as included in that idea) should, in any case of conflict, give way. But I hold that the very question, what constitutes this elevation of character, is itself to be decided by a reference to happiness as the standard. The character itself should be, to the individual, a paramount end, simply because the existence of this ideal nobleness of character, or of a near approach to it, in any abundance, would go further than all things else towards making human life happy, both in the comparatively humble sense of pleasure and freedom from pain, and in the higher meaning of rendering life, not what it now is almost universally, puerile and insignificant, but such as human beings with highly developed faculties can care to have.

V I I I

With these remarks we must close this summary view of the application of the general logic of scientific inquiry to the moral and social departments of science. Notwithstanding the extreme generality of the principles of method which I have laid down (a generality which, I trust, is not, in this instance, synonymous with vagueness), I have indulged the hope that to some of those on whom the task will devolve of bringing those most important of all sciences into a more satisfactory state, these observations may be useful, both in removing erroneous, and in clearing up the true, conceptions of the means by which, on subjects of so high a degree of complication, truth can be attained. Should this hope be realized, what is probably destined to be the great intellectual achievement of the next two or three generations of European thinkers will have been in some degree forwarded.

Dr. Whewell on Moral Philosophy

[William Whewell, D.D. (1794–1866), was Knightbridge Professor of Moral Philosophy and Master of Trinity College, at Cambridge. He was a member of practically every important scientific association of the time, and a copious writer on scientific as well as philosophical and theological topics. His influence in academic circles was considerable. His books were widely used as texts, and Mill himself had found Whewell's *History of the Inductive Sciences* an invaluable aid in writing certain portions of his own *System of Logic*, though he disagreed radically with Whewell's theories as set forth in his *Philosophy of the Inductive Sciences*. Whewell seemed to Mill to be the archetypal representative of all that he most disliked in philosophical theory—to represent in person all the defects involved in being an "intuitionist." Mill stated his estimate of that sort of position quite bluntly in the *Autobiography* (ch. VII):

> The notion that truths external to the mind may be known by intuition or consciousness, independently of observation and experience, is, I am persuaded, in these times, the great intellectual support of false doctrines and bad institutions. By the aid of this theory, every inveterate belief and every intense feeling, of which the origin is not remembered, is enabled to dispense with the obligation of justifying itself by reason, and is erected into its own all-sufficient voucher and justification. There never was such an instrument devised for consecrating all deep-seated prejudices.

The *System of Logic* had been intended, in part, to deprive intuitionism in moral and political theory of the support it derived from the view that intuitions are indispensable in mathematics and the physical sciences, by showing that they are not needed there. In the essay on Whewell's moral philosophy, Mill pressed the attack more directly.

The essay was first published in the *Westminster Review* in October, 1852, as a review of two books by Whewell, the *Lectures on the History of Moral Philosophy in England*, 1852, and the *Elements of Morality, including Polity*, 2 vols.,

1845. It was reprinted in Mill's *Dissertations and Discussions*, from which the present text is taken.]

IF THE WORTH of Dr. Whewell's writings could be measured by the importance and amplitude of their subjects, no writer of the age could vie with him in merit or usefulness. He has aspired to be not only the historian, but the philosopher and legislator, of almost all the great departments of human knowledge, reducing each to its first principles, and showing how it might be scientifically evolved from these as a connected whole. After endeavoring, in his *History* and *Philosophy of the Inductive Sciences*, to place physics, and incidentally metaphysics, on a philosophic foundation, he has made an almost equally ambitious attempt on the subjects of morals and government, of which the two works before us are the results. He is thus entitled to the praise of having done his best to wipe off from the two endowed universities, in one of which he holds a high place, the reproach to which they have so long been justly liable, of neglecting the higher regions of philosophy. By his writings and influence, he has been an agent in that revival of speculation on the most difficult and highest subjects, which has been noticeable for some years past within as well as without the pale of Oxford and Cambridge. And inasmuch as mental activity of any kind is better than torpidity, and bad solutions of the great questions of philosophy are preferable to a lazy ignoring of their existence, whoever has taken so active a part as Dr. Whewell in this intellectual movement may lay claim to considerable merit.

Unfortunately, it is not in the nature of bodies constituted like the English Universities, even when stirred up into something like mental activity, to send forth thought of any but one description. There have been universities (those of France and Germany have at some periods been practically conducted on this principle) which brought together into a body the most vigorous thinkers and the ablest teachers, whatever the conclusions to which their thinking might have led them. But in the English Universities no thought can find place except that which can reconcile itself with orthodoxy. They are ecclesiastical institutions; and it is the essence of all churches to vow adherence to a set of opinions made up and prescribed, it matters little whether three or thirteen centuries ago. Men will some day open their eyes, and perceive how fatal a thing it is that the instruction of those who are intended to be the guides and governors of mankind should be confided to a collection of persons thus pledged. If the opinions they are pledged to were every one as true as any fact in physical science, and had been adopted, not as they almost always are, on trust and authority, but as the result of the most diligent and impartial examination of which the mind of the recipient was capable, even then, the engagement under penalties always to adhere to the opinions once assented to would debilitate and lame the mind, and unfit it for progress, still more for assisting the progress of others. The person who has to think more of what an opinion leads to, than of what is the evidence of it, cannot be a philosopher, or a teacher of philosophers. Of what value is the opinion, on any subject, of a man of whom every one knows that by his profession he must hold that opinion? and how can intellectual vigor be fostered by the teaching of those who, even as a matter of duty, would rather that their pupils were weak and orthodox, then strong with freedom of thought? Whoever thinks that persons thus tied are fitting depositories of the trust of educating a people must think that the proper object of intellectual education is not to strengthen and cultivate the intellect, but to make sure of its adopting certain conclusions; that, in short, in the exercise of the thinking faculty, there is something, either religion, or conservatism, or peace, or whatever it be, more important than truth. Not to dilate further on this topic, it is nearly inevitable that, when persons bound by the vows and placed in the circumstances of an established clergy enter into the paths of higher speculation, and endeavor to make a philosophy, either purpose or instinct will direct them to the kind of philosophy best fitted to prop up the doctrines to which they are pledged. And when these doctrines are so prodigiously in arrear of the general progress of thought as the doctrines of the Church of England now are, the philosophy resulting will have a tendency not to promote, but to arrest progress.

Without the slightest wish to speak in disparagement of Dr. Whewell's labors, and with no ground for questioning his sincerity of purpose, we think the preceding remark thoroughly applicable to his philosophical speculations. We do not say the intention, but certainly the tendency, of his efforts, is to shape the whole of philosophy, physical as well as moral, into a form adapted to serve as a support and a justification to any opinions which happen to be established. A writer who has gone beyond all his predecessors in the manufacture of necessary truths, that is, of propositions which, according to him, may be known to be true independently of proof; who ascribes this self-evidence to the larger generalities of all sciences (however little obvious at first) as soon as they have become familiar—was still more certain to regard all moral propositions familiar to him from his early years as self-evident truths. His *Elements of Morality* could be nothing better than a classification and systematizing of the opinions which he found prevailing among those who had been educated according to the approved methods of his own country, or, let us rather say, an apparatus for converting those prevailing opinions, on matters of morality, into reasons for themselves.

This, accordingly, is what we find in Dr. Whewell's volumes, while we have sought in vain for the numerous minor merits which give a real scientific value to his previous works. If the *Philosophy of the Inductive Sciences* was, as we think, an erroneous philosophy, it contained much that was not unfit to find place in a better, and was often calculated to suggest deeper thoughts than it possessed of its own. But in the *Elements of Morality* he leaves the subject so exactly as he found it—the book is so mere a catalogue of received opinions, containing nothing to correct any of them, and little which can work with any potency even to confirm them —that it can scarcely be counted as anything more than one of the thousand waves on the dead sea of commonplace, affording nothing to invite or to reward a separate examination. We should not, therefore, have felt called upon to concern ourselves specially about it, if Dr. Whewell had not, in his more recent publication *Lectures on the History of Moral Philosophy in England*, undertaken to characterize and criticize, from his own point of view, all other English writers on moral philosophy, and particularly those who derive their ethical conclusions, not from internal intuition, but from an external standard. So long as he contented himself with giving what we think bad reasons for common opinions, there was not much inducement to interfere with them, but assaults on the only methods of philosophizing from which any improvement in ethical opinions can be looked for ought to be repelled. And in doing this it is necessary to extend our comments to some of Dr. Whewell's substantive opinions also. When he argues in condemnation of any external standard, and especially of utility, or tendency to happiness, as the principle or test of morality, it is material to examine how he gets on without it, how he fares in the attempt to construct a coherent theory of morals on any other basis. We shall make use of his larger work in so far only as it is evidence on this point.

Even with the *Lectures*, considered as giving an account of English speculations on moral philosophy previous to the age of Bentham and Paley, it is not our purpose to meddle; Hobbes, therefore, and Locke, must be left in the hands of Dr. Whewell, without any attempt either to correct his estimate of their opinions, or to offer any judgment of our own. This historical sketch suggests, however, one remark of an historical character, not new to any one who is conversant with the writings of English thinkers on ethical subjects. During the greater part of the eighteenth century, the received opinions in religion and ethics were chiefly attacked, as by Shaftesbury, and even by Hume, on the ground of instinctive feelings of virtue, and the theory of a moral taste or sense. As a consequence of this, the defenders of established opinions, both lay and clerical, commonly professed utilitarianism. To the many writers on the side of orthodoxy, of the utilitarian school, mentioned by Dr. Whewell, might be added several of at least equal note, whom he has omitted: as John Brown, the author of *Essays on the Characteristics*; Soame Jenyns and his more celebrated reviewer, Dr. Johnson; all of whom, as explicitly as Bentham, laid down the doctrine that utility is the foundation of morals. This series of writers attained its culmination in Paley, whose treatise, proclaiming without evasion or circumlocution, not only expediency as the end, but (a very different doctrine) simple self-interest as the motive, of virtue, and deducing from these premises all the orthodox conclusions, became the textbook of moral philosophy in one of the two Universities of the Church of England. But a change ensued, and the utilitarian doctrine, which had been the favorite theory of the defenders of orthodoxy, began to be used by its assailants. In the hands of the French philosophers, and in those of Godwin and of Bentham—who, though earlier than Godwin in date, was later in acquiring popular influence—a moral philosophy founded on utility led to many conclusions very unacceptable to the orthodox. For a whole generation, so effectual a fight was kept up against those conclusions by bayonets in the field and prosecutions in the courts of justice, that there seemed no necessity for taking much concern about the premises; but when those carnal weapons fell into disuse, and the spirit which had wielded them was laid—when the battle of established opinions in Church and State had again to be fought by argument, a demand arose for metaphysics and moral philosophy, of the kind most remote from that which appeared so full of danger to received opinions. Utility was now abjured as a deadly heresy, and the doctrine of *a priori* or self-evident morality, an end in itself, independent of all consequences, became the orthodox theory. Having once entered into this course, and gone in search of a philosophical system to be extracted from the mind itself, without any external evidence, the defenders of orthodoxy were insensibly led to seek their system where it exists in the most elaborate shape—in the German metaphysicians. It was not without reluctance that they found themselves engaged in this path, for German metaphysics in Germany lay under as grave a suspicion of religious skepticism, as the rival philosophy in England or France. But it was found, on trial, that philosophy of this cast admitted of easy adaptation, and would bend to the very Thirty-nine Articles, as it is the essence of a philosophy which seeks its evidence in internal conviction, that it bears its testimony with equal ease for any conclusions in favor of which there is a predisposition, and is skeptical with the skeptical, and mystical with the mystical. Accordingly, the tone of religious metaphysics, and of the ethical speculations connected with religion, is now altogether Germanized, and Dr. Whewell, by his writings, has done no little to impress upon the metaphysics of orthodoxy this change of character.

It has always been indistinctly felt that the doctrine of *a priori* principles is one and the same doctrine, whether applied to the $\overset{\text{γ}}{o}\nu$ or the $\delta\acute{e}o\nu$—to the knowledge of truth or to that of duty; that it belongs to the same general tendency of thought: to extract from the mind itself, without any outward standard, principles and rules of morality, and to deem it possible to discover, by mere introspection into our minds, the laws of external nature. Both forms of this mode of thought attained a brilliant development in Descartes, the real founder of the modern anti-inductive school of philosophy. The Cartesian tradition was never lost, being kept alive by direct descent through Spinoza, Leibnitz, and Kant, to Schelling and Hegel, but the speculations of Bacon and Locke, and the progress of the experimental sciences, gave a long period of predominance to the philosophy of experience; and though many followed out that philosophy into its natural alliances, and acknowledged not only observation and experiment as rulers of the speculative world, but utility of the practical, others thought that it was scientifically possible to separate the two opinions, and professed themselves Baconians in the physical department, remaining Cartesians in the moral. It will probably be thought by posterity to be the principal merit of the German metaphysicans of the last and present age that they have proved the impossibility of resting on this middle ground of compromise, and have convinced all thinkers of any force that, if they adhere to the doctrine of *a priori* principles of morals, they must follow Descartes and Hegel in ascribing the same character to the principles of physics.

On the present occasion, it is only with the moral branch of the subject that we have to deal, and we shall begin by showing in what manner Dr. Whewell states the question between us.

Schemes of morality, that is, modes of deducing the rules of human action, are of two kinds: those which assert it to be the law of human action to aim at some external object (external, that is, to the mind which aims), as, for example, those which in ancient or modern times have asserted pleasure, or utility, or the greatest happiness of the greatest number, to be the true end of human action; and those which would regulate human action by an internal principle or relation, as conscience or a moral faculty, or duty, or rectitude, or the superiority of reason to desire. These two kinds of schemes may be described respectively as *dependent* and *independent* morality. Now it is here held that independent morality is the true scheme. We maintain with Plato that reason has a natural and rightful authority over desire and affection; with Butler, that there is a difference of kind in our principles of action; with the general voice of mankind, that we must do what is right, at whatever cost of pain and loss. We deny the doctrine of the ancient Epicureans, that pleasure is the supreme good; of Hobbes, that moral rules are only the work of men's mutual fear; of Paley, that what is expedient is right, and that there is no difference among pleasures except their intensity and duration; and of Bentham, that the rules of human action are to be obtained by casting up the pleasures which actions produce. But though we thus take our stand upon the ground of independent morality, as held by previous writers, we hope that we are (by their aid mainly) able to present it in a more systematic and connected form than has yet been done.—*Introductory Lecture,* pp. ix–x.

There is, in this mode of stating the question, great unfairness to the doctrine of "dependent morality," as Dr. Whewell terms it, though the word independent is fully as applicable to it as to the intuition doctrine. He appropriates to his own side of the question all the expressions, such as conscience, duty, rectitude, with which the reverential feelings of mankind towards moral ideas are associated, and cries out, *I* am for these noble things, *you* are for pleasure, or utility. We cannot accept this as a description of the matter in issue. Dr. Whewell is assuming to himself what belongs quite as rightfully to his antagonists. We are as much for conscience, duty, rectitude, as Dr. Whewell. The terms, and all the feelings connected with them, are as much a part of the ethics of utility as of that of intuition. The point in dispute is what acts are the proper objects of those feelings, whether we ought to take the feelings as we find them, as accident or design has made them, or whether the tendency of actions to promote happiness affords a test to which the feelings of morality should conform. In the same spirit, Dr. Whewell announces it as *his* opinion, as the side *he* takes in this great controversy, "that we must do what is right, at whatever cost of pain and loss." As if this was not everybody's opinion; as if it was not the very meaning of the word right. The matter in debate is, what *is* right, not whether what is right ought to be done. Dr. Whewell represents his opponents as denying an identical proposition, in order that he may claim a monopoly of high principle for his own opinions. The same unfairness pervades the whole phraseology. It is not only Dr. Whewell who "maintains, with Plato, that reason has a rightful authority over desire and affection." Everybody maintains it; only, what *is* reason? and by what rule is it to guide and govern the desires and affections? The description of Bentham as obtaining his rule of conduct by "casting up the pleasures which actions produce," ought to be "casting up the pleasures and pains which actions produce," a very different thing.

As might be expected from the historical character of the *Lectures*, the discussion of opinions mostly assumes the form of criticism on writers. Dr. Whewell's objections to utility or the "greatest happiness" as the standard of morals, are chiefly contained in his animadversions on Paley and on Bentham. It would be quite open to a defender of the principle of utility, to refuse encumbering himself with a defense of either of those authors. The principle is not bound up with what they have said in its behalf, nor with the degree of felicity which they may have shown in applying it. As for Paley, we resign him without compunction to the tender mercies of Dr. Whewell. It concerns Dr. Whewell more than ourselves to uphold the reputation of a writer who, whatever principle of morals he professed, seems to have had no object but to insert it as a foundation underneath the existing set of opinions, ethical and political; who, when he had laid down utility as the fundamental axiom, and the recognition of general rules as the condition of its application, took his leave of scientific analysis, and betook himself to picking up utilitarian reasons by the wayside, in proof of all accredited doctrines, and in defense of most tolerated practices. Bentham was a moralist of another stamp. With him, the first use to be made of his ultimate principle, was to erect on it, as a foundation, secondary or middle principles, capable of serving as premises for a body of ethical doctrine not derived from existing opinions, but fitted to be their test. Without such middle principles, an universal principle, either in science or in morals, serves for little but a thesaurus of commonplaces for the discussion of questions, instead of a means of deciding them. If Bentham has been regarded, by subsequent adherents of a morality grounded on the "greatest happiness," as in a peculiar sense the founder of that system of ethics, it is not because, as Dr. Whewell imagines (p. 190), he either thought himself or was thought by others to be the "discoverer of the principle," but because he was the first who, keeping clear of the direct and indirect influences of all doctrines inconsistent with it, deduced a set of subordinate generalities from utility alone, and by these consistently tested all particular questions. This great service, previously to which a scientific doctrine of ethics on the foundation of utility was impossible, has been performed by Bentham (though with a view to the exigencies of legislation more than to those of morals) in a manner, as far as it goes, eminently meritorious, and so as to indicate clearly the way to complete the scheme. We must at the same time qualify our approbation by adding, not that his practical conclusions in morals were often wrong, for we think that as far as they went they were mostly right, but that there were large deficiencies and hiatuses in his scheme of human nature and life, and a consequent want of breadth and comprehension in his secondary principles, which led him often to deduce just conclusions from premises so narrow as to provoke many minds to a rejection of what was nevertheless truth. It is by his *method* chiefly that Bentham, as we think, justly earned a position in moral science analogous to that of Bacon in physical. It is because he was the first to enter into the right mode of working ethical problems, though he worked many of them, as Bacon did physical, on insufficient data. Dr. Whewell's shafts, however, seldom touch Bentham where he is really vulnerable; they are mostly aimed at his strong points.

Before commencing his attack on Bentham's opinions, Dr. Whewell gives a sketch of his life. In this there is an apparent desire to be just to Bentham, as far as the writer's opinions allow. But there is in some of the strictures a looseness of expression, scarcely excusable in an extemporaneous lecture, and still less in a printed book. "He (Bentham) showed very early that peculiar onesidedness in his mode of asserting and urging his opinions, which made him think all moderation with regard to his opponents superfluous and absurd" (p. 189). What is here called "onesidedness in his mode of asserting and urging his opinions" must mean onesidedness in the opinions themselves. It could not be Bentham's "mode of asserting his opinions" that "made him think" whatever he did think. This is as if any one should say, "his speaking only English made him unable to understand French," or "his peculiar habit of fighting made him think it superfluous and absurd to keep the peace." Again

(p. 190), "Bentham appears to have been one of those persons to whom everything which passes through their own thoughts assumes quite a different character and value from that which the same thing had when it passed through the thoughts of other persons." If a thought in a person's own mind did not assume a different character from what the same thought had in other minds, people might as well think by deputy.

A more serious injustice to Bentham is that of citing, as is constantly done in this volume, the book called *Deontology*, as the authentic exposition of Bentham's philosophy of morals. Dr. Whewell would no doubt justify this by saying that the book in question is the only treatise expressly and exclusively on morals, which we have from Bentham. It is true that we have no other, but the *Deontology* was not, and does not profess to be, written by Bentham. Still less ought that book to be represented as the embodiment of the opinions and mental characteristics of all who share Bentham's general conception of ethics. After charging the compiler of the *Deontology* with profound ignorance, and saying that it is almost "superfluous to notice misstatements so gross and partiality so blind," Dr. Whewell adds that "such misrepresentations and such unfairness are the usual style of controversy of him (Bentham) and his disciples; and it is fit that we, in entering upon the consideration of their writings, should be aware of this." Who are the persons here included under the name of Bentham's "disciples," we are not enabled to judge, nor are we aware that Bentham ever had any disciples, in Dr. Whewell's sense of the term. As far as our means of observation have gone, which in this matter are considerably greater than Dr. Whewell's, those who, from the amount of their intellectual obligations to Bentham, would be the most likely to be classed by Dr. Whewell as Benthamites, were and are persons in an unusual degree addicted to judging and thinking for themselves, persons remarkable for learning willingly from all masters, but swearing blind fealty to none. It is also a fact, with which Dr. Whewell cannot be altogether unacquainted, that among them there have been men of the widest and most accurate acquirements in history and philosophy, against whom the accusation of ignorance of the opinions which they controverted would be as unfounded as the imputation of blind partiality. We protest against including them and Bentham in an imaginary sect, of which the *Deontology* is to be considered the gospel. Bentham's merits or demerits must stand on what is contained in the books written by himself.

Among these, the one in which the doctrine of utility is expressly discussed, and contrasted with the various ethical doctrines opposed to it, is the *Introduction to the Principles of Morals and Legislation*, published in 1789. On this Dr. Whewell comments as follows:

The first chapter of this work is "On the Principle of Utility," the second, "On Principles adverse to that of Utility." These adverse principles are stated to be two: the Principle of Asceticism, and the Principle of Sympathy. [Bentham calls it the Principle of Sympathy and Antipathy, which is already a considerable difference.] The principle of asceticism is that principle which approves of actions in proportion as they tend to *diminish* human happiness and, conversely, disapproves of them as they tend to augment it. The principle of sympathy is that which approves or disapproves of certain actions "merely because a man finds himself disposed to approve or disapprove of them, holding up that approbation or disapprobation as a sufficient reason for itself, and disclaiming the necessity of looking out for any extrinsic ground." And these two principles are, it seems, according to Bentham's view, the only principles which are, or which can be, opposed to the principle of utility!

Now it is plain that these are not only not fair representations of any principles ever held by moralists, or by any persons speaking gravely and deliberately, but that they are too extravagant and fantastical to be accepted even as caricatures of any such principles. For who ever approved of actions because they tend to make mankind miserable? or who ever said anything which could, even in an intelligible way of exaggeration, be so represented? . . . But who then are the ascetic school who are thus ridiculed? We could not, I think, guess from the general description thus given but, from a note, it appears that he had the Stoical philosophers and the religious ascetics in his mind. With regard to the Stoics, it would of course be waste of time and thought to defend them from such coarse buffoonery as this, which does not touch their defects, whatever these may be, etc.— (p. 202.)

Not solely for the due estimation of Bentham, but for the right understanding of the utilitarian controversy, it is important to know what the truth is, respecting the points here in issue between Bentham and Dr. Whewell.

Undoubtedly no one has set up, in opposition to the "greatest happiness" principle, a "greatest unhappiness" principle, as the standard of virtue. But it was Bentham's business not merely to discuss the avowed principles of his opponents, but to draw out those which, without being professed as principles, were implied in detail, or were essential to support the judgments passed in particular cases. His own doctrine being that the increase of pleasure and the prevention of pain were the proper ends of all moral rules, he had for his opponents all who contended that pleasure could ever be an evil or pain a good in itself, apart from its consequences. Now this, whatever Dr. Whewell may say, the religious ascetics really did. They held that self-mortification, or even self-torture, practised for its own sake and not for the sake of any useful end, was meritorious. It matters not that they may have expected to be rewarded for these merits by consideration in this world, or by the favor of an invisible tyrant in a world to come. So far as this life was concerned, their doctrine required it to be supposed that pain was a thing to be sought, and pleasure to be avoided. Bentham generalized this into a maxim which he called the principle of asceticism. The Stoics did not go so far as the ascetics; they stopped halfway. They did not say that pain is a good, and pleasure an evil. But they said, and boasted of saying, that pain is no evil, and pleasure no good; and this is all and more than all that Bentham imputes to them, as may be seen by any one who reads that chapter of his book. This, however, was enough to place them, equally with the ascetics, in direct opposition to Bentham, since they denied his supreme end to be an end at all. And hence he classed them and the ascetics together, as professing the direct negation of the utilitarian standard.

In the other division of his opponents he placed those who, though they did not deny pleasure to be a good and pain an evil, refused to consider the pain or the pleasure which an action or a class of actions tends to produce, as the criterion of its morality. As the former category of opponents were described by Bentham as followers of the "principle of asceticism," so he described these as followers of "the principle of sympathy and antipathy," not because they had themselves generalized their principle of judgment, or would have acknowledged it when placed undisguised before them, but because, at the bottom of what they imposed on themselves and others as reasons, he could find nothing else; because they all, in one phrase or another, placed the test of right and wrong in a feeling of approbation or disapprobation, thus making the feeling its own reason and its own justification. This portion of Bentham's doctrine can only be fairly exhibited in his own words.

It is manifest that this [the principle of sympathy and antipathy] is rather a principle in name than in reality; it is not a positive principle of itself, so much as a term employed to signify the negation of all principle. What one expects to find in a principle is something that points out some external consideration as a means of warranting and guiding the internal sentiments of approbation and disapprobation; this expectation is but ill fulfilled by a proposition which does neither more nor less than hold up each of these sentiments as a ground and standard for itself.

In looking over the catalogue of human actions (says a partisan of this principle) in order to determine which of them are to be marked with the seal of disapprobation, you need but to take counsel of your own feelings; whatever you find in yourself a propensity to condemn is wrong for that very reason. For the same reason it is also meet for punishment; in what proportion it is adverse to utility, or whether it be adverse to utility at all, is a matter that makes no difference. In that same proportion also is it meet for punishment: if you hate much, punish much, if you hate little, punish little; punish as you hate. If you hate not at all, punish not at all; the fine feelings of the soul are not to be overborne and tyrannized by the harsh and rugged dictates of political utility.

The various systems that have been formed concerning the standard of right and wrong may all be reduced to the principle of sympathy and antipathy. One account may serve for all of them. They consist, all of them, in so many contrivances for avoiding the obligation of appealing to any external standard, and for prevailing upon the reader to accept of the author's sentiment or opinion as a reason for itself. The phrase is different, but the principle the same.

It is curious enough to observe the variety of inventions men have hit upon and the variety of phrases they have brought forward, in order to conceal from the world and if possible from themselves this very general and therefore very pardonable self-sufficiency.

One man says he has a thing made on purpose to tell him what is right and what is wrong, and that it is called a *moral sense*; and then he goes to work at his ease, and says, such a thing is right, and such a thing is wrong—why? "because my moral sense tells me it is."

Another man comes and alters the phrase, leaving out *moral*, and putting in *common* in the room of it. He then tells you that his common sense teaches him what is right and wrong, as much as the other's moral sense did, meaning, by common sense, a sense of some kind or other which, he says, is possessed by all mankind, the sense of those whose sense is not the same as the author's being struck out of the account as not worth taking. This contrivance does better than the other; for, a moral sense being a new thing, a man may feel about him a good while without being able to find it out, but common sense is as old as the creation, and there is no man but would be ashamed to be thought not to have as much of it as his neighbors. It has another great advantage: by appearing to share power, it lessens envy; for when a man gets up upon this ground, in order to anathematize those who differ from him, it is not by a *sic volo sic jubeo*, but by a *velitis jubeatis*.

Another man comes and says that, as to a moral sense indeed, he cannot find that he has any such thing; that, however, he has an *understanding*, which will do quite as well. This understanding, he says, is the standard of right and wrong; it tells him so and so. All good and wise men understand as he does; if other men's understandings differ in any point from his, so much the worse for them: it is a sure sign they are either defective or corrupt.

Another man says that there is an eternal and immutable rule of right, that that rule of right dictates so and so; and then he begins giving you his sentiments upon anything that comes uppermost, and these sentiments (you are to take for granted) are so many branches of the eternal rule of right.

Another man, or perhaps the same man (it's no matter), says that there are certain practices conformable, and others repugnant, to the fitness of things; and then he tells you, at his leisure, what practices are conformable and what repugnant, just as he happens to like a practice or dislike it.

A great multitude of people are continually talking of the law of nature, and then they go on giving you their sentiments about what is right and what is wrong; and these sentiments, you are to understand, are so many chapters and sections of the law of nature.

We have one philosopher who says there is no harm in

anything in the world but in telling a lie, and that if, for example, you were to murder your own father, this would only be a particular way of saying he was not your father. Of course, when this philosopher sees anything that he does not like, he says, it is a particular way of telling a lie. It is saying that the act ought to be done or may be done, when *in truth* it ought not to be done.—(chap. ii.)

To this Dr. Whewell thinks it a sufficient answer to call it extravagant ridicule, and to ask, "Who ever asserted that he approved or disapproved of actions merely because he found himself disposed to do so, and that this was reason sufficient in itself for his moral judgments?" Dr. Whewell will find that this by no means disposes of Bentham's doctrine. Bentham did not mean that people "ever asserted" that they approved or condemned actions only because they felt disposed to do so. He meant that they do it without asserting it: that they find certain feelings of approbation and disapprobation in themselves, take for granted that these feelings are the right ones, and when called on to say anything in justification of their approbation or disapprobation, produce phrases which mean nothing but the fact of the approbation or disapprobation itself. If the hearer or reader feels in the same way, the phrases pass muster; and a great part of all the ethical reasoning in books and in the world is of this sort. All this is not only true, but cannot consistently be denied by those who, like Dr. Whewell, consider the moral feelings as their own justification. Dr. Whewell will doubtless say that the feelings they appeal to are not their own individually, but a part of universal human nature. Nobody denies that they say so; a feeling of liking or aversion to an action, confined to an individual, would have no chance of being accepted as a reason. The appeal is always to something which is assumed to belong to all mankind. But it is not of much consequence whether the feeling which is set up as its own standard is the feeling of an individual human being, or of a multitude. A feeling is not proved to be right, and exempted from the necessity of justifying itself, because the writer or speaker is not only conscious of it in himself, but expects to find it in other people, because, instead of saying "I" he says "you and I." If it is alleged that the intuitive school require, as an authority for the feeling, that it should *in fact* be universal, we deny it. They assume the utmost latitude of arbitrarily determining whose votes deserve to be counted. They either ignore the existence of dissentients, or leave them out of the account, on the pretext that they have the feeling which they deny having or, if not, that they ought to have it. This falsification of the universal suffrage which is ostensibly appealed to is not confined, as is often asserted, to cases in which the only dissentients are barbarous tribes. The same measure is dealt out to whole ages and nations, the most conspicuous for the cultivation and development of their mental faculties, and to individuals among the best and wisest of their respective countries. The explanation of the matter is the inability of persons in general to conceive that feelings of right and wrong which have been deeply implanted in their minds by the teaching they have from infancy received from all around them, can be sincerely thought by any one else to be mistaken or misplaced. This is the mental infirmity which Bentham's philosophy tends especially to correct, and Dr. Whewell's to perpetuate. Things which were really believed by all mankind, and for which all were convinced that they had the unequivocal evidence of their senses, have been proved to be false: as that the sun rises and sets. Can immunity from similar error be claimed for the moral feelings? when all experience shows that those feelings are eminently artificial and the product of culture; that, even when reasonable, they are no more spontaneous than the growth of corn and wine (which are quite as natural), and that the most senseless and pernicious feelings can as easily be raised to the utmost intensity by inculcation, as hemlock and thistles could be reared to luxuriant growth by sowing them instead of wheat. Bentham, therefore, did not judge too severely a kind of ethics whereby any implanted sentiment which is tolerably general may be erected into a moral law, binding, under penalties, on all mankind. The contest between the morality which appeals to an external standard and that which grounds itself on internal conviction, is the contest of progressive morality against stationary—of reason and argument against the deification of mere opinion and habit. The doctrine that the existing order of things is the natural order, and that, being natural, all innovation upon it is criminal, is as vicious in morals as it is now at last admitted to be in physics, and in society and government.

Let us now consider Dr. Whewell's objections to utility as the foundation of ethics.

Let it be taken for granted as a proposition which is true, if the terms which it involves be duly understood, that actions are right and virtuous in proportion as they promote the happiness of mankind, the actions being considered upon the whole, and with regard to all their consequences. Still, I say, we cannot make this truth the basis of morality, for two reasons: first, we cannot calculate all the consequences of any action, and thus cannot estimate the degree in which it promotes human happiness; second, happiness is derived from moral elements, and therefore we cannot properly derive morality from happiness. The calculable happiness resulting from actions cannot determine their virtue: first, because the resulting happiness is not calculable; and secondly, because the virtue is one of the things which determine the resulting happiness.—(p. 210.)

The first of these arguments is an irrelevant truism. "We cannot calculate *all* the consequences of any action." If Dr. Whewell can point out any department of human affairs in which we can do *all* that would be desirable, he will have found something new. But because we cannot foresee everything, is there no such thing as foresight? Does Dr. Whewell mean to say that no estimate can be formed of consequences which can be any guide for our conduct, unless we can calculate *all* consequences? that because we cannot predict every effect which may follow from a person's death, we cannot know that the liberty of murder would be destructive to human happiness? Dr. Whewell, in his zeal against the morality of consequences, commits the error of proving too much. Whether morality is or is not a question of consequences, he cannot deny that prudence is; and if there is such a thing as prudence, it is because the consequences of actions *can* be calculated. Prudence, indeed, depends on a calculation of the consequences of individual actions, while for the establishment of moral rules it is only necessary to calculate the consequences of classes of actions—a much easier matter. It is certainly a very effectual way of proving that morality does not depend on expediency, to maintain that there is no such thing as expediency—that we have no means of knowing whether anything is expedient or not. Unless Dr. Whewell goes this length, to what purpose is what he says about the uncertainty of consequences? Uncertain or certain, we are able to guide ourselves by them, otherwise human life could not exist. And there is hardly any one concerned in the business of life who has not daily to decide questions of expediency far more knotty than those which Dr. Whewell so coolly pronounces to be insoluble.

But let us examine more closely what Dr. Whewell finds to say for the proposition that "if we ask whether a given action will increase or diminish the total amount of human happiness, it is impossible to answer with any degree of certainty."

Take ordinary cases. I am tempted to utter a flattering falsehood: to gratify some sensual desire contrary to ordinary moral rules. How shall I determine, on the greatest happiness principle, whether the act is virtuous, or the contrary? In the first place, the direct effect of each act is to give pleasure, to another by flattery, to myself by sensual gratification; and pleasure is the material of happiness, in the scheme we are now considering. But by the flattering lie I promote falsehood, which is destructive of confidence and so of human comfort. Granted that I do this in some degree—although I may easily say that I shall never allow myself to speak falsely, except when it will give pleasure, and thus I may maintain that I shall not shake confidence in any case in which it is of any value. But granted that I do in some degree shake the general fabric of mutual human confidence by my flattering lie—still the question remains, *how much* I do this; whether in such a degree as to overbalance the pleasure, which is the primary and direct consequence of the act. How small must be the effect of my solitary act upon the whole scheme of human action and habit! how clear and decided is the direct effect of increasing the happiness of my hearer! And in the same way we may reason concerning the sensual gratification. Who will know it? Who will be influenced by it of those who do know it? What appreciable amount of pain will it produce in its consequences, to balance the palpable pleasure which, according to our teachers, is the only real good? It appears to me that it is impossible to answer these questions in any way which will prove, on these principles, mendacious flattery and illegitimate sensuality, to be vicious and immoral. They may possibly produce, take in all their effects, a balance of evil, but if they do, it is by some process which we cannot trace with any clearness, and the result is one which we cannot calculate with any certainty or even probability; and therefore, on this account, because the resulting evil of such falsehood and sensuality is not calculable or appreciable, we cannot, by calculation of resulting evil, show falsehood and sensuality to be vices. And the like is true of other vices; and, on this ground, the construction of a scheme of morality on Mr. Bentham's plan is plainly impossible.—(p. 211.)

Dr. Whewell supposes his self-deceiving utilitarian to be very little master of his own principles. If the effect of a "solitary act upon the whole scheme of human action and habit" is small, the addition which the accompanying pleasure makes to the general mass of human happiness is small likewise. So small, in the great majority of cases, are both, that we have no scales to weigh them against each other, taken singly. We must look at them multiplied and in large masses. The portion of the tendencies of an action which belong to it not individually but as a violation of a general rule, are as certain and as calculable as any other consequences; only they must be examined not in the individual case, but in classes of cases. Take, for example, the case of murder. There are many persons to kill whom would be to remove men who are a cause of no good to any human being, of cruel physical and moral suffering to several, and whose whole influence tends to increase the mass of unhappiness and vice. Were such a man to be assassinated, the balance of traceable consequences would be greatly in favor of the act. The counter-consideration, on the principle of utility, is that, unless persons were punished for killing and taught not to kill, that if it were thought allowable for any one to put to death at pleasure any human being whom he believes that the world would be well rid of, nobody's life would be safe. To this Dr. Whewell answers:

How does it appear that the evil, that is, the pain, arising from violating a general rule once, is too great to be over-balanced by the pleasurable consequences of that single violation? The actor says, I acknowledge the general rule—I do not deny its value; but I do not intend that this one act should be drawn into consequence.—(p. 212.)

But it does not depend on him whether or not it shall be drawn into consequence. If one person may break through the rule on his own judgment, the same liberty cannot be refused to others and, since no one could rely on the rule's being observed, the rule would cease to exist. If a hundred infringements would produce all the mischief implied in the abrogation of the rule, a hundredth part of that mischief must be debited to each one of the infringements, though we may not be able to trace it home individually. And this hundredth part will generally far outweigh any good expected to arise from the individual act. We say generally, not universally, for the admission of exceptions to rules is a necessity equally felt in all systems of morality. To take an obvious instance, the rule against homicide, the rule against deceiving, the rule against taking advantage of superior physical strength, and various other important moral rules, are suspended against enemies in the field, and partially against malefactors in private life; in each case, suspended as far as is required by the peculiar nature of the case. That the moralities arising from the special circumstances of the action may be so important as to overrule those arising from the class of acts to which it belongs, perhaps to take it out of the category of virtues into that of crimes, or *vice versa*, is a liability common to all ethical systems.

And here it may be observed that Dr. Whewell, in his illustration drawn from flattering lies, gives to the side he advocates a color of rigid adherence to principle, which the fact does not bear out. Is none of the intercourse of society carried on by those who hold the common opinions, by means of what is here meant by "flattering lies"? Does no one of Dr. Whewell's way of thinking say, or allow it to be thought, that he is glad to see a visitor whom he wishes away? Does he never ask acquaintances or relatives to stay when he would prefer them to go, or invite them when he hopes that they will refuse? Does he never show any interest in persons and things he cares nothing for, or send people away believing in his friendly feeling, to whom his real feeling is indifference or even dislike? Whether these things are right, we are not now going to discuss. For our part, we think that flattery should be only permitted to those who can flatter without lying, as all persons of sympathizing feelings and quick perceptions can. At all events, the existence of exceptions to moral rules is no stumbling-block peculiar to the principle of utility. The essential is that the exception should be itself a general rule, so that, being of definite extent, and not leaving the expediencies to the partial judgment of the agent in the individual case, it may not shake the stability of the wider rule in the cases to which the reason of the exception does not extend. This is an ample foundation for "the construction of a scheme of morality." With respect to the means of inducing people to conform in their actions to the scheme so formed, the utilitarian system depends, like all other schemes of morality, on the external motives supplied by law and opinion, and the internal feelings produced by education or reason. It is thus no worse off in this respect than any other scheme—we might rather say, much better; inasmuch as people are likely to be more willing to conform to rules when a reason is given for them.

Dr. Whewell's second argument against the happiness principle is that the morality of actions cannot depend on the happiness they produce, because the happiness depends on the morality.

Why should a man be truthful and just? Because acts of veracity and justice, even if they do not produce immediate gratification to him and his friends in other ways (and it may easily be that they do not), at least produce pleasure in this way, that they procure him his own approval and that of all good men. To us this language is intelligible and significant, but the Benthamite must analyze it further. What does it mean according to him? A man's own approval of his act means that he thinks it virtuous. And therefore the matter stands thus. He (being a Benthamite) thinks it virtuous because it gives him pleasure, and it gives him pleasure because he thinks it virtuous. This is a vicious circle, quite as palpable as any of those in which Mr. Bentham is so fond of representing his adversaries as revolving. And in like manner with regard to the approval of others. The action is virtuous, says the Benthamite, because it produces pleasure, namely, the pleasure arising from the approval of neighbors; they approve it and think it virtuous, he also says, because it gives pleasure. The virtue depends upon the pleasure, the pleasure depends upon the virtue. Here again is a circle from which there is no legitimate egress. We may grant that, taking into account all the elements of happiness—the pleasures of self-approval—of peace of mind and harmony within us, and of the approval of others—of the known sympathy of all good men—we may grant that, including these elements, virtue always does produce an overbalance of happiness; but then we cannot make this moral truth the basis of morality, because we cannot extricate the happiness and the virtue the one from the other, so as to make the first, the happiness, the foundation of the second, the virtue.—(p. 215.)

In Dr. Whewell's first argument against utility, he was obliged to assert that it is impossible for human beings to know that some actions are useful and others hurtful. In the present, he forgets against what principle he is combating, and draws out an elaborate argument against something else. What he now appears to be contending against is the doctrine (whether really held by any one or not) that the test of morality is the greatest happiness of the agent himself. It argues total ignorance of Bentham, to represent him as saying that an action is virtuous because it produces "the approbation of neighbors," and as making so "fluctuating" a thing as "public opinion," and such a "loose and wide abstraction as education," the "basis of morality." When Bentham talks of public opinion in connection with morality, he is not talking of the "basis of morality" at all. He was the last person to found the morality of actions upon anybody's opinion of them. He founded it upon facts, namely, upon the observed tendencies of the actions. Nor did he ever dream of defining morality to be the self-interest of the agent. His "greatest-happiness principle" was the greatest happiness of mankind, and of all sensitive beings. When he talks of education, and of "the popular or moral sanction," meaning the opinion of our fellow-creatures, it is not as constituents or tests of virtue, but as *motives* to it, as means of making the self-interest of the individual *accord* with the greatest happiness principle.*

---

* It is curious that while Dr. Whewell here confounds the Happiness theory of Morals with the theory of Motives sometimes called the Selfish System, and attacks the latter as Bentham's, under the name of the former, Dr. Whewell himself, in his larger work, adopts the Selfish theory. Happiness, he says (meaning, as he explains, our own happiness), is "our being's end and aim"; we cannot desire anything else unless by identifying it with our happiness.—(*Elements,* i. 359.) To this we should have nothing to object, if by identification was meant that what we desire unselfishly must first, by a mental process, become an actual part of what we seek as our own happiness; that the good of others becomes our pleasure because we have learnt to find pleasure in it; this is, we think, the true philosophical account of the matter. But we do not understand this to be Dr. Whewell's meaning; for, in an argument to prove that there is no virtue without religion, he says that religion alone can assure us of the identity of happiness with duty. Now, if the happiness connected with duty were the happiness we find *in* our duty, self-consciousness would give us a full

Dr. Whewell's remark, therefore, that the approval of our fellow creatures, presupposing moral ideas, cannot be the foundation of morality, has no application against Bentham, nor against the principle of utility. It may, however, be pertinently remarked that the moral ideas which this approval presupposes are no other than those of utility and hurtfulness. There is no great stretch of hypothesis in supposing that, in proportion as mankind are aware of the tendencies of actions to produce happiness or misery, they will like and commend the first, abhor and reprobate the second. How these feelings of natural complacency and natural dread and aversion directed towards actions come to assume the peculiar character of what we term *moral* feelings is not a question of ethics but of metaphysics, and very fit to be discussed in its proper place. Bentham did not concern himself with it. He left it to other thinkers. If sufficed him that the perceived influence of actions on human happiness is cause enough, both in reason and in fact, for strong feelings of favor to some actions and of hatred towards others. From the sympathetic reaction of these feelings in the imagination and self-consciousness of the agent naturally arise the more complex feelings of self-approbation and self-reproach or, to avoid all disputed questions, we will merely say of satisfaction and dissatisfaction with ourselves. All this must be admitted, whatever else may be denied. Whether the greatest happiness is the principle of morals or not, people do desire their own happiness, and do consequently like the conduct in other people which they think promotes it, and dislike that which visibly endangers it. This is absolutely all that Bentham postulates. Grant this, and you have his popular sanction and its reaction on the agent's own mind, two influences tending, in proportion to mankind's enlightenment, to keep the conduct of each in the line which promotes the general happiness.

---

account of this, without religion. The happiness, therefore, which Dr. Whewell means, must consist, not in the thing itself, but in a reward appended to it; and when he says that there can be no morality unless we believe that happiness is identical with duty, and that we cannot believe this apart from "the belief in God's government of the world," he must mean that no one would act virtuously unless he believed that God would reward him for it. In Dr. Whewell's view of morality, therefore, disinterestedness has no place.

Bentham thinks that there is no other true morality than this, and that the so-called moral sentiments, whatever their origin or composition, should be trained to act in this direction only. And Dr. Whewell's attempt to find anything illogical or incoherent in this theory only proves that he does not yet understand it.

Dr. Whewell puts the last hand to his supposed refutation of Bentham's principle by what he thinks a crushing *reductio ad absurdum*. The reader might make a hundred guesses before discovering what this is. We have not yet got over our astonishment, not at Bentham, but at Dr. Whewell. See, he says, to what consequences your "greatest-happiness principle" leads! Bentham says that it is as much a moral duty to regard the pleasures and pains of other animals as those of human beings. We cannot resist quoting the admirable passage which Dr. Whewell cites from Bentham, with the most *naïf* persuasion that everybody will regard it as reaching the last pitch of paradoxical absurdity.

Under the Gentoo and Mahometan religion, the interests of the rest of the animal kingdom seem to have met with some attention. Why have they not, universally, with as much as those of human creatures, allowance made for the difference in point of sensibility? Because the laws that are, have been the work of mutual fear, a sentiment which the less rational animals have not had the same means as man has of turning to account. Why ought they not? No reason can be given. The day may come when the rest of the animal creation may acquire those rights which never could have been withholden from them but by the hand of tyranny. It may come one day to be recognized that the number of the legs, the villosity of the skin, or the termination of the *os sacrum*, are reasons insufficient for abandoning a sensitive being to the caprice of a tormentor. What else is it that should trace the insuperable line? Is it the faculty of reason, or perhaps the faculty of discourse? But a full-grown horse or dog is beyond comparison a more rational, as well as a more conversable animal, than an infant of a day, a week, or even a month old. But suppose the case were otherwise, what would it avail? The question is not can they reason? nor can they speak? but can they suffer?

This noble anticipation, in 1780, of the better morality of which a first dawn has been seen in the laws enacted nearly fifty years afterwards against cruelty to animals, is in Dr. Whewell's eyes the finishing proof that the morality of happiness is absurd!

The pleasures of animals are elements of a very different order from the pleasures of man. We are bound to endeavor to augment the pleasures of men, not only because they are pleasures, but because they are human pleasures. We are bound to men by the universal tie of humanity, of human brotherhood. We have no such tie to animals.

This then is Dr. Whewell's noble and disinterested ideal of virtue. Duties, according to him, are only duties of ourselves and our like.

We are to be *humane* to them, because we are *human*, not because we and they alike feel *animal* pleasures. . . . The morality which depends upon the increase of pleasure alone would make it our duty to increase the pleasure of pigs or of geese rather than that of men, if we were sure that the pleasures we could give them were greater than the pleasures of men. . . . It is not only not an obvious, but to most persons not a tolerable doctrine, that we may sacrifice the happiness of men provided we can in that way produce an overplus of pleasure to cats, dogs, and hogs.— (pp. 223–5.)

It is "to most persons" in the Slave States of America not a tolerable doctrine that we may sacrifice any portion of the happiness of white men for the sake of a greater amount of happiness to black men. It would have been intolerable five centuries ago "to most persons" among the feudal nobility, to hear it asserted that the greatest pleasure or pain of a hundred serfs ought not to give way to the smallest of a nobleman. According to the standard of Dr. Whewell, the slavemasters and the nobles were right. They too felt themselves "bound" by a "tie of brotherhood" to the white men and to the nobility, and felt no such tie to the Negroes and serfs. And if a feeling on moral subjects is right because it is natural, their feeling was justifiable. Nothing is more natural to human beings nor, up to a certain point in cultivation, more universal, than to estimate the pleasures and pains of others as deserving of regard exactly in proportion to their likeness to ourselves. These superstitions of selfishness had the char-

acteristics by which Dr. Whewell recognizes his moral rules,
and his opinion on the rights of animals shows that, in this
case at least, he is consistent. We are perfectly willing to
stake the whole question on this one issue. Granted that any
practice causes more pain to animals than it gives pleasure
to man, is that practice moral or immoral? And if, exactly
in proportion as human beings raise their heads out of the
slough of selfishness, they do not with one voice answer
"immoral," let the morality of the principle of utility be for
ever condemned.

There cannot be a fitter transition than this subject affords
from the Benthamic standard of ethics to that of Dr. Whewell.
It is not enough to object to the morality of utility. It is necessary also to show that there is another and a better morality.
This is what Dr. Whewell proposes to himself in his *Introductory Lecture,* and in the whole of his previous work,
Elements of Morality. We shall now, therefore, proceed to
examine Dr. Whewell's achievements as the constructor of a
scientific foundation for the theory of morals.

"The moral rule of human action," Dr. Whewell says, is that
"we must do what is right." (*Lectures*, p. xi.) Here, at all
events, is a safe proposition, since to deny it would be a
contradiction in terms. But what is meant by "right?" According to Dr. Whewell, "what we must do." This, he says,
is the very definition of right.

> The definition of *rightful*, or of the adjective *right*, is, I
> conceive, contained in the maxim which I have already
> quoted as proceeding from the general voice of mankind;
> namely this, that we must do what is right at whatever cost.
> That an action is right, is a reason for doing it which is
> paramount to all other reasons, and overweighs them all
> when they are on the contrary side. It is painful, but it is
> right; therefore we must do it. It is a loss, but it is right;
> therefore we must do it. It is unkind, but it is right; there-
> fore we must do it. These are self-evident [he might have
> said identical] propositions. That a thing is right, is a *su-
> preme* reason for doing it. *Right* implies this supreme, un-
> conquerable reason, and does this especially and exclusively.
> No other word does imply such an irresistible cogency in its
> effect, except in so far as it involves the same notion. What
> we *ought* to do, what we *should* do, that we *must* do,
> though it bring pain and loss. But why? *Because* it is *right*.

The expressions all run together in their meaning. And this *supreme* rule, that we must do what is right, is also the *moral* rule of human action. —(pp. x–xi.)

Right means that which we *must* do, and the rule of action is that we must do what is right, that we must do that which we must do. This we will call vicious circle the first. But let us not press hardly on Dr. Whewell at this stage; perhaps he only means that the foundation of morals is the conviction that there is *something* which we must do at all risks, and he admits that we have still to find what this something is. "What *is* right, what it is that we ought to do, we must have some means of determining, in order to complete our moral scheme." (p. xi.)

Attempting then to pick out Dr. Whewell's leading propositions, and exhibit them in connection, we find, first, that "the supreme rule of human action, Rightness," ought to control the desires and affections, or otherwise that these are "to be regulated so that they may be right." (pp. xii–xiii.) This does not help towards showing what *is* right.

But secondly, we come to a "condition which is obviously requisite." In order that the desires and affections which relate to "other men" may be right, "they must conform to this primary and universal condition, that they do not violate the *rights* of others. This condition may not be sufficient, but it is necessary." (p. xiii.)

This promises something. In tracing to its elements the idea of Right, the adjective, we are led to the prior, and it is to be presumed more elementary idea, of Rights, the substantive. But now, what are rights? and how came they to be rights?

Before answering these questions, Dr. Whewell gives a classification of rights "commonly recognized among men." He says they are of five sorts, "those of person, property, family, state, and contract." (p. xv.) But how do we discover that they are rights? and what is meant by calling them rights? Much to our surprise, Dr. Whewell refers us, on both these points, to the law. And he asks, "in what manner do we rise from mere legal rights to moral rightness?" and replies, "we do so in virtue of this principle: that the supreme rule of man's actions must be a rule which has authority over the whole of man, over his intentions as well as his actions, over

his affections, his desires, his habits, his thoughts, his wishes."
We must not only not violate the rights of others, but we
must not desire to violate them. "And thus we rise from
legal obligation to moral duty, from legality to virtue, from
blamelessness in the forum of man to innocence in the court
of conscience."

And this Dr. Whewell actually gives as his scheme of morality. His rule of right is, to infringe no rights conferred by
the law, and to cherish no dispositions which could make us
desire such infringements! According to this, the early Christians, the religious reformers, the founders of all free governments, Clarkson, Wilberforce, and all enemies of the rights of
slaveowners, must be classed among the wicked. If this is Dr.
Whewell's morality, it is the very Hobbism which he repro-
bates, and this in its worst sense. But though Dr. Whewell
says that this is his morality, he presently unsays it.

> Our morality is not derived from the special commands
> of existing laws, but from the fact that laws exist, and from
> our classification of their subjects. Personal safety, prop-
> erty, contracts, family and civil relations, are everywhere
> the subjects of law, and are everywhere protected by law;
> therefore we judge that these things must be the subjects of
> morality and must be reverently regarded by morality. But
> we are not thus bound to approve of all the special appoint-
> ments with regard to those subjects, which may exist at a
> given time in the laws of a given country. On the contrary,
> we may condemn the laws as being contrary to morality.
> We cannot frame a morality without recognizing property,
> and property exists through law; but yet the law of prop-
> erty, in a particular country, may be at variance with that
> moral purpose for which, in our eyes, laws exist. Law is
> the foundation and necessary condition of justice, but yet
> laws may be unjust and when unjust ought to be changed.
> —(p. xvii.)

The practical enormities consequent on Dr. Whewell's theory are thus got rid of, but when these are gone, there is
nothing of the theory left. He undertook to explain how we
may know what is right. It appeared at first that he was about
to give a criterion, when he said that it is not right to violate
legal rights. According to this, when we want to know what
is right, we have to consult the law, and see what rights it
recognizes. But now it seems that these rights may be contrary

to right, and all we can be sure of is that it is right there should be rights of some sort. And we learn that, after all, it is for a "moral purpose" that in Dr. Whewell's opinion "laws exist." So that while the meaning of *ought* is that we ought to respect rights, it is a previous condition that these rights must be such as *ought* to be respected. Morality must conform to law, but law must first conform to morality. This is vicious circle the second. Dr. Whewell has broken out of the first; he has made, this time, a larger sweep; the curve he describes is wider, but it still returns into itself.

An adherent of "dependent morality" would say that, instead of deriving right from rights, we must have a rule of right before it can be decided what ought to be rights, and that, both in law and in morals, the rights which ought to exist are those which for the general happiness it is expedient should exist. And Dr. Whewell anticipates that some one may even do him what he thinks the injustice of supposing this to be his opinion. He introduces an objector as saying that "by making our morality begin from rights, we really do found it upon expediency, notwithstanding our condemnation of systems so founded. For, it may be said, rights such as property exist only because they are expedient." Dr. Whewell hastens to repel this imputation, and here is his theory. "We reply, as before, that rights are founded on the whole nature of man, in such a way that he cannot have a human existence without them. He is a moral being, and must have rights, *because morality cannot exist where rights are not.*" Was ever an unfortunate metaphysician driven into such a corner? We wanted to know what morality is, and Dr. Whewell said that it is conforming to rights. We ask how he knows that there are rights, and he answers, because otherwise there could be no morality. This is vicious circle the third, and the most wonderful of the three. The Indians placed their elephant on the back of a tortoise, but they did not at the same time place the tortoise on the back of the elephant.

Dr. Whewell has failed in what it was impossible to succeed in. Every attempt to dress up an appeal to intuition in the forms of reasoning must break down in the same manner. The system must, from the conditions of the case, revolve in a circle. If morality is not to gravitate to any end, but to hang self-balanced in space, it is useless attempting to suspend one point of it upon another point. The fact of moral rules supposes a certain assemblage of ideas. It is to no purpose detaching these ideas one from another, and saying that one of them must exist because another does. Press the moralist a step farther, and he can only say that the other must exist because of the first. The house must have a center because it has wings, and wings because it has a center. But the question was about the whole house, and how it comes to exist. It would be much simpler to say plainly, that it exists because it exists. This is what Dr. Whewell is in the end obliged to come to, and he would have saved himself a great deal of bad logic, if he had begun with it.*

So much as to the existence of moral rules: now as to what they are.

> We do not rest our rules of action upon the tendency of actions to produce the happiness of others, or of mankind in general, because we cannot solve a problem so difficult as to determine which of two courses of human action will produce the greatest amount of human happiness, and we see a simpler and far more satisfactory mode of deducing such rules: namely, by considering that there must be such rules, that they must be rules for man, for man living among men, and for the whole of man's being. Since we are thus led directly to moral rules, by the consideration of the internal condition of man's being, we cannot think it wise to turn away from this method, and to try to determine such rules by reference to an obscure and unmanageable external condition, the amount of happiness produced.—(p. xx.)

If these were not Dr. Whewell's own words, we should expect to be charged, as he charges Bentham, with caricature. This is given as a scientific statement of the proper mode of

---

* In Dr. Whewell's larger work, we find him resorting, after all, to an "external object" as the ultimate ground for acknowledging any moral rules whatever. He there says that "the reason for doing what is absolutely right is that it is the will of God, through whom the condition and destination of mankind are what they are."— (*Elements*, i. 225.) In the *Lectures*, however, he admits that this renders nugatory the ascribing any moral attributes to God. "If we make holiness, justice, and purity the mere result of God's commands, we can no longer find any force in the declaration that God is holy, just, and pure, since the assertion then becomes merely an empty identical proposition."—(p. 58.) We hope that this indicates a change of opinion since the publication of the earlier work.

discovering what are the rules of morality! We are to "deduce such rules" from four considerations. First, "that there must be such rules"; a necessary preliminary, certainly. If we are to build a wall, it is because it has been previously decided that there must be a wall. But we must know what the wall is for, what end it is intended to serve, or we shall not know what sort of wall is required. What end are moral rules intended to serve? No end, according to Dr. Whewell. They do not exist for the sake of an end. To have them is part of man's nature, like (it is Dr. Whewell's own illustration) the circulation of the blood. It is now then to be inquired *what* rules are part of our nature. This is to be discovered from three things: that they must be "rules for man, for man living among men, and for the whole of man's being." This is only saying over again, in a greater number of words, what we want, not how we are to find it. First, they must be "rules for man"; but we are warned not to suppose that this means for man's benefit, it only means that they are for man to obey. This leaves us exactly where we were before. Next, they are for "man living among men," that is, for the conduct of man to men; but *how* is man to conduct himself to men? Thirdly, they are "for the whole of man's being"; that is, according to Dr. Whewell's explanation, they are for the regulation of our desires as well as of our actions; but what we wanted to know was, *how* we are to regulate our desires and our actions? Of the four propositions given as premises from which all moral rules are to be deduced, not one points to any difference between one kind of moral rules and another. Whether the rule is to love or to hate our neighbor, it will equally answer all Dr. Whewell's conditions. These are the premises which are more "simple and satisfactory" than such "obscure and unmanageable" propositions, so utterly impossible to be assured of, as that some actions are favorable, and others injurious, to human happiness! Try a parallel case. Let it be required to find the principles of the art of navigation. Bentham says we must look to an "external end": getting from place to place on the water. No, says Dr. Whewell, there is a "simpler and more satisfactory" mode, viz. to consider that there must be such an art, that it must be for a ship, for a ship at sea, and for all the parts of a ship. Would Dr. Whewell prevail on any one to suppose that these considerations made it unnecessary to consider, with Bentham, what a ship is intended to do?

This account is all we get from Dr. Whewell, in the *Lectures*, of the mode of discovering and recognizing the rules of morality. But perhaps he succeeds better in doing the thing than in explaining how it ought to be done. At all events, having written two volumes of *Elements of Morality*, he must have performed this feat, either well or ill, he must have found a way of "deducing moral rules." We will now, therefore, dismiss Dr. Whewell's generalities, and try to estimate his method, not by what he says about it, but by what we see him doing when he carries it into practice.

We turn, then, to his *Elements of Morality*, and to the third chapter of that work, which is entitled "Moral Rules Exist Necessarily." And here we at once find something well calculated to surprise us. That moral rules must exist, was, it may be remembered, the first of Dr. Whewell's four fundamental axioms, and has been presented hitherto as a law of human nature, requiring no proof. It must puzzle some of his pupils to find him here proving it, and still more, to find him proving it from utility.

> In enumerating and describing, as we have done, certain desires as among the most powerful springs of human action, we have stated that man's life is scarcely tolerable if these desires are not in some degree gratified; that man cannot be at all satisfied without some security in such gratification; that without property, which gratifies one of these desires, man's free agency cannot exist; that without marriage, which gratifies another, there can be no peace, comfort, tranquillity, or order. And the same may be said of all those springs of actions which we enumerated as mental desires. Without some provision for the tranquil gratification of these desires, society is disturbed, unbalanced, painful. The gratification of such desires must be a part of the order of the society. There must be rules which direct the course and limits of such gratification. Such rules are necessary for the peace of society.—(*Elements*, i. 32.)

This is a very different mode of treating the subject from that which we observed in the *Lectures*. We are now among reasons; good or bad they may be, but still reasons. Moral rules are here spoken of as means to an end. We now hear of the peace and comfort of society, of making man's life tolerable, of the satisfaction and gratification of human beings, of preventing a disturbed and painful state of society. This is utility—this is pleasure and pain. When real reasons are wanted, the repudiated "happiness principle" is always the resource. It is true, this is soon followed by a recurrence to the old topics, of the necessity of rules "for the action of man as man," and the impossibility to "conceive man as man without conceiving him as subject to rules." But any meaning it is possible to find in these phrases (which is not much) is all reflected from the utilitarian reasons given just before. Rules are necessary because mankind would have no security for any of the things which they value, for anything which gives them pleasure or shields them from pain, unless they could rely on one another for doing, and in particular for abstaining from, certain acts. And it is true that man could not be conceived "as man," that is, with the average human intelligence, if he were unable to perceive so obvious an utility.

Almost all the *generalia* of moral philosophy prefixed to the *Elements* are in like manner derived from utility. For example: that the desires, until subjected to general rules, bring mankind into conflict and opposition; but that, when general rules are established, the feelings which gather round these "are sources not of opposition, but of agreement"; that they "tend to make men unanimous, and that such rules with regard to the affections and desires as tend to control the repulsive and confirm the attractive forces which operate in human society, such as tend to unite men, to establish concord, unanimity, sympathy, agree with that which is the character of moral rules." (i. 35). This is Benthamism—even approaching to Fourierism.

And again, in attempting a classification and definition of virtues, and a parallel one of duties corresponding to them, the definitions of both the one and the other are deduced from utility. After classing virtues under the several heads of benevolence, justice, truth, purity, and order, Benevolence is defined as "desire of the good of all men"; and in a wider sense, as the "absence of all the affections which tend to separate men, and the aggregate of the affections which unite them" (i. 137–8.), Justice, as "the desire that each person should have his own." (p. 138.) Truth is defined "an agreement of the verbal expression with the thought," and is declared to be a duty because "lying and deceit tend to separate and disunite men, and to make all actions implying mutual dependence, that is, all social action and social life, impossible."

(pp. 138–9.) Purity is defined "the control of the appetites by the moral sentiments and the reason." Order, as a conformity of our internal dispositions to the laws and to moral rules (why not rather to good laws, and good moral rules?) All these definitions, though very open to criticism in detail, are in principle utilitarian.* Though Dr. Whewell will not recognize the promotion of happiness as the ultimate principle, he deduces his secondary principles from it, and supports his propositions by utilitarian reasons as far as they will go. He is chiefly distinguished from utilitarian moralists of the more superficial kind, by this, that he ekes out his appeals to utility with appeals to "our idea of man as man"; and when reasons fail, or are not sufficiently convincing, then "all men think," or "we cannot help feeling," serves as a last resort, and closes the discussion.

Of this hybrid character is the ethics of Dr. Whewell's *Elements of Morality*. And in this he resembles all other writers of the intuitive school of morals. They are none of them frankly and consistently intuitive. To use a happy expression of Bentham in a different case, they draw from a double fountain—utility and internal conviction, the tendencies of actions and the feelings with which mankind regard them. This is not a matter of choice with these writers, but of necessity. It arises from the nature of the morality of internal conviction. Utility, as a standard, is capable of being carried out singly and consistently; a moralist can deduce from it his whole system of ethics, without calling to his assistance any foreign principle. It is not so with one who relies on moral intuition,

---

* The enumeration of duties does not always follow accurately the definition of the corresponding virtues. For example, the definition of purity is one which suits temperance, "the control of the appetites by the moral sentiments and the reason"; but the scheme of duties set forth under this head is rather as if the definition had been "the conformity of the appetites to the moral opinions and customs of the country." It is remarkable that a writer who uses the word purity so much out of its common meaning as to make it synonymous with temperance, should charge Bentham (*Lectures*, p. 208), because he employs the word in another of its acknowledged senses, with arbitrarily altering its signification. Bentham understands by the purity of a pleasure, its freedom from admixture of pain; as we speak of pure gold, pure water, pure truth, of things purely beneficial or purely mischievous, meaning, in each case, freedom from alloy with any other ingredient.

for where will he find his moral intuitions? How many ethical propositions can be enumerated, of which the most reckless assertor will venture to affirm that they have the adhesion of all mankind? Dr. Whewell declares unhesitatingly that the moral judgment of mankind, when it is unanimous, must be right. "What are universally held as virtues must be dispositions in conformity with this [the supreme] law; what are universally reckoned vices, must be wrong." This is saying much, when we consider the worth, in other matters nearly allied to these, of what is complimentarily called the general opinion of mankind, when we remember what groveling superstitions, what witchcraft, magic, astrology, what oracles, ghosts, what gods and demons scattered through all nature, were once universally believed in, and still are so by the majority of the human race. But where are these unanimously recognized vices and virtues to be found? Practices the most revolting to the moral feelings of some ages and nations do not incur the smallest censure from others, and it is doubtful whether there is a single virtue which is held to be a virtue by all nations, in the same sense, and with the same reservations. There are, indeed, some moralities of an utility so unmistakable, so obviously indispensable to the common purposes of life that, as general rules, mankind could no more differ about them than about the multiplication table; but even here, there is the widest difference of sentiment about the exceptions. The universal voice of mankind, so often appealed to, is universal only in its discordance. What passes for it is merely the voice of the majority or, failing that, of any large number having a strong feeling on the subject, especially if it be a feeling of which they cannot give any account, and which, as it is not consciously grounded on any reasons, is supposed to be better than reasons and of higher authority. With Dr. Whewell, a strong feeling, shared by most of those whom he thinks worth counting, is always an *ultima ratio* from which there is no appeal. He forgets that as much might have been pleaded, and in many cases might still be pleaded, in defense of the absurdest superstitions.

It seems to be tacitly supposed that however liable mankind are to be wrong in their opinions, they are generally right in their feelings, and especially in their antipathies. On the contrary, there is nothing which it is more imperative that they should be required to justify by reasons. The antipathies of mankind are mostly derived from three sources. One of these is an impression, true or false, of utility. They dislike what is painful or dangerous, or what is apparently so. These antipathies, being grounded on the "happiness principle," must be required to justify themselves by it. The second class of antipathies are against what they are taught, or imagine, to be displeasing to some visible or invisible power capable of doing them harm, and whose wrath, once kindled, may be wreaked on those who tolerated, as well as on those who committed, the offense. The third kind of antipathies, often as strong as either of the others, are directed towards mere differences of opinion, or of taste. Any of the three, when nourished by education and deriving confidence from mutual encouragement, assumes to common minds the character of a moral feeling. But to pretend that any such antipathy, were it ever so general, gives the smallest guarantee of its own justice and reasonableness, or has any claim to be binding on those who do not partake in the sentiment, is as irrational as to adduce the belief in ghosts or witches as a proof of their real existence. I am not bound to abstain from an action because another person dislikes it, however he may dignify his dislike with the name of disapprobation.

We cannot take leave of Dr. Whewell's strictures on Bentham without adverting to some observations made by him on Bentham's character as a jurist rather than as a moralist. In this capacity Dr. Whewell does more justice to Bentham, than in the department of moral philosophy. But he finds fault with him for two things: first, for not sufficiently recognizing what Dr. Whewell calls the historical element of legislation, and imagining "that to a certain extent his schemes of law might be made independent of local conditions." Dr. Whewell admits it to be part of Bentham's doctrine that different countries must to a certain extent have different laws, and is aware that he wrote an *Essay on the Influence of Time and Place in Matters of Legislation*, but thinks him wrong in maintaining that there should be a general plan, of which the details only should be modified by local circumstances, and contends that different countries require different ground-plans of legislation.

> There is in every national code of law a necessary and fundamental historical element; not a few supplementary provisions which may be added or adapted to the local circumstances after the great body of the code has been con-

structed; not a few touches of local coloring to be put in after the picture is almost painted; but an element which belongs to law from its origin, and penetrates to its roots, a part of the intimate structure, a cast in the original design. The national views of personal status, property and the modes of acquisition, bargains and the modes of concluding them, family and its consequences, government and its origin, these affect even the most universal aspects and divisions of penal offenses, these affect still more every step of the expository process which the civil law applies to rights in defining penal offenses.—(*Lectures,* p. 254.)

What Dr. Whewell designates by the obscure and misleading expression "an historical element," and accuses Bentham of paying too little regard to, is the existing opinions and feelings of the people. These may, without doubt, in some sense be called historical, as being partly the product of their previous history, but whatever attention is due to those opinions and feelings in legislation, is due to them not as matter of history, but as social forces in present being. Now Bentham, in common with all other rational persons, admitted that a legislator is obliged to have regard to the opinions and feelings of the people to be legislated for, but with this difference, that he did not look upon those opinions and feelings as affecting, in any great degree, what was desirable to be done, but only what could be done. Take one of Dr. Whewell's instances, "the national views of personal status." The "national views" may regard slavery as a legitimate condition of human beings, and Mr. Livingstone, in legislating for Louisiana, may have been obliged to recognize slavery as a fact, and to make provision for it, and for its consequences, in his code of laws; but he was bound to regard the equality of human beings as the foundation of his legislation, and the concession to the "historical element" as a matter of temporary expediency and, while yielding to the necessity, to endeavor, by all the means in his power, to educate the nation into better things. And so of the other subjects mentioned by Dr. Whewell—property, contracts, family, and government. The fact that, in any of these matters, a people prefer some particular mode of legislation, on historical grounds—that is, because they have been long used to it—is no proof of any original adaptation in it to their nature or circumstances, and goes a very little way in recommendation of it as for their benefit now. But it may be a very important element in determining what the legislator can do, and still more, the manner in which he should do it, and in both these respects Bentham allowed it full weight. What he is at issue with Dr. Whewell upon is in deeming it right for the legislator to keep before his mind an ideal of what he would do if the people for whom he made laws were entirely devoid of prejudice or accidental prepossession, while Dr. Whewell, by placing their prejudices and accidental prepossessions "at the basis of the system," enjoins legislation not in simple recognition of existing popular feelings, but in obedience to them.

The other objection made by Dr. Whewell to Bentham as a writer on legislation (for we omit the criticism on his classification of offenses, as too much a matter of detail for the present discussion) is that he does not fully recognize "the moral object of law" (p. 257). Dr. Whewell says, in phraseology which we considerably abridge, that law ought not only to preserve and gratify man, but to improve and teach him, not only to take care of him as an animal, but to raise him to a moral life. Punishment, therefore, he says, "is to be, not merely a means of preventing suffering, but is also to be a moral lesson." But Bentham, as Dr. Whewell is presently forced to admit, says the same; and in fact carries this doctrine so far as to maintain that legal punishment ought sometimes to be attached to acts for the mere purpose of stigmatizing them, and turning the popular sentiment against them. No one more than Bentham recognizes that most important but most neglected function of the legislator, the office of an instructor, both moral and intellectual. But he receives no credit for this from Dr. Whewell, except that of being false to his principles; for Dr. Whewell seems to reckon it an impertinence in anybody to recognize morality as a good, who thinks, as Bentham does, that it is a means to an end. If any one who believes that the moral sentiments should be guided by the happiness of mankind, proposes that moral sentiments, so guided, should be cultivated and fostered, Dr. Whewell treats this as a deserting of utilitarian principles, and borrowing or stealing from his.

As an example of "Bentham's attempt to exclude morality, as such, in his legislation," Dr. Whewell refers to "what he says respecting the laws of marriage, and especially in favor of a liberty of divorce by common consent." As this is the only opportunity Dr. Whewell gives his readers of comparing his mode of discussing a specific moral question with Bentham's, we shall devote a few words to it.

Having quoted from Bentham the observation that a government which interdicts divorce "takes upon itself to decide that it understands the interests of individuals better than they do themselves," Dr. Whewell answers that this is an objection to all laws; that in many other cases, "government, both in its legislation and administration, does assume that it understands the interests of individuals, *and the public interest as affected by them,* better than they do themselves." The words which we have put in italics, adroitly change the question. Government is entitled to assume that it will take better care than individuals of the public interest, but not better care of their own interest. It is one thing for the legislator to dictate to individuals what they shall do for their own advantage, and another thing to protect the interest of other persons who may be injuriously affected by their acts. Dr. Whewell's own instances suffice: "What is the meaning of restraints imposed for the sake of public health, cleanliness, and comfort? Why are not individuals left to do what they like with reference to such matters? Plainly because carelessness, ignorance, indolence, would prevent their doing what is most for their own interest."—(p. 258.) Say rather, would lead them to do what is contrary to the interest of other people. The proper object of sanitary laws is not to compel people to take care of their own health, but to prevent them from endangering that of others. To prescribe by law what they should do for their own health alone would by most people be justly regarded as something very like tyranny.

Dr. Whewell continues:

> But is Mr. Bentham ready to apply consistently the principle which he thus implies, that in such matters individuals are the best judges of their own interests? Will he allow divorce to take place whenever the two parties agree in desiring it? . . . Such a facility of divorce as this, leaves hardly any difference possible between marriage and concubinage. If a pair may separate when they please, why does the legislator take the trouble to recognize their living together?

Apply this to other cases. If a man can pay his tailor when he and his tailor choose, why does the law take the trouble to recognize them as debtor and creditor? Why recognize as partners in business, as landlords and tenants, as servants and employers, people who are not tied to each other for life?

Dr. Whewell finds what he thinks an inconsistency in Bentham's view of the subject. He thus describes Bentham's opinions:

> Marriage for life is, he [Bentham] says, the most natural marriage; if there were no laws except the ordinary law of contracts, this would be the most ordinary arrangement. So far, good. But Mr. Bentham, having carried his argument so far, does not go on with it. What conclusion are we to suppose him to intend? This arrangement would be very *general* without law, therefore the legislator should pass a law to make it *universal*? . . . No. The very next sentence is employed in showing the absurdity of making the engagement one from which the parties cannot liberate themselves by mutual consent. And there is no attempt to reduce these arguments, or their results, to a consistency.—(p. 259.)

Dr. Whewell's ideas of inconsistency seem to be peculiar. Bentham, he says, is of opinion that, in the majority of cases, it is best for the happiness of married persons that they should remain together. Is it so? (says Dr. Whewell)—then why not force them to remain together, even when it would be best for their happiness to separate?

Try again parallel cases. In choosing a profession, a sensible person will fix on one in which he will find it agreeable to remain; therefore, it should not be lawful to change a profession once chosen. A landlord, when he has a good tenant, best consults his own interest by not changing him; therefore, all tenancy should be for life. Electors who have found a good representative will probably do wisely in reelecting him; therefore, members of parliament should be irremovable.

Dr. Whewell intended to show into what errors Bentham was led by treating the question of marriage apart from "moral grounds." Yet part of his complaint is that Bentham does consider moral grounds which, according to Dr. Whewell, he has no right to do. If one married person maltreats the other to procure consent to a divorce—

> Bentham's decision is, that liberty should be allowed to the party maltreated and not to the other. . . . Now to this decision I have nothing to object; but I must remark that the view which makes it tolerable is its being a decision on

moral grounds, such as Mr. Bentham would not willingly acknowledge. The man may not take advantage of his own wrong; *that* is a maxim which quite satisfies *us*. But Mr. Bentham, who only regards wrong as harm, would, I think, find it difficult to satisfy the man that he was fairly used.

Mr. Bentham would have found it difficult to conceive that any one attempting to criticize his philosophy could know so little of its elements. Dr. Whewell wonders what the reason can be, on Bentham's principles, for not allowing a man to benefit by his own wrong. Did it never occur to him that it is to take away from the man his inducement to commit the wrong?

Finally, Dr. Whewell says, "No good rule can be established on this subject without regarding the marriage union in a moral point of view, without assuming it as one great object of the law to elevate and purify men's idea of marriage, to lead them to look upon it as an entire union of interests and feelings, enjoyments and hopes, between the two parties." We cannot agree in the doctrine that it should be an object of the law to "lead men to look upon" marriage as being what it is not. Neither Bentham nor any one who thinks with him would deny that this entire union is the completest ideal of marriage, but it is bad philosophy to speak of a relation as if it always *was* the best thing that it possibly can be, and then infer that, when it is notoriously not such, as in an immense majority of cases, and even when it is the extreme contrary, as in a considerable minority, it should nevertheless be treated exactly as if the fact corresponded with the theory. The liberty of divorce is contended for because marriages are not what Dr. Whewell says they should be looked upon as being, because a choice made by an inexperienced person, and not allowed to be corrected, cannot, except by a happy accident, realize the conditions essential to this complete union.

We give these observations not as a discussion of the question, but of Dr. Whewell's treatment of it, as part of the comparison which he invites his readers to institute between his method and that of Bentham. Were it our object to confirm the general character we have given of Dr. Whewell's philosophy by a survey in detail of the morality laid down by him, the two volumes of *Elements* afford abundant materials. We could show that Dr. Whewell not only makes no improvement on the old moral doctrines, but attempts to set up afresh several of them which have been loosened or thrown down by the stream of human progress.

Thus we find him everywhere inculcating, as one of the most sacred duties, reverence for superiors, even when personally undeserving (i. 176–7), and obedience to existing laws, even when bad. "The laws of the state are to be observed even when they enact slavery."—(i. 351.) "The morality of the individual," he says (i. 58), "depends on his not violating the law of his nation." It is not even the spirit of the law, but the letter (i. 213), to which obedience is due. The law, indeed, is accepted by Dr. Whewell as the fountain of rights, of those rights which it is the primary moral duty not to infringe. And mere custom is of almost equal authority with express enactment. Even in a matter so personal as marriage, the usage and practice of the country is to be a paramount law. "In some countries, the marriage of the child is a matter usually managed by the parents; in such cases, it is the child's duty to bring the affections, as far as possible, into harmony with the custom."—(i. 211.) "Reverence and affection" towards "the constitution of each country," he holds (ii. 204) as "one of the duties of a citizen."

Again, Dr. Whewell affirms, with a directness not usually ventured on in these days by persons of his standing and importance, that to disbelieve either a providential government of the world, or revelation, is morally criminal, for that "men are blameable in disbelieving truths after they have been promulgated, though they are ignorant without blame before the promulgation."—(ii. 91–94.) This is the very essence of religious intolerance, aggravated by the fact that, among the persons thus morally stigmatized, are notoriously included many of the best men who ever lived. He goes still further and lays down the principle of intolerance in its broad generality, saying that "the man who holds false opinions" is morally condemnable "when he has had the means of knowing the truth" (ii. 102); that it is "his duty to think rationally" (*i.e.* to think the same as Dr. Whewell); that "it is to no purpose his saying that he has done all he could to arrive at truth, since a man has never done *all he can* to arrive at truth."—(ii. 106.) If a man has never done all he can, neither has his judge done all he can, and the heretic may have more grounds for believing his opinion true, than the judge has for affirming it to be false. But the judge is on the side of received opinions, which, according to Dr. Whewell's standard, makes all right.

It is not, however, our object to criticize Dr. Whewell as a teacher of the details of morality. Our design goes no farther than to illustrate his controversy with Bentham respecting its first principle. It may, perhaps, be thought that Dr. Whewell's arguments against the philosophy of utility are too feeble to require so long a refutation. But feeble arguments easily pass for convincing, when they are on the same side as the prevailing sentiment; and readers in general are so little acquainted with that or any other system of moral philosophy, that they take the word of anybody, especially an author in repute, who professes to inform them what it is, and suppose that a doctrine must be indeed absurd, to which mere truisms are offered as a sufficient reply. It was, therefore, not unimportant to show, by a minute examination, that Dr. Whewell has misunderstood and misrepresented the philosophy of utility, and that his attempts to refute it, and to construct a moral philosophy without it, have been equally failures.

Of Liberty and Necessity

[In a letter written early in 1843 to a Robert Barclay Fox, a friend to whom a copy of his newly published *System of Logic* was being sent, Mill said, "If I could fix on any part as capable of being read with interest apart from the rest, it would be the fifth book, on Fallacies, and especially the chapter in the sixth book, on Liberty and Necessity, which is short, and in my judgment the best chapter in the two volumes." Mill expressed a similar opinion at greater length in a letter to Alexis de Tocqueville, thanking him for the flattering remarks de Tocqueville had made about the *Logic*. Writing in French, Mill said:

> Your approval of the point of view from which I have envisaged the question of human liberty is also very precious to me. I myself regard that chapter as the most important of the book; it is the faithful expression of ideas at which I arrived almost fifteen years ago, which I have never written down, but in which I can say that I have found peace, because they alone have fully satisfied in me the need to put intelligence and conscience in harmony, in resting the feeling of human responsibility on a solid intellectual base. I do not believe that any even slightly serious thinker can enjoy true tranquillity of mind and soul until he has found some satisfactory solution to this great problem. I do not wish to impose my own solution on those who are satisfied with theirs, but I believe that there are many men for whom it will be, as it has been for me, a veritable anchor of salvation.

(This letter may be found in J. P. Mayer's edition of de Tocqueville's *Oeuvres Complètes*, vol. VI, part 1, Paris, 1954, pp. 340–41.)

The chapter of which Mill speaks in these letters (Book VI, ch. ii) is here reprinted complete, in the text of the eighth (and final) edition, published in 1872. It will be of some use to the reader to have at hand Mill's definition of "action," given in Book I, ch. iii. It is as follows:

> Now what is an action? Not one thing, but a series of two things; the state of mind called a volition, followed by an

effect. The volition or intention to produce the effect, is one thing; the effect produced in consequence of the intention, is another thing; the two together constitute the action. I form the purpose of instantly moving my arm, that is a state of my mind; my arm (not being tied or paralytic) moves in obedience to my purpose, that is a physical fact, consequent on a state of mind. The intention, followed by the fact, or (if we prefer the expression) the fact when preceded and caused by the intention, is called the action of moving my arm.]

I

THE QUESTION whether the law of causality applies in the same strict sense to human actions as to other phenomena, is the celebrated controversy concerning the freedom of the will which, from at least as far back as the time of Pelagius, has divided both the philosophical and the religious world. The affirmative opinion is commonly called the doctrine of Necessity, as asserting human volitions and actions to be necessary and inevitable. The negative maintains that the will is not determined, like other phenomena, by antecedents, but determines itself, that our volitions are not, properly speaking, the effects of causes, or at least have no causes which they uniformly and implicitly obey.

I have already made it sufficiently apparent that the former of these opinions is that which I consider the true one, but the misleading terms in which it is often expressed, and the indistinct manner in which it is usually apprehended, have both obstructed its reception and perverted its influence when received. The metaphysical theory of free will, as held by philosophers (for the practical feeling of it, common in a greater or less degree to all mankind, is in no way inconsistent with the contrary theory) was invented because the supposed alternative of admitting human actions to be *necessary* was deemed inconsistent with every one's instinctive consciousness, as well as humiliating to the pride and even degrading to the moral nature of man. Nor do I deny that the doctrine, as sometimes held, is open to these imputations, for the misapprehension in which I shall be able to show that they originate unfortunately is not confined to the opponents of the doctrine, but participated in by many, perhaps we might say by most, of its supporters.

I I

Correctly conceived, the doctrine called Philosophical Necessity is simply this: that, given the motives which are present to an individual's mind, and given likewise the character and disposition of the individual, the manner in which he will act might be unerringly inferred; that if we knew the person thoroughly, and knew all the inducements which are acting upon him, we could foretell his conduct with as much certainty as we can predict any physical event. This proposition I take to be a mere interpretation of universal experience, a statement in words of what every one is internally convinced of. No one who believed that he knew thoroughly the circumstances of any case, and the characters of the different persons concerned, would hesitate to foretell how all of them would act. Whatever degree of doubt he may in fact feel, arises from the uncertainty whether he really knows the circumstances, or the character of some one or other of the persons, with the degree of accuracy required, but by no means from thinking that, if he did know these things, there could be any uncertainty what the conduct would be. Nor does this full assurance conflict in the smallest degree with what is called our feeling of freedom. We do not feel ourselves the less free because those to whom we are intimately known are well assured how we shall will to act in a particular case. We often, on the contrary, regard the doubt what our conduct will be as a mark of ignorance of our character, and sometimes even resent it as an imputation. The religious metaphysicians who have asserted the freedom of the will, have always maintained it to be consistent with divine foreknowledge of our actions, and if with divine, then with any other foreknowledge. We may be free, and yet another may have reason to be perfectly certain what use we shall make of our freedom. It is not, therefore, the doctrine that our volitions and actions are invariable consequents of our antecedent states of mind, that is either contradicted by our consciousness or felt to be degrading.

But the doctrine of causation, when considered as obtaining between our volitions and their antecedents, is almost universally conceived as involving more than this. Many do not believe, and very few practically feel, that there is nothing in causation but invariable, certain, and unconditional sequence. There are few to whom mere constancy of succession appears a sufficiently stringent bond of union for so peculiar a relation as that of cause and effect. Even if the reason repudiates, the imagination retains, the feeling of some more intimate connection, of some peculiar tie, or mysterious constraint exercised by the antecedent over the consequent. Now this it is which, considered as applying to the human will, conflicts with our consciousness and revolts our feelings. We are certain that, in the case of our volitions, there is not this mysterious constraint. We know that we are not compelled, as by a magical spell, to obey any particular motive. We feel that, if we wished to prove that we have the power of resisting the motive, we could do so (that wish being, it needs scarcely be observed, a *new antecedent*); and it would be humiliating to our pride, and (what is of more importance) paralyzing to our desire of excellence if we thought otherwise. But neither is any such mysterious compulsion now supposed, by the best philosophical authorities, to be exercised by any other cause over its effect. Those who think that causes draw their effects after them by a mystical tie are right in believing that the relation between volitions and their antecedents is of another nature. But they should go farther, and admit that this is also true of all other effects and their antecedents. If such a tie is considered to be involved in the word necessity, the doctrine is not true of human actions, but neither is it then true of inanimate objects. It would be more correct to say that matter is not bound by necessity than that mind is so.

That the free-will metaphysicians, being mostly of the school which rejects Hume's and Brown's analysis of Cause and Effect, should miss their way for want of the light which that analysis affords, cannot surprise us. The wonder is, that the Necessitarians, who usually admit that philosophical theory, should in practice equally lose sight of it. The very same misconception of the doctrine called Philosophical Necessity, which prevents the opposite party from recognizing its truth, I believe to exist more or less obscurely in the minds of most Necessitarians, however they may in words disavow it. I am much mistaken if they habitually feel that the necessity which they recognize in actions is but uniformity of order, and capability of being predicted. They have a feeling as if there were at bottom a stronger tie between the volitions and their causes; as if, when they asserted that the will is governed by the balance of motives, they meant something more cogent than if they had only said that whoever knew the motives, and our habitual susceptibilities to them, could predict how we should will to act. They commit, in opposition to their own scientific system, the very same mistake which their adversaries commit in obedience to theirs, and in consequence do really in some instances suffer those depressing consequences which their opponents erroneously impute to the doctrine itself.

I I I

I am inclined to think that this error is almost wholly an effect of the associations with a word, and that it would be prevented by forbearing to employ, for the expression of the simple fact of causation, so extremely inappropriate a term as Necessity. That word, in its other acceptations, involves much more than mere uniformity of sequence; it implies irresistibleness. Applied to the will, it only means that the given cause will be followed by the effect, subject to all possibilities of counteraction by other causes, but in common use it stands for the operation of those causes exclusively, which are supposed too powerful to be counteracted at all. When we say that all human actions take place of necessity, we only mean that they will certainly happen if nothing prevents: when we say that dying of want, to those who cannot get food, is a necessity, we mean that it will certainly happen whatever may be done to prevent it. The application of the same term to the agencies on which human actions depend, as is used to express those agencies of nature which are really uncontrollable, cannot fail, when habitual, to create a feeling of uncontrollableness in the former also. This, however, is a mere illusion. There are physical sequences which we call necessary, as death for want of food or air; there are others which, though as much cases of causation as the former, are not said to be necessary, as death from poison, which an antidote, or the use of the stomach pump, will sometimes avert. It is apt to be forgotten by people's feelings, even if remembered by their understandings, that human actions are in this last predicament: they are never (except in some cases of mania) ruled by any one motive with such absolute sway, that there is no room for the influence of any other. The causes, therefore, on which action depends are never uncontrollable, and any given effect is only necessary provided that the causes tending to produce it are not controlled. That whatever happens could not have happened otherwise, unless something had taken place which was capable of preventing it, no one surely needs hesitate to admit. But to call this by the name necessity is to use the term in a sense so different from its primitive and familiar meaning, from that which it bears in the common occasions of life, as to amount almost to a play upon words. The associations derived from the ordinary sense of the term will adhere to it in spite of all we can do, and though the doctrine of Necessity, as stated by most who hold it, is very remote from fatalism, it is probable that most Necessitarians are fatalists, more or less, in their feelings.

A Fatalist believes, or half believes (for nobody is a consistent Fatalist), not only that whatever is about to happen, will be the infallible result of the causes which produce it (which is the true Necessitarian doctrine), but moreover that there is no use in struggling against it, that it will happen however we may strive to prevent it. Now, a Necessitarian believing that our actions follow from our characters, and that our characters follow from our organization, our education, and our circumstances, is apt to be, with more or less of consciousness on his part, a Fatalist as to his own actions, and to believe that his nature is such, or that his education and circumstances have so molded his character, that nothing can now prevent him from feeling and acting in a particular way, or at least that no effort of his own can hinder it. In the words of the sect which in our own day has most perseveringly inculcated and most perversely misunderstood this great doctrine, his character is formed *for* him, and not *by* him; therefore his wishing that it had been formed differently is of no use: he has no power to alter it. But this is a grand error. He has, to a certain extent, a power to alter his character. Its being, in the ultimate resort, formed for him, is not inconsistent with its being, in part, formed *by* him as one of the intermediate agents. His character is formed by his circumstances (including among these his particular organization); but his own desire to mould it in a particular way is one of those circumstances, and by no means one of the least influential. We cannot, indeed, directly will to be different from what we are. But neither did those who are supposed to have formed our characters directly will that we should be what we are. Their will had no direct power except over their own actions. They made us what they did make us, by willing, not the end but the requisite means; and we, when our habits are not too inveterate, can, by similarly willing the requisite means, make ourselves different. If they could place us under the influence of certain circumstances, we, in like manner, can place ourselves under the influence of other circumstances. We are exactly as capable of making our own character, *if we will,* as others are of making it for us.

Yes (answers the Owenite), but these words "if we will" surrender the whole point, since the will to alter our own character is given us, not by any efforts of ours, but by circumstances which we cannot help: it comes to us either from external causes, or not at all. Most true; if the Owenite stops here, he is in a position from which nothing can expel him. Our character is formed by us as well as for us; but the wish which induces us to attempt to form it is formed for us, and how? Not, in general, by our organization, nor wholly by our education, but by our experience—experience of the painful consequences of the character we previously had—or by some strong feeling of admiration or aspiration accidentally aroused. But to think that we have no power of altering our character, and to think that we shall not use our power unless we desire to use it, are very different things, and have a very different effect on the mind. A person who does not wish to alter his character cannot be the person who is supposed to feel discouraged or paralyzed by thinking himself unable to do it. The depressing effect of the fatalist doctrine can only be felt where there *is* a wish to do what that doctrine represents as impossible. It is of no consequence what we think forms our character, when we have no desire of our own about forming it, but it is of great consequence that we should not be prevented from forming such a desire by thinking the attainment impracticable, and that if we have the desire, we should know that the work is not so irrevocably done as to be incapable of being altered.

And indeed, if we examine closely, we shall find that this feeling of our being able to modify our own character *if we wish,* is itself the feeling of moral freedom which we are conscious of. A person feels morally free who feels that his habits or his temptations are not his masters, but he theirs, who even in yielding to them knows that he could resist, that were he desirous of altogether throwing them off, there would not be required for that purpose a stronger desire than he knows himself to be capable of feeling. It is of course necessary, to render our consciousness of freedom complete, that we should have succeeded in making our character all we have hitherto attempted to make it; for if we have wished and not attained, we have, to that extent, not power over our own character—we are not free. Or at least we must feel that our wish, if not strong enough to alter our character, is strong enough to conquer our character when the two are brought into conflict in any particular case of conduct. And hence it is said with truth that none but a person of confirmed virtue is completely free.

The application of so improper a term as Necessity to the doctrine of cause and effect in the matter of human character seems to me one of the most signal instances in philosophy of the abuse of terms, and its practical consequences one of the most striking examples of the power of language over our associations. The subject will never be generally understood, until that objectionable term is dropped. The free-will doctrine, by keeping in view precisely that portion of the truth which the word Necessity puts out of sight—namely the power of the mind to cooperate in the formation of its own character—has given to its adherents a practical feeling much nearer to the truth than has generally (I believe) existed in the minds of Necessitarians. The latter may have had a stronger sense of the importance of what human beings can do to shape the characters of one another, but the free-will doctrine has, I believe, fostered in its supporters a much stronger spirit of self-culture.

I V

There is still one fact which requires to be noticed (in addition to the existence of a power of self-formation), before the doctrine of the causation of human actions can be freed from the confusion and misapprehensions which surround it in many minds. When the will is said to be determined by motives, a motive does not mean always, or solely, the anticipation of a pleasure or of a pain. I shall not here inquire whether it be true that, in the commencement, all our voluntary actions are mere means consciously employed to obtain some pleasure, or avoid some pain. It is at least certain that we gradually, through the influence of association, come to desire the means without thinking of the end; the action itself becomes an object of desire, and is performed without reference to any motive beyond itself. Thus far, it may still be objected that, the action having through association become pleasurable, we are, as much as before, moved to act by the anticipation of a pleasure, namely the pleasure of the action itself. But granting this, the matter does not end here. As we proceed in the formation of habits, and become accustomed to will a particular act or a particular course of conduct because it is pleasurable, we at last continue to will it without any reference to its being pleasurable. Although, from some change in us or in our circumstances, we have ceased to find any pleasure in the action, or perhaps to anticipate any pleasure as the consequence of it, we still continue to desire the action, and consequently to do it. In this manner it is that habits of hurtful excess continue to be practiced, although they have ceased to be pleasurable, and in this manner also it is that the habit of willing to persevere in the course which he has chosen, does not desert the moral hero, even when the reward, however real, which he doubtless receives from the consciousness of well-doing is anything but an equivalent for the sufferings he undergoes, or the wishes which he may have to renounce.

A habit of willing is commonly called a purpose, and among the causes of our volitions, and of the actions which flow from them, must be reckoned not only likings and aversions, but also purposes. It is only when our purposes have become independent of the feelings of pain or pleasure from which they originally took their rise, that we are said to have a confirmed character. "A character," says Novalis, "is a completely fashioned will"; and the will, once so fashioned, may be steady and constant, when the passive susceptibilities of pleasure and pain are greatly weakened, or materially changed.

With the corrections and explanations now given, the doctrine of the causation of our volitions by motives, and of motives by the desirable objects offered to us, combined with our particular susceptibilities of desire, may be considered, I hope, as sufficiently established for the purposes of this treatise.*

* Some arguments and explanations, supplementary to those in the text, will be found in *An Examination of Sir William Hamilton's Philosophy*, chap. xxvi.

On the Freedom of the Will

[In his *Examination of Sir William Hamilton's Philosophy*, Mill dealt at great length with a number of metaphysical questions which he handled nowhere else, and expanded his views on other topics previously discussed. Chapter XXVI, "On the Freedom of the Will," presents a valuable supplement to the opinions expressed in the *System of Logic*. In the selection given here, the first few pages, which contain a criticism of Hamilton's view that denial of the doctrine of free will entails denial of the existence of God, have been omitted, as have some of Mill's controversial footnotes. The text is taken from the sixth edition, 1889.

The following excerpt from a letter to Dr. W. G. Ward, written in the Spring of 1849, may provide a useful supplement to the other selections on freedom of the will (this letter is to be found in the *Letters*, ed. Elliot, Vol. I, pp. 140–142).

Dear Sir,—You have given me six months to answer all your questions. I think you ought to allow me six volumes too; for if the questions occupy so many pages, what must the answers? . . .

1st. Your explanations do not at all clear up, to my apprehension, what I think the inconsistency of blending high moral praise with the strongest language of moral reprobation. You say that certain states of mind are sinful in the greatest degree, yet that for those states the individual may possibly be not at all responsible. I can understand that persons may hold false and pernicious opinions conscientiously, and may have defects or peculiarities of character which, both in themselves and in their consequences, are extremely undesirable, yet to which their own wishes or voluntary conduct having in no way contributed, they are not morally accountable for them. But to call anything a sin and yet say that the sinner is not accountable for it, seems to me, if the word sin means anything, a direct contradiction. It is you who appear to be chargeable with what my opinions are usually charged with, viz., confounding the distinction between moral badness and mere aberration in a person or thing from the ideal perfection of the kind of being it belongs to. I recognize two kinds of imperfections:

those which come independently of our will, and which our will could not prevent, and for these we are not accountable; and those which our will has either positively or negatively assisted in producing, and for which we *are* accountable. The former may be very hurtful to ourselves and offensive to others, but in *us* they are not morally culpable. The latter *are*. You ride over this (as it seems to me) perfectly definite distinction by the ambiguous word *sin*, under which a third class of defects of character finds entrance which is supposed to unite both attributes—to be culpable and ultra-culpable, although the person thus morally guilty cannot help it. This seems to me to exemplify the unmeaningness of the word sin, which, if it is anything other than the theological synonym of "morally wrong," is a name for something which I do not admit to exist.]

So MUCH FOR Sir W. Hamilton's attempt to prove that one who disbelieves free will, has no business to believe in a God. Let us now consider his view of the doctrine itself, and of the evidence for it.

His view of the controversy is peculiar, but harmonizes with his Philosophy of the Conditioned, which seems indeed to have been principally suggested to him by the supposed requirements of this question. He is of opinion that Free Will and Necessity are both inconceivable. Free Will, because it supposes volitions to originate without cause;* because it affirms an absolute commencement, which, as we are aware,

---

* Sir W. Hamilton thinks it a fair statement of the Free Will doctrine, that it supposes our volitions to be uncaused. But the "Inquirer" (p. 45) considers this a misstatement, and thinks the real free will doctrine to be that "I" am the cause. I prefer the other language, as being more consistent with the use of the word cause in other cases. If we take the word, we must take the acknowledged Law of Causation along with it, viz., that a cause which is the same in every respect, is always followed by the same effects. But on the free will theory, the "I" is the same, and all the other conditions the same, and yet the effect may not only be different, but contrary. For instead of saying that "I" am the cause, the "Inquirer" should at least say, some state or mode of me, which is different when the effect is different; though what state or mode this could be, unless it were a will to will (the notion so justly ridiculed by Hobbes), it is difficult to imagine. I persist, therefore, in saying, with Sir W. Hamilton, that, on the free will doctrine, volitions are emancipated from causation altogether.

our author deems it impossible for the human mind to conceive. On the other hand, the mind is equally unable to conceive an infinite regress, a chain of causation going back to all eternity. Both the one and the other theory, thus involve difficulties insurmountable by the human faculties. But, as Sir W. Hamilton has so often told us, the inconceivability of a thing by us is no proof that it is objectively impossible by the laws of the universe; on the contrary, it often happens that both sides of an alternative are alike incomprehensible to us, while from their nature we are certain that the one or the other must be true. Such an alternative, according to Sir W. Hamilton, exists between the conflicting doctrines of Free Will and Necessity. By the law of Excluded Middle, one or other of them must be true, and inconceivability, as common to both, not operating more against one than against the other, does not operate against either. The balance, therefore, must turn in favor of the side for which there is positive evidence. In favor of Free Will we have the distinct testimony of consciousness, perhaps directly, though of this he speaks with some appearance of doubt,* but at all events, indirectly, freedom being implied in the consciousness of moral responsibility. As there is no corresponding evidence in favor of the other theory, the Free Will doctrine must prevail. "How† the will can possibly be free must remain to us, under the present limitation of our faculties, wholly incomprehensible. We cannot conceive absolute commencement; we cannot, therefore, conceive a free volition. But as little can we conceive the alternative on which liberty is denied, on which necessity is affirmed. And in favor of our moral nature, the fact that we are free is given us in the consciousness of an uncompromising law of Duty, in the consciousness of our moral accountability; and this fact of liberty cannot be re-argued on the ground that it is incomprehensible, for the doctrine of the Conditioned proves, against the Necessitarian, that something may, nay must, be true, of which the mind is wholly unable to construe to itself the possibility, whilst it shows that the objection of incomprehensibility applies no less to the doctrine of fatalism than to the doctrine of moral freedom."

The inconceivability of the Free Will doctrine is main-

* Footnotes to Reid, pp. 509, 602, 624.
† *Lectures*, ii. 412, 413.

tained by our author, not only on the general ground just stated, of our incapacity to conceive an absolute commencement, but on the further and special ground, that the will is determined by motives. In rewriting the preceding passage for the Appendix to his *Discussions*, he made the following addition to it: * "A determination by motives cannot, to our understanding, escape from necessitation. Nay, were we even to admit as true what we cannot think as possible, still the doctrine of a motiveless volition would be only casualism; and the free acts of an indifferent, are, morally and rationally, as worthless as the preordered passions of a determined will. *How*, therefore, I repeat, moral liberty is possible in man or God, we are utterly unable speculatively to understand. But . . . the scheme of freedom is not more inconceivable than the scheme of necessity. For whilst fatalism is a recoil from the more obtrusive inconceivability of an *absolute* commencement, on the fact of which commencement the doctrine of liberty proceeds, the fatalist is shown to overlook the equal, but less obtrusive, inconceivability of an *infinite* non-commencement, on the assertion of which non-commencement his own doctrine of necessity must ultimately rest." It rests on no such thing, if he believes in a First Cause, which a Necessitarian may. What is more, even if he does not believe in a First Cause, he makes no "assertion of non-commencement"; he only declines to make an assertion of commencement, and, therefore, is not in the position of asserting what is inconceivable, which, however, as Sir W. Hamilton is perpetually declaring, is a position perfectly tenable, and the position he avowedly chooses for himself on this very subject. But to resume the quotation: "As equally unthinkable, the two counter, the two one-sided, schemes are thus theoretically balanced. But, practically, our consciousness of the moral law, which, without a moral liberty in man, would be a mendacious imperative, gives a decisive preponderance to the doctrine of freedom over the doctrine of fate. We are free in act, if we are accountable for our actions."

Sir W. Hamilton is of opinion that both sides are alike unsuccessful in repelling each other's attacks. The arguments against both are, he thinks, to the human faculties, irrefutable. "The champions† of the opposite doctrines are at once resistless in assault and impotent in defense. Each is hewn down,

* Appendix to *Discussions*, pp. 624-625.
† Footnote to Reid, p. 602.

and appears to die under the home thrusts of his adversary, but each again recovers life from the very death of his antagonist, and to borrow a simile, both are like the heroes in Valhalla, ready in a moment to amuse themselves anew in the same bloodless and interminable conflict. The doctrine of Moral Liberty cannot be made conceivable, for we can only conceive the determined and the relative. As already stated, all that can be done is to show: 1. That, for the *fact* of Liberty, we have, immediately or mediately, the evidence of Consciousness; and 2. That there are, among the phenomena of mind, many facts which we *must* admit as actual, but of whose possibility we are wholly unable to form any notion. I may merely observe that the fact of *Motion* can be shown to be impossible, on grounds not less strong than those on which it is attempted to disprove the fact of Liberty." These "grounds no less strong" are the mere paralogisms which we examined in a recent chapter, and with regard to which our author showed so surprising a deficiency in the acuteness and subtlety to be expected from the general quality of his mind.

Conformably to these views, Sir W. Hamilton, in his footnotes on Reid, promptly puts an extinguisher on several of that philosopher's arguments against the doctrine of so-called Necessity. When Reid affirms that Motives are not causes—that they may influence to action, but do not act, Sir W. Hamilton observes:* "If Motives influence to action, they must cooperate in producing a certain effect upon the agent; and the determination to act, and to act in a certain manner, is that effect. They are thus, on Reid's own view, in this relation, *causes*, and *efficient* causes. It is of no consequence in the argument whether motives be said to determine a man to act, or to influence (that is, to determine) him to determine himself to act."† This is one of the neatest specimens in our author's writings of a fallacy cut clean through by a single stroke.

Again, when Reid says that acts are often done without any motive, or when there is no motive for preferring the means used, rather than others by which the same end might have been attained, Sir W. Hamilton asks,‡ "Can we con-

* Ibid. p. 608.

† To the same effect see *Discussions*, Appendix on Causality, p. 614.

‡ Footnote to Reid, p. 609.

ceive any act of which there was not a sufficient cause or concourse of causes why the man performed it and no other? If not, call this cause, or these concauses, the *motive* and there is no longer a dispute."

Reid asks, "Is there no such thing as wilfulness, caprice, or obstinacy among mankind?" Sir W. Hamilton, *e contra*:* "But are not these all tendencies, and fatal tendencies, to act or not to act? By contradistinguishing such tendencies from motives strictly so called or rational impulses, we do not advance a single step towards rendering liberty comprehensible."

According to Reid, the determination is made by the man and not by the motive. "But," asks Sir W. Hamilton,† "was the *man* determined by no motive to that determination? Was his specific volition to this or to that without a cause? Or the supposition that the sum of influences (motives, dispositions, and tendencies) to volition A, is equal to 12, and the sum of influences to counter-volition B equal to 8—can we conceive that the determination of volition A should not be necessary?—We can only conceive the volition B to be determined by supposing that the man *creates* (calls from non-existence into existence) a certain supplement of influences. But this creation as actual, or in itself, is inconceivable, and even to conceive the possibility of this inconceivable act, we must suppose some cause by which the man is determined to exert it. We thus, in *thought*, never escape determination and necessity. It will be observed that I do not consider this inability to the *notion*, any disproof of the *fact* of Free Will." Nor is it; but if, as our author so strongly inculcates, "every effort to bring the fact of liberty within the compass of our conceptions only results in the substitution in its place of some more or less disguised form of necessity," it is a strong indication that some form of necessity is the opinion naturally suggested by our collective experience of life.§

* Ibid. p. 610.
† Ibid. p. 611.
‡ *Lectures*, i. 34.
§ So difficult is it to escape from this fact that Sir W. Hamilton himself says (*Lectures*, i. 188), "Voluntary conation is a faculty which can only be determined to energy through a pain or pleasure—through an estimate of the relative worth of objects." If I am determined to prefer innocence to the satisfaction of a particular desire, through an estimate of the relative worth of innocence and of the gratification, can this estimate, while unchanged, leave me at liberty to choose the gratification in preference to innocence?

Sir W. Hamilton having thus, as is often the case (and it is one of the best things he does), saved his opponents the trouble of answering his friends, his doctrine is left resting exclusively on the supports which he has himself provided for it. In examining them, let us place ourselves, in the first instance, completely at his point of view, and concede to him the coequal inconceivability of the conflicting hypotheses, an uncaused commencement, and an infinite egress. But this choice of inconceivabilities is not offered to us in the case of volitions only. We are held, as he not only admits but contends, to the same alternative in all cases of causation whatsoever. But we find our way out of the difficulty, in other cases, in quite a different manner. In the case of every other kind of fact, we do not elect the hypothesis that the event took place without a cause; we accept the other supposition, that of a regress, not indeed to infinity, but either generally into the region of the Unknowable, or back to an Universal Cause, regarding which, as we are only concerned with it in respect of attributes bearing relation to what it preceded, and not as itself preceded by anything, we can afford to consider this reference as ultimate.

Now, what is the reason which, in the case of all things within the range of our knowledge except volitions, makes us choose this side of the alternative? Why do we, without scruple, register all of them as depending on causes, by which (to use our author's language) they are determined necessarily, though, in believing this, we, according to Sir W. Hamilton, believe as utter an inconceivability as if we supposed them to take place without a cause? Apparently it is because the causation hypothesis, inconceivable as he may think it, possesses the advantage of having experience on its side. And how or by what evidence does experience testify to it? Not by disclosing any *nexus* between the cause and the effect, any Sufficient Reason in the cause itself why the effect should follow it. No philosopher now makes this supposition, and Sir W. Hamilton positively disclaims it. What experience makes known is the fact of an invariable sequence between every event and some special combination of antecedent conditions, in such sort that wherever and whenever that union of antecedents exists, the event does not fail to occur. Any *must* in the case, any necessity, other than the unconditional universality of the fact, we know nothing of. Still, this *a posteriori* "does," though not confirmed by an *a priori* "must," decides our choice between the two inconceivables, and leads us to the belief that every event within the phenomenal universe, except human volitions, is determined to take place by a cause. Now, the so-called Necessitarians demand the application of the same rule of judgment to our volitions. They maintain that there is the same evidence for it. They affirm, as a truth of experience, that volitions do, in point of fact, follow determinate moral antecedents with the same uniformity, and (when we have sufficient knowledge of the circumstances) with the same certainty, as physical effects follow their physical causes. These moral antecedents are desires, aversions, habits, and dispositions, combined with outward circumstances suited to call those internal incentives into action. All these again are effects of causes, those of them which are mental being consequences of education, and of other moral and physical influences. This is what Necessitarians affirm, and they court every possible mode in which its truth can be verified. They test it by each person's observation of his own volitions. They test it by each person's observation of the voluntary actions of those with whom he comes into contact, and by the power which every one has of foreseeing actions, with a degree of exactness proportioned to his previous experience and knowledge of the agents, and with a certainty often quite equal to that with which we predict the commonest physical events. They test it further, by the statistical results of the observation of human beings acting in numbers sufficient to eliminate the influences which operate only on a few, and which on a large scale neutralize one another, leaving the total result about the same as if the volitions of the whole mass had been affected by such only of the determining causes as were common to them all. In cases of this description the results are as uniform, and may be as accurately foretold, as in any physical inquires in which the effect depends upon a multiplicity of causes. The cases in which volitions seem too uncertain to admit of being confidently predicted are those in which our knowledge of the influences antecedently in operation is so incomplete, that with equally imperfect data there would be the same uncertainty in the predictions of the astronomer and the chemist. On these grounds it is contended that our choice between the conflicting inconceivables should be the same in the case of volitions as of all other phenomena: we must reject equally in both cases the hypothesis of spontaneousness, and consider them all as caused. A volition is a moral effect, which follows the corresponding moral causes as certainly and invariably as physical effects follow their physical causes. Whether it *must* do so, I acknowledge myself to be entirely ignorant, be the phenomenon moral or physical; and I condemn, accordingly, the word Necessity as applied to either case. All I know is, that it always *does*.*

This argument from experience Sir W. Hamilton passes unnoticed, but urges, on the opposite side of the question, the argument from Consciousness. We are conscious, he affirms, either of our freedom, or at all events (it is odd that, on his theory, there should be any doubt) of something which implies freedom. If this is true, our internal consciousness tells us that we have a power which the whole outward experience of the human race tells us that we never use. This is surely a very unfortunate predicament we are in, and a sore trial to the puzzled metaphysician. Philosophy is far from having so easy a business before her as our author thinks; the arbiter Consciousness is by no means invoked to turn the scale between two equally balanced difficulties; on the contrary, she has to sit in judgment between herself and a complete induction from experience. Consciousness, it will probably be said, is the best evidence, and so it would be, if we were always certain what is Consciousness. But while there are so many varying testimonies respecting this, when Sir W. Hamilton can himself say,† "many philosophers have attempted to establish, on the principles of common sense, propositions which are not original data of consciousness,

---

* The "Inquirer" accuses this argument (p. 45) of "gratuitously assuming that free will is inconsistent with foreknowledge." This is a misapprehension. That vexed question is not even approached in the text. All that is maintained is that the possibility to human intelligence, of predicting human actions, implies a constancy of observed sequence between the same antecedents and the same consequents, which, in the case of all events except volitions, is deemed to justify the assertion of a law of nature (called in the language of the free will philosophers Necessity). This constancy of sequence between motives, mental dispositions, and actions, is a strong reason against admitting free will as a fact, but I have not meddled, and do not intend to meddle, with the metaphysical question whether a contingent event can be foreknown.

† *Dissertations on Reid*, p. 749.

while the original data of consciousness from which these propositions were derived, and to which they owed all their necessity and truth, these same philosophers were (strange to say) not disposed to admit"; when M. Cousin and nearly all Germany find the Infinite and the Absolute in Consciousness, Sir W. Hamilton thinking them utterly repugnant to it; when philosophers, for many generations, fancied that they had Abstract Ideas—that they could conceive a triangle which was neither equilateral, isosceles, nor scalene,* which Sir W. Hamilton and all other people now consider to be simply absurd; with all these conflicting opinions respecting the things to which Consciousness testifies, what is the perplexed inquirer to think? Does all philosophy end, as in our author's opinion Hume believed it to do, in a persistent contradiction between one of our mental faculties and another? We shall find there is a solution, which relieves the human mind from this embarrassment: namely, that the question to which experience says yes, and that to which consciousness says no, are different questions.

Let us cross-examine the alleged testimony of consciousness. And first, it is left in some uncertainty by Sir W. Hamilton whether Consciousness makes only one deliverance on the subject, or two: whether we are conscious only of moral responsibility, in which free will is implied, or are directly conscious of free will. In his *Lectures*, Sir W. Hamilton speaks only of the first. In the notes on Reid, which were written subsequently, he seems to affirm both, but the latter of the two in a doubtful and hesitating manner, so difficult, in

---

* Does it not require," says Locke (*Essay on the Human Understanding*, Book iv. chap. 7, sect. 9), "some pains and skill to form the general idea of a triangle (which yet is none of the most abstract, comprehensive and difficult?) for it must be neither oblique nor rectangle, neither equilateral, equicrural, nor scalene; but all and none of these at once. In effect, it is something imperfect, that cannot exist; an idea wherein some parts of several different and inconsistent ideas are put together." Yet this union of contradictory elements such a philosopher as Locke was able to fancy that he conceived. I scarcely know a more striking example of the tendency of the human mind to believe that things can exist separately because they can be separately named; a tendency strong enough, in this case, to make a mind like Locke's believe itself to be conscious of that which by the laws of mind cannot be a subject of consciousness to any one.

reality, does he find it to ascertain with certainty what it is that Consciousness certifies. But as there are many who maintain with a confidence far greater than his that we are directly conscious of free will,* it is necessary to examine that question.

To be conscious of free will, must mean to be conscious, before I have decided, that I am able to decide either way. Exception may be taken *in limine* to the use of the word consciousness in such an application. Consciousness tells me what I do or feel. But what I am *able* to do, is not a subject of consciousness. Consciousness is not prophetic; we are conscious of what is, not of what will or can be. We never know that we are able to do a thing, except from having done it, or something equal and similar to it. We should not know that we were capable of action at all, if we had never acted. Having acted, we know, as far as that experience reaches, how we are able to act, and this knowledge, when it has become familiar, is often confounded with, and called by the name of, consciousness. But it does not derive any increase of authority from being misnamed; its truth is not supreme over, but depends on, experience. If our so-called consciousness of what we are able to do is not borne out by experience, it is a delusion. It has no title to credence but as an interpretation of experience, and if it is a false interpretation, it must give way.†

* Mr. Mansel, among others, makes the assertion in the broadest form it is capable of saying, "In every act of volition, I am fully conscious that I can at this moment act in either of two ways and that, all the antecedent phenomena being precisely the same, I may determine one way today and another way tomorrow." (*Prolegomena Logica*, p. 152.) Yes, though the antecedent phenomena remain the same; but not if my judgment of the antecedent phenomena remains the same. If my conduct changes, either the external inducements or my estimate of them must have changed.

Mr. Mansel (as I have already observed) goes so far as to maintain that our immediate intuition of Power is given us by the ego producing its own volitions, not by its volitions producing bodily movements (pp. 139–140, and 151).

† In answer to the statement that what I am *able* to do is not a subject of consciousness, Mr. Alexander says (pp. 22 *et seq.*), "Perhaps it is not; but what I *feel* I am able to do is surely a subject of consciousness. . . . As to 'consciousness is not prophetic, we are conscious of what is, not of what will or can be,' it seems

But this conviction, whether termed consciousness or only belief, that our will is free—what is it? Of what are we convinced? I am told that whether I decide to do or to abstain, I feel that I could have decided the other way. I ask my consciousness what I do feel, and I find, indeed, that I feel

---

enough to say that if we are conscious of a free force of volition continuously inherent in us, we are conscious of what *is*." If we can be conscious of a force, and can feel an ability, independently of any present or past exercise thereof, the fact has nothing similar or analogous in all the rest of our nature. We are not conscious of a muscular force continuously inherent in us. If we were born with a cataract, we are not conscious, previous to being couched, of our ability to see. We should not feel able to walk if we had never walked, nor to think if we had never thought. Ability and force are not real entities, which can be felt as present when no effect follows; they are abstract names for the happening of the effect on the occurrence of the needful conditions, or for our expectation of its happening. It is of course possible that this may be all wrong, and that there may be a concrete real thing called ability, of which consciousness discloses to us the positive existence in this one case, though there is no evidence of it in any other. But it is surely, to say the least, much more probable that we mistake for consciousness our habitual affirmation to ourselves of an acquired knowledge or belief. This very common mistake may have escaped the notice of Mr. Alexander, who (p. 23) considers knowledge to be the same thing as direct consciousness! but it is a possibility which it will not do to overlook, when one takes for one's standard (p. 25) the "general consciousness of the race"; especially if, with Mr. Alexander, one restricts "the race" to those who are not philosophers, on the ground that no philosopher "unless he be one of a thousand," can see or feel anything that is inconsistent with his preconceived opinion. If this be the normal effect of philosophy on the human mind; if, nine hundred and ninety-nine times against one, the effect of cultivating our power of mental discrimination is to pervert it; let us close our books, and accept Hodge as a better authority in metaphysics than Locke or Kant, and, I suppose, in astronomy than Newton. An appeal to consciousness, however, to be of any value, must be to those who have formed a habit of sifting their consciousness, and distinguishing what they perceive or feel from what they infer, to those who can be made to understand that they do not see the sun move; and, to have attained this power of criticising their own consciousness on metaphysical subjects, they must have reflected on those subjects, in a manner and degree which quite entitle any one to the name of a philosopher.

(or am convinced) that I could, and even should, have chosen the other course if I had preferred it, that is, if I had liked it better, but not that I could have chosen one course while I preferred the other. When I say preferred, I of course include, with the thing itself, all that accompanies it. I know that I can, because I know that I often do, elect to do one thing, when

---

Mr. Alexander denies that the belief that I was free to act can possibly be tested by experience *a posteriori*, since experience only tells me the way in which I did act, and says nothing about my having been able to act otherwise. Mr. Alexander's idea of the conditions of proof by experience is not a very enlarged one. Suppose that my experience of myself afforded two undeniable cases, alike in all the mental and physical antecedents, in one of which cases I acted in one way, and in the other in the direct opposite; there would then be proof by experience that I had been able to act either in the one way or in the other. It is by experience of this sort I learn that I can act at all, viz., by finding that an event takes place or not, according as (other circumstances being the same) a volition of mine does or does not take place. But when this power of my volitions over my actions has become a familiar fact, the knowledge of it is so constantly present to my mind as to be popularly called, and habitually confounded with, consciousness. And the supposed power of myself over my volitions, which is termed Free Will, though it cannot be a fact of consciousness, yet if true, or even if believed, would similarly work itself into our inmost knowledge of ourselves, in such a manner as to be mistaken for consciousness.

It would hardly be worth while to notice a pretended inconsistency discovered by Mr. Alexander between what is here said, and my recognition in a former work of a "practical feeling of Free Will"—"a feeling of Moral Freedom which we are conscious of," if Mr. Alexander had not inferred from it that I "was at one time conscious" of what I now, for the convenience of my argument, deny to be a subject of consciousness. Mr. Alexander himself quotes the words in which I spoke of this practical feeling of free will as not one of free will at all, in a sense implying the theory, and took pains to describe what it really is, expressly declaring our feeling of moral freedom to be a feeling of our being able to modify our own character *if we wish*. When I applied the words feeling and consciousness to this acquired knowledge, I did not use those terms in their strict psychological meaning, there being no necessity for doing so in that place but, agreeably to popular usage, extended them to (what there is no appropriate scientific name for) the whole of our familiar and intimate knowledge concerning ourselves.

I should have preferred another in itself, apart from its consequences, or from a moral law which it violates. And this preference for a thing in itself, abstractedly from its accompaniments, is often loosely described as preference for the thing. It is this unprecise mode of speech which makes it not seem absurd to say that I act in opposition to my preference, that I do one thing when I would rather do another, that my conscience prevails over my desires—as if conscience were not itself a desire—the desire to do right. Take any alternative: say to murder or not to murder. I am told, that if I elect to murder, I am conscious that I could have elected to abstain; but am I conscious that I could have abstained if my aversion to the crime, and my dread of its consequences, had been weaker than the temptation? If I elect to abstain, in what sense am I conscious that I could have elected to commit the crime? Only if I had desired to commit it with a desire stronger than my horror of murder, not with one less strong. When we think of ourselves hypothetically as having acted otherwise than we did, we always suppose a difference in the antecedents; we picture ourselves as having known something that we did not know, or not known something that we did know, which is a difference in the external inducements, or as having desired something, or disliked something, more or less than we did, which is a difference in the internal inducements.

In refutation of this it is said that, in resisting a desire, I am conscious of making an effort; that, after I have resisted, I have the remembrance of having made an effort; that, "if the temptation was long continued, or if I have been resisting the strong will of another, I am as sensibly exhausted by that effort, as after any physical exertion I ever made"; and it is added, "If my volition is wholly determined by the strongest present desire, it will be decided without any effort. . . . When the greater weight goes down, and the lesser up, no effort is needed on the part of the scale."* It is implied in this argument that, in a battle between contrary impulses, the victory must always be decided in a moment, that the force which is really the strongest, and prevails ultimately, must prevail instantaneously. The fact is not quite thus even in inanimate nature: the hurricane does not level the house or blow down

* *The Battle of the Two Philosophies*, pp. 13, 14.

the tree without resistance; even the balance trembles, and the scales oscillate for a short time, when the difference of the weights is not considerable. Far less does victory come without a contest to the strongest of two moral, or even two vital forces, whose nature it is to be never fixed, but always flowing, quantities. In a struggle between passions, there is not a single instant in which there does not pass across the mind some thought, which adds strength to, or takes it from, one or the other of the contending powers. Unless one of them was, from the beginning, out of all proportion stronger than the other, some time must elapse before the balance adjusts itself between forces neither of which is for any two successive instants the same. During that interval, the agent is in the peculiar mental and physical state which we call a conflict of feelings; and we all know that a conflict between strong feelings *is*, in an extraordinary degree, exhaustive of the nervous energies.* The consciousness of effort which we are told of, is this state of conflict. The author I am quoting considers what he calls, I think improperly, an effort, to be only on one side, because he represents to himself the conflict as taking place between me and some foreign power, which I conquer, or by which I am overcome. But it is obvious that "I" am both parties in the contest; the conflict is between me and myself, between (for instance) me desiring a pleasure, and me dreading self-reproach. What causes Me, or, if you please, my Will, to be identified with one side rather than with the other, is that one of the Me's represents a more permanent state of my feelings than the other does. After the temptation has been yielded to, the desiring "I" will come to an end, but the conscience-stricken "I" may endure to the end of life.

I therefore dispute altogether that we are conscious of being able to act in opposition to the strongest present desire or aversion. The difference between a bad and a good man is

* The writer I quote says, "Balancing one motive against another is not willing but judging." The state of mind I am speaking of is by no means a state of judging. It is an emotional, not an intellectual state, and the judging may be finished before it commences. If there were any indispensable act of judging in this stage, it could only be judging which of the two pains or pleasures was the greatest, and to regard this as the operative force would be conceding the point in favor of Necessitarianism.

not that the latter acts in opposition to his strongest desires; it is that his desire to do right, and his aversion to doing wrong, are strong enough to overcome, and in the case of perfect virtue to silence, any other desire or aversion which may conflict with them. It is because this state of mind is possible to human nature that human beings are capable of moral government; and moral education consists in subjecting them to the discipline which has most tendency to bring them into this state. The object of moral education is to educate the will; but the will can only be educated through the desires and aversions, by eradicating or weakening such of them as are likeliest to lead to evil, exalting to the highest pitch the desire of right conduct and the aversion to wrong, cultivating all other desires and aversions of which the ordinary operation is auxiliary to right, while discountenancing so immoderate an indulgence of them, as might render them too powerful to be overcome by the moral sentiment, when they chance to be in opposition to it. The other requisites are a clear intellectual standard of right and wrong, that moral desire and aversion may act in the proper places, and such general mental habits as shall prevent moral considerations from being forgotten or overlooked, in cases to which they are rightly applicable.

Rejecting, then, the figment of a direct consciousness of the freedom of the will, in other words, our ability to will in opposition to our strongest preference, it remains to consider whether, as affirmed by Sir W. Hamilton, a freedom of this kind is implied in what is called our consciousness of moral responsibility. There must be something very plausible in this opinion, since it is shared even by Necessitarians. Many of these—in particular Mr. Owen and his followers—from a recognition of the fact that volitions are effects of causes, have been led to deny human responsibility. I do not mean that they denied moral distinctions. Few persons have had a stronger sense of right and wrong, or been more devoted to the things they deemed right. What they denied was the rightfulness of inflicting punishment. A man's actions, they said, are the result of his character, and he is not the author of his own character. It is made *for* him, not *by* him. There is no justice in punishing him for what he cannot help. We should try to convince or persuade him that he had better act in a different manner, and should educate all, especially the young, in the habits and dispositions which lead to well-doing; though how this is to be effected without any use whatever of punishment as a means of education, is a question they have failed to resolve. The confusion of ideas which makes the subjection of human volitions to the law of Causation seem inconsistent with accountability, must thus be very natural to the human mind; but this may be said of a thousand errors, and even of some merely verbal fallacies. In the present case there is more than a verbal fallacy, but verbal fallacies also contribute their part.

What is meant by moral responsibility? Responsibility means punishment. When we are said to have the feeling of being morally responsible for our actions, the idea of being punished for them is uppermost in the speaker's mind. But the feeling of liability to punishment is of two kinds. It may mean expectation that, if we act in a certain manner, punishment will actually be inflicted upon us, by our fellow creatures or by a Supreme Power. Or it may only mean knowing that we shall deserve that infliction.

The first of these cannot, in any correct meaning of the term, be designated as a consciousness. If we believe that we shall be punished for doing wrong, it is because the belief has been taught to us by our parents and tutors, or by our religion, or is generally held by those who surround us, or because we have ourselves come to the conclusion, by reasoning or from the experience of life. This is not Consciousness. And, by whatever name it is called, its evidence is not dependent on any theory of the spontaneousness of volition. The punishment of guilt in another world is believed with undoubting conviction by Turkish fatalists, and by professed Christians who are not only Necessitarians, but believe that the majority of mankind were divinely predestined from all eternity to sin and to be punished for sinning. It is not, therefore, the belief that we shall be *made* accountable, which can be deemed to require or presuppose the free-will hypothesis; it is the belief that we ought so to be, that we are justly accountable, that guilt deserves punishment. It is here that issue is joined between the two opinions.

In discussing it, there is no need to postulate any theory respecting the nature or criterion of moral distinctions. It matters not, for this purpose, whether the right and wrong of actions depends on the consequences they tend to produce, or on an inherent quality of the actions themselves. It is indifferent whether we are utilitarians or anti-utilitarians, whether our ethics rest on intuition or on experience. It is sufficient if we believe that there is a difference between right and wrong, and a natural reason for preferring the former, that people in general, unless when they expect personal benefit from a wrong, naturally and usually prefer what they think to be right; whether because we are all dependent, for what makes existence tolerable, upon the right conduct of other people, while their wrong conduct is a standing menace to our security, or for some more mystical and transcendental reason. Whatever be the cause, we are entitled to assume the fact; and its consequence is that, whoever cultivates a disposition to wrong places his mind out of sympathy with the rest of his fellow creatures and, if they are aware of his disposition, becomes a natural object of their active dislike. He not only forfeits the pleasure of their good will, and the benefit of their good offices, except when compassion for the human being is stronger than distaste towards the wrongdoer, but he also renders himself liable to whatever they may think it necessary to do in order to protect themselves against him; which may probably include punishment, as such, and will certainly involve much that is equivalent in its operation on himself. In this way he is certain to be made accountable, at least to his fellow creatures, through the normal action of their natural sentiments. And it is well worth consideration, whether the practical expectation of being thus called to account, has not a great deal to do with the internal feeling of being accountable, a feeling, assuredly, which is seldom found existing in any strength in the absence of that practical expectation. It is not usually found that Oriental despots, who cannot be called to account by anybody, have much consciousness of being morally accountable. And (what is still more significant) in societies in which caste or class distinctions are really strong—a state so strange to us now, that we seldom realize it in its full force—it is a matter of daily experience that persons may show the strongest sense of moral accountability as regards their equals, who can make them accountable, and not the smallest vestige of a similar feeling towards their inferiors, who cannot.

This does not imply that the feeling of accountability,

even when porportioned very exactly to the chance of being called to account, is a mere interested calculation, having nothing more in it than an expectation and dread of external punishment. When pain has long been thought of as a consequence of a given fact, the fact becomes wrapt up in associations which make it painful in itself, and cause the mind to shrink from it even when, in the particular case, no painful consequences are apprehended; just as the dislike to spending money, which grows up while money can ill be spared, may be an absorbing passion after the professor has grown so rich that the expenditure would not really cause him the most trifling inconvenience. On this familiar principle of association it is abundantly certain that, even if wrong meant merely what is forbidden, a disinterested detestation of doing wrong would naturally grow up, and might become, in its strength and promptitude, and in the immediateness of its action, without reflection or ulterior purpose, undistinguishable from any of our instincts or natural passions.

Another fact, which it is of importance to keep in view, is that the highest and strongest sense of the worth of goodness, and the odiousness of its opposite, is perfectly compatible with even the most exaggerated form of Fatalism. Suppose that there were two peculiar breeds of human beings —one of them so constituted from the beginning that, however educated or treated, nothing could prevent them from always feeling and acting so as to be a blessing to all whom they approached; another, of such original perversity of nature that neither education nor punishment could inspire them with a feeling of duty, or prevent them from being active in evil doing. Neither of these races of human beings would have free will; yet the former would be honored as demigods, while the latter would be regarded and treated as noxious beasts, not punished perhaps, since punishment would have no effect on them, and it might be thought wrong to indulge the mere instinct of vengeance, but kept carefully at a distance, and killed like other dangerous creatures when there was no other convenient way of being rid of them. We thus see that even under the utmost possible exaggeration of the doctrine of Necessity, the distinction between moral good and evil in conduct would not only subsist, but would stand out in a more marked manner than now, when the good and the wicked, however unlike, are still regarded as of one common nature.

An opponent may say this is not a distinction between *moral* good and evil, and I am far from intending to beg the question against him. But neither can he be permitted to beg the question, by assuming that the distinction is not moral because it does not imply free will. The reality of moral distinctions, and the freedom of our volitions, are questions independent of one another. My position is that a human being who loves, disinterestedly and consistently, his fellow creatures and whatever tends to their good, who hates with a vigorous hatred that causes them evil, and whose actions correspond in character with these feelings, is naturally, necessarily, and reasonably an object to be loved, admired, sympathized with, and in all ways cherished and encouraged by mankind, while a person who has none of these qualities, or so little, that his actions continually jar and conflict with the good of others, and that for purposes of his own he is ready to inflict on them a great amount of evil, is a natural and legitimate object of their fixed aversion, and of conduct conformable thereto; and this, whether the will be free or not, and even independently of any theory of the difference between right and wrong, whether right means productive of happiness, and wrong productive of misery, or right and wrong are intrinsic qualities of the actions themselves—provided only we recognize that there is a difference, and that the difference is highly important. What I maintain is that this is a sufficient distinction between moral good and evil, sufficient for the ends of society and sufficient for the individual conscience; that we need no other distinction; that if there be any other distinction, we can dispense with it, and that, supposing acts in themselves good or evil to be as unconditionally determined from the beginning of things as if they were phenomena of dead matter, still, if the determination from the beginning of things has been that they shall take place through my love of good and hatred of evil, I am a proper object of esteem and affection, and if that they shall take place through my love of self and indifference to good, I am a fit object of aversion which may rise to abhorrence. And no competently informed person will deny that, as a matter of fact, those who have held this creed have had as strong a feeling, both emotional and practical, of moral distinctions, as any other people.*

But these considerations, however pertinent to the subject, do not touch the root of the difficulty. The real question is one of justice—the legitimacy of retribution, or punishment. On the theory of Necessity (we are told) a man cannot help acting as he does, and it cannot be just that he should be punished for what he cannot help.

Not if the expectation of punishment enables him to help it, and is the only means by which he can be enabled to help it?

* Mr. Alexander draws a woeful picture of the pass which mankind would come to, if belief in so-called Necessity became general. All "our current moralities" would come to be regarded "as a form of superstition," all "moral ideas as illusions," by which "it is plain we get rid of them as motives"; consequently the internal sanction of conscience would no longer exist. "The external sanctions remain, but not quite as they were. That important section of them which rests on the *moral* approval or disapproval of our fellow men has, of course, evaporated"; and "in virtue of a deadly moral indifference," the remaining external sanctions "might come to be much more languidly enforced them as now they are," and "the progressive degradation would in a sufficient time "succeed in reproducing the real original gorilla" (pp. 118–121). A formidable prospect; but Mr. Alexander must not suppose that other people's feelings about the matters of highest importance to them are bound up with a certain speculative dogma, and even a certain form of words, because, it seems, his are. As long as guilt is thoroughly regarded as an evil, it would be quite safe even to hold, with Plato, that it is the mental equivalent of bodily disease; people would be none the less anxious to avoid it for themselves, and to cure it in others. Whatever else may be an illusion, it is no illusion that some types of conduct and character are salutary, and others pernicious, to the race and to each of its members, and there is no fear that mankind will not retain the property of their nature by which they prefer what is salutary to what is pernicious, and proclaim and act upon the preference. It is no illusion that human beings are objects of sympathy or of antipathy as they belong to the one type or to the other, and that the sympathies and antipathies excited in us by others react on ourselves. The qualities which each man feels to be odious in others are odious, without illusion, in himself. The basis of Mr. Alexander's gloomy prophecy thus fails him. I might add, that even if his groundless anticipations came to pass in some other manner, and disinterested love of virtue and hatred of guilt

To say that he cannot help it is true or false, according to the qualification with which the assertion is accompanied. Supposing him to be of a vicious disposition, he cannot help doing the criminal act, if he is allowed to believe that he will be able to commit it unpunished. If, on the contrary, the impression is strong in his mind that a heavy punishment will follow, he can, and in most cases does, help it.

The question deemed to be so puzzling is how punishment can be justified, if men's actions are determined by motives, among which motives punishment is one. A more difficult question would be how it can be justified if they are not so determined. Punishment proceeds on the assumption that the will is governed by motives. If punishment had no power of acting on the will, it would be illegitimate, however natural might be the inclination to inflict it. Just so far as the will is supposed free, that is, capable of acting *against* motives, punishment is disappointed of its object, and deprived of its justification.

There are two ends which, on the Necessitarian theory, are sufficient to justify punishment: the benefit of the offender himself, and the protection of others. The first justifies it, because to benefit a person cannot be to do him an injury. To punish him for his own good, provided the inflictor has any proper title to constitute himself a judge, is no more unjust than to administer medicine. As far, indeed, as respects the criminal himself, the theory of punishment is that, by counterbalancing the influence of present temptations or acquired bad habits, it restores the mind to that normal preponderance of the love of right, which many moralists and theologians consider to constitute the true definition of our

---

faded away from the earth, though the human race, thus degenerated, would be little worth preserving, it would probably find the means of preserving itself notwithstanding. The external sanctions, instead of being more languidly, would probably be far more rigidly enforced than at present; for more rigorous penalties would be necessary when there was less inward sentiment to aid them, and however destitute of pure virtuous feeling mankind might be, each one of them would be far too well aware of the importance of other people's conduct to his own interest, not to exact those penalties without stint, and without any of the scruples which at present make conscientious men afraid of carrying repression too far.

freedom.* In its other aspect, punishment is a precaution taken by society in self-defense. To make this just, the only condition required is that the end which society is attempting to enforce by punishment should be a just one. Used as a means of aggression by society on the just rights of the individual, punishment is unjust. Used to protect the just rights of others against unjust aggression by the offender, it is just. If it is possible to have just rights (which is the same thing as to have rights at all), it cannot be unjust to defend them. Free will or no free will, it is just to punish

* "La liberté complète, réelle, de l'homme, est la perfection humaine, le but à atteindre." From a paper by M. Albert Réville, in the *Revue Germanique* for September, 1863, in which the question of free will is discussed (though only parenthetically) with a good sense and philosophy seldom found in recent writings on that subject.

The "Inquirer" accuses me (pp. 49–51) of throwing aside a "well-considered and deliberate opinion, because it refuses to fit in with a foregone conclusion on another subject," when I affirm that the good of the person punished can ever be one of the ends of punishment, and he quotes, on that subject, my essay on Liberty. I am responsible for the Essay, but not for this absurd perversion of its doctrines. Does it anywhere assert that children ought not to be punished for their own good? that parents, and even the magistrate, when dealing with that class of delinquents, are not entitled to constitute themselves judges of the delinquent's good, and even bound to make it the principal consideration? Did I not expressly leave open, as similar to the case of children, that of adult communities which are still in the infantile stage of development? And did I say, or did any one ever say, that when, for the protection of society, we punish those who have done injury to society, the reformation of the offenders is not one of the ends to be aimed at, in the kind and mode at least, of the punishment?

The "Inquirer" adds (p. 49), "If I deserve punishment, only because my love of right is too weak, and my desire for wrong pleasures is too strong, and therefore punishment will help me to dislike the latter the most, then I equally deserve rewards; 'by counterbalancing the influence of present temptation or bad habits,' rewards 'restore the mind to the normal preponderance of the love of right.' . . . And the more wicked I am, the greater reward I deserve. . . . For children, and for all so far as their own improvement is concerned, rewards for evildoers must be more moral than punishments, as tending directly to diminish misery, and increase the sum of human happiness."

so far as is necessary for this purpose, as it is just to put a wild beast to death (without unnecessary suffering) for the same object.

Now, the primitive consciousness we are said to have, that we are accountable for our actions, and that if we violate the rule of right we shall deserve punishment, I contend is nothing else than our knowledge that punishment will be

---

Supposing even that the matter of reward were sufficiently plentiful to allow of compensating everybody for every temptation he foregoes, I submit that this plan would scarcely fulfil the other, and still more important end of punishment, the discouragement of future offenders. And even in the case of children, whose own improvement, as long as their education lasts, is the main end to be considered, every one knows, though he may forget it in confuting an adversary, that pain is a stronger thing than pleasure, and punishment vastly more efficacious than reward. Punishment, too, can alone produce the associations which make the conduct that incurs it, ultimately hateful in itself, and which, by rendering that which is injurious to society sincerely distasteful to its individual members, produces the fellowship of feeling which gives them a sense of common interest and enables them to sympathize and cooperate as creatures of one kin. Thus much to show (if it needs showing) that the preference of punishment to reward as a protection against violations of right is no inconsistency in the conception of social justice laid down in the text. If the objector now asks—But, supposing this were not so, and that rewarding an offender were as effectual a means of improving his own character and protecting society as punishing him, would it equally commend itself to our feeling of desert? I answer, no. It would conflict with that natural, and even animal, desire of retaliation—of hurting those who have hurt us, either in ourselves or in anything we care for—which, as I have elsewhere maintained, is the root of all that distinguishes our feeling of justice from our ordinary sense of expediency. This natural feeling, whether instinctive or acquired, though in itself it has nothing moral in it, yet when moralized by being allied with, and limited by, regard for the general welfare, becomes, in my view of the matter, our moral sentiment of justice. And this sentiment is necessarily offended by rewarding delinquents, and gratified by their punishment. The sentiment is entitled to consideration in a world like ours, in which punishment is really necessary; but granting the absurd supposition of a state of human affairs in which rewarding offenders would really be more expedient than punishing them, there would be no need of this particular moral sentiment and, like other sentiments

just; that by such conduct we shall place ourselves in the position in which our fellow creatures, or the Deity, or both, will naturally, and may justly, inflict punishment upon us. By using the word *justly*, I am not assuming, in the explanation, the thing I profess to explain. As before observed, I am entitled to postulate the reality, and the knowledge and feeling, of moral distinctions. These, it is both evident metaphysically and notorious historically, are independent of any

---

the use of which is superseded by changes in the circumstances of mankind, it might, and probably would, die away.

The chapter in which I have discussed this question (*Utilitarianism*, chap. v.) is quite familiar to Mr. Alexander, who shows himself extremely well acquainted with all parts of it, except those which tell against his own side. Even when he accomplishes (pp. 52 and 59) the great fact of finding in it the two statements—that justice, in the general mind, has a great deal to do with the notion of desert, and that justice is not synonymous with expediency—no one who reads him would suspect that I had explained in the same chapter what, in my view, the notion of desert is, and what there is in our idea of justice besides expediency. Mr. Alexander's perpetual insinuations, and more than insinuations, of bad faith, since he makes a kind of retraction of their grossest meaning in one line of his essay, I pardon, as one of the incidents of his rollicking style, but it is well that he should be aware how easy, if any one were disposed, it would be to retaliate them.

How far Mr. Alexander understands the first elements of the ethical system which he denounces is shown by one of his arguments, which he is so fond of that he repeats it several times: that if the protection of society is a sufficient reason for hanging any one, it holds good for hanging an innocent person, or a madman (pp. 36, 37, 65, 89). He repeatedly says that this has just as deterring an effect as hanging a real criminal, being of opinion, apparently, that hanging a person who is not guilty gives people a motive to abstain from being guilty. As to the madman he asks (p. 65), "How should the state of mind of the maniac, as unamenable to motive, any way affect the efficacy of our hanging him for murder, as a means to deter others from murder?" Mr. Alexander really has no claim to be answered, until he has got a step or two beyond this. Perhaps, however, he may be able to see that all the deterring effect which hanging can produce on men who are amenable to motive is produced by hanging men who are amenable to motive. Hanging, in addition, those who are not amenable to motive adds nothing to the deterring effect, and is therefore a gratuitous brutality.

theory concerning the will. We are supposed capable of understanding that other people have rights, and all that follows from this. The mind which possesses this idea, if capable of placing itself at the point of view of another person, must recognize it as not unjust that others should protect themselves against any disposition on his part to infringe their rights, and he will do so the more readily, because he also has rights, and his rights continually require the same protection. This, I maintain, is our feeling of accountability, in so far as it can be separated from the associations engendered by the prospect of being actually called to account. No one who understands the power of the principle of association can doubt its sufficiency to create out of these elements the whole of the feeling of which we are conscious. To rebut this view of the case would require positive evidence; as, for example, if it could be proved that the feeling of accountability precedes, in the order of development, all experience of punishment. No such evidence has been produced, or is producible. Owing to the limited accessibility to observation of the mental processes of infancy, direct proof can as little be produced on the other side; but if there is any validity in Sir W. Hamilton's Law of Parsimony, we ought not to assume any mental phenomenon as an ultimate fact, which can be accounted for by other known properties of our mental nature.

I ask any one who thinks that the justice of punishment is not sufficiently vindicated by its being for the protection of just rights, how he reconciles his sense of justice to the punishment of crimes committed in obedience to a perverted conscience? Ravaillac and Balthasar Gérard, did not regard themselves as criminals, but as heroic martyrs. If they were justly put to death, the justice of punishment has nothing to do with the state of mind of the offender, further than as this may affect the efficacy of punishment as a means to its end. It is impossible to assert the justice of punishment for crimes of fanaticism, on any other ground than its necessity for the attainment of a just end. If that is not a justification, there is no justification. All other imaginary justifications break down in their application to this case.

If, indeed, punishment is inflicted for any other reason than in order to operate on the will, if its purpose be other than that of improving the culprit himself, or securing the just rights of others against unjust violation, then, I admit, the case is totally altered. If any one thinks that there is justice in the infliction of purposeless suffering, that there is a natural affinity between the two ideas of guilt and punishment, which makes it intrinsically fitting that wherever there has been guilt, pain should be inflicted by way of retribution, I acknowledge that I can find no argument to justify punishment inflicted on this principle. As a legitimate satisfaction to feelings of indignation and resentment which are on the whole salutary and worthy of cultivation, I can in certain cases admit it, but here it is still a means to an end. The merely retributive view of punishment derives no justification from the doctrine I support. But it derives quite as little from the free-will doctrine. Suppose it true that the will of a malefactor, when he committed an offense, was free, or in other words, that he acted badly, not because he was of a bad disposition, but from no cause in particular; it is not easy to deduce from this the conclusion that it is just to punish him. That his acts were beyond the command of motives might be a good reason for keeping out of his way, or placing him under bodily restraint, but no reason for inflicting pain upon him, when that pain, by supposition, could not operate as a deterring motive.

While the doctrine I advocate does not support the idea that punishment in mere retaliation is justifiable, it at the same time fully accounts for the general and natural sentiment of its being so. From our earliest childhood, the idea of doing wrong (that is, of doing what is forbidden, or what is injurious to others) and the idea of punishment are presented to our mind together, and the intense character of the impressions causes the association between them to attain the highest degree of closeness and intimacy. Is it strange, or unlike the usual processes of the human mind, that in these circumstances we should retain the feeling, and forget the reason on which it is grounded? But why do I speak of forgetting? In most cases the reason has never, in our early education, been presented to the mind. The only ideas presented have been those of wrong and punishment, and an inseparable association has been created between these directly, without the help of any intervening idea. This is quite enough to make the spontaneous feelings of mankind regard punishment and a wrongdoer as naturally fitted to each other—as a conjunction appropriate in itself, independently of any consequences. Even

Sir W. Hamilton recognizes as one of the common sources of error, that "the associations of thought are mistaken for the connections of existence."* If this is true anywhere, it is truest of all in the associations into which emotions enter. A strong feeling, directly excited by an object, is felt (except when contradicted by the feelings of other people) as its own sufficient justification—no more requiring the support of a reason than the fact that ginger is hot in the mouth; and it almost requires a philosopher to recognize the need of a reason for his feelings, unless he has been under the practical necessity of justifying them to persons by whom they are not shared.

That a person holding what is called the Necessitarian doctrine should on that account *feel* that it would be unjust to punish him for his wrong actions, seems to me the veriest of chimeras. Yes, if he really "could not help" acting as he did, that is, if it did not depend on his will, if he was under physical constraint, or even if he was under the action of such a violent motive that no fear of punishment could have any effect; which, if capable of being ascertained, is a just ground of exemption, and is the reason why by the laws of most countries people are not punished for what they were compelled to do by immediate danger of death. But if the criminal was in a state capable of being operated upon by the fear of punishment, no metaphysical objection, I believe, will make him feel his punishment unjust. Neither will he feel that because his act was the consequence of motives, operating upon a certain mental disposition, it was not his own fault. For first, it was at all events his own defect or infirmity, for which the expectation of punishment is the appropriate cure. And secondly, the word "fault," so far from being inapplicable, is the specific name for the kind of defect or infirmity which he has displayed—insufficient love of good and aversion to evil. The weakness of these feelings or their strength is in every one's mind the standard of fault or merit, of degrees of fault and degrees of merit. Whether we are judging of particular actions, or of the character of a person, we are wholly guided by the indications afforded of the energy of these influences. If the desire of right and aversion to wrong have yielded to a small temptation, we judge them to be weak, and our disapprobation is strong. If the temptation to which they have

* *Lectures*, iii. 47.

yielded is so great that even strong feelings of virtue might have succumbed to it, our moral reprobation is less intense. If, again, the moral desires and aversions have prevailed, but not over a very strong force, we hold that the action was good, but that there was little merit in it, and our estimate of the merit rises, in exact proportion to the greatness of the obstacle which the moral feeling proved strong enough to overcome.

Mr. Mansel* has furnished what he thinks a refutation of the Necessitarian argument, of which it is well to take notice, the more so, perhaps, as it is directed against some remarks on the subject by the present writer in a former work,† remarks which were not intended as an argument for so-called Necessity, but only to place the nature and meaning of that ill-understood doctrine in a truer light. With this purpose in view, it was remarked that "by saying that a man's actions necessarily follow from his character, all that is really meant (for no more is meant in any case whatever of causation) is that he invariably does act in conformity to his character, and that any one who thoroughly knew his character could certainly predict how he would act in any supposable case. No more than this is contended for by any one but an Asiatic fatalist." "And no more than this," observes Mr. Mansel, "is needed to construct a system of fatalism as rigid as any Asiatic can desire."

Mr. Mansel is mistaken in thinking that the doctrine of the causation of human actions is fatalism at all, or resembles fatalism in any of its moral or intellectual effects. To call it by that name is to break down a fundamental distinction. Real fatalism is of two kinds. Pure, or Asiatic fatalism—the fatalism of the Oedipus—holds that our actions do not depend upon our desires. Whatever our wishes may be, a superior power, or an abstract destiny, will overrule them, and compel us to act, not as we desire, but in the manner predestined. Our love of good and hatred of evil are of no efficacy and, though in themselves they may be virtuous, as far as conduct is concerned it is unavailing to cultivate them. The other kind —Modified Fatalism I will call it—holds that our actions are determined by our will, our will by our desires, and our de-

---

* *Prolegomena Logica*, Note C at the end.
† *System of Logic*, Book vi, ch. 2.

sires by the joint influence of the motives presented to us and of our individual character, but that, our character having been made for us and not by us, we are not responsible for it, nor for the actions it leads to, and should in vain attempt to alter them. The true doctrine of the Causation of human actions maintains, in opposition to both, that not only our conduct but our character is in part amenable to our will, that we can, by employing the proper means, improve our character, and that if our character is such that while it remains what it is, it necessitates us to do wrong, it will be just to apply motives which will necessitate us to strive for its improvement, and so emancipate ourselves from the other necessity. In other words, we are under a moral obligation to seek the improvement of our moral character. We shall not indeed do so unless we desire our improvement, and desire it more than we dislike the means which must be employed for the purpose. But does Mr. Mansel, or any other of the free-will philosophers, think that we can will the means if we do not desire the end, or if our desire of the end is weaker than our aversion to the means?*

* This vital truth in moral psychology, that we can improve our character if we will, is a great stumbling block both to the "Inquirer" and to Mr. Alexander. They maintain that this fact makes no difference at all, and that the Causation of human actions is exactly the same thing as Modified Fatalism. That the "Inquirer" cannot see any difference excites no surprise, since he professes himself (p. 46) unable to understand "how our conduct is amenable to our will if it is wholly caused by our character and circumstances." Is not the very doctrine he is contending against, that our character and circumstances cause it *through* our will? Both he and Mr. Alexander protest vehemently, and Mr. Alexander at much length, that the Causation doctrine is as incompatible with Free Will as Fatalism is. As if anybody had denied that. In the very next paragraph, when arguing against Kant, I expressly affirmed it. But if it is not too much to ask, let them try to put their own opinion in abeyance, and condescend for a few moments to look at the question from mine. Suppose (I have as much right to make the supposition as they have) that a person dislikes some part of his own character, and would be glad to change it. He cannot, as he well knows, change it by a mere act of volition. He must use the means which nature gives to ourselves, as she gave to our parents and teachers, of influencing our character by appropriate circumstances. If he is a Modified Fatalist, he will not

Mr. Mansel is more rigid in his ideas of what the free-will theory requires, than one of the most eminent of the thinkers who have adopted it. According to Mr. Mansel, the belief that whoever knew perfectly our character and our circumstances could predict our actions, amounts to Asiatic fatalism. According to Kant, in his *Metaphysics of Ethics*, such capability of prediction is quite compatible with the freedom of the will. This seems, at first sight, to be an admission of everything which the rational supporters of the opposite theory could desire. But Kant avoids this consequence, by changing (as lawyers would say) the *venue* of free will, from our actions generally, to the formation of our character. It is in that, he thinks, we are free, and he is almost willing to admit that while our character is what it is, our actions are necessitated by it. In drawing this distinction, the philosopher of Königsberg saves inconvenient facts at the expense of the consistency of his theory. There cannot be one theory for one kind of voluntary actions, and another theory for the other kinds.

---

use those means, for he will not believe in their efficacy, but will remain passively discontented with himself, or what is worse, will learn to be contented, thinking that his character has been made for him, and that he cannot make it over again, however willing. If, on the contrary, he is a Moral Causationist, he will know that the work is not finally and irrevocably done, that the improvement of his character is still possible by the proper means, the only needful condition being that he should desire, what by the supposition he does desire; consequently, if the desire is stronger than the means are disagreeable, he will set about doing that which, if done, will improve his character. I cannot suppose my critics capable of maintaining that such a difference as this, between the two theories, is of no practical importance, and I must, with all courtesy, decline to recognize as entitled to any voice in the question, whoever is not able to seize a distinction so broad and obvious.

Mr. Alexander's curious dictum (pp. 18–20) that a motive is itself an act, can only have a true meaning, or any meaning at all, if understood of this indirect influence of our voluntary acts over our mental dispositions. That a person can, by an act of will, either give to himself, or take away from himself, a desire or an aversion, I suppose even Mr. Alexander will hardly affirm; but we can, by a course of self-culture, finally modify, to a greater or less extent, our desires and aversions, which is the doctrine of Moral Causation, as distinguished from Modified Fatalism.

When we voluntarily exert ourselves, as it is our duty to do, for the improvement of our character, or when we act in a manner which (either consciously on our part or unconsciously) deteriorates it, these, like all other voluntary acts, presuppose that there was already something in our character, or in that combined with our circumstances, which led us to do so, and accounts for our doing so. The person, therefore, who is supposed able to predict our actions from our character as it now is, would, under the same conditions of perfect knowledge, be equally able to predict what we should do to change our character: and if this be the meaning of necessity, that part of our conduct is as necessary as all the rest. If necessity means more than this abstract possibility of being foreseen; if it means any mysterious compulsion, apart from simple invariability of sequence, I deny it as strenuously as any one in the case of human volitions, but I deny just as much of all other phenomena. To enforce this distinction was the principal object of the remarks which Mr. Mansel has criticized. If an unessential distinction from Mr. Mansel's point of view, it is essential from mine, and of supreme importance in a practical aspect.

The free-will metaphysicians have made little endeavor to prove that we can will in opposition to our strongest desire, but have strenuously maintained that we can will when we have no strongest desire. With this view Dr. Reid formerly, and Mr. Mansel now, have thrown in the teeth of Necessitarians the famous *asinus Buridani*. If, say they, the will were solely determined by motives, the ass, between two bundles of hay, exactly alike, and equally distant from him, would remain undecided until he died of hunger. From Sir W. Hamilton's notes on this chapter of Reid,* I infer that he did not countenance this argument, and it is surprising that writers of talent should have seen anything in it. I waive the objection that, if it applies at all, it proves that the ass also has free will, for perhaps he has. But the ass, it is affirmed, would starve before he decided. Yes, possibly, if he remained all the time in a fixed attitude of deliberation, if he never for an instant ceased to balance one against another the rival attractions, and if they really were so exactly equal that no dwelling on them could detect any difference. But this is not the way

* Pp. 609–611.

in which things take place on our planet. From mere lassitude, if from no other cause, he would intermit the process, and cease thinking of the rival objects at all, until a moment arrived when he would be seeing or thinking of one only, and that fact, combined with the sensation of hunger, would determine him to a decision.

But the argument on which Mr. Mansel lays most stress (it is also one of Reid's) is the following. Necessitarians say that the will is governed by the strongest motive: "but I only know the strength of motives in relation to the will by the test of ultimate prevalence, so that this means no more than that the prevailing motive prevails." I have heretofore complimented Mr. Mansel on seeing farther, in some things, than his master. In the present instance I am compelled to remark that he has not seen so far. Sir W. Hamilton was not the man to neglect an argument like this, had there been no flaw in it. The fact is that there are two. First, those who say that the will follows the strongest motive, do not mean the motive which is strongest in relation to the will, or in other words, that the will follows what it does follow. They mean the motive which is strongest in relation to pain and pleasure, since a motive, being a desire or aversion, is proportional to the pleasantness, as conceived by us, of the thing desired, or the painfulness of the thing shunned. And when what was at first a direct impulse towards pleasure, or recoil from pain, has passed into a habit or a fixed purpose, then the strength of the motive means the completeness and promptitude of the association which has been formed between an idea and an outward act. This is the first answer to Mr. Mansel. The second is, that even supposing there were no test of the strength of motives but their effect on the will, the proposition that the will follows the strongest motive would not, as Mr. Mansel supposes, be identical and unmeaning. We say, without absurdity that, if two weights are placed in opposite scales, the heavier will lift the other up, yet we mean nothing by the heavier, except the weight which will lift up the other. The proposition, nevertheless, is not unmeaning, for it signifies that in many or most cases there *is* a heavier, and that this is always the same one, not one or the other as it may happen. In like manner, even if the strongest motive meant only the motive which prevails, yet if there is a prevailing motive—if, all other antecedents being the same, the motive which pre-

vails today will prevail tomorrow and every subsequent day—
Sir W. Hamilton was acute enough to see that the free-will
theory is not saved. I regret that I cannot, in this instance,
credit Mr. Mansel with the same acuteness.

Before leaving the subject, it is worth while to remark that
not only the doctrine of Necessity, but Predestination in its
coarsest form—the belief that all our actions are divinely preordained—though, in my view, inconsistent with ascribing any
moral attributes whatever to the Deity, yet if combined with
the belief that God works according to general laws, which
have to be learnt from experience, has no tendency to make
us act in any respect otherwise than we should do if we
thought our actions really contingent. For if God acts according to general laws, then, whatever he may have preordained,
he has preordained that it shall take place through the causes
on which experience shows it to be consequent, and if he has
predestined that I shall attain my ends, he has predestined
that I shall do so by studying and putting in practice the
means which lead to their attainment. When the belief in predestination has a paralyzing effect on conduct, as is sometimes
the case with Mohammedans, it is because they fancy they
can infer what God has predestined, without waiting for the
result. They think that either by particular signs of some sort,
or from the general aspect of things, they can perceive the
issue towards which God is working and, having discovered
this, naturally deem useless any attempt to defeat it. Because
something will certainly happen if nothing is done to prevent
it, they think it will certainly happen whatever may be done
to prevent it; in a word, they believe in Necessity in the only
proper meaning of the term—an issue unalterable by human
efforts or desires.

ELEVEN

On the Moral Sentiments:
Two Comments

[The question of the nature and psychological origin of the moral sentiments is one to which Mill returned frequently, but which he never handled in a separate work. In a letter to Dr. W. G. Ward, an old acquaintance and philosophical opponent, Mill gave his views on the feeling of moral obligation quite clearly, and his theory of approval and disapproval is clarified by a long footnote to a remark in James Mill's *Analysis of the Phenomena of the Human Mind*, of which John Stuart Mill published a new edition in 1869.]

1. To Dr. W. G. Ward, November 28, 1859

NOW, AS TO THE still more important subject of the meaning of *ought*. I will endeavor to explain the sense I attach to it, though this cannot be done in very few words. I believe that the word has in some respects a different meaning to different people. We must first distinguish between those who have themselves a moral feeling—a feeling of approving and condemning conscience—and those who have not, or in whom what they may have is dormant. I believe that those who have no *feeling* of right and wrong cannot possibly intue [sic] the rightness or wrongness of anything. They may assent to the proposition that a certain rule of conduct is right, but they really mean nothing except that such is the conduct which other people expect and require at their hands, with perhaps the addition that they have a strong motive for themselves requiring the same from other people. This you will probably agree with, and I will therefore pass to the case of those who have a true moral feeling, that is, a feeling of pain in the fact of violating a certain rule, quite independently of any expected consequences to themselves. It appears to me that to them the word *ought* means that, if they act otherwise, they shall be punished by this internal and perfectly disinterested feeling. Unless they would be so punished, or unless they think they would, any assertion they make to themselves that they ought so to act seems to me to lose its proper meaning, and to refer only to the sentiments of others, or of themselves at some other time or in some other case.

If I am asked what is the nature of this feeling, and whence it comes, I do not think that it is exactly of the same nature or has exactly the same origin in all who have it. My father's theory of it, which you quote, seems to me a sufficient account of it, as it exists in many minds. I certainly do not accept that theory as an exhaustive analysis of the phenomenon; yet I do not think your refutation, even of that theory, a sufficient one, inasmuch as the generation of a complex feeling from simple ones, being a sort of chemical union, not a mechanical juxtaposition, it is quite to be expected that the compound will be to appearance unlike the elements it is formed from. The pains of conscience are certainly very different from those of the dread of disapprobation; yet it might well be that the innumerable associations of pain with doing wrong which have been riveted by a long succession of pains undergone, or pains feared or imagined as the consequence of wrong things done, or of wrong things which we have been tempted to do (especially in early life), may produce a general and intense feeling of recoil from wrongdoing in which no conscious influence of other people's disapprobation may be perceptible.

However, I do not hold this to be the normal form of moral feeling. I conceive that feeling to be a natural outgrowth from the social nature of man; a state of society is so eminently natural to human beings that anything which is an obviously indispensable condition of social life easily comes to act upon their minds almost like a physical necessity. Now it is an indispensable condition of all society, except between master and slave, that each shall pay regard to the other's happiness. On this basis, combined with a human creature's capacity of fellow-feeling, the feelings of morality properly so-called seem to me to be grounded, and their main constituent to be the idea of punishment. I feel conscious that, if I violate certain laws, other people must necessarily and naturally desire that I should be punished for the violation. I also feel that I should desire them to be punished if they violated the same laws towards me. From these feelings and from the sociality of my nature I place myself in their situation, and sympathize in their desire that I should be punished, and (even apart from benevolence) the painfulness of not being in union with them makes me shrink from pursuing a line of conduct which would make my ends, wishes, and purposes habitually conflict with theirs. To this fellow-feeling with man may of course be added (if I may so express myself) fellow-feeling with God, and recoil from the idea of not being in unison with Him. May I add that even to an unbeliever there may be a feeling similar in nature towards an *ideal* God, as there may be towards an ideally perfect man, or towards our friends who are no more, even if we do not feel assured of their immortality? All these feelings are immensely increased in strength by a reflected influence from other persons who feel the same.

This is the nearest approach I am able to make to a theory of our moral feelings. I have written it out, much more fully, in a little manuscript treatise which I propose to publish. . . .

2. Footnote to Chapter XXIII of James Mill's *Analysis of the Phenomena of the Human Mind*, 1869

I

IT HAD BEEN POINTED OUT in a preceding chapter that Wealth, Power, Dignity, and many other things which are not in their own nature pleasures, but only causes of pleasures and of exemption from pains, become so closely associated with the pleasures of which they are causes, and their absence or loss becomes so closely associated with the pains to which it exposes us, that the things become objects of love and desire, and their absence an object of hatred and aversion, for their own sake, without reference to their consequences. By virtue of the same law of association, it is pointed out in the present chapter that human actions, both our own and those of other people, standing so high as they do among the causes both of pleasure and of pain to us (sometimes by their direct operation, and sometimes through the sentiments they give birth to in other persons towards ourselves) tend naturally to become inclosed in a web of associated ideas of pleasures or of pains at a very early period of life, in such sort that the ideas of acts beneficial to ourselves and to others become pleasurable in themselves, and the ideas of acts hurtful to ourselves and to others become painful in themselves; and both kinds of acts become objects of a feeling, the former of love, the latter of aversion, which having, in our minds, become independent of any pleasures or pains actually expected to result to ourselves from the acts, may be truly said to be disinterested. It is no less obvious that acts which are not really beneficial, or not really hurtful, but which, through some false opinion prevailing among mankind, or some extraneous agency operating on their sentiments, incur their praise or blame, may and often do come to be objects of a quite similar disinterested love or hatred, exactly as if they deserved it. This disinterested love and hatred of actions, generated by the association of praise or blame with them, constitute, in the author's opinion, the feelings of moral approbation and disapprobation, which the majority of psychologists have thought it necessary to refer to an original and ultimate principle of our nature. Mr. Bain, in the preceding note, makes in this theory a correction, to which the author himself would probably not have objected, namely, that the mere idea of a pain or pleasure, by whomsoever felt, is intrinsically painful or pleasurable, and when raised in the mind with intensity is capable of becoming a stimulus to action, independent, not merely of expected consequences to ourselves, but of any reference whatever to Self; so that care for others is, in an admissible sense, as much an ultimate fact of our nature, as care for ourselves, though one which greatly needs strengthening by the concurrent force of the manifold associations insisted on in the author's text. Though this of Mr. Bain is rather an account of disinterested Sympathy, than of the moral feeling, it is undoubtedly true that the *foundation* of the moral feeling is the adoption of the pleasures and pains of others as our own, whether this takes place by the natural force of sympathy, or by the association which has grown up in our mind between our own good or evil and theirs. The moral feeling rests upon this identification of the feelings of others with our own, but is not the same thing with it. To constitute the moral feeling, not only must the good of others have become in itself a pleasure to us, and their suffering a pain, but this pleasure or pain must be associated with our own acts as producing it, and must in this manner have become a motive, prompting us to the one sort of acts, and restraining us from the other sort. And this is, in brief, the author's theory of the Moral Sentiments.

The exhaustive treatment of this subject would require a length and abundance of discussion disproportioned to the compass and purposes of a treatise like the present, which was intended to expound what the author believed to be the real mode of formation of our complex states of consciousness, but not to say all that may and ought to be said in refutation of other views of the subject. There are, however, some important parts of the author's own theory, which are not stated in this work, but in a subsequent one, of a highly polemical character, the *Fragment on Mackintosh*, and it may be both instructive and interesting to the reader to find the statement here. I therefore subjoin the passages containing it.

Nature makes no classes. Nature makes individuals. Classes are made by men, and rarely with such marks as determine certainly what is to be included in them.

Men make classifications, as they do every thing else, for some end. Now, for what end was it that men, out of their innumerable acts, selected a class to which they gave the name of moral, and another class to which they gave the name of immoral? What was the motive of this act? What its final cause?

Assuredly the answer to this question is the first step, though Sir James saw it not, towards the solution of his two questions, comprehending the whole of ethical science: first, what makes an act to be moral? and secondly, what are the sentiments with which we regard it?

We may also be assured, that it was some very obvious interest which recommended this classification, for it was performed, in a certain rough way, in the very rudest states of society.

Farther, we may easily see how, even in very rude states, men were led to it, by little less than necessity. Every day of their lives they had experience of acts, some of which were agreeable, or the cause of what was agreeable, to them, others disagreeable, or the cause of what was disagreeable to them, in all possible degrees.

They had no stronger interest than to obtain the repetition of the one sort, and to prevent the repetition of the other.

The acts in which they were thus interested were of two sorts: first, those to which the actor was led by a natural interest of his own; secondly, those to which the actor was not led by any interest of his own. About the first sort there was not occasion for any particular concern. They were pretty sure to take place, without any stimulus from without. The second sort, on the contrary, were not likely to take place, unless an interest was artificially created, sufficiently strong to induce the actor to perform them.

And here we clearly perceive the origin of that important case of classification . . . the classification of acts as moral and immoral. The acts which it was important to other men that each individual should perform, but in which the individual had not a sufficient interest to secure the performance of them, were constituted one class. The acts, which it was important to other men that each individual should abstain from, but in regard to which he had not a personal interest sufficiently strong to secure his abstaining from them, were constituted another class. The first class were distinguished by the name moral acts; the second by the name immoral.

The interest which men had in securing the performance of the one set of acts, the non-performance of the other, led them by a sort of necessity to think of the means. They had to create an interest, which the actor would not otherwise have, in the performance of the one sort, the non-performance of the other. And in proceeding to this end, they could not easily miss their way. They had two powers applicable to the purpose. They had a certain quantity of good at their disposal, and they had a certain quantity of evil. If they could apply the good in such a manner as to afford a motive both for the performance and non-performance which they desired, or the evil, in such a manner as to afford a motive against the performance and non-performance which they wished to prevent, their end was attained.

And this is the scheme which they adopted, and which, in every situation, they have invariably pursued. The whole business of the moral sentiments, moral approbation, and disapprobation, has this for its object: the distribution of the good and evil we have at command, for the production of acts of the useful sort, the prevention of acts of the contrary sort. Can there be a nobler object?

But though men have been thus always right in their general aim, their proceedings have been cruelly defective in the detail; witness the consequence—the paucity of good acts, the frequency of bad acts, which there is in the world.

A portion of acts having been thus classed into good and bad, and the utility having been perceived of creating motives to incite to the one, and restrain from the other, a subclassification was introduced. One portion of these acts was such that the good and evil available for their production and prevention, could be applied by the community in its conjunct capacity. Another portion was such that the good and evil available could be applied only by individuals in their individual capacity. The first portion was placed under the control of what is called law; the other remained under the control of the moral sentiments, that is, the distribution of good and evil, made by individuals in their individual capacity.

No sooner was the class made than the rule followed. Moral acts are to be performed; immoral acts are to be abstained from.

Beside this the general rule, there was needed, for more precise direction, particular rules.

We must remember the fundamental condition, that all rules of action must be preceded by a corresponding classification of actions. All moral rules, comprehended in the great moral rule, must relate to a class of actions comprehended within the grand class, constituted and marked by the term moral. This is the case with grand classes in general. They are subdivided into minor classes, each of the minor classes being a portion of the larger. Thus, the grand class of acts called moral has been divided into certain convenient portions, or subclasses, and marked by particular names: Just, Beneficent, Brave, Prudent, Temperate, to each of which classes belongs its appropriate rule that men should be just, that they should be beneficent, and so on. . . .

In the performance of our duties two sets of cases may be distinguished. There is one set in which a direct estimate of the good of the particular act is inevitable, and the man acts immorally who acts without making it. There are other cases in which it is not necessary.

The first are those, which have in them so much of singularity, as to prevent their coming within the limits of any established class. In such cases a man has but one guide: he must consider the consequences, or act not as a moral or rational agent at all.

The second are cases of such ordinary and frequent occurrence as to be distinguished into classes. And everybody knows . . . that when a class of acts are performed regularly and frequently, they are at last performed by habit; in other words, the idea of the act and the performance of it follow so easily and speedily that they seem to cohere, and to be but one operation. It is only necessary to recall some of the more familiar instances, to see the mode of this formation. In playing on a musical instrument, every note at first is found by an effort. Afterwards, the proper choice is made so rapidly as to appear as if made by a mechanical process in which the mind has no concern. The same is the case with moral acts. When they have been performed with frequency and uniformity, for a sufficient length of time, a habit is generated. . . .

When a man acts from habit, he does not act without reflection. He only acts with a very rapid reflection. In no class of acts does a man begin to act by habit. He begins without habit, and acquires the habit by frequency of acting. The consideration on which the act is founded, and the act itself, form a sequence. And it is obvious, from the familiar cases of music and of speaking, that it is a sequence at first not very easily performed. By every repetition, however, it becomes easier. The consideration occurs with less effort; the action follows with less effort; they take place with greater and greater rapidity, till they seem blended. To say that this is acting without reflection is only ignorance, for it is thus seen to be a case of acting by reflection so easily and rapidly that the reflection and the act cannot be distinguished from one another. . . .

Since moral acts are not performed at first by habit, but each upon the consideration which recommends it, upon what considerations, we may be asked, do moral acts begin to be performed?

The question has two meanings, and it is necessary to reply to both. It may be asked upon what consideration the men of our own age and country, for example, at first, and before a habit is formed, perform moral acts? Or, it may be asked, upon what consideration did men originally perform moral acts?

To the first of these questions every one can reply from his own memory and observation. We perform moral acts at first from authority. Our parents tell us that we ought to do this, ought not to do that. They are anxious that we should obey their precepts. They have two sets of influences with which to work upon us: praise and blame, reward and punishment. All the acts which they say we ought to do are praised in the highest degree, all those which they say we ought not to do are blamed in the highest degree. In this manner, the ideas of praise and blame become associated with certain classes of acts, at a very early age, so closely that they cannot easily be disjoined. No sooner does the idea of the act occur than the idea of praise springs up along with it and clings to it. And generally these associations exert a predominant influence during the whole of life.

Our parents not only praise certain kinds of acts, blame other kinds; but they praise us when we perform those of the one sort, blame us when we perform those of the other. In this manner other associations are formed. The idea of ourselves performing certain acts is associated with the idea of our being praised, performing certain other acts with the idea of our being blamed, so closely that the ideas become at last indissoluble. In this association consist the very important complex ideas of praiseworthiness, and blameworthiness. An act which is praiseworthy is an act with the idea of which the idea of praise is indissolubly joined; an agent who is praiseworthy is an agent with the idea of whom the idea of praise is indissolubly joined. And in the converse case, that of blameworthiness, the formation of the idea is similar.

Many powerful circumstances come in aid of these important associations, at an early age. We find that not only our parents act in this manner, but all other parents. We find that grown people act in this manner, not only towards children but towards one another. The associations, therefore, are unbroken, general, and all-comprehending.

Our parents administer not only praise and blame, to induce us to perform acts of one sort, abstain from acts of another sort, but also rewards and punishments. They do so directly, and, further, they forward all our inclinations in the one case, balk them in the other. So does everybody else. We find our comforts excessively abridged by other people, when we act in one way, enlarged when we act in another way. Hence another most important class of associations: that of an increase of well-being from the goodwill of our fellow creatures, if we perform acts of one sort, of an increase of misery from their ill will, if we perform those of another sort.

In this manner it is that men born in the social state acquire the habits of moral acting, and certain affections connected with it, before they are capable of reflecting upon the grounds which recommend the acts either to praise or blame. Nearly at this point the greater part of them remain, continuing to perform moral acts and to abstain from the contrary, chiefly from the habits they have acquired and the authority upon which they originally acted, though it is not possible that any man should come to the years and blessing of reason without perceiving, at least in an indistinct and general way, the advantage which mankind derive from their acting towards one another in one way rather than another.

We come now to the second question, viz. what are the considerations upon which men originally performed moral acts? The answer to this question is substantially contained in the explanation already given of the classification of acts as moral and immoral.

When men began to mark the distinction between acts, and were prompted to praise one class, blame another, they did so, either because the one sort benefited, the other hurt them, or for some other reason. If for the first reason, the case is perfectly intelligible. The men had a motive which they understood, and which was adequate to the end. If it was not on account of utility that men classed some acts as moral, others as immoral, on what other account was it?

To this question, an answer consisting of anything but words has never been returned.

It has been said that there is a beauty and a deformity in moral and immoral acts, which recommended them to the distinctions they have met with.

It is obvious to reply to this hypothesis that the mind of a savage, that is, a mind in the state in which the minds of all men were when they began to classify their acts, was not likely to be much affected by the ideal something called the beauty of acts. To receive pain or pleasure from an act, to obtain, or be deprived of, the means of enjoyment by an act; to like the acts and the actors whence the good proceeded, dislike those whence the evil proceeded—all these were things which they understood.

But we must endeavor to get a little nearer to the bottom of this affair.

In truth, the term beauty as applied to acts is just as unintelligible to the philosopher as to the savage. Is the beauty of an act one thing, the morality of it another? Or are they two names for the same thing? If they are two things, what is the beauty, distinct from the morality? If they are the same thing, what is the use of the name morality? It only tends to confusion.

But this is not all. The beautiful is that which excites in us the emotion of beauty, a state of mind with which we are acquainted by experience. This state of mind has been successfully analyzed, and shown to consist of a train of pleasurable ideas, awakened in us by the beautiful object.

But is it in this way only that we are concerned in moral acts? Do we value them for nothing, but as we value a picture or a piece of music, for the pleasure of looking at them or hearing them? Everybody knows the contrary. Acts are objects of importance to us, on account of their consequences and nothing else. This constitutes a radical distinction between them and the things called beautiful. Acts are hurtful or beneficial, moral or immoral, virtuous or vicious. But it is only an abuse of language to call them beautiful or ugly.

That it is jargon, the slightest reflection is sufficient to evince, for what is the beauty of an act, detached from its consequences? We shall be told, perhaps, that the beauty of an act was never supposed to be detached from its consequences. The beauty consists in the consequences. I am contented with the answer. But observe to what it binds you. The consequences of acts are the good or evil they do. According to you, therefore, the beauty of acts is either the utility of them or it is nothing at all—a beautiful ground on which to dispute with us that acts are classed as moral, not on account of their utility, but on account of their beauty.

It will be easily seen, from what has been said, that they who ascribe the classification of acts as moral and immoral, to a certain taste, an agreeable or disagreeable sentiment which they excite (among whom are included the Scottish professors Hutcheson, and Brown, and David Hume himself, though on his part with wonderful inconsistency)— hold the same theory with those who say that beauty is the source of the classification of moral acts. Things are classed as beautiful, or deformed, on account of a certain taste, or inward sentiment. If acts are classed in the same way, on account of a certain taste or inward sentiment, they deserve to be classed under the names beautiful and deformed; otherwise not.

I hope it is not necessary for me to go minutely into the exposure of the other varieties of jargon by which it has been endeavored to account for the classification of acts as moral and immoral. "Fitness" is one of them. Acts are approved on account of their fitness. When fitness is hunted down, it is brought to bay exactly at the place where beauty was. Fitness is either the goodness of the consequences or it is nothing at all.

The same is the case with "Right Reason," or "Moral Reason." An act according to moral reason is an act the consequences of which are good. Moral reason, therefore, is another name, and not a bad name, for the principle of utility.[a]

[a] *Fragment on Mackintosh*, pp. 247–265.

The following passage from another part of the same work, is also very much to the purpose:

> The terms moral and immoral were applied by men, primarily, not to their own acts, but the acts of other men. Those acts, the effects of which they observed to be beneficial, they desired should be performed. To make them be performed, they, among other things they did, affixed to them marks of their applause; they called them, good, moral, well-deserving, and behaved accordingly.
>
> Such is the source of the moral approbation we bestow on the acts of other men. The source of that which we bestow on our own is twofold. First, every man's beneficial acts, like those of every other man, form part of that system of beneficial acting in which he, in common with all other men, finds his account. Secondly, he strongly associates with his own beneficial acts both that approbation of other men, which is of so much importance to him, and that approbation which he bestows on other men's beneficial acts.
>
> It is also easy to show what takes place in the mind of a man, before he performs an act which he morally approves or condemns.
>
> What is called the approbation of an act not yet performed, is only the idea of future approbation; and it is not excited by the act itself, it is excited by the idea of the act. The idea of approbation or disapprobation is excited by the idea of an act, because the approbation would be excited by the act itself. But what excites moral approbation or disapprobation of an act is neither the act itself nor the motive of the act, but the consequences of the act, good or evil, and their being within the intention of the agent.
>
> Let us put a case. A man with a starving wife and family is detected wiring a hare on my premises. What happens? I call up the idea of sending him to prison. I call up the ideas of the consequences of that act, the misery of the helpless creatures whom his labor supported, their agonizing feelings, their corporal wants, their hunger, cold, their destitution of hope, their despair; I call up the ideas of the man himself in jail, the sinking of heart which attends incarceration, the dreadful thought of his family deprived of his support, his association with vicious characters, the natural consequences—his future profligacy, the consequent profligacy of his ill-fated children, and hence the permanent wretchedness and ruin of them all. I next have the idea of my own intending all these consequences. And only then am I in a condition to perform, as Sir James says, the "op-

eration of conscience." I perform it. But in this case, it is, to use another of his expressions, "defeated." Notwithstanding the moral disapprobation, which the idea of such intended consequences excites in me, I perform the act.

Here, at all events, any one may see, that conscience and the motive of the act are not the same, but opposed to one another. The motive of the act is the pleasure of having hares, not in itself a thing anywise bad. The only thing bad is the producing so much misery to others, for securing that pleasure to myself.

The state of the case, then, is manifest. The act of which I have the idea has two sets of consequences: one set pleasurable, another hurtful. I feel an aversion to produce the hurtful consequences. I feel a desire to produce the pleasurable. The one prevails over the other. . . .

. . . Nothing in an act is voluntary but the consequences that are intended. The idea of good consequences intended is the pleasurable feeling of moral approbation; the idea of bad consequences intended is the painful feeling of moral disapprobation. The very term voluntary, therefore, applied to an act which produces good or evil consequences, expresses the antecedence of moral approbation or disapprobation.[a]

I will quote one short passage more, in correction of the very vulgar error that to analyze our disinterested affections and resolve them into associations with the ideas of our own elementary pleasures and pains is to deny their reality:

Sir James must mean, if he means anything, that to trace up the motive affections of human nature to pain and pleasure, is to make personal advantage the only motive. This is to affirm that he who analyzes any of the complicated phenomena of human nature, and points out the circumstances of their formation, puts an end to them.

Sir James was totally ignorant of this part of human nature. Gratitude remains gratitude, resentment remains resentment, generosity generosity in the mind of him who feels them, after analysis, the same as before. The man who can trace them to their elements does not cease to feel them as much as the man who never thought about the matter. And whatever effects they produce, as motives, in the mind of the man who never thought about the matter, they produce equally in the minds of those who have analyzed them the most minutely.

[a] *Fragment on Mackintosh*, pp. 375–378.

They are constituent parts of human nature. How we are actuated, when we feel them, is matter of experience, which every one knows within himself. Their action is what it is, whether they are simple or compound. Does a complex motive cease to be a motive whenever it is discovered to be complex? The analysis of the active principles leaves the nature of them untouched. To be able to assert that a philosopher who finds some of the active principles of human nature to be compound and traces them to their origin does on that account exclude them from human nature, and deny their efficiency as constituent parts of that nature, discovers a total incapacity of thinking upon these subjects. When Newton discovered that a white ray of light is not simple but compound, did he for that reason exclude it from the denomination of light, and deny that it produced its effects, with respect to our perception, as if it were of the same nature with the elementary rays of which it is composed?[a]

I I

The reluctance of many persons to receive as correct this analysis of the sentiments of moral approbation and disapprobation, though a reluctance founded more on feeling than on reasoning, is accustomed to justify itself intellectually, by alleging the total unlikeness of those states of mind to the elementary ones from which, according to the theory, they are compounded. But this is no more than what is observed in every similar case. When a complex feeling is generated out of elements very numerous and various, and in a corresponding degree indeterminate and vague, but so blended together by a close association, the effect of a long series of experiences, as to have become inseparable, the resulting feeling always seems not only very unlike any one of the elements composing it but very unlike the sum of those elements. The pleasure of acquiring, or of consciously possessing, a sum of money (supposed not to be desired for application to some specific purpose) is a feeling, to our consciousness, very different from the pleasure of protection against hunger and cold, the pleasure of ease and rest from labor, the pleasure of receiving consideration from our fellow creatures, and the other miscellaneous pleasures the association with which is admitted to be the real and only source of the pleasure of pos-

[a] *Fragment on Mackintosh*, pp. 51, 52.

sessing money. In the case, then, of the moral sentiments, we have, on the one hand, a *vera causa* or set of causes, having a positive tendency to generate a sentiment of love for certain actions, and of aversion for certain others, and on the other hand, those sentiments of love and aversion, actually produced. This coincidence between the sentiments and a power adequate to produce them, goes far towards proving causation. That the sentiments are not obviously like the causes, is no reason for postulating the existence of another cause, in the shape of an original principle of our nature.

In a case, however, of so great interest and importance, a rigid adherence to the canons of inductive proof must be insisted on. Those who dispute the theory are entitled to demand that it shall conform strictly to the general law of cause and effect, which is, that the effect shall occur with the cause, shall not occur without the cause, and shall bear some proportion to the cause. Unless it can be shown that when the effect is not produced, the cause is either absent or counteracted by some more powerful agency, and unless, when there is any marked difference in the effect, a difference can be shown in the cause, sufficient to account for it, the theory must give way, or at least, cannot be considered as proved.

The principal case in which the effect is absent, notwithstanding the apparent presence of the cause assigned for it, is anticipated by the author, and provided for after his manner, in the first of the passages quoted from the *Fragment on Mackintosh*. There are actions (he observes) as beneficial as any others, which yet do not excite the moral sentiment of approbation, but it is because the spontaneous motives to those beneficial acts are in general sufficient: as to eat when we are hungry, or to do a service for which we are to be amply paid. There are, again, actions of a very hurtful character, but such that the spontaneous motives for abstaining from them may be relied on, without any artificial addition: such, in general, are acts destructive of one's own life or property. But even in these cases the hurtful acts may become objects of moral reprobation when, in any particular case, the natural deterrents prove insufficient for preventing them.

The author seems to think that the difference here pointed out is explained by the fact that the moral sentiment is in the one case needed, in the other not needed, for producing the useful or averting the hurtful act; that, in short, we are made to have the feeling, by a foresight that our having it will operate usefully on the conduct of our fellow creatures. I cannot accept this explanation. It seems to me to explain everything about the moral feelings except the feelings themselves. It explains praise and blame, because these may be administered with the express design of influencing conduct. It explains reward and punishment, and every other distinction which we make in our behavior between what we desire to encourage and what we are anxious to check. But these things we might do from a deliberate policy, without having any moral feeling in our minds at all. When there is a moral feeling in our minds, our praise or blame is usually the simple expression of that feeling, rather than an instrument purposely employed for an end. We may give expression to the feeling without really having it, in the belief that our praise or blame will have a salutary effect, but no anticipation of salutary effects from our feeling will ever avail to give us the feeling itself; except indeed, what may be said of every other mental feeling —that we may talk ourselves into it, that the habitual use of the modes of speech that are associated with it has some tendency to call up the feeling in the speaker himself, and a great tendency to engender it in other people.

I apprehend, however, that there is another and more adequate reason why the feeling of moral approbation is usually absent in the case of actions (or forbearances) for which there are sufficient motives without it. These actions are done, and are seen to be done, by everybody alike. The pleasant associations derived from their usefulness merge, therefore, in our feelings towards human life and towards our fellow creatures generally, and do not give rise to any special association of pleasure with given individuals. But when we find that a certain person does beneficial acts which the general experience of life did not warrant us in counting upon—acts which would not have been done by everybody, or even by most people, in his place, we associate the pleasure which the benefit gives us with the character and disposition of that individual, and with the act, conceived as proceeding from that specially beneficent disposition. And obversely, if a person acts in a manner from which we suffer, but which is such as we should expect from most other people in a parallel case, the associations which his acts create in our minds are associations with human life, or with mankind in general; but if the acts, besides being of a hurtful kind, betoken a disposition in the agent more hurtful than we are accustomed to look for in average men, we associate the injury with that very man, and with that very disposition, and have the feeling of moral disapprobation and repugnance.

There is, as already intimated, another condition which those who hold the Association theory of the moral sentiments are bound to fulfil. The class of feelings called moral embraces several varieties, materially different in their character. Wherever this difference manifests itself, the theory must be required to show that there is a corresponding difference in the antecedents. If pleasurable or painful associations are the generating cause, those associations must differ in some proportion to the difference which exists in what they generate.

The principal case in point is the case of what is called Duty, or Obligation. It will probably be admitted that beneficial acts, when done because they are beneficial, excite in us favorable sentiments towards the agent, for which the utility or beneficial tendency of the actions is sufficient to account. But it is only some, not all, of these beneficial acts, that we regard as duties, as acts which the agent, or we ourselves if we are the persons concerned, are bound to do. This feeling of duty or obligation, it is contended, is a very different state of mind from mere liking for the action and goodwill to the agent. The Association theory may account for the two last, but not for the former.

I have examined this question in the concluding chapter of a short treatise entitled *Utilitarianism*. The subject of the chapter is "The Connection between Justice and Utility." I have there endeavored to show what the association is which exists in the case of what we regard as a duty, but does not exist in the case of what we merely regard as useful, and which gives to the feeling in the former case the strength, the gravity, and pungency which in the other case it has not.

I believe that the element in the association which gives this distinguishing character to the feeling, and which constitutes the difference of the antecedents in the two cases, is the idea of Punishment. I mean the association with punishment, not the expectation of it.

No case can be pointed out in which we consider anything as a duty, and any act or omission as immoral or wrong, without regarding the person who commits the wrong and violates the duty as a fit object of punishment. We think that the general good requires that he should be punished, if not by the law, by the displeasure and ill offices of his fellow creatures; we at any rate feel indignant with him, that is, it would give us pleasure that he should suffer for his misconduct, even if there are preponderant reasons of another kind against inflicting the suffering. This feeling of indignation, or resentment is, I conceive, a case of the animal impulse (I call it animal because it is common to us with the other animals) to defend our own life or possessions, or the persons whom we care for, against actual or threatened attack. All conduct which we class as wrong or criminal is, or we suppose it to be, an attack upon some vital interest of ourselves or of those we care for (a category which may include the public, or the whole human race); conduct which, if allowed to be repeated, would destroy or impair the security and comfort of our lives. We are prompted to defend these paramount interests by repelling the attack, and guarding against its renewal, and our earliest experience gives us a feeling which acts with the rapidity of an instinct, that the most direct and efficacious protection is retaliation. We are therefore prompted to retaliate by inflicting pain on the person who has inflicted or tried to inflict it upon ourselves. We endeavor, as far as possible, that our social institutions shall render us this service. We are gratified when, by that or other means, the pain is inflicted, and dissatisfied if from any cause it is not. This strong association of the idea of punishment and the desire for its infliction, with the idea of the act which has hurt us, is not in itself a moral sentiment, but it appears to me to be the element which is present when we have the feelings of obligation and of injury, and which mainly distinguishes them from simple distaste or dislike for anything in the conduct of another that is disagreeable to us, that distinguishes, for instance, our feeling towards the person who steals our goods, from our feeling towards him who offends our senses by smoking tobacco. This impulse to self-defense by the retaliatory infliction of pain, only becomes a moral sentiment when it is united with a conviction that the infliction of punishment in such a case is conformable to the general good, and when the impulse is not allowed to carry us beyond the point at which that conviction ends. For further illustration, I must refer to the little Treatise already mentioned.—*Ed.*

TWELVE

Utilitarianism

[Although *Utilitarianism* was not published until 1861, Mill had been working on various sections comprising it at least since 1854. A comment in a letter to his close friend Alexander Bain, dated Nov. 14, 1859, is interesting:

. . . I do not think of publishing my "Utilitarianism" till next winter at the earliest, though it is now finished, subject to any correction or enlargement which may suggest itself in the interval. It will be but a small book, about a fifth less than the "Liberty," if I make no addition to it. But small books are so much more read than large ones, that it is an advantage when one's matter will go into a small space. I have not written it in any hostile spirit towards Christianity, though undoubtedly both good ethics and good metaphysics will sap Christianity if it persists in allying itself with bad. The best thing to do in the present state of the human mind is to go on establishing positive truths (principles and rules of evidence of cause included) and leave Christianity to reconcile itself with them the best way it can. By that course, in so far as we have any success, we are at least doing something to improve Christianity.

The chapters of *Utilitarianism* were first published in *Fraser's Magazine* in 1861 as follows: I and II in October; III and IV in November; and V in December. It was reprinted as a book in 1863. For the second edition, published in 1864, Mill made a few, but only a few, changes. He added a long footnote to Chapter II, he rewrote a paragraph on etymology in Chapter V, and he changed a word here and there. The fourth edition (1871) shows no further changes. The text here given is that of the first publication, in *Fraser's*. I have given the two major changes in the footnotes, and indicated one or two of the minor verbal changes. Capitalization and punctuation (which had not been standardized at the time, and on which Mill does not seem to have had any particular feelings) have been slightly modified.]

1. General Remarks

THERE ARE FEW circumstances, among those which make up the present condition of human knowledge, more unlike what might have been expected, or more significant of the backward state in which speculation on the most important subjects still lingers, than the little progress which has been made in the decision of the controversy respecting the criterion of right and wrong. From the dawn of philosophy, the question concerning the *summum bonum* or, what is the same thing, concerning the foundation of morality, has been accounted the main problem in speculative thought, has occupied the most gifted intellects and divided them into sects and schools, carrying on a vigorous warfare against one another. And, after more than two thousand years, the same discussions continue, philosophers are still ranged under the same contending banners, and neither thinkers nor mankind at large seem nearer to being unanimous on the subject than when the youth Socrates listened to the old Protagoras, and asserted (if Plato's dialogue be grounded on a real conversation) the theory of utilitarianism against the popular morality of the so-called Sophist.

It is true that similar confusion and uncertainty, and in some cases similar discordance, exist respecting the first principles of all the sciences, not excepting that which is deemed the most certain of them—mathematics—without much impairing, generally indeed without impairing at all, the trustworthiness of the conclusions of those sciences. An apparent anomaly, the explanation of which is that the detailed doctrines of a science are not usually deduced from, nor depend for their evidence upon, what are called its first principles. Were it not so, there would be no science more precarious, or whose conclusions were more insufficiently made out, than algebra, which derives none of its certainty from what are commonly taught to learners as its elements, since these, as laid down by some of its most eminent teachers, are as full of fictions as English law, and of mysteries as theology. The truths which are ultimately accepted as the first principles of a science are really the last results of metaphysical analysis practiced on the elementary notions with which the science is conversant, and their relation to the science is not that of foundations to an edifice, but of roots to a tree, which may perform their office equally well though they be never dug down to and exposed to light. But though, in science the particular truths precede the general theory, the contrary might be expected to be the case with a practical art, such as morals or legislation. All action is for the sake of some end; and rules of action, it seems natural to suppose, must take their whole character and color from the end to which they are subservient. When we engage in a pursuit, a clear and precise conception of what we are pursuing would seem to be the first thing we need, instead of the last we are to look forward to. A test of right and wrong must be the means, one would think, of ascertaining what is right or wrong, and not a consequence of having already ascertained it.

The difficulty is not avoided by having recourse to the popular theory of a natural faculty, a sense or instinct, informing us of right and wrong. For, besides that the existence of such a moral instinct is itself one of the matters in dispute, those believers in it who have any pretensions to philosophy have been obliged to abandon the idea that it discerns what is right or wrong in the particular case in hand, as our other senses discern the sight or sound actually present. Our moral faculty, according to all those of its interpreters who are entitled to the name of thinkers, supplies us only with the general principles of moral judgments; it is a branch of our reason, not of our sensitive faculty, and must be looked to for the abstract doctrines of morality, not for perception of it in the concrete. The intuitive, no less than what may be termed the inductive, school of ethics, insists on the necessity of general laws. They both agree that the morality of an individual action is not a question of direct perception, but of the application of a law to an individual case. They recognize also, to a great extent, the same moral laws, but differ as to their evidence, and the source from which they derive their authority. According to the one opinion, the principles of morals are evident *a priori*, requiring nothing to command assent, except that the meaning of the terms be understood. According to the other doctrine, right and wrong, as well as truth and falsehood, are questions of observation and experience. But both hold equally that morality must be deduced from principles, and the intuitive school affirm, as strongly as the inductive, that there is a science of morals. Yet they seldom attempt to make out a list of the *a priori* principles which are to serve as the premises of the science; still more rarely do they make any effort to reduce those various principles to one first principle, or common ground of obligation. They either assume the ordinary precepts of morals as of *a priori* authority, or they lay down as the common groundwork of those maxims some generality much less obviously authoritative than the maxims themselves, and which has never succeeded in gaining popular acceptance. Yet, to support their pretensions, there ought either to be some one fundamental principle or law at the root of all morality, or, if there be several, there should be a determinate order of precedence among them, and the one principle, or the rule for deciding between the various principles when they conflict, ought to be self-evident.

To inquire how far the bad effects of this deficiency have been mitigated in practice, or to what extent the moral beliefs of mankind have been vitiated or made uncertain by the absence of any distinct recognition of an ultimate standard, would imply a complete survey and criticism of past and present ethical doctrine. It would, however, be easy to show that whatever steadiness or consistency these moral beliefs have attained has been mainly due to the tacit influence of a standard not recognized. Although the nonexistence of an acknowledged first principle has made ethics not so much a guide as a consecration of men's actual sentiments, still, as men's sentiments, both of favor and of aversion, are greatly influenced by what they suppose to be the effects of things upon their happiness, the principle of utility, or, as Bentham latterly called it, the greatest-happiness principle, has had a large share in forming the moral doctrines even of those who most scornfully reject its authority. Nor is there any school of thought which refuses to admit that the influence of actions on happiness is a most material and even predominant consideration in many of the details of morals, however unwilling to acknowledge it as the fundamental principle of morality and the source of moral obligation. I might go much further, and say that, to all those *a priori* moralists who deem it necessary to argue at all, utilitarian arguments are indispensable. It is not my present purpose to criticize these thinkers, but I cannot help referring, for illustration, to a systematic treatise by one of the most illustrious of them—the *Metaphysics of Ethics*, by Kant. This remarkable man, whose system of thought will long remain one of the landmarks in the history of philosophical speculation, does, in the treatise in question, lay down an universal first principle as the origin and ground of moral obligation. It is this: "So act, that the rule on which thou actest would admit of being adopted as a law by all rational beings." But when he begins to deduce from this precept any of the actual duties of morality, he fails, almost grotesquely, to show that there would be any contradiction, any logical (not to say physical) impossibility, in the adoption by all rational beings of the most outrageously immoral rules of conduct. All he shows is that the *consequences* of their universal adoption would be such as no one would choose to incur.

On the present occasion, I shall, without further discussion of the other theories, attempt to contribute something towards the understanding and appreciation of the Utilitarian or Happiness theory and towards such proof as it is susceptible of. It is evident that this cannot be proof in the ordinary and popular meaning of the term. Questions of ultimate ends are not amenable to direct proof. Whatever can be proved to be good, must be so by being shown to be a means to something admitted to be good without proof. The medical art is proved to be good by its conducing to health, but how is it possible to prove that health is good? The art of music is good, for the reason, among others, that it produces pleasure, but what proof is it possible to give that pleasure is good? If, then, it is asserted that there is a comprehensive formula, including all things which are in themselves good, and that whatever else is good is not so as an end, but as a mean, the formula may be accepted or rejected, but is not a subject of what is commonly understood by proof. We are not, however, to infer that its acceptance or rejection must depend on blind impulse or arbitrary choice. There is a larger meaning of the word "proof," in which this question is as amenable to it as any other of the disputed questions of philosophy. The subject is within the cognizance of the rational faculty, and neither does that faculty deal with it solely in the way of intuition. Considerations may be presented capable of determining the intellect either to give or withhold its assent to the doctrine, and this is equivalent to proof.

We shall examine presently of what nature are these considerations, in what manner they apply to the case, and what rational grounds, therefore, can be given for accepting or rejecting the utilitarian formula. But it is a preliminary condition of rational acceptance or rejection that the formula should be correctly understood. I believe that the very imperfect notion ordinarily formed of its meaning is the chief obstacle which impedes its reception, and that, could it be cleared even from only the grosser misconceptions, the question would be greatly simplified, and a large proportion of its difficulties removed. Before, therefore, I attempt to enter into the philosophical grounds which can be given for assenting to the utilitarian standard, I shall offer some illustrations of the doctrine itself, with the view of showing more clearly what it is, distinguishing it from what it is not, and disposing of such of the practical objections to it as either originate in, or are closely connected with, mistaken interpretations of its meaning. Having thus prepared the ground, I shall afterwards endeavor to throw such light as I can upon the question, considered as one of philosophical theory.

2. What Utilitarianism Is

A passing remark is all that needs be given to the ignorant blunder of supposing that those who stand up for utility, as the test of right and wrong, use the term in that restricted and merely colloquial sense in which utility is opposed to pleasure. An apology is due to the philosophical opponents of utilitarianism for even the momentary appearance of confounding them with any one capable of so absurd a misconception, which is the more extraordinary, inasmuch as the contrary accusation, of referring every thing to pleasure, and that, too, in its grossest form, is another of the common charges against utilitarianism, and, as has been pointedly remarked by an able writer, the same sort of persons, and often the very same persons, denounce the theory "as impracticably dry when the word 'utility' precedes the word 'pleasure,' and as too practicably voluptuous when the word 'pleasure' precedes the word 'utility.'" Those who know any thing about the matter are aware that every writer from Epicurus to Bentham who maintained the theory of utility meant by it, not something to be contradistinguished from pleasure, but pleasure itself, together with exemption from pain, and, instead of opposing the useful to the agreeable or the ornamental, have always declared that the useful means these, among other things. Yet the common herd, including the herd of writers, not only in newspapers and periodicals, but in books of weight and pretension, are perpetually falling into this shallow mistake. Having caught up the word "utilitarian," while knowing nothing whatever about it but its sound, they habitually express by it the rejection or the neglect of pleasure in some of its forms, of beauty, of ornament, or of amusement. Nor is the term thus ignorantly misapplied solely in disparagement, but occasionally in compliment, as though it implied superiority to frivolity and the mere pleasures of the moment. And this perverted use is the only one in which the word is popularly known, and the one from which the new generation are acquiring their sole notion of its meaning. Those who introduced the word, but who had for many years discontinued it as a distinctive appellation, may well feel themselves called upon to resume it, if by doing so they can hope to contribute any thing towards rescuing it from this utter degradation.*

The creed which accepts as the foundation of morals Utility, or the Greatest-happiness Principle, holds that actions are right in proportion as they tend to promote happiness, wrong as they tend to produce the reverse of happiness. By happiness is intended pleasure and the absence of pain, by unhappiness, pain and the privation of pleasure. To give a clear view of the moral standard set up by the theory, much more requires to be said, in particular, what things it includes in the ideas of pain and pleasure, and to what extent this is left an open question. But these supplementary explanations do not affect the theory of life on which this theory of morality is grounded—namely, that pleasure and freedom from pain are the only things desirable as ends, and that all desirable things (which are as numerous in the utilitarian as in any other scheme) are desirable either for the pleasure inherent in themselves, or as means to the promotion of pleasure and the prevention of pain.

* The author of this essay has reason for believing himself to be the first person who brought the word "utilitarian" into use. He did not invent it, but adopted it from a passing expression in Mr. Galt's *Annals of the Parish*. After using it as a designation for several years, he and others abandoned it from a growing dislike to any thing resembling a badge or watchword of sectarian distinction. But as a name for one single opinion, not a set of opinions—to denote the recognition of utility as a standard, not any particular way of applying it—the term supplies a want in the language, and offers, in many cases, a convenient mode of avoiding tiresome circumlocution.

Now, such a theory of life excites in many minds, and among them in some of the most estimable in feeling and purpose, inveterate dislike. To suppose that life has (as they express it) no higher end than pleasure—no better and nobler object of desire and pursuit—they designate as utterly mean and groveling, as a doctrine worthy only of swine, to whom the followers of Epicurus were, at a very early period, contemptuously likened; and modern holders of the doctrine are occasionally made the subject of equally polite comparisons by its German, French, and English assailants.

When thus attacked, the Epicureans have always answered, that it is not they, but their accusers, who represent human nature in a degrading light, since the accusation supposes human beings to be capable of no pleasures except those of which swine are capable. If this supposition were true, the charge could not be gainsaid but would then be no longer an imputation; for, if the sources of pleasure were precisely the same to human beings and to swine, the rule of life which is good enough for the one would be good enough for the other. The comparison of the Epicurean life to that of beasts is felt as degrading, precisely because a beast's pleasures do not satisfy a human being's conceptions of happiness. Human beings have faculties more elevated than the animal appetites, and, when once made conscious of them, do not regard any thing as happiness which does not include their gratification. I do not, indeed, consider the Epicureans to have been by any means faultless in drawing out their scheme of consequences from the utilitarian principle. To do this in any sufficient manner, many Stoic as well as Christian elements require to be included. But there is no known Epicurean theory of life which does not assign to the pleasures of the intellect, of the feelings and imagination, and of the moral sentiments, a much higher value as pleasures than to those of mere sensation. It must be admitted, however, that utilitarian writers in general have placed the superiority of mental over bodily pleasures chiefly in the greater permanency, safety, uncostliness, etc., of the former—that is, in their circumstantial advantages rather than in their intrinsic nature. And, on all these points, utilitarians have fully proved their case, but they might have taken the other, and, as it may be called, higher ground, with entire consistency. It is quite compatible with the principle of utility to recognize the fact that some *kinds* of pleasure are more desirable and more valuable than others. It would be absurd that while, in estimating all other things, quality is considered as well as quantity, the estimation of pleasures should be supposed to depend on quantity alone.

If I am asked what I mean by difference of quality in pleasures, or what makes one pleasure more valuable than another, merely as a pleasure, except its being greater in amount, there is but one possible answer. Of two pleasures, if there be one to which all or almost all who have experience of both give a decided preference, irrespective of any feeling of moral obligation to prefer it, that is the more desirable pleasure. If one of the two is, by those who are competently acquainted with both, placed so far above the other that they prefer it, even though knowing it to be attended with a greater amount of discontent, and would not resign it for any quantity of the other pleasure which their nature is capable of, we are justified in ascribing to the preferred enjoyment a superiority in quality so far outweighing quantity, as to render it, in comparison, of small account.

Now, it is an unquestionable fact, that those who are equally acquainted with and equally capable of appreciating and enjoying both do give a most marked preference to the manner of existence which employs their higher faculties. Few human creatures would consent to be changed into any of the lower animals for a promise of the fullest allowance of a beast's pleasures; no intelligent human being would consent to be a fool, no instructed person would be an ignoramus, no person of feeling and conscience would be selfish and base, even though they should be persuaded that the fool, the dunce, or the rascal is better satisfied with his lot than they are with theirs. They would not resign what they possess more than he for the most complete satisfaction of all the desires which they have in common with him. If they ever fancy they would, it is only in cases of unhappiness so extreme that, to escape from it, they would exchange their lot for almost any other, however undesirable in their own eyes. A being of higher faculties requires more to make him happy, is capable probably of more acute suffering, and certainly accessible to it at more points, than one of an inferior type, but, in spite of these liabilities, he can never really wish to sink into what he feels to be a lower grade of existence. We may give what explanation we please of this unwillingness: we may attribute it to pride, a name which is given indiscriminately to some of the most and to some of the least estimable feelings of which mankind are capable; we may refer it to the love of liberty and personal independence—an appeal to which was with the Stoics one of the most effective means for the inculcation of it; to the love of power, or to the love of excitement, both of which do really enter into and contribute to it; but its most appropriate appellation is a sense of dignity, which all human beings possess in one form or other, and in some, though by no means in exact, proportion to their higher faculties, and which is so essential a part of the happiness of those in whom it is strong, that nothing which conflicts with it could be, otherwise than momentarily, an object of desire to them. Whoever supposes that this preference takes place at a sacrifice of happiness, that the superior being, in any thing like equal circumstances, is not happier than the inferior—confounds the two very different ideas of happiness and content. It is indisputable that the being whose capacities of enjoyment are low has the greatest chance of having them fully satisfied, and a highly endowed being will always feel that any happiness which he can look for, as the world is constituted, is imperfect. But he can learn to bear its imperfections, if they are at all bearable, and they will not make him envy the being who is indeed unconscious of the imperfections, but only because he feels not at all the good which those imperfections qualify. It is better to be a human being dissatisfied than a pig satisfied, better to be Socrates dissatisfied than a fool satisfied. And if the fool or the pig are of a different opinion, it is because they only know their own side of the question. The other party to the comparison knows both sides.

It may be objected that many who are capable of the higher pleasures occasionally, under the influence of temptation, postpone them to the lower. But this is quite compatible with a full appreciation of the intrinsic superiority of the higher. Men often, from infirmity of character, make their election for the nearer good, though they know it to be the less valuable, and this no less when the choice is between two bodily pleasures than when it is between bodily and mental. They pursue sensual indulgences to the injury of health, though perfectly aware that health is the greater good. It may be further objected, that many who begin with youthful enthusiasm for everything noble, as they advance in years sink into indolence and selfishness. But I do not believe that those who undergo this very common change voluntarily choose the lower description of pleasures in preference to the higher. I believe that, before they devote themselves exclusively to the one, they have already become incapable of the other. Capacity for the nobler feelings is in most natures a very tender plant, easily killed, not only by hostile influences but by mere want of sustenance, and, in the majority of young persons, it speedily dies away if the occupations to which their position in life has devoted them, and the society into which it has thrown them, are not favorable to keeping that higher capacity in exercise. Men lose their high aspirations as they lose their intellectual tastes, because they have not time or opportunity for indulging them, and they addict themselves to inferior pleasures, not because they deliberately prefer them, but because they are either the only ones to which they have access or the only ones which they are any longer capable of enjoying. It may be questioned whether any one who has remained equally susceptible to both classes of pleasures ever knowingly and calmly preferred the lower, though many in all ages have broken down in an ineffectual attempt to combine both.

From this verdict of the only competent judges, I apprehend there can be no appeal. On a question which is the best worth having of two pleasures, or which of two modes of existence is the most grateful to the feelings, apart from its moral attributes and from its consequences, the judgment of those who are qualified by knowledge of both, or, if they differ, that of the majority among them, must be admitted as final. And there needs be the less hesitation to accept this judgment respecting the quality of pleasures, since there is no other tribunal to be referred to even on the question of quantity. What means are there of determining which is the acutest of two pains, or the intensest of two pleasurable sensations, except the general suffrage of those who are familiar with both? Neither pains nor pleasures are homogeneous, and pain is always heterogeneous with pleasure. What is there to decide whether a particular pleasure is worth purchasing at the cost of a particular pain, except the feelings and judgment of the experienced? When, therefore, those feelings and judgment declare the pleasures derived from the higher faculties to be preferable *in kind*, apart from the question of intensity, to those of which the animal nature disjoined from the higher faculties is susceptible, they are entitled on this subject to the same regard.

I have dwelt on this point, as being a necessary part of a perfectly just conception of Utility or Happiness, considered as the directive rule of human conduct. But it is by no means an indispensable condition to the acceptance of the utilitarian standard, for that standard is not the agent's own greatest happiness, but the greatest amount of happiness altogether; and if it may possibly be doubted whether a noble character is always the happier for its nobleness, there can be no doubt that it makes other people happier, and that the world in general is immensely a gainer by it. Utilitarianism, therefore, could only attain its end by the general cultivation of nobleness of character, even if each individual were only benefited by the nobleness of others, and his own, so far as happiness is concerned, were a sheer deduction from the benefit. But the bare enunciation of such an absurdity as this last renders refutation superfluous.

According to the Greatest-happiness Principle, as above explained, the ultimate end with reference to and for the sake of which all other things are desirable (whether we are considering our own good or that of other people) is an existence exempt as far as possible from pain, and as rich as possible in enjoyments, both in point of quantity and quality; the test of quality, and the rule for measuring it against quantity, being the preference felt by those who in their opportunities of experience, to which must be added their habits of self-consciousness and self-observation, are best furnished with the means of comparison. This being, according to the utilitarian opinion, the end of human action is necessarily also the standard of morality; which may accordingly be defined, the rules and precepts for human conduct by the observance of which an existence such as has been described might be, to the greatest extent possible, secured to all mankind, and not to them only but, so far as the nature of things admits, to the whole sentient creation.

Against this doctrine, however, arises another class of objectors who say that happiness, in any form, cannot be the rational purpose of human life and action, because, in the first place, it is unattainable; and they contemptuously ask,

What right hast thou to be happy? a question which Mr. Carlyle clinches by the addition, What right, a short time ago, hadst thou even *to be*? Next they say that men can do *without* happiness, that all noble human beings have felt this, and could not have become noble but by learning the lesson of *Entsagen* or renunciation, which lesson, thoroughly learnt and submitted to, they affirm to be the beginning and necessary condition of all virtue.

The first of these objections would go to the root of the matter, were it well founded; for, if no happiness is to be had at all by human beings, the attainment of it cannot be the end of morality, or of any rational conduct. Though, even in that case, something might still be said for the utilitarian theory, since utility includes not solely the pursuit of happiness, but the prevention or mitigation of unhappiness; and, if the former aim be chimerical, there will be all the greater scope and more imperative need for the latter, so long at least as mankind think fit to live, and do not take refuge in the simultaneous act of suicide recommended under certain conditions by Novalis. When, however, it is thus positively asserted to be impossible that human life should be happy, the assertion, if not something like a verbal quibble, is at least an exaggeration. If by happiness be meant a continuity of highly pleasurable excitement, it is evident enough that this is impossible. A state of exalted pleasure lasts only moments, or in some cases, and with some intermissions, hours or days, and is the occasional brilliant flash of enjoyment, not its permanent and steady flame. Of this the philosophers who have taught that happiness is the end of life were as fully aware as those who taunt them. The happiness which they meant was not a life of rapture, but moments of such, in an existence made up of few and transitory pains, many and various pleasures, with a decided predominance of the active over the passive, and having, as the foundation of the whole, not to expect more from life than it is capable of bestowing. A life thus composed, to those who have been fortunate enough to obtain it, has always appeared worthy of the name of "happiness." And such an existence is even now the lot of many, during some considerable portion of their lives. The present wretched education and wretched social arrangements are the only real hindrance to its being attainable by almost all.

The objectors, perhaps, may doubt whether human beings, if taught to consider happiness as the end of life, would be satisfied with such a moderate share of it. But great numbers of mankind have been satisfied with much less. The main constituents of a satisfied life appear to be two, either of which by itself is often found sufficient for the purpose—tranquillity and excitement. With much tranquillity, many find that they can be content with very little pleasure; with much excitement, many can reconcile themselves to a considerable quantity of pain. There is assuredly no inherent impossibility in enabling even the mass of mankind to unite both, since the two are so far from being incompatible, that they are in natural alliance, the prolongation of either being a preparation for, and exciting a wish for, the other. It is only those in whom indolence amounts to a vice that do not desire excitement after an interval of repose; it is only those in whom the need of excitement is a disease, that feel the tranquillity which follows excitement dull and insipid, instead of pleasurable in direct proportion to the excitement which preceded it. When people who are tolerably fortunate in their outward lot do not find in life sufficient enjoyment to make it valuable to them, the cause generally is caring for nobody but themselves. To those who have neither public nor private affections, the excitements of life are much curtailed and, in any case, dwindle in value as the time approaches when all selfish interests must be terminated by death; while those who leave after them objects of personal affection, and especially those who have also cultivated a fellow feeling with the collective interests of mankind, retain as lively an interest in life on the eve of death as in the vigor of youth and health. Next to selfishness, the principal cause which makes life unsatisfactory is want of mental cultivation. A cultivated mind—I do not mean that of a philosopher, but any mind to which the fountains of knowledge have been opened, and which has been taught, in any tolerable degree, to exercise its faculties—finds sources of inexhaustible interest in all that surrounds it, in the objects of nature, the achievements of art, the imaginations of poetry, the incidents of history, the ways of mankind past and present, and their prospects in the future. It is possible, indeed, to become indifferent to all this, and that, too, without having exhausted a thousandth part of it, but only when one has had from the beginning no moral or human interest in these things, and has sought in them only the gratification of curiosity.

Now, there is absolutely no reason in the nature of things why an amount of mental culture sufficient to give an intelligent interest in these objects of contemplation should not be the inheritance of every one born in a civilized country. As little is there an inherent necessity that any human being should be a selfish egotist, devoid of every feeling or care but those which center in his own miserable individuality. Something far superior to this is sufficiently common even now to give ample earnest of what the human species may be made. Genuine private affections and a sincere interest in the public good are possible, though in unequal degrees, to every rightly brought up human being. In a world in which there is so much to interest, so much to enjoy, and so much also to correct and improve, every one who has this moderate amount of moral and intellectual requisites is capable of an existence which may be called enviable; and unless such a person, through bad laws or subjection to the will of others, is denied the liberty to use the sources of happiness within his reach, he will not fail to find this enviable existence, if he escape the positive evils of life, the great sources of physical and mental suffering—such as indigence, disease, and the unkindness, worthlessness, or premature loss, of objects of affection. The main stress of the problem lies, therefore, in the contest with these calamities, from which it is a rare good fortune entirely to escape, which, as things now are, cannot be obviated, and often cannot be in any material degree mitigated. Yet no one whose opinion deserves a moment's consideration can doubt that most of the great positive evils of the world are in themselves removable, and will, if human affairs continue to improve, be in the end reduced within narrow limits. Poverty, in any sense implying suffering, may be completely extinguished by the wisdom of society, combined with the good sense and providence of individuals. Even that most intractable of enemies, disease, may be indefinitely reduced in dimensions by good physical and moral education, and proper control of noxious influence, while the progress of science holds out a promise for the future of still more direct conquests over this detestable foe. And every advance in that direction relieves us from some, not only of the chances which cut short our own lives but, what concerns us still more, which deprive us of those in whom our happiness is wrapped up. As for vicissitudes of fortune and other disappointments connected with worldly circumstances, these are principally the effect either of gross imprudence, of ill-regulated desires, or of bad or imperfect social institutions. All the grand sources, in short, of human suffering are in a great degree, many of them almost entirely, conquerable by human care and effort; and though their removal is grievously slow, though a long succession of generations will perish in the breach before the conquest is completed, and this world becomes all that, if will and knowledge were not wanting, it might easily be made—yet every mind sufficiently intelligent and generous to bear a part, however small and unconspicuous, in the endeavor will draw a noble enjoyment from the contest itself, which he would not, for any bribe in the form of selfish indulgence, consent to be without.

And this leads to the true estimation of what is said by the objectors concerning the possibility and the obligation of learning to do without happiness. Unquestionably, it is possible to do without happiness; it is done involuntarily by nineteen-twentieths of mankind, even in those parts of our present world which are least deep in barbarism, and it often has to be done voluntarily by the hero or the martyr, for the sake of something which he prizes more than his individual happiness. But this something—what is it, unless the happiness of others, or some of the requisites of happiness? It is noble to be capable of resigning entirely one's own portion of happiness, or chances of it; but, after all, this self-sacrifice must be for some end; it is not its own end, and if we are told that its end is not happiness but virtue, which is better than happiness, I ask, Would the sacrifice be made if the hero or martyr did not believe that it would earn for others immunity from similar sacrifices? Would it be made if he thought that his renunciation of happiness for himself would produce no fruit for any of his fellow-creatures but to make their lot like his, and place them also in the condition of persons who have renounced happiness? All honor to those who can abnegate for themselves the personal enjoyment of life, when by such renunciation they contribute worthily to increase the amount of happiness in the world, but he who does it, or professes to do it, for any other purpose is no more deserving of admiration than the ascetic mounted on his pillar. He may be an inspiriting proof of what men *can* do, but assuredly not an example of what they *should*.

Though it is only in a very imperfect state of the world's arrangements that any one can best serve the happiness of others by the absolute sacrifice of his own, yet, so long as the world is in that imperfect state, I fully acknowledge that the readiness to make such a sacrifice is the highest virtue which can be found in man. I will add that in this condition of the world, paradoxical as the assertion may be, the conscious ability to do without happiness gives the best prospect of realizing such happiness as is attainable. For nothing except that consciousness can raise a person above the chances of life, by making him feel that, let fate and fortune do their worst, they have not power to subdue him; which, once felt, frees him from excess of anxiety concerning the evils of life, and enables him, like many a Stoic in the worst times of the Roman Empire, to cultivate in tranquillity the sources of satisfaction accessible to him, without concerning himself about the uncertainty of their duration, any more than about their inevitable end.

Meanwhile, let utilitarians never cease to claim the morality of self-devotion as a possession which belongs by as good a right to them as either to the Stoic or to the Transcendentalist. The utilitarian morality does recognize in human beings the power of sacrificing their own greatest good for the good of others. It only refuses to admit that the sacrifice is itself a good. A sacrifice which does not increase, or tend to increase, the sum total of happiness, it considers as wasted. The only self-renunciation which it applauds is devotion to the happiness, or to some of the means of happiness, of others, either of mankind collectively, or of individuals within the limits imposed by the collective interests of mankind.

I must again repeat what the assailants of utilitarianism seldom have the justice to acknowledge, that the happiness which forms the utilitarian standard of what is right in conduct is not the agent's own happiness but that of all concerned. As between his own happiness and that of others, utilitarianism requires him to be as strictly impartial as a disinterested and benevolent spectator. In the golden rule of Jesus of Nazareth, we read the complete spirit of the ethics of utility. To do as you would be done by, and to love your neighbor as yourself, constitute the ideal perfection of utilitarian morality. As the means of making the nearest approach to this ideal, utility would enjoin, first, that laws and social arrangements should place the happiness or (as, speaking practically, it may be called) the interest of every individual as nearly as possible in harmony with the interest of the whole; and secondly, that education and opinion, which have so vast a power over human character, should so use that power as to establish in the mind of every individual an indissoluble association between his own happiness and the good of the whole—especially between his own happiness, and the practice of such modes of conduct, negative and positive, as regard for the universal happiness prescribes—so that not only he may be unable to conceive the possibility of happiness to himself consistently with conduct opposed to the general good, but also that a direct impulse to promote the general good may be in every individual one of the habitual motives of action, and the sentiments connected therewith may fill a large and prominent place in every human being's sentient existence. If the impugners of the utilitarian morality represented it to their own minds in this its true character, I know not what recommendation possessed by any other morality they could possibly affirm to be wanting to it, what more beautiful or more exalted developments of human nature any other ethical system can be supposed to foster, or what springs of action, not accessible to the utilitarian, such systems rely on for giving effect to their mandates.

The objectors to utilitarianism cannot always be charged with representing it in a discreditable light. On the contrary, those among them who entertain any thing like a just idea of its disinterested character sometimes find fault with its standard as being too high for humanity. They say it is exacting too much to require that people shall always act from the inducement of promoting the general interests of society. But this is to mistake the very meaning of a standard of morals, and confound the rule of action with the motive of it. It is the business of ethics to tell us what are our duties or by what test we may know them, but no system of ethics requires that the sole motive of all we do shall be a feeling of duty; on the contrary, ninety-nine hundredths of all our actions are done from other motives, and rightly so done, if the rule of duty does not condemn them. It is the more unjust to utilitarianism that this particular misapprehension should be made a ground of objection to it, inasmuch as utilitarian moralists have gone beyond almost all others in affirming that the motive has nothing to do with the morality of the action though much with the worth of the agent. He who saves a fellow creature from drowning does what is morally right, whether his motive be duty or the hope of being paid for his trouble; he who betrays the friend that trusts him is guilty of a crime, even if his object be to serve another friend to whom he is under greater obligations.[1] But to speak only of actions done from the motive of duty, and in direct obedience to principle: it is a misapprehension of the utilitarian mode of thought to conceive it as implying that people should fix their minds upon so wide a generality as the world or society at large. The great majority of good actions are intended, not for the benefit of the world but for that of individuals, of which the good of the world is made up; and the thoughts of the most virtuous man need not on these occasions travel beyond the particular persons concerned, except so far as is necessary to assure himself that, in benefiting them, he is not violating the rights—that is, the legitimate and authorized expectations—of any one else. The multiplication of happiness is, according to the utilitarian ethics, the object of virtue; the occasions on which any person (except one in a thousand) has it in his power to do this on an extended scale—in other words, to be a public benefactor—are but exceptional, and on these occasions alone is he called on to consider public utility; in every other case, private utility, the interest or happiness of some few persons, is all he has to attend to. Those alone, the influence of whose actions extends to society in general, need concern themselves habitually about so large an object. In the case of abstinences indeed—of things which people forbear to do from moral considerations, though the consequences in the particular case might be beneficial—it would be unworthy of an intelligent agent not to be consciously aware that the action is of a class which, if practised generally, would be generally injurious, and that this is the ground of the obligation to abstain from it. The amount of regard for the public interest implied in this recognition is no greater than is demanded by every system of morals, for they all enjoin to abstain from whatever is manifestly pernicious to society.

The same considerations dispose of another reproach

against the doctrine of utility, founded on a still grosser misconception of the purpose of a standard of morality, and of
the very meaning of the words "right" and "wrong." It is
often affirmed that utilitarianism renders men cold and un-
sympathizing, that it chills their moral feelings towards individuals, that it makes them regard only the dry and hard
consideration of the consequences of actions, not taking into
their moral estimate the qualities from which those actions
emanate. If the assertion means that they do not allow their
judgment respecting the rightness or wrongness of an action
to be influenced by their opinion of the qualities of the person
who does it, this is a complaint, not against utilitarianism but
against having any standard of morality at all; for certainly
no known ethical standard decides an action to be good or
bad because it is done by a good or a bad man, still less because done by an amiable, a brave, or a benevolent man, or
the contrary. These considerations are relevant, not to the
estimation of actions, but of persons, and there is nothing in
the utilitarian theory inconsistent with the fact that there are
other things which interest us in persons besides the rightness
and wrongness of their actions. The Stoics indeed, with the
paradoxical misuse of language which was part of their system and by which they strove to raise themselves above all
concern about any thing but virtue, were fond of saying that
he who has that has everything, that he, and only he, is
rich, is beautiful, is a king. But no claim of this description
is made for the virtuous man by the utilitarian doctrine.
Utilitarians are quite aware that there are other desirable
possessions and qualities besides virtue, and are perfectly willing to allow to all of them their full worth. They are also
aware that a right action does not necessarily indicate a
virtuous character, and that actions which are blamable often
proceed from qualities entitled to praise. When this is apparent in any particular case, it modifies their estimation, not
certainly of the act but of the agent. I grant that they are
notwithstanding of opinion that, in the long run, the best
proof of a good character is good actions, and resolutely refuse to consider any mental disposition as good, of which
the predominant tendency is to produce bad conduct. This
makes them unpopular with many people; but it is an un-
popularity which they must share with every one who regards
the distinction between right and wrong in a serious light,

and the reproach is not one which a conscientious utilitarian need be anxious to repel.

If no more be meant by the objection than that many utilitarians look on the morality of actions, as measured by the utilitarian standards, with too exclusive a regard, and do not lay sufficient stress upon the other beauties of character which go towards making a human being lovable or admirable, this may be admitted. Utilitarians who have cultivated their moral feelings but not their sympathies nor their artistic perceptions, do fall into this mistake, and so do all other moralists under the same conditions. What can be said in excuse for other moralists is equally available for them, namely that, if there is to be any error, it is better that it should be on that side. As a matter of fact, we may affirm that among utilitarians, as among adherents of other systems, there is every imaginable degree of rigidity and of laxity in the application of their standard; some are even puritanically rigorous, while others are as indulgent as can possibly be desired by sinner or by sentimentalist. But on the whole, a doctrine which brings prominently forward the interest that mankind have in the repression and prevention of conduct which violates the moral law, is likely to be inferior to no other in turning the sanctions of opinion against such violations. It is true, the question, What does violate the moral law? is one on which those who recognize different standards of morality are likely now and then to differ. But difference of opinion on moral questions was not first introduced into the world by utilitarianism, while that doctrine does supply, if not always an easy, at all events a tangible and intelligible mode of deciding such differences.

It may not be superfluous to notice a few more of the common misapprehensions of utilitarian ethics, even those which are so obvious and gross that it might appear impossible for any person of candor and intelligence to fall into them, since persons even of considerable mental endowments often give themselves so little trouble to understand the bearings of any opinion against which they entertain a prejudice, and men are in general so little conscious of this voluntary ignorance as a defect, that the vulgarest misunderstandings of ethical doctrines are continually met with in the deliberate writings of persons of the greatest pretensions both to high principle and to philosophy. We not uncommonly hear the doctrine of utility inveighed against as a *godless* doctrine. If it be necessary to say any thing at all against so mere an assumption, we may say that the question depends upon what idea we have formed of the moral character of the Deity. If it be a true belief that God desires, above all things, the happiness of his creatures, and that this was his purpose in their creation, utility is not only not a godless doctrine but more profoundly religious than any other. If it be meant that utilitarianism does not recognize the revealed will of God as the supreme law of morals, I answer that an utilitarian, who believes in the perfect goodness and wisdom of God, necessarily believes that whatever God has thought fit to reveal on the subject of morals must fulfil the requirements of utility in a supreme degree. But others besides utilitarians have been of opinion that the Christian revelation·was intended, and is fitted, to inform the hearts and minds of mankind with a spirit which should enable them to find for themselves what is right and incline them to do it when found, rather than to tell them, except in a very general way, what it is, and that we need a doctrine of ethics, carefully followed out, to *interpret* to us the will of God. Whether this opinion is correct or not, it is superfluous here to discuss, since whatever aid religion, either natural or revealed, can afford to ethical investigation, is as open to the utilitarian moralist as to any other. He can use it as the testimony of God to the usefulness or hurtfulness of any given course of action, by as good a right as others can use it for the indication of a transcendental law, having no connection with usefulness or with happiness.

Again: Utility is often summarily stigmatized as an immoral doctrine by giving it the name of Expediency and, taking advantage of the popular use of that term, to contrast it with Principle. But the Expedient, in the sense in which it is opposed to the Right, generally means that which is expedient for the particular interest of the agent himself, as when a minister sacrifices the interests of his country to keep himself in place. When it means any thing better than this, it means that which is expedient for some immediate object, some temporary purpose, but which violates a rule whose observance is expedient in a much higher degree. The Expedient, in this sense, instead of being the same thing with the useful, is a branch of the hurtful. Thus it would often be expedient, for the purpose of getting over some momentary embarrassment or attaining some object immediately useful to ourselves or others, to tell a lie. But inasmuch as the cultivation in ourselves of a sensitive feeling on the subject of veracity is one of the most useful, and the enfeeblement of that feeling one of the most hurtful, things to which our conduct can be instrumental, and inasmuch as any, even unintentional, deviation from truth does that much towards weakening the trustworthiness of human assertion, which is not only the principal support of all present social well-being, but the insufficiency of which does more than any one thing that can be named to keep back civilization, virtue, every thing on which human happiness on the largest scale depends—we feel that the violation, for a present advantage, of a rule of such transcendent expediency is not expedient, and that he who, for the sake of a convenience to himself or to some other individual, does what depends on him to deprive mankind of the good, and inflict upon them the evil, involved in the greater or less reliance which they can place in each other's word, acts the part of one of their worst enemies. Yet that even this rule, sacred as it is, admits of possible exceptions is acknowledged by all moralists, the chief of which is, when the withholding of some fact (as of information from a malefactor, or of bad news from a person dangerously ill) would save an individual (especially an individual other than one's self) from great and unmerited evil and when the withholding can only be effected by denial. But in order that the exception may not extend itself beyond the need and may have the least possible effect in weakening reliance on veracity, it ought to be recognized and, if possible, its limits defined, and, if the principle of utility is good for any thing, it must be good for weighing these conflicting utilities against one another, and marking out the region within which one or the other preponderates.

Again: defenders of utility often find themselves called upon to reply to such objections as this—that there is not time, previous to action, for calculating and weighing the effects of any line of conduct on the general happiness. This is exactly as if any one were to say that it is impossible to guide our conduct by Christianity, because there is not time, on every occasion on which any thing has to be done, to read through the Old and New Testaments. The answer to the objection is that there has been ample time, namely, the whole past duration of the human species. During all that time, mankind have been learning by experience the tendencies of actions, on which experience all the prudence as well as all the morality of life are dependent. People talk as if the commencement of this course of experience had hitherto been put off and as if, at the moment when some man feels tempted to meddle with the property or life of another, he had to begin considering for the first time whether murder and theft are injurious to human happiness. Even then, I do not think that he would find the question very puzzling, but at all events the matter is now done to his hand. It is truly a whimsical supposition that, if mankind were agreed in considering utility to be the test of morality, they would remain without any agreement as to what *is* useful, and would take no measures for having their notions on the subject taught to the young and enforced by law and opinion. There is no difficulty in proving any ethical standard whatever to work ill, if we suppose universal idiocy to be conjoined with it; but on any hypothesis short of that, mankind must by this time have acquired positive beliefs as to the effects of some actions on their happiness, and the beliefs which have thus come down are the rules of morality for the multitude, and for the philosopher, until he has succeeded in finding better. That philosophers might easily do this, even now, on many subjects, that the received code of ethics is by no means of divine right, and that mankind have still much to learn as to the effects of actions on the general happiness—I admit or, rather, earnestly maintain. The corollaries from the principle of utility, like the precepts of every practical art, admit of indefinite improvement and, in a progressive state of the human mind, their improvement is perpetually going on. But to consider the rules of morality as improvable is one thing; to pass over the intermediate generalizations entirely, and endeavor to test each individual action directly by the first principle, is another. It is a strange notion, that the acknowledgment of a first principle is inconsistent with the admission of secondary ones. To inform a traveler respecting the place of his ultimate destination is not to forbid the use of landmarks and direction posts on the way. The proposition that happiness is the end and aim of morality does not mean that no road ought to be laid down to that goal, or that persons going thither should not be advised to take one direction rather than another. Men really ought to leave off talking a kind of nonsense on this subject which they would neither talk nor listen to on other matters of practical concernment. Nobody argues that the art of navigation is not founded on astronomy, because sailors cannot wait to calculate the "Nautical Almanac." Being rational creatures, they go to sea with it ready calculated, and all rational creatures go out upon the sea of life with their minds made up on the common questions of right and wrong, as well as on many of the far more difficult questions of wise and foolish. And this, as long as foresight is a human quality, it is to be presumed they will continue to do. Whatever we adopt as the fundamental principle of morality, we require subordinate principles to apply it by; the impossibility of doing without them, being common to all systems, can afford no argument against any one in particular; but gravely to argue as if no such secondary principles could be had, and as if mankind had remained till now and always must remain without drawing any general conclusions from the experience of human life, is as high a pitch, I think, as absurdity has ever reached in philosophical controversy.

The remainder of the stock arguments against utilitarianism mostly consist in laying to its charge the common infirmities of human nature, and the general difficulties which embarrass conscientious persons in shaping their course through life. We are told that an utilitarian will be apt to make his own particular case an exception to moral rules and, when under temptation, will see an utility in the breach of a rule greater than he will see in its observance. But is utility the only creed which is able to furnish us with excuses for evil-doing, and means of cheating our own conscience? They are afforded in abundance by all doctrines which recognize as a fact in morals the existence of conflicting considerations, which all doctrines do that have been believed by sane persons. It is not the fault of any creed, but of the complicated nature of human affairs, that rules of conduct cannot be so framed as to require no exceptions, and that hardly any kind of action can safely be laid down as either always obligatory or always condemnable. There is no ethical creed which does not temper the rigidity of its laws by giving a certain latitude, under the moral responsibility of the agent, for accommodation to peculiarities of circumstances and, under every creed, at the opening thus made, self-deception and dishonest casuistry get in. There exists no moral system under which there do not arise unequivocal cases of conflicting obligation. These are the real difficulties, the knotty points both in the theory of ethics and in the conscientious guidance of personal conduct. They are overcome practically with greater or with less success according to the intellect and virtue of the individual, but it can hardly be pretended that any one will be the less qualified for dealing with them, from possessing an ultimate standard to which conflicting rights and duties can be referred. If utility is the ultimate source of moral obligations, utility may be invoked to decide between them when their demands are incompatible. Though the application of the standard may be difficult, it is better than none at all; while in other systems, the moral laws all claiming independent authority, there is no common umpire entitled to interfere between them, their claims to precedence one over another rest on little better than sophistry, and unless determined, as they generally are, by the unacknowledged influence of considerations of utility, afford a free scope for the action of personal desires and partialities. We must remember that only in these cases of conflict between secondary principles is it requisite that first principles should be appealed to. There is no case of moral obligation in which some secondary principle is not involved and, if only one, there can seldom be any real doubt which one it is, in the mind of any person by whom the principle itself is recognized.

3. Of the Ultimate Sanction of the Principle of Utility

The question is often asked, and properly so, in regard to any supposed moral standard, What is its sanction? what are the motives to obey it? or, more specifically, what is the source of its obligation? whence does it derive its binding force? It is a necessary part of moral philosophy to provide the answer to this question, which, though frequently assuming the shape of an objection to the utilitarian morality, as if it had some special applicability to that above others, really arises in regard to all standards. It arises, in fact, whenever a person is called on to *adopt* a standard or refer morality to any basis on which he has not been accustomed to rest it. For the customary morality, that which education and opinion have consecrated, is the only one which presents itself to the mind with the feeling of being *in itself* obligatory; and, when a person is asked to believe that this morality *derives* its obligation from some general principle round which custom has not thrown the same halo, the assertion is to him a paradox: the supposed corollaries seem to have a more binding force than the original theorem; the superstructure seems to stand better without than with what is represented as its foundation. He says to himself, "I feel that I am bound not to rob or murder, betray or deceive, but why am I bound to promote the general happiness? If my own happiness lies in something else, why may I not give that the preference?"

If the view adopted by the utilitarian philosophy of the nature of the moral sense be correct, this difficulty will always present itself, until the influences which form moral character have taken the same hold of the principle which they have taken of some of the consequences, until, by the improvement of education, the feeling of unity with our fellow creatures shall be (what it cannot be denied that Christ intended it to be) as deeply rooted in our character and, to our own consciousness, as completely a part of our nature, as the horror of crime is in an ordinarily well brought up young person. In the mean time, however, the difficulty has no peculiar application to the doctrine of utility, but is inherent in every attempt to analyze morality, and reduce it to principles, which, unless the principle is already in men's minds invested with as much sacredness as any of its applications, always seems to divest them of a part of their sanctity.

The principle of utility either has, or there is no reason why it might not have, all the sanctions which belong to any other system of morals. Those sanctions are either external or internal. Of the external sanctions it is not necessary to speak at any length. They are the hope of favor and the fear of displeasure from our fellow creatures, or from the Ruler of the universe, along with whatever we may have of sympathy or affection for them or of love and awe of him, inclining us to do his will independently of selfish consequences. There is evidently no reason why all these motives for observance should not attach themselves to the utilitarian morality as completely and as powerfully as to any other. Indeed, those of them which refer to our fellow creatures are sure to do so, in proportion to the amount of general intelligence; for, whether there be any other ground of moral obligation than the general happiness or not, men do desire happiness and, however imperfect may be their own practice, they desire and commend all conduct in others towards themselves by which they think their happiness is promoted. With regard to the religious motive, if men believe, as most profess to do, in the goodness of God, those who think that conduciveness to the general happiness is the essence, or even only the criterion of good, must necessarily believe that it is also that which God approves. The whole force, therefore, of external reward and punishment, whether physical or moral, and whether proceeding from God or from our fellow men, together with all that the capacities of human nature admit of disinterested devotion to either, become available to enforce the utilitarian morality, in proportion as that morality is recognized, and the more powerfully, the more the appliances of education and general cultivation are bent to the purpose.

So far as to external sanctions. The internal sanction of duty, whatever our standard of duty may be, is one and the same—a feeling in our own mind, a pain, more or less intense, attendant on violation of duty, which, in properly cultivated moral natures, rises in the more serious cases into shrinking from it as an impossibility. This feeling, when disinterested, and connecting itself with the pure idea of duty and not with some particular form of it, or with any of the merely accessory circumstances, is the essence of Conscience; though in that complex phenomenon, as it actually exists, the simple fact is, in general, all incrusted over with collateral associations, derived from sympathy, from love, and still more from fear, from all the forms of religious feeling, from the recollections of childhood, and of all our past life, from self-esteem, desire of the esteem of others, and occasionally even self-abasement. This extreme complication is, I apprehend, the origin of the sort of mystical character which, by a tendency of the human mind of which there are many other examples, is apt to be attributed to the idea of moral obligation, and which leads people to believe that the idea cannot possibly attach itself to any other objects than those which, by a supposed mysterious law, are found in our present experience to excite it. Its binding force, however, consists in the existence of a mass of feeling which must be broken through in order to do what violates our standard of right, and which, if we do nevertheless violate that standard, will probably have to be encountered afterwards in the form of remorse. Whatever theory we have of the nature or origin of conscience, this is what essentially constitutes it.

The ultimate sanction, therefore, of all morality (external motives apart) being a subjective feeling in our own minds, I see nothing embarrassing, to those whose standard is utility, in the question, What is the sanction of that particular standard? We may answer, The same as of all other moral standards—the conscientious feelings of mankind. Undoubtedly this sanction has no binding efficacy on those who do not possess the feelings it appeals to, but neither will these persons be more obedient to any other moral principle than to the utilitarian one. On them, morality of any kind has no hold but through the external sanctions. Meanwhile the feelings exist—a fact in human nature, the reality of which, and the great power with which they are capable of acting on those in whom they have been duly cultivated, are proved by experience. No reason has ever been shown why they may not be cultivated to as great intensity in connection with the utilitarian as with any other rule of morals.

There is, I am aware, a disposition to believe that a person who sees in moral obligation a transcendental fact, an objective reality belonging to the province of "things in themselves," is likely to be more obedient to it than one who believes it to be entirely subjective, having its seat in human consciousness only. But, whatever a person's opinion may be on this point of ontology, the force he is really urged by is his own subjective feeling and is exactly measured by its strength. No one's belief that Duty is an objective reality is stronger than the belief that God is so, yet the belief in God, apart from the expectation of actual reward and punishment, only operates on conduct through, and in proportion to, the subjective religious feeling. The sanction, so far as it is disinterested, is always in the mind itself; and the notion, therefore, of the transcendental moralists must be that this sanction will not exist *in* the mind, unless it is believed to have its root out of the mind, and that if a person is able to say to himself, "This which is restraining me, and which is called my conscience, is only a feeling in my own mind," he may possibly draw the conclusion that, when the feeling ceases, the obligation ceases, and that, if he find the feeling inconvenient, he may disregard it and endeavor to get rid of it. But is this danger confined to the utilitarian morality? Does the belief that moral obligation has its seat outside the mind make the feeling of it too strong to be got rid of? The fact is so far otherwise that all moralists admit and lament the ease with which, in the generality of minds, conscience can be silenced or stifled. The question, Need I obey my conscience? is quite as often put to themselves by persons who never heard of the principle of utility as by its adherents. Those whose conscientious feelings are so weak as to allow of their asking this question, if they answer it affirmatively, will not do so because they believe in the transcendental theory but because of the external sanctions.

It is not necessary, for the present purpose, to decide whether the feeling of duty is innate or implanted. Assuming it to be innate, it is an open question to what objects it naturally attaches itself, for the philosophic supporters of that theory are now agreed that the intuitive perception is of principles of morality and not of the details. If there be any thing innate in the matter, I see no reason why the feeling which is innate should not be that of regard to the pleasures and pains of others. If there is any principle of morals which is intuitively obligatory, I should say it must be that. If so, the intuitive ethics would coincide with the utilitarian, and there would be no further quarrel between them. Even as it is, the intuitive moralists, though they believe that there are other intuitive moral obligations, do already believe this to be one, for they unanimously hold that a large *portion* of morality turns upon the consideration due to the interests of our fellow creatures. Therefore, if the belief in the transcendental origin of moral obligation gives any additional efficacy to the internal sanction, it appears to me that the utilitarian principle has already the benefit of it.

On the other hand, if, as is my own belief, the moral feelings are not innate but acquired, they are not for that reason the less natural. It is natural to man to speak, to reason, to build cities, to cultivate the ground, though these are acquired faculties. The moral feelings are not indeed a part of our nature, in the sense of being in any perceptible degree present in all of us, but this, unhappily, is a fact admitted by those who believe the most strenuously in their transcendental origin. Like the other acquired capacities above referred to, the moral faculty, if not a part of our nature, is a natural outgrowth from it, capable like them, in a certain small degree, of springing up spontaneously, and susceptible of being brought by cultivation to a high degree of development. Unhappily, it is also susceptible, by a sufficient use of the external sanctions and of the force of early impressions, of being cultivated in almost any direction, so that there is hardly any thing so absurd or so mischievous that it may not, by means of these influences, be made to act on the human mind with all the authority of conscience. To doubt that the same potency might be given by the same means to the principle of utility, even if it had no foundation in human nature, would be flying in the face of all experience.

But moral associations which are wholly of artificial creation, when intellectual culture goes on, yield by degrees to the dissolving force of analysis; and if the feeling of duty, when associated with utility, would appear equally arbitrary, if there were no leading department of our nature, no powerful class of sentiments, with which that association would harmonize, which would make us feel it congenial, and incline us not only to foster it in others (for which we have abundant interested motives), but also to cherish it in ourselves, if there were not, in short, a natural basis of sentiment for utilitarian morality— it might well happen that this association also, even after it had been implanted by education, might be analyzed away.

But there *is* this basis of powerful natural sentiment, and this it is, which, when once the general happiness is recognized as the ethical standard, will constitute the strength of the utilitarian morality. This firm foundation is that of the social feelings of mankind: the desire to be in unity with our fellow creatures, which is already a powerful principle in human nature, and happily one of those which tend to become stronger, even without express inculcation from the influences of advancing civilization. The social state is at once so natural, so necessary, and so habitual to man, that except in some unusual circumstances, or by an effort of voluntary abstraction, he never conceives himself otherwise than as a member of a body, and this association is riveted more and more as mankind are further removed from the state of savage independence. Any condition, therefore, which is essential to a state of society, becomes more and more an inseparable part of every person's conception of the state of things which he is born into, and which is the destiny of a human being. Now, society between human beings, except in the relation of master and slave, is manifestly impossible on any other footing than that the interests of all are to be consulted. Society between equals can only exist on the understanding that the interests of all are to be regarded equally. And since, in all states of civilization, every person except an absolute monarch has equals, every one is obliged to live on these terms with somebody, and in every age, some advance is made towards a state in which it will be impossible to live permanently on other terms with anybody. In this way, people grow up unable to conceive as possible to them a state of total disregard of other people's interests. They are under a necessity of conceiving themselves as at least abstaining from all the grosser injuries, and (if only for their own protection) living in a state of constant protest against them. They are also familiar with the fact of cooperating with others, and proposing to themselves a collective, not an individual, interest as the aim (at least for the time being) of their actions. So long as they are cooperating, their ends are identified with those of others; there is at least a temporary feeling that the interests of others are their own interests. Not only does all strengthening of social ties, and all healthy growth of society, give to each individual a stronger personal interest in practically consulting the welfare of others; it also leads him to identify his *feelings* more and more with their good, or at least with an ever greater degree of practical consideration for it. He comes, as though instinctively, to be conscious of himself as a being who *of course* pays regard to others. The good of others becomes to him a thing naturally and necessarily to be attended to, like any of the physical conditions of our existence. Now, whatever amount of this feeling a person has, he is urged by the strongest motives, both of interest and of sympathy, to demonstrate it and, to the utmost of his power, encourage it in others, and, even if he has none of it himself, he is as greatly interested as any one else that others should have it. Consequently, the smallest germs of the feeling are laid hold of and nourished by the contagion of sympathy and the influences of education, and a complete web of corroborative association is woven round it by the powerful agency of the external sanctions. This mode of conceiving ourselves and human life, as civilization goes on, is felt to be more and more natural. Every step in political improvement renders it more so, by removing the sources of opposition of

interest and leveling those inequalities of legal privilege between individuals or classes, owing to which there are large
portions of mankind whose happiness it is still practicable to
disregard. In an improving state of the human mind, the influences are constantly on the increase which tend to generate in
each individual a feeling of unity with all the rest, which, if
perfect, would make him never think of or desire any beneficial condition for himself, in the benefits of which they are
not included. If we now suppose this feeling of unity to be
taught as a religion, and the whole force of education, of institutions, and of opinion directed, as it once was in the case
of religion, to make every person grow up from infancy surrounded on all sides both by the profession and the practice
of it, I think that no one who can realize this conception will
feel any misgiving about the sufficiency of the ultimate sanction for the Happiness morality. To any ethical student who
finds the realization difficult, I recommend, as a means of
facilitating it, the second of M. Comte's two principal works,
the *Traité de Politique Positive*. I entertain the strongest objections to the system of politics and morals set forth in that
treatise; but I think it has superabundantly shown the possibility of giving to the service of humanity, even without the
aid of belief in a Providence, both the psychological power
and the social efficacy of a religion, making it take hold of
human life, and color all thought, feeling, and action, in a
manner of which the greatest ascendancy ever exercised by
any religion may be but a type and foretaste, and of which
the danger is, not that it should be insufficient, but that it
should be so excessive as to interfere unduly with human
freedom and individuality.

Neither is it necessary to the feeling which constitutes the
binding force of the utilitarian morality on those who recognize it, to wait for those social influences which would make
its obligation felt by mankind at large. In the comparatively
early state of human advancement in which we now live, a
person cannot indeed feel that entireness of sympathy with all
others which would make any real discordance in the general
direction of their conduct in life impossible, but already a person in whom the social feeling is at all developed cannot bring
himself to think of the rest of his fellow-creatures as struggling rivals with him for the means of happiness, whom he
must desire to see defeated in their object in order that he

may succeed in his. The deeply rooted conception which every individual even now has of himself as a social being tends to make him feel it one of his natural wants that there should be harmony between his feelings and aims and those of his fellow creatures. If differences of opinion and of mental culture make it impossible for him to share many of their actual feelings—perhaps make him denounce and defy those feelings—he still needs to be conscious that his real aim and theirs do not conflict, that he is not opposing himself to what they really wish for—namely, their own good—but is, on the contrary, promoting it. This feeling in most individuals is much inferior in strength to their selfish feelings, and is often wanting altogether. But to those who have it, it possesses all the characters of a natural feeling. It does not present itself to their minds as a superstition of education, or a law despotically imposed by the power of society, but as an attribute which it would not be well for them to be without. This conviction is the ultimate sanction of the greatest-happiness morality. This it is which makes any mind of well-developed feelings work with, and not against, the outward motives to care for others, afforded by what I have called the external sanctions, and when those sanctions are wanting, or act in an opposite direction, constitutes in itself a powerful internal binding force, in proportion to the sensitiveness and thoughtfulness of the character; since few but those whose mind is a moral blank could bear to lay out their course of life on the plan of paying no regard to others, except so far as their own private interest compels.

4. Of What Sort of Proof the Principle of Utility Is Susceptible

It has already been remarked that questions of ultimate ends do not admit of proof, in the ordinary acceptation of the term. To be incapable of proof by reasoning is common to all first principles, to the first premises of our knowledge, as well as to those of our conduct. But the former, being matters of fact, may be the subject of a direct appeal to the faculties which judge of fact, namely, our senses, and our internal consciousness. Can an appeal be made to the same faculties on questions of practical ends? Or by what other faculty is cognizance taken of them?

Questions about ends are, in other words, questions what things are desirable. The utilitarian doctrine is that happiness is desirable, and the only thing desirable, as an end, all other things being only desirable as means to that end. What ought to be required of this doctrine—what conditions is it requisite that the doctrine should fulfil—to make good its claim to be believed?

The only proof capable of being given that an object is visible is that people actually see it, the only proof that a sound is audible is that people hear it, and so of the other sources of our experience. In like manner, I apprehend, the sole evidence it is possible to produce that any thing is desirable is that people do actually desire it. If the end which the utilitarian doctrine proposes to itself were not, in theory and in practice, acknowledged to be an end, nothing could ever convince any person that it was so. No reason can be given why the general happiness is desirable, except that each person, so far as he believes it to be attainable, desires his own happiness. This, however, being a fact, we have not only all the proof which the case admits of, but all which it is possible to require, that happiness is a good, that each person's happiness is a good to that person, and the general happiness, therefore, a good to the aggregate of all persons.[2] Happiness has made out its title as *one* of the ends of conduct, and consequently one of the criteria of morality.

But it has not, by this alone, proved itself to be the sole criterion. To do that, it would seem, by the same rule, necessary to show, not only that people desire happiness, but that they never desire any thing else. Now, it is palpable that they do desire things, which, in common language, are decidedly distinguished from happiness. They desire, for example, virtue and the absence of vice, no less really than pleasure and the absence of pain. The desire of virtue is not as universal, but it is as authentic a fact, as the desire of happiness, and hence the opponents of the utilitarian standard deem that they have a right to infer that there are other ends of human action besides happiness, and that happiness is not the standard of approbation and disapprobation.

But does the utilitarian doctrine deny that people desire virtue, or maintain that virtue is not a thing to be desired? The very reverse. It maintains not only that virtue is to be desired, but that it is to be desired disinterestedly, for itself. Whatever may be the opinion of utilitarian moralists as to the original conditions by which virtue is made virtue, however they may believe (as they do) that actions and dispositions are only virtuous because they promote another end than virtue—yet, this being granted, and it having been decided, from considerations of this description, what *is* virtuous, they not only place virtue at the very head of the things which are good as means to the ultimate end, but they also recognize, as a psychological fact, the possibility of its being to the individual a good in itself, without looking to any end beyond it, and hold that the mind is not in a right state, not in a state conformable to utility, not in the state most conducive to the general happiness, unless it does love virtue in this manner— as a thing desirable in itself, even although, in the individual instance, it should not produce those other desirable consequences which it tends to produce, and on account of which it is held to be virtue. This opinion is not, in the smallest degree, a departure from the Happiness principle. The ingredients of happiness are very various, and each of them is desirable in itself and not merely when considered as swelling an aggregate. The principle of utility does not mean that any given pleasure—as music, for instance—or any given exemption from pain—as, for example, health—are to be looked upon as means to a collective something termed happiness, and to be desired on that account. They are desired and desirable in and for themselves; besides being means, they are a part of the end. Virtue, according to the utilitarian doctrine, is not naturally and originally part of the end, but it is capable of becoming so and, in those who love it disinterestedly, it has become so, and is desired and cherished, not as a means to happiness, but as a part of their happiness.

To illustrate this further: we may remember that virtue is not the only thing, originally a means, and which, if it were not a means to anything else, would be and remain indifferent, but which, by association with what it is a means to, comes to be desired for itself, and that, too, with the utmost intensity. What, for example, shall we say of the love of money? There is nothing originally more desirable about money than about any heap of glittering pebbles. Its worth is solely that of the things which it will buy, the desires for other things than itself, which it is a means of gratifying. Yet the love of money is not only one of the strongest moving forces of human life, but money is, in many cases, desired in and for itself; the desire to possess it is often stronger than the desire to use it, and goes on increasing when all the desires which point to ends beyond it, to be compassed by it, are falling off. It may, then, be said truly, that money is desired, not for the sake of an end but as part of the end. From being a means to happiness, it has come to be itself a principal ingredient of the individual's conception of happiness. The same may be said of the majority of the great objects of human life—power, for example, or fame, except that to each of these there is a certain amount of immediate pleasure annexed, which has at least the semblance of being naturally inherent in them, a thing which cannot be said of money. Still, however, the strongest natural attraction, both of power and of fame, is the immense aid they give to the attainment of our other wishes, and it is the strong association thus generated between them and all our objects of desire which gives to the direct desire of them the intensity it often assumes, so as in some characters to surpass in strength all other desires. In these cases, the means have become a part of the end, and a more important part of it than any of the things which they are means to. What was once desired as an instrument for the attainment of happiness has come to be desired for its own sake. In being desired for its own sake, it is, however, desired as *part* of happiness. The person is made, or thinks he would be made, happy by its mere possession, and is made unhappy by failure to obtain it. The desire of it is not a different thing from the desire of happiness, any more than the love of music or the desire of health. They are included in happiness. They are some of the elements of which the desire of happiness is made up. Happiness is not an abstract idea but a concrete whole, and these are some of its parts. And the utilitarian standard sanctions and approves their being so. Life would be a poor thing, very ill provided with sources of happiness, if there were not this provision of nature, by which things originally indifferent, but conducive to, or otherwise associated with, the satisfaction of our primitive desires, become in themselves sources of pleasure more valuable than the primitive pleasures, both in permanency, in the space of human existence that they are capable of covering, and even in intensity.

Virtue, according to the utilitarian conception, is a good of this description. There was no original desire of it, or motive to it, save its conduciveness to pleasure, and especially to protection from pain. But through the association thus formed, it may be felt a good in itself, and desired as such with as great intensity as any other good, and with this difference between it and the love of money, of power, or of fame—that all of these may, and often do, render the individual noxious to the other members of the society to which he belongs, whereas there is nothing which makes him so much a blessing to them as the cultivation of the disinterested love of virtue. And consequently the utilitarian standard, while it tolerates and approves those other acquired desires, up to the point beyond which they would be more injurious to the general happiness than promotive of it, enjoins and requires the cultivation of the love of virtue up to the greatest strength possible, as being above all things important to the general happiness.

It results from the preceding considerations that there is in reality nothing desired except happiness. Whatever is desired otherwise than as a means to some end beyond itself, and ultimately to happiness, is desired as itself a part of happiness, and is not desired for itself until it has become so. Those who desire virtue for its own sake desire it either because the consciousness of it is a pleasure, or because the consciousness of being without it is a pain, or for both reasons united; as in truth the pleasure and pain seldom exist separately, but almost always together, the same person feeling pleasure in the degree of virtue attained, and pain in not having attained more. If one of these gave him no pleasure, and the other no pain, he would not love or desire virtue, or would desire it only for the other benefits which it might produce to himself or to persons whom he cared for.

We have now, then, an answer to the question of what sort of proof the principle of utility is suceptible. If the opinion which I have now stated is psychologically true, if human nature is so constituted as to desire nothing which is not either a part of happiness or a means of happiness—we can have no other proof, and we require no other, that these are the only things desirable. If so, happiness is the sole end of human action, and the promotion of it the test by which to judge of all human conduct, from whence it necessarily follows that it must be the criterion of morality, since a part is included in the whole.

And, now, to decide whether this is really so, whether mankind do desire nothing for itself but that which is a pleasure to them, or of which the absence is a pain—we have evidently arrived at a question of fact and experience, dependent, like all similar questions, upon evidence. It can only be determined by practised self-consciousness and self-observation, assisted by observation of others. I believe that these sources of evidence, impartially consulted, will declare that desiring a thing and finding it pleasant, aversion to it and thinking of it as painful, are phenomena entirely inseparable, or rather two parts of the same phenomenon—in strictness of language, two different modes of naming the same psychological fact; that to think of an object as desirable (unless for the sake of its consequences), and to think of it as pleasant, are one and the same thing; and that to desire any thing, except in proportion as the idea of it is pleasant, is a physical and metaphysical impossibility.

So obvious does this appear to me that I expect it will hardly be disputed, and the objection made will be, not that desire can possibly be directed to any thing ultimately except pleasure and exemption from pain, but that the will is a different thing from desire; that a person of confirmed virtue, or any other person whose purposes are fixed, carries out his purposes without any thought of the pleasure he has in contemplating them, or expects to derive from their fulfilment, and persists in acting on them, even though these pleasures are much diminished by changes in his character, or decay of his passive sensibilities, or are outweighed by the pains which the pursuit of the purposes may bring upon him. All this I fully admit, and have stated it elsewhere as positively and emphatically as any one. Will, the active phenomenon, is a different thing from desire, the state of passive sensibility and, though originally an offshoot from it, may in time take root and detach itself from the parent stock; so much so, that in the case of an habitual purpose, instead of willing the thing because we desire it, we often desire it only because we will it. This, however, is but an instance of that familiar fact, the power of habit, and is nowise confined to the case of virtuous actions. Many indifferent things, which men originally did from a motive of some sort, they continue to do from habit. Sometimes this is done unconsciously, the consciousness coming only after the action; at other times with conscious volition, but volition which has become habitual, and is put in operation by the force of habit, in opposition, perhaps, to the deliberate preference, as often happens with those who have contracted habits of vicious or hurtful indulgence. Third and last comes the case in which the habitual act of will in the individual instance is not in contradiction to the general intention prevailing at other times, but in fulfilment of it, as in the case of the person of confirmed virtue, and of all who pursue deliberately and consistently any determinate end. The distinction between will and desire, thus understood, is an authentic and highly important psychological fact, but the fact consists solely in this—that will, like all other parts of our constitution, is amenable to habit, and that we may will from habit what we no longer desire for itself, or desire only because we will it. It is not the less true that will, in the beginning, is entirely produced by desire, including in that term the repelling influence of pain, as well as the attractive one of pleasure. Let us take into consideration no longer the person who has a confirmed will to do right, but him in whom that virtuous will is still feeble, conquerable by temptation, and not to be fully relied on; by what means can it be strengthened? How can the will to be virtuous, where it does not exist in sufficient force, be implanted or awakened? Only by making the person *desire* virtue, by making him think of it in a pleasurable light, or of its absence in a painful one. It is by associating the doing right with pleasure, or the doing wrong with pain, or by eliciting and impressing and bringing home to the person's experience the pleasure naturally involved in the one or the pain in the other, that it is possible to call forth that will to be virtuous which, when confirmed, acts without any thought of either pleasure or pain. Will is the child of desire, and passes out of the domination of its parent only to come under that of habit. That which is the result of habit affords no presumption of being intrinsically good, and there would be no reason for wishing that the purpose of virtue should become independent of pleasure and pain, were it not that the influence of the pleasurable and painful associations which prompt to virtue is not sufficiently to be depended on for unerring constancy of action until it has acquired the support of habit. Both in feeling and in conduct, habit is the only thing which imparts certainty, and it is because of the importance to others of being able to rely absolutely on one's feelings and conduct, and to one's self of being able to rely on one's own, that the will to do right ought to be cultivated into this habitual independence. In other words, this state of the will is a means to good, not intrinsically a good, and does not contradict the doctrine that nothing is a good to human beings but in so far as it is either itself pleasurable or a means of attaining pleasure or averting pain.

But if this doctrine be true, the principle of utility is proved. Whether it is so or not, must now be left to the consideration of the thoughtful reader.

5. On the Connection Between Justice and Utility

In all ages of speculation, one of the strongest obstacles to the reception of the doctrine that Utility or Happiness is the criterion of right and wrong, has been drawn from the idea of Justice. The powerful sentiment and apparently clear perception which that word recalls, with a rapidity and certainty resembling an instinct, have seemed to the majority of thinkers to point to an inherent quality in things, to show that the Just must have an existence in nature as something absolute, generically distinct from every variety of the Expedient and, in idea, opposed to it, though (as is commonly acknowledged) never, in the long run, disjoined from it in fact.

In the case of this, as of our other moral sentiments, there is no necessary connection between the question of its origin and that of its binding force. That a feeling is bestowed on us by Nature does not necessarily legitimate all its promptings. The feeling of justice might be a peculiar instinct, and might yet require, like our other instincts, to be controlled and enlightened by a higher reason. If we have intellectual instincts leading us to judge in a particular way, as well as animal instincts that prompt us to act in a particular way, there is no necessity that the former should be more infallible in their sphere than the latter in theirs; it may as well happen that wrong judgments are occasionally suggested by those, as wrong actions by these. But though it is one thing to believe that we have natural feelings of justice and another to acknowledge them as an ultimate criterion of conduct, these

two opinions are very closely connected in point of fact.
Mankind are always predisposed to believe that any subjective feeling not otherwise accounted for, is a revelation of
some objective reality. Our present object is to determine
whether the reality to which the feeling of justice corresponds, is one which needs any such special revelation,
whether the justice or injustice of an action is a thing intrinsically peculiar, and distinct from all its other qualities,
or only a combination of certain of those qualities, presented
under a peculiar aspect. For the purpose of this inquiry, it is
practically important to consider whether the feeling itself
of justice and injustice is *sui generis* like our sensations of
color and taste, or a derivative feeling, formed by a combination of others. And this it is the more essential to examine, as
people are in general willing enough to allow that, objectively, the dictates of Justice coincide with a part of the field
of General Expediency; but inasmuch as the subjective mental
feeling of Justice is different from that which commonly
attaches to simple expediency and, except in the extreme
cases of the latter, is far more imperative in its demands,
people find it difficult to see, in Justice, only a particular kind
or branch of general utility, and think that its superior binding force requires a totally different origin.

To throw light upon this question, it is necessary to attempt to ascertain what is the distinguishing character of
justice or of injustice; what is the quality, or whether there is
any quality, attributed in common to all modes of conduct
designated as unjust (for justice, like many other moral attributes, is best defined by its opposite), and distinguishing
them from such modes of conduct as are disapproved, but
without having that particular epithet of disapprobation applied to them. If, in everything which men are accustomed
to characterize as just or unjust, some one common attribute
or collection of attributes is always present, we may judge
whether this particular attribute, or combination of attributes,
would be capable of gathering round it a sentiment of that
peculiar character and intensity by virtue of the general laws
of our emotional constitution, or whether the sentiment is inexplicable and requires to be regarded as a special provision
of nature. If we find the former to be the case, we shall, in
resolving this question, have resolved also the main problem;
if the latter, we shall have to seek for some other mode of
investigating it.

To find the common attributes of a variety of objects, it is necessary to begin by surveying the objects themselves in the concrete. Let us therefore advert successively to the various modes of action, and arrangements of human affairs, which are classed, by universal or widely spread opinion, as Just or as Unjust. The things well known to excite the sentiments associated with those names are of a very multifarious character. I shall pass them rapidly in review, without studying any particular arrangement.

In the first place, it is mostly considered unjust to deprive any one of his personal liberty, his property, or any other thing which belongs to him by law. Here, therefore, is one instance of the application of the terms Just and Unjust in a perfectly definite sense, namely, that it is just to respect, unjust to violate, the *legal rights* of any one. But this judgment admits of several exceptions, arising from the other forms in which the notions of justice and injustice present themselves. For example: the person who suffers the deprivation may (as the phrase is) have *forfeited* the rights which he is so deprived of; a case to which we shall return presently. But also,

Secondly, The legal rights of which he is deprived may be rights which *ought* not to have belonged to him; in other words, the law which confers on him these rights may be a bad law. When it is so, or when (which is the same thing for our purpose) it is supposed to be so, opinions will differ as to the justice or injustice of infringing it. Some maintain that no law, however bad, ought to be disobeyed by an individual citizen, that his opposition to it, if shown at all, should only be shown in endeavoring to get it altered by competent authority. This opinion (which condemns many of the most illustrious benefactors of mankind, and would often protect pernicious institutions against the only weapons which, in the state of things existing at the time, have any chance of succeeding against them) is defended, by those who hold it, on grounds of expediency, principally on that of the importance, to the common interest of mankind, of maintaining inviolate the sentiment of submission to law. Other persons, again, hold the directly contrary opinion that any law judged to be bad may blamelessly be disobeyed, even though it be not judged to be unjust, but only inexpedient, while others would confine the license of disobedience to the case of unjust laws. But, again, some say that all laws which are inexpedient are unjust, since every law imposes some restriction on the natural liberty of mankind, which restriction is an injustice, unless legitimated by tending to their good. Among these diversities of opinion, it seems to be universally admitted that there may be unjust laws, and that law, consequently, is not the ultimate criterion of justice, but may give to one person a benefit, or impose on another an evil, which justice condemns. When, however, a law is thought to be unjust, it seems always to be regarded as being so in the same way in which a breach of law is unjust— namely, by infringing somebody's right; which, as it cannot in this case be a legal right, receives a different appellation and is called a moral right. We may say, therefore, that a second case of injustice consists in taking or withholding from any person that to which he has a *moral right*.

Thirdly, It is universally considered just that each person should obtain that (whether good or evil) which he *deserves*, and unjust, that he should obtain a good, or be made to undergo an evil, which he does not deserve. This is, perhaps, the clearest and most emphatic form in which the idea of justice is conceived by the general mind. As it involves the notion of desert, the question arises, What constitutes desert? Speaking in a general way, a person is understood to deserve good if he does right, evil, if he does wrong; and, in a more particular sense, to deserve good from those to whom he does or has done good, and evil from those to whom he does or has done evil. The precept of returning good for evil has never been regarded as a case of the fulfilment of justice, but as one in which the claims of justice are waived, in obedience to other considerations.

Fourthly, It is confessedly unjust to *break faith* with any one, to violate an engagement, either express or implied, or disappoint expectations raised by our own conduct, at least if we have raised those expectations knowingly and voluntarily. Like the other obligations of justice already spoken of, this one is not regarded as absolute, but as capable of being overruled by a stronger obligation of justice on the other side, or by such conduct on the part of the person concerned as is deemed to absolve us from our obligation to him and to constitute a *forfeiture* of the benefit which he has been led to expect.

Fifthly, It is, by universal admission, inconsistent with justice to be *partial*, to show favor or preference to one person over another in matters to which favor and preference do not properly apply. Impartiality, however, does not seem to be regarded as a duty in itself, but rather as instrumental to some other duty, for it is admitted that favor and preference are not always censurable, and indeed the cases in which they are condemned are rather the exception than the rule. A person would be more likely to be blamed than applauded for giving his family or friends no superiority in good offices over strangers, when he could do so without violating any other duty, and no one thinks it unjust to seek one person in preference to another as a friend, connection, or companion. Impartiality, where rights are concerned, is of course obligatory, but this is involved in the more general obligation of giving to every one his right. A tribunal, for example, must be impartial, because it is bound to award, without regard to any other consideration, a disputed object to the one of two parties who has the right to it. There are other cases in which impartiality means, being solely influenced by desert, as with those who, in the capacity of judges, preceptors, or parents, administer reward and punishment as such. There are cases, again, in which it means being solely influenced by consideration for the public interest, as in making a selection among candidates for a government employment. Impartiality, in short, as an obligation of justice, may be said to mean being exclusively influenced by the considerations which it is supposed ought to influence the particular case in hand, and resisting the solicitation of any motives which prompt to conduct different from what those considerations would dictate.

Nearly allied to the idea of impartiality is that of *equality*, which often enters as a component part both into the conception of justice and into the practice of it and, in the eyes of many persons, constitutes its essence. But, in this still more than in any other case, the notion of justice varies in different persons, and always conforms in its variations to their notion of utility. Each person maintains that equality is the dictate of justice, except where he thinks that expediency requires inequality. The justice of giving equal protection to the rights of all is maintained by those who support the most outrageous inequality in the rights themselves. Even in slave countries, it is theoretically admitted that the rights of the slave, such as they are, ought to be as sacred as those of the master, and that a tribunal which fails to enforce them with equal strictness is wanting in justice, while, at the same time, institutions which leave to the slave scarcely any rights to enforce are not deemed unjust, because they are not deemed inexpedient. Those who think that utility requires distinctions of rank do not consider it unjust that riches and social privileges should be unequally dispensed, but those who think this inequality inexpedient think it unjust also. Whoever thinks that government is necessary sees no injustice in as much inequality as is constituted by giving to the magistrate powers not granted to other people. Even among those who hold leveling doctrines, there are as many questions of justice as there are differences of opinion about expediency. Some Communists consider it unjust that the produce of the labor of the community should be shared on any other principle than that of exact equality, others think it just that those should receive most whose wants[3] are greatest, while others hold that those who work harder, or who produce more, or whose services are more valuable to the community, may justly claim a larger quota in the division of the produce. And the sense of natural justice may be plausibly appealed to in behalf of every one of these opinions.

Among so many diverse applications of the term Justice, which yet is not regarded as ambiguous, it is a matter of some difficulty to seize the mental link which holds them together, and on which the moral sentiment adhering to the term essentially depends. Perhaps, in this embarrassment, some help may be derived from the history of the word, as indicated by its etymology.

[In most, if not in all languages, the etymology of the word which corresponds to Just points distinctly to an origin connected with the ordinance of law. *Justum* is a form of *jussum* —that which has been ordered. Δίκαιον comes directly from δίκη, a suit at law. *Recht*, from which came *right* and *righteous*, is synonymous with law. The courts of justice, the administration of justice, are the courts and the administration of law. *La justice*, in French, is the established term for judicature. I am not committing the fallacy imputed with some show of truth to Horne Tooke, of assuming that a word must still continue to mean what it originally meant. Etymology is slight evidence of what the idea now signified is, but the very best evidence of how it sprang up.][4] There can,

I think, be no doubt that the *idée mère*, the primitive element, in the formation of the notion of justice, was conformity to law. It constituted the entire idea among the Hebrews up to the birth of Christianity, as might be expected in the case of a people whose laws attempted to embrace all subjects on which precepts were required, and who believed those laws to be a direct emanation from the Supreme Being. But other nations, and in particular the Greeks and Romans, who knew that their laws had been made originally, and still continued to be made, by men, were not afraid to admit that those men might make bad laws, might do, by law, the same things, and from the same motives, which, if done by individuals without the sanction of law, would be called unjust. And hence the sentiment of injustice came to be attached, not to all violations of law, but only to violations of such laws as *ought* to exist, including such as ought to exist, but do not, and to laws themselves, if supposed to be contrary to what ought to be law. In this manner, the idea of law and of its injunctions was still predominant in the notion of justice, even when the laws actually in force ceased to be accepted as the standard of it.

It is true that mankind consider the idea of justice and its obligations as applicable to many things which neither are, nor is it desired that they should be, regulated by law. Nobody desires that laws should interfere with the whole detail of private life, yet every one allows that, in all daily conduct, a person may and does show himself to be either just or unjust. But even here, the idea of the breach of what ought to be law still lingers in a modified shape. It would always give us pleasure, and chime in with our feelings of fitness, that acts which we deem unjust should be punished, though we do not always think it expedient that this should be done by the tribunals. We forego that gratification on account of incidental inconveniences. We should be glad to see just conduct enforced, and injustice repressed, even in the minutest details, if we were not with reason afraid of trusting the magistrate with so unlimited an amount of power over individuals. When we think that a person is bound in justice to do a thing, it is an ordinary form of language to say that he ought to be compelled to do it. We should be gratified to see the obligation enforced by anybody who had the power. If we see that its enforcement by law would be inexpedient, we lament the impossibility, we consider the impunity given to injustice as an evil, and strive to make amends for it by bringing a strong expression of our own and the public disapprobation to bear upon the offender. Thus the idea of legal constraint is still the generating idea of the notion of justice, though undergoing several transformations before that notion, as it exists in an advanced state of society, becomes complete.

The above is, I think, a true account, as far as it goes, of the origin and progressive growth of the idea of justice. But we must observe that it contains, as yet, nothing to distinguish that obligation from moral obligation in general. For the truth is that the idea of penal sanction, which is the essence of law, enters not only into the conception of injustice, but into that of any kind of wrong. We do not call anything wrong, unless we mean to imply that a person ought to be punished in some way or other for doing it, if not by law, by the opinion of his fellow-creatures, if not by opinion, by the reproaches of his own conscience. This seems the real turning point of the distinction between morality and simple expediency. It is a part of the notion of Duty in every one of its forms that a person may rightfully be compelled to fulfil it. Duty is a thing which may be *exacted* from a person, as one exacts a debt. Unless we think that it may be exacted from him, we do not call it his duty. Reasons of prudence, or the interest of other people, may militate against actually exacting it, but the person himself, it is clearly understood, would not be entitled to complain. There are other things, on the contrary, which we wish that people should do, which we like or admire them for doing, perhaps dislike or despise them for not doing, but yet admit that they are not bound to do; it is not a case of moral obligation; we do not blame them, that is, we do not think that they are proper objects of punishment. How we come by these ideas of deserving and not deserving punishment, will appear, perhaps, in the sequel; but I think there is no doubt that this distinction lies at the bottom of the notions of right and wrong, that we call any conduct wrong, or employ instead some other term of dislike or disparagement, according as we think that the person ought or ought not to be punished for it, and we say it would be right to do so and so, or merely that it would be desirable or laudable, according as we would wish to see the person whom it concerns compelled, or only persuaded and exhorted, to act in that manner.*

This, therefore, being the characteristic difference which marks off, not justice but morality in general, from the remaining provinces of Expediency and Worthiness, the character is still to be sought which distinguishes justice from other branches of morality. Now, it is known that ethical writers divide moral duties into two classes, denoted by the ill-chosen expressions, duties of perfect and of imperfect obligation; the latter being those in which, though the act is obligatory, the particular occasions of performing it are left to our choice, as in the case of charity or beneficence, which we are indeed bound to practise, but not towards any definite person, nor at any prescribed time. In the more precise language of philosophic jurists, duties of perfect obligation are those duties in virtue of which a correlative *right* resides in some person or persons; duties of imperfect obligation are those moral obligations which do not give birth to any right. I think it will be found that this distinction exactly coincides with that which exists between justice and the other obligations of morality. In our survey of the various popular acceptations of justice, the term appeared generally to involve the idea of a personal right—a claim on the part of one or more individuals, like that which the law gives when it confers a proprietary or other legal right. Whether the injustice consists in depriving a person of a possession, or in breaking faith with him, or in treating him worse than he deserves, or worse than other people who have no greater claims, in each case the supposition implies two things—a wrong done, and some assignable person who is wronged. Injustice may also be done by treating a person better than others, but the wrong in this case is to his competitors, who are also assignable persons. It seems to me that this feature in the case —a right in some person, correlative to the moral obligation— constitutes the specific difference between justice and generosity or beneficence. Justice implies something which it is not only right to do and wrong not to do, but which some individual person can claim from us as his moral right. No one

* See this point enforced and illustrated by Professor Bain, in an admirable chapter (entitled "The Ethical Emotions, or the Moral Sense") of the second of the two treatises composing his elaborate and profound work on the Mind.

has a moral right to our generosity or beneficence, because we are not morally bound to practise those virtues towards any given individual. And it will be found, with respect to this as to every correct definition, that the instances which seem to conflict with it are those which most confirm it, for if a moralist attempts, as some have done, to make out that mankind generally, though not any given individual, have a right to all the good we can do them, he at once, by that thesis, includes generosity and beneficence within the category of justice. He is obliged to say that our utmost exertions are *due* to our fellow creatures, thus assimilating them to a debt, or that nothing less can be a sufficient *return* for what society does for us, thus classing the case as one of gratitude, both of which are acknowledged cases of justice. Wherever there is a right, the case is one of justice, and not of the virtue of beneficence, and whoever does not place the distinction between justice and morality in general where we have now placed it will be found to make no distinction between them at all, but to merge all morality in justice.

Having thus endeavored to determine the distinctive elements which enter into the composition of the idea of justice, we are ready to enter on the inquiry, whether the feeling which accompanies the idea is attached to it by a special dispensation of nature, or whether it could have grown up by any known laws out of the idea itself, and, in particular, whether it can have originated in considerations of general expediency.

I conceive that the sentiment itself does not arise from anything which would commonly or correctly be termed an idea of expediency, but that, though the sentiment does not, whatever is moral in it does.

We have seen that the two essential ingredients in the sentiment of justice are the desire to punish a person who has done harm, and the knowledge or belief that there is some definite individual or individuals to whom harm has been done.

Now, it appears to me that the desire to punish a person who has done harm to some individual is a spontaneous outgrowth from two sentiments, both in the highest degree natural, and which either are or resemble instincts—the impulse of self-defense, and the feeling of sympathy.

It is natural to resent, and to repel or retaliate, any harm done or attempted against ourselves or against those with whom we sympathize. The origin of this sentiment it is not necessary here to discuss. Whether it be an instinct or a result of intelligence, it is, we know, common to all animal nature, for every animal tries to hurt those who have hurt, or who it thinks are about to hurt, itself or its young. Human beings, on this point, only differ from other animals in two particulars: first, in being capable of sympathizing, not solely with their offspring or, like some of the more noble animals, with some superior animal who is kind to them, but with all human and even with all sentient beings; secondly, in having a more developed intelligence, which gives a wider range to the whole of their sentiments, whether self-regarding or sympathetic. By virtue of his superior intelligence, even apart from his superior range of sympathy, a human being is capable of apprehending a community of interest between himself and the human society of which he forms a part, such that any conduct which threatens the security of the society generally is threatening to his own, and calls forth his instinct (if instinct it be) of self-defense. The same superiority of intelligence, joined to the power of sympathizing with human beings generally, enables him to attach himself to the collective idea of his tribe, his country, or mankind, in such a manner that any act hurtful to them raises his instinct of sympathy, and urges him to resistance.

The sentiment of justice, in that one of its elements which consists of the desire to punish, is thus, I conceive, the natural feeling of retaliation or vengeance, rendered by intellect and sympathy applicable to those injuries—that is, to those hurts —which wound us through, or in common with, society at large. This sentiment in itself has nothing moral in it; what is moral is the exclusive subordination of it to the social sympathies, so as to wait on and obey their call. For the natural feeling would make us resent indiscriminately whatever any one does that is disagreeable to us, but, when moralized by the social feeling, it only acts in the directions conformable to the general good: just persons resenting a hurt to society, though not otherwise a hurt to themselves, and not resenting a hurt to themselves, however painful, unless it be of the kind which society has a common interest with them in the repression of.

It is no objection against this doctrine to say that, when we feel our sentiment of justice outraged, we are not thinking of society at large, or of any collective interest, but only of the individual case. It is common enough, certainly, though the reverse of commendable, to feel resentment merely because we have suffered pain, but a person whose resentment is really a moral feeling—that is, who considers whether an act is blamable before he allows himself to resent it—such a person, though he may not say expressly to himself that he is standing up for the interest of society, certainly does feel that he is asserting a rule which is for the benefit of others as well as for his own. If he is not feeling this, if he is regarding the act solely as it affects him individually—he is not consciously just, he is not concerning himself about the justice of his actions. This is admitted even by anti-utilitarian moralists. When Kant (as before remarked) propounds as the fundamental principle of morals, "So act that thy rule of conduct might be adopted as a law by all rational beings," he virtually acknowledges that the interest of mankind collectively, or at least of mankind indiscriminately, must be in the mind of the agent when conscientiously deciding on the morality of the act. Otherwise he uses words without a meaning, for that a rule even of utter selfishness could not *possibly* be adopted by all rational beings —that there is any insuperable obstacle in the nature of things to its adoption—cannot be even plausibly maintained. To give any meaning to Kant's principle, the sense put upon it must be that we ought to shape our conduct by a rule which all rational beings might adopt *with benefit to their collective interest*.

To recapitulate: the idea of justice supposes two things—a rule of conduct and a sentiment which sanctions the rule. The first must be supposed common to all mankind, and intended for their good; the other (the sentiment) is a desire that punishment may be suffered by those who infringe the rule. There is involved, in addition, the conception of some definite person who suffers by the infringement, whose rights (to use the expression appropriated to the case) are violated by it. And the sentiment of justice appears to me to be the animal desire to repel or retaliate a hurt or damage to one's self or to those with whom one sympathizes, widened so as to include all persons, by the human capacity of enlarged sympathy, and the human conception of intelligent self-interest. From the latter elements, the feeling derives its morality; from the former, its peculiar impressiveness and energy of self-assertion.

I have throughout treated the idea of a *right* residing in the injured person, and violated by the injury, not as a separate element in the composition of the idea and sentiment, but as one of the forms in which the other two elements clothe themselves. These elements are a hurt to some assignable person or persons on the one hand, and a demand for punishment on the other. An examination of our own minds, I think, will show that these two things include all that we mean when we speak of violation of a right. When we call any thing a person's right, we mean that he has a valid claim on society to protect him in the possession of it, either by the force of law, or by that of education and opinion. If he has what we consider a sufficient claim, on whatever account, to have something guaranteed to him by society, we say that he has a right to it. If we desire to prove that anything does not belong to him by right, we think this done as soon as it is admitted that society ought not to take measures for securing it to him, but should leave him to chance or to his own exertions. Thus a person is said to have a right to what he can earn in fair professional competition, because society ought not to allow any other person to hinder him from endeavoring to earn in that manner as much as he can. But he has not a right to three hundred a year, though he may happen to be earning it, because society is not called on to provide that he shall earn that sum. On the contrary, if he owns ten thousand pounds three-per-cent stock, he *has* a right to three hundred a year, because society has come under an obligation to provide him with an income of that amount.

To have a right then is, I conceive, to have something which society ought to defend me in the possession of. If the objector goes on to ask why it ought, I can give him no other reason than general utility. If that expression does not seem to convey a sufficient feeling of the strength of the obligation, nor to account for the peculiar energy of the feeling, it is because there goes to the composition of the sentiment, not a rational only but also an animal element—the thirst for retaliation, and this thirst derives its intensity, as well as its moral justification, from the extraordinarily important and impressive kind of utility which is concerned. The interest involved is that of security, to every one's feelings, the most vital of all interests. All other earthly benefits are needed by one person, not needed by another, and many of them can, if necessary, be cheerfully foregone, or replaced by something else. But security no human being can possibly do without; on it we depend for all our immunity from evil, and for the whole value of all and every good, beyond the passing moment, since nothing but the gratification of the instant could be of any worth to us if we could be deprived of everything the next instant by whoever was momentarily stronger than ourselves. Now, this most indispensable of all necessaries, after physical nutriment, cannot be had, unless the machinery for providing it is kept unintermittedly in active play. Our notion, therefore, of the claim we have on our fellow creatures to join in making safe for us the very groundwork of our existence, gathers feelings around it so much more intense than those concerned in any of the more common cases of utility, that the difference in degree (as is often the case in psychology) becomes a real difference in kind. The claim assumes that character of absoluteness, that apparent infinity and incommensurability with all other considerations, which constitute the distinction between the feeling of right and wrong and that of ordinary expediency and inexpediency. The feelings concerned are so powerful, and we count so positively on finding a responsive feeling in others (all being alike interested), that *ought* and *should* grow into *must*, and recognized indispensability becomes a moral necessity, analogous to physical, and often not inferior to it in binding force.

If the preceding analysis, or something resembling it, be not the correct account of the notion of justice, if justice be totally independent of utility, and be a standard *per se*, which the mind can recognize by simple introspection of itself—it is hard to understand why that internal oracle is so ambiguous, and why so many things appear either just or unjust, according to the light in which they are regarded.

We are continually informed that Utility is an uncertain standard, which every different person interprets differently, and that there is no safety but in the immutable, ineffaceable, and unmistakable dictates of Justice, which carry their evidence in themselves and are independent of the fluctuations of opinion. One would suppose from this that, on questions of justice, there could be no controversy, that, if we take that for our rule, its application to any given case could leave us in as little doubt as a mathematical demonstration. So far is this from being the fact, that there is as much[5] difference of opinion and as much discussion about what is just as about what is useful to society. Not only have different nations and individuals different notions of justice but, in the mind of one and the same individual, justice is not some one rule, principle, or maxim, but many, which do not always coincide in their dictates, and, in choosing between which, he is guided either by some extraneous standard, or by his own personal predilections.

For instance: there are some who say that it is unjust to punish any one for the sake of example to others, that punishment is just, only when intended for the good of the sufferer himself. Others maintain the extreme reverse, contending that to punish persons who have attained years of discretion, for their own benefit, is despotism and injustice, since, if the matter at issue is solely their own good, no one has a right to control their own judgment of it, but that they may justly be punished to prevent evil to others, this being the exercise of the legitimate right of self-defense. Mr. Owen, again, affirms that it is unjust to punish at all, for the criminal did not make his own character; his education, and the circumstances which surrounded him, have made him a criminal, and for these he is not responsible. All these opinions are extremely plausible, and so long as the question is argued as one of justice simply, without going down to the principles which lie under justice, and are the source of its authority, I am unable to see how any of these reasoners can be refuted. For, in truth, every one of the three builds upon rules of justice confessedly true. The first appeals to the acknowledged injustice of singling out an individual, and making him a sacrifice, without his consent, for other people's benefit. The second relies on the acknowledged justice of self-defense, and the admitted injustice of forcing one person to conform to another's notions of what constitutes his good. The Owenite invokes the admitted principle that it is unjust to punish any one for what he cannot help. Each is triumphant so long as he is not compelled to take into consideration any other maxims of justice than the one he has selected but, as soon as their several maxims are brought face to face, each disputant seems to have exactly as much to say for himself as the others. No one of them can carry out his own notion of justice without trampling upon another equally binding. These are difficulties, they have always been felt to be such, and many devices have been invented to turn rather than to overcome them. As a refuge from the last of the three, men imagined what they called the "freedom of the will," fancying that they could not justify punishing a man whose will is in a thoroughly hateful state, unless it be supposed to have come into that state through no influence of anterior circumstances. To escape from the other difficulties, a favorite contrivance has been the fiction of a contract, whereby at some unknown period all the members of society engaged to obey the laws, and consented to be punished for any disobedience to them, thereby giving to their legislators the right, which it is assumed they would not otherwise have had, of punishing them, either for their own good or for that of society. This happy thought was considered to get rid of the whole difficulty, and to legitimate the infliction of punishment, in virtue of another received maxim of justice, *Volenti non fit injuria,* "That is not unjust which is done with the consent of the person who is supposed to be hurt by it." I need hardly remark that, even if the consent were not a mere fiction, this maxim is not superior in authority to the others which it is brought in to supersede. It is, on the contrary, an instructive specimen of the loose and irregular manner in which supposed principles of justice grow up. This particular one evidently came into use as a help to the coarse exigencies of courts of law, which are sometimes obliged to be content with very uncertain presumptions, on account of the greater evils which would often arise from any attempt on their part to cut finer. But even courts of law are not able to adhere consistently to the maxim, for they allow voluntary engagements to be set aside on the ground of fraud, and sometimes on that of mere mistake or misinformation.

Again: when the legitimacy of inflicting punishment is admitted, how many conflicting conceptions of justice come to light in discussing the proper apportionment of punishments to offenses! No rule on the subject recommends itself so strongly to the primitive and spontaneous sentiment of justice, as the *lex talionis,* "An eye for an eye, and a tooth for a tooth." Though this principle of the Jewish and of the Mohammedan law has been generally abandoned in Europe as a practical maxim, there is, I suspect, in most minds, a secret hankering after it and, when retribution accidentally falls on

an offender in that precise shape, the general feeling of satisfaction evinced bears witness how natural is the sentiment to
which this repayment in kind is acceptable. With many, the
test of justice in penal infliction is that the punishment should
be proportioned to the offense—meaning that it should be exactly measured by the moral guilt of the culprit (whatever be
their standard for measuring moral guilt), the consideration,
what amount of punishment is necessary to deter from the offense, having nothing to do with the question of justice, in
their estimation; while there are others to whom that consideration is all in all, who maintain that it is not just, at least
for man, to inflict on a fellow creature, whatever may be his
offenses, any amount of suffering beyond the least that will
suffice to prevent him from repeating, and others from imitat-
ing, his misconduct.

To take another example from a subject already once referred to. In a cooperative industrial association, is it just or
not that talent or skill should give a title to superior remuner-
ation? On the negative side of the question it is argued that
whoever does the best he can deserves equally well, and ought
not in justice to be put in a position of inferiority for no fault
of his own, that superior abilities have already advantages
more than enough, in the admiration they excite, the personal
influence they command, and the internal sources of satisfaction attending them, without adding to these a superior share
of the world's goods, and that society is bound in justice
rather to make compensation to the less favored, for this unmerited inequality of advantages, than to aggravate it. On the
contrary side it is contended that society receives more from
the more efficient laborer, that, his services being more useful,
society owes him a larger return for them, that a greater share
of the joint result is actually his work, and not to allow his
claim to it is a kind of robbery, that, if he is only to receive
as much as others, he can only be justly required to produce
as much, and to give a smaller amount of time and exertion,
proportioned to his superior efficiency. Who shall decide between these appeals to conflicting principles of justice? Justice
has in this case two sides to it, which it is impossible to bring
into harmony, and the two disputants have chosen opposite
sides: the one looks to what it is just that the individual
should receive, the other, to what it is just that the community
should give. Each, from his own point of view, is unanswer-
able, and any choice between them, on grounds of justice,

must be perfectly arbitrary. Social utility alone can decide the preference.

How many, again, and how irreconcilable, are the standards of justice to which reference is made in discussing the repartition of taxation! One opinion is that payment to the State should be in numerical proportion to pecuniary means. Others think that justice dictates what they term "graduated taxation"—taking a higher percentage from those who have more to spare. In point of natural justice, a strong case might be made for disregarding means altogether, and taking the same absolute sum (whenever it could be got) from every one, as the subscribers to a mess, or to a club, all pay the same sum for the same privileges, whether they can all equally afford it or not. Since the protection (it might be said) of law and government is afforded to and is equally required by all, there is no injustice in making all buy it at the same price. It is reckoned justice, not injustice, that a dealer should charge to all customers the same price for the same article, not a price varying according to their means of payment. This doctrine, as applied to taxation, finds no advocates, because it conflicts so strongly with man's feelings of humanity and of social expediency, but the principle of justice which it invokes is as true and as binding as those which can be appealed to against it. Accordingly, it exerts a tacit influence on the line of defense employed for other modes of assessing taxation. People feel obliged to argue that the State does more for the rich than for the poor, as a justification for its taking more from them; though this is in reality not true, for the rich would be far better able to protect themselves, in the absence of law or government, than the poor, and indeed would probably be successful in converting the poor into their slaves. Others, again, so far defer to the same conception of justice as to maintain that all should pay an equal capitation tax for the protection of their persons (these being of equal value to all), and an unequal tax for the protection of their property, which is unequal. To this others reply that the all of one man is as valuable to him as the all of another. From these confusions, there is no other mode of extrication than the utilitarian.

Is, then, the difference between the Just and the Expedient a merely imaginary distinction? Have mankind been under a delusion in thinking that justice is a more sacred thing than policy, and that the latter ought only to be listened to after the former has been satisfied? By no means. The exposition we have given of the nature and origin of the sentiment recognizes a real distinction, and no one of those who profess the most sublime contempt for the consequences of actions as an element in their morality attaches more importance to the distinction than I do. While I dispute the pretensions of any theory which sets up an imaginary standard of justice not grounded on utility, I account the justice which is grounded on utility to be the chief part, and incomparably the most sacred and binding part, of all morality. Justice is a name for certain classes of moral rules which concern the essentials of human well-being more nearly, and are therefore of more absolute obligation, than any other rules for the guidance of life, and the notion which we have found to be of the essence of the idea of justice, that of a right residing in an individual, implies and testifies to this more binding obligation.

The moral rules which forbid mankind to hurt one another (in which we must never forget to include wrongful interference with each other's freedom) are more vital to human well-being than any maxims, however important, which only point out the best mode of managing some department of human affairs. They have also the peculiarity that they are the main element in determining the whole of the social feelings of mankind. It is their observance which alone preserves peace among human beings; if obedience to them were not the rule, and disobedience the exception, every one would see in every one else an enemy, against whom he must be perpetually guarding himself. What is hardly less important, these are the precepts which mankind have the strongest and the most direct inducements for impressing upon one another. By merely giving to each other prudential instruction or exhortation, they may gain, or think they gain, nothing; in inculcating on each other the duty of positive beneficence, they have an unmistakable interest, but far less in degree: a person may possibly not need the benefits of others, but he always needs that they should not do him hurt. Thus the moralities which protect every individual from being harmed by others, either directly or by being hindered in his freedom of pursuing his own good, are at once those which he himself has most at heart, and those which he has the strongest interest in publishing and enforcing by word and deed. It is by a person's observance of these that his fitness to exist as one of the fellowship of human beings is tested and decided, for on that depends his being a nuisance or not to those with whom he is in contact. Now, it is these moralities, primarily, which compose the obligations of justice. The most marked cases of injustice, and those which give the tone to the feeling of repugnance which characterizes the sentiment, are acts of wrongful aggression, or wrongful exercise of power over some one; the next are those which consist in wrongfully withholding from him something which is his due, in both cases inflicting on him a positive hurt, either in the form of direct suffering, or of the privation of some good which he had reasonable ground, either of a physical or of a social kind, for counting upon.

The same powerful motives which command the observance of these primary moralities enjoin the punishment of those who violate them, and as the impulses of self-defense, of defense of others, and of vengeance, are all called forth against such persons, retribution, or evil for evil, becomes closely connected with the sentiment of justice and is universally included in the idea. Good for good is also one of the dictates of justice; and this, though its social utility is evident, and though it carries with it a natural human feeling, has not at first sight that obvious connection with hurt or injury, which, existing in the most elementary cases of just and unjust, is the source of the characteristic intensity of the sentiment. But the connection, though less obvious, is not less real. He who accepts benefits, and denies a return of them when needed, inflicts a real hurt, by disappointing one of the most natural and reasonable of expectations, and one which he must at least tacitly have encouraged, otherwise the benefits would seldom have been conferred. The important rank, among human evils and wrongs, of the disappointment of expectation, is shown in the fact, that it constitutes the principal criminality of two such highly immoral acts as a breach of friendship and a breach of promise. Few hurts which human beings can sustain are greater, and none wound more, than when that on which they habitually and with full assurance relied fails them in the hour of need, and few wrongs are greater than this mere withholding of good; none excite more resentment, either in the person suffering, or in a sympathizing spectator. The principle, therefore, of giving to each what

they deserve—that is, good for good, as well as evil for evil—
is not only included within the idea of Justice as we have defined it, but is a proper object of that intensity of sentiment
which places the Just, in human estimation, above the simply
Expedient.

Most of the maxims of justice current in the world, and
commonly appealed to in its transactions, are simply instrumental to carrying into effect the principles of justice which
we have now spoken of. That a person is only responsible for
what he has done voluntarily, or could voluntarily have
avoided, that it is unjust to condemn any person unheard, that
the punishment ought to be proportioned to the offense, and
the like—are maxims intended to prevent the just principle of
evil for evil from being perverted to the infliction of evil without that justification. The greater part of these common maxims have come into use from the practice of courts of justice,
which have been naturally led to a more complete recognition
and elaboration than was likely to suggest itself to others, of
the rules necessary to enable them to fulfil their double function, of inflicting punishment when due, and of awarding to
each person his right.

That first of judicial virtues, impartiality, is an obligation of
justice, partly for the reason last mentioned, as being a necessary condition of the fulfilment of the other obligations of
justice. But this is not the only source of the exalted rank,
among human obligations, of those maxims of equality and
impartiality, which, both in popular estimation and in that of
the most enlightened, are included among the precepts of justice. In one point of view, they may be considered as corollaries from the principles already laid down. If it is a duty to
do to each according to his deserts, returning good for good
as well as repressing evil by evil, it necessarily follows that we
should treat all equally well (when no higher duty forbids)
who have deserved equally well of *us*, and that society should
treat all equally well who have deserved equally well of *it*—
that is, who have deserved equally well absolutely. This is the
highest abstract standard of social and distributive justice, towards which all institutions, and the efforts of all virtuous
citizens, should be made in the utmost possible degree to con-
verge. But this great moral duty rests upon a still deeper foundation, being a direct emanation from the first principle of
morals, and not a mere logical corollary from secondary or
derivative doctrines. It is involved in the very meaning of Util-

ity, or the Greatest-happiness Principle. That principle is a mere form of words without rational signification, unless one person's happiness, supposed equal in degree (with the proper allowance made for kind), is counted for exactly as much as another's. Those conditions being supplied, Bentham's dictum, "Everybody to count for one, nobody for more than one," might be written under the principle of utility as an explanatory commentary.* The equal claim of everybody to happi-

* This implication, in the first principle of the utilitarian scheme, of perfect impartiality between persons is regarded by Mr. Herbert Spencer (in his *Social Statics*) as a disproof of the pretensions of utility to be a sufficient guide to right, since (he says) the principle of utility presupposes the anterior principle, that everybody has an equal right to happiness. It may be more correctly described as supposing that equal amounts of happiness are equally desirable, whether felt by the same or by different persons. This, however, is not a *pre*-supposition, not a premise needful to support the principle of utility, but the very principle itself; for what is the principle of utility, if it be not that "happiness" and "desirable" are synonymous terms? If there is any anterior principle implied, it can be no other than this—that the truths of arithmetic are applicable to the valuation of happiness, as of all other measurable quantities.
[Mr. Herbert Spencer, in a private communication on the subject of the preceding note, objects to being considered an opponent of Utilitarianism, and states that he regards happiness as the ultimate end of morality, but deems that end only partially attainable by empirical generalizations from the observed results of conduct, and completely attainable only by deducing, from the laws of life and the conditions of existence, what kinds of action necessarily tend to produce happiness, and what kinds to produce unhappiness. With the exception of the word "necessarily," I have no dissent to express from this doctrine, and (omitting that word) I am not aware that any modern advocate of Utilitarianism is of a different opinion. Bentham certainly, to whom, in the *Social Statics*, Mr. Spencer particularly referred, is, least of all writers, chargeable with unwillingness to deduce the effect of actions on happiness from the laws of human nature and the universal conditions of human life. The common charge against him is of relying too exclusively upon such deductions, and declining altogether to be bound by the generalizations from specific experience which Mr. Spencer thinks that utilitarians generally confine themselves to. My own opinion (and, as I collect, Mr. Spencer's) is, that in ethics, as in all other branches of scientific study, the consilience of the results of both these processes, each corroborating and verifying the other, is requisite to give to any general proposition the kind and degree of evidence which constitutes scientific proof.][6]

ness, in the estimation of the moralist and the legislator, involves an equal claim to all the means of happiness, except in so far as the inevitable conditions of human life, and the general interest, in which that of every individual is included, set limits to the maxim, and those limits ought to be strictly construed. As every other maxim of justice, so this, is by no means applied or held applicable universally; on the contrary, as I have already remarked, it bends to every person's ideas of social expediency. But, in whatever case it is deemed applicable at all, it is held to be the dictate of justice. All persons are deemed to have a *right* to equality of treatment, except when some recognized social expediency requires the reverse. And hence all social inequalities, which have ceased to be considered expedient, assume the character, not of simple inexpediency but of injustice, and appear so tyrannical that people are apt to wonder how they ever could have been tolerated, forgetful that they themselves perhaps tolerate other inequalities under an equally mistaken notion of expediency, the correction of which would make that which they approve seem quite as monstrous as what they have at last learnt to condemn. The entire history of social improvement has been a series of transitions, by which one custom or institution after another, from being a supposed primary necessity of social existence, has passed into the rank of an universally stigmatized injustice and tyranny. So it has been with the distinctions of slaves and freemen, nobles and serfs, patricians and plebeians, and so it will be, and in part already is, with the aristocracies of color, race, and sex.

It appears, from what has been said, that justice is a name for certain moral requirements which, regarded collectively, stand higher in the scale of social utility, and are therefore of more paramount obligation, than any others, though particular cases may occur in which some other social duty is so important as to overrule any one of the general maxims of justice. Thus, to save a life, it may not only be allowable, but a duty, to steal, or take by force, the necessary food or medicine, or to kidnap and compel to officiate, the only qualified medical practitioner. In such cases, as we do not call any thing justice which is not a virtue, we usually say, not that justice must give way to some other moral principle, but that what is just in ordinary cases is, by reason of that other principle, not just in the particular case. By this useful accommodation of language, the character of indefeasibility attributed to justice is kept up, and we are saved from the necessity of maintaining that there can be laudable injustice.

The considerations which have now been adduced, resolve, I conceive, the only real difficulty in the utilitarian theory of morals. It has always been evident that all cases of justice are also cases of expediency; the difference is in the peculiar sentiment which attaches to the former, as contradistinguished from the latter. If this characteristic sentiment has been sufficiently accounted for, if there is no necessity to assume for it any peculiarity of origin, if it is simply the natural feeling of resentment, moralized by being made coextensive with the demands of social good, and if this feeling not only does but ought to exist in all the classes of cases to which the idea of justice corresponds—that idea no longer presents itself as a stumbling-block to the utilitarian ethics. Justice remains the appropriate name for certain social utilities which are vastly more important, and therefore more absolute and imperative, than any others are as a class (though not more so than others may be in particular cases), and which therefore ought to be, as well as naturally are, guarded by a sentiment not only different in degree, but also in kind, distinguished from the milder feeling which attaches to the mere idea of promoting human pleasure or convenience, at once by the more definite nature of its commands, and by the sterner character of its sanctions.

N O T E S

1. The following footnote was added by Mill in the second edition:

An opponent, whose intellectual and moral fairness it is a pleasure to acknowledge (the Rev. J. Llewellyn Davies), has objected to this passage, saying, "Surely the rightness or wrongness of saving a man from drowning does depend very much upon the motive with which it is done. Suppose that a tyrant, when his enemy jumped into the sea to escape from him, saved him from drowning simply in order that he might inflict upon him more exquisite tortures, would it tend to clearness to speak of that rescue as 'a morally right action'? Or suppose again, according to one of the stock illustrations of ethical inquiries, that a man betrayed a trust received from a friend, because the discharge of it would fatally injure that friend himself or someone belonging to him, would Utilitarianism compel one to call the betrayal 'a crime' as much as if it had been done from the meanest motive?"

I submit that he who saves another from drowning in order to kill him by torture afterwards does not differ only in motive from him who does the same thing from duty or benevolence; the act itself is different. The rescue of the man is, in the case supposed, only the necessary first step of an act far more atrocious than leaving him to drown would have been. Had Mr. Davies said, "The rightness or wrongness of saving a man from drowning does depend very much"—not upon the motive, but—"upon the *intention*," no utilitarian would have differed from him. Mr. Davies, by an oversight too common not to be quite venial, has in this case confounded the very different ideas of Motive and Intention. There is no point which utilitarian thinkers (and Bentham preeminently) have taken more pains to illustrate than this. The morality of the action depends entirely upon the intention—that is, upon what the agent *wills to do*. But the motive, that is, the feeling which makes him will so to do, if it makes no difference in the act, makes none in the morality; though it makes a great difference in our moral estimation of the agent, especially if it indicates a good or a bad habitual *disposition*—a bent of character from which useful, or from which hurtful actions are likely to arise.

2. In a letter written in 1868 to an unidentified correspondent, and published in the second volume of *Letters* (ed. Elliot), Mill said:

"As to the sentence you quote from my *Utilitarianism*: when I said that the general happiness is a good to the aggregate of all persons I did not mean that every human being's happiness is a good to every other human being, though I think in a good state of society and education it would be so. I merely meant in this particular sentence to argue that since A's happiness is a good, B's a good, C's a good, etc., the sum of all these goods must be a good."

3. In the second and later editions, "wants" is changed to "needs."

4. In the second and later editions, the passage enclosed in brackets reads as follows:

In most if not in all languages, the etymology of the word which corresponds to "just" points distinctly to an origin connected either with positive law, or with that which was in most cases the primitive form of law—authoritative custom. *Justum* is a form of *jussum*, that which has been ordered. *Jus* is of the same origin. Δίκαιον comes from δίκη, of which the principal meaning, at least in the historical ages of Greece, was a suit at law. Originally, indeed, it meant only the mode or *manner* of doing things, but it early came to mean the *prescribed* manner, that which the recognized authorities, patriarchal, judicial, or political, would enforce. *Recht*, from which came *right* and *righteous*, is synonymous with law. The original meaning indeed of *recht* did not point to law, but to physical straightness, as *wrong* and its Latin equivalents meant twisted or *tortuous*; and from this it is argued that right did not originally mean law, but on the contrary law meant right. But however this may be, the fact that *recht* and *droit* became restricted in their meaning to positive law, although much which is not required by law is equally necessary to moral straightness or rectitude, is as significant of the original character of moral ideas as if the derivation had been the reverse way.

5. In the second and later editions "much" is changed to "fierce."

6. The section of this note enclosed in brackets was added by Mill after the first publication of the chapter.

THIRTEEN

Mill's Journal: Excerpts

[In 1854 Mill, who was quite ill, kept a daily journal for a few months. The entries are usually quite brief. They touch on many topics on which he was later to write as well as on problems on which he had already written. The Journal was published in the second volume of the *Letters of J. S. Mill*, edited by H. S. R. Elliot, London, 1910, from which the present selections are taken.]

JANUARY 20

Is IT TRUE, as Carlyle says, that nobody ever did a good thing by reason of his bad qualities, but always and necessarily in spite of them? Surely this can only be made true by an arbitrary limitation of the term "good" to *morally* good, which reduces the brilliantly sounding assertion to a mere identical proposition. Useful and even permanently valuable things are continually done from vanity, or a selfish desire of riches or power; sometimes even from envy or jealousy, and the desire to lower others. What is true is that such good things would almost always have been *better* done, and would have produced greatly more good, if they had been done from a more virtuous motive.

JANUARY 22

In this age a far better ideal of human society can be formed, and by some persons both here and in France has been formed, than at any former time. But to discern the road to it—the series of transitions by which it must be reached, and what can be done, either under existing institutions or by a wise modification of them, to bring it nearer—is a problem no nearer being resolved than formerly. The only means of which the efficacy and the necessity are evident, is universal Education; and who will educate the educators?

JANUARY 23

There is no doctrine really worth laboring at, either to construct or to inculcate, except the Philosophy of Life. A

Philosophy of Life, in harmony with the noblest feelings and cleared of superstition, is the great want of these times. There has always been talent enough in the world when there was earnestness enough, and always earnestness enough when there were strong convictions. There seems to be so little talent now, only because there is universal uncertainty about the great questions, and the field for talent is narrowed to things of subaltern interest. Ages of belief, as Goethe says, have been the only ages in which great things have been done. Ages of belief have hitherto always been religious ages, but Goethe did not mean that they must necessarily be so in future. Religion of one sort or another has been at once the spring and the regulator of energetic actions, chiefly because religion has hitherto supplied the only Philosophy of Life, or the only one which differed from a mere theory of self-indulgence. Let it be generally known what life is and might be, and how to make it what it might be, and there will be as much enthusiasm and as much energy as there has ever been.

FEBRUARY 22

Carlyle is abundantly contemptuous of all who make their intellects bow to their moral timidity by endeavoring to believe Christianity. But his own creed—that everything is right and good which accords with the laws of the universe— is either the same or a worse perversion. If it is not a resignation of intellect into the hands of fear, it is the subornation of it by a bribe—the bribe of being on the side of Power—irresistible and eternal Power.

FEBRUARY 27

The doctrines of free will and of necessity rightly understood are both true. It is necessary, that is, it was inevitable from the beginning of things, that I should freely will whatever things I do will.

MARCH 2

It is a common saying that the only true test of a person's character is actions. There is much error in this. Actions, even habitual ones, are as fallacious a test of character as any other. A person's actions are often an indication not so much of what the person is as of what he desires to be thought or, in the case of a better sort of persons, of what he desires to think himself. Actions, no doubt, are the fittest test for the world at large, because all they want to know of a man is the actions they may expect from him. But to his intimates, who care about what he is and not merely what he does, the involuntary indications of feeling and disposition are a much surer criterion of them than voluntary acts.

MARCH 23

The only true or definite rule of conduct or standard of morality is the greatest happiness, but there is needed first a philosophical estimate of happiness. Quality as well as quantity of happiness is to be considered; less of a higher kind is preferable to more of a lower. The test of quality is the preference given by those who are acquainted with both. Socrates would rather choose to be Socrates dissatisfied than to be a pig satisfied. The pig probably would not, but then the pig knows only one side of the question; Socrates knows both.

APRIL 8

Moral regenerators in this age mostly aim at setting up a new form either of Stoicism or of Puritanism—persuading men to sink altogether earthly happiness as a pursuit. This might be practicable in the ages in which myriads fled to the Thebaid to get into any solitude out of such a world, but must be a failure now when an earthly life both pleasant and innocent can be had by many and might by all. What is wanted now is the creed of Epicurus warmed by the additional element of an enthusiastic love of the general good.

APRIL 9

All systems of morals agree in prescribing to do that, and only that, which accords with self-respect. The difference between one person and another is mainly in that with which their self-respect is associated. In some it is with worldly or selfish success. In others, with the supposed favor of the supernal powers. In others, with the indulgence of mere self-will. In others, with self-conceit. In the best, with the sympathy of those they respect and a just regard for the good of all.

APRIL 15

The remedies for all our diseases will be discovered long after we are dead; and the world will be made a fit place to live in, after the death of most of those by whose exertions it will have been made so. It is to be hoped that those who live in those days will look back with sympathy to their known and unknown benefactors.

Bibliography

I

WORKS.   There is no complete edition of Mill's writings, but the University of Toronto Press has announced plans to publish the Collected Works, in approximately thirteen volumes. Their edition will present previously unpublished material, collect hitherto uncollected reviews, essays, and letters to newspapers, and give adequate scholarly attention to the texts of Mill's writings.

The most nearly complete bibliography of Mill's work is the one Mill himself kept. It has been published under the editorship of Ney MacMinn, J.R. Hainds, and James McNab, as *Bibliography of the published writings of John Stuart Mill*, Northwestern University Studies in the Humanities, No. 12, 1945.

The following list of Mill's works does not contain his shorter essays, and of his pamphlets only those of general interest are included.

The Rationale of Judicial Evidence. From the MSS. of Jeremy Bentham. Edited, with a Preface, by J. Stuart Mill. 5 vols., London, 1827.

A System of Logic. 2 vols., London, 1843. (The definitive edition is the 8th, published in 1872.)

Essays on Some Unsettled Questions of Political Economy. London, 1844. (These essays were written in 1830–1831.)

Principles of Political Economy. 2 vols., London, 1848. (The last edition Mill revised is the 7th, 1871. The edition produced by Sir W. J. Ashley, London, 1909, has an Introduction and contains many of the variant readings from the earlier editions.)

On Liberty. London, 1859. (This has been reprinted many times. In *Prefaces to Liberty*, Boston, 1959, Bernard Wishy has collected a number of Mill's newspaper articles and letters which touch on the themes dealt with in *On Liberty*. The edition published by R. B. McCallum, Oxford, 1946, has a long introduction.)

Thoughts on Parliamentary Reform. London, 1859.

Dissertations and Discussions. 2 vols., London, 1859. 3 vols., 1867. 4 vols., 1875.

Considerations on Representative Government. London, 1861.

Utilitarianism. Reprinted from *Fraser's Magazine*, Oct.–Dec. 1861. London, 1863. 2nd ed., 1864.

An Examination of Sir William Hamilton's Philosophy. London,

1865. (In subsequent editions Mill replied to critics, mostly in footnotes. There was a 4th edition, 1872, corrected by Mill.)

Auguste Comte and Positivism. Reprinted from the *Westminster Review*, April and July, 1865. London, 1865. (There were later, slightly revised, editions.)

Inaugural Address to the University of St. Andrews. Feb. 1, 1867. London, 1867.

Speech on the Admission of Women to the Electoral Franchise. May 20, 1867. London, 1867.

Analysis of the Phenomena of the Human Mind, by James Mill. Edited, with additional notes, by John Stuart Mill. 2 vols., London, 1869.

The Subjection of Women. London, 1869. (This was written in 1861.)

Autobiography. Ed. Helen Taylor. London, 1873. (The version published by John Jacob Coss, New York, 1924, is more complete. It has been reprinted with an introduction by Currin V. Shields, New York, 1957. The first draft has been published as *The Early Draft of John Stuart Mill's Autobiography,* ed. J. Stillinger, Urbana, 1961.)

Three Essays on Religion: Nature, The Utility of Religion, and Theism. London, 1874.

Chapters on Socialism. Reprinted from the *Fortnightly Review,* 1879, under the title *Socialism,* and including selections from his other works. Edited by W. D. P. Bliss. New York, 1891.

(An essay entitled "On Social Freedom" and attributed to Mill has been edited by Dorothy Fosdick and published by the Columbia University Press, 1941. But it has been quite convincingly argued by J. C. Rees that this essay is *not* by Mill. See Rees's *Mill and His Early Critics,* Leicester, 1956. On this subject see also H. D. Aiken's essay "Utilitarianism and Liberty: John Stuart Mill's Defense of Freedom," reprinted in his *Reason and Conduct,* New York, 1962.)

I I

LIFE AND LETTERS.   Alexander Bain—himself a distinguished psychologist and philosopher, and a friend of Mill's—wrote a critical biography, *John Stuart Mill,* London, 1882, which is charming and valuable; W. L. Courtney's *Life of John Stuart Mill,* London, 1889, is still useful; but the standard biography is now M. St.J. Packe, *The Life of John Stuart Mill,* London, 1954, which is very good in spite of the weakness of the author's philosophical comments.

There is no collection of Mill's letters which even begins to approach completeness. The University of Toronto Press plans the production of several volumes of letters as part of its edition of Mill's *Works*. F. E. Mineka's two-volume edition of *Earlier Letters*, covering the period up to 1848, has now been published. But until the remainder appear the reader must consult numerous biographies, collections, and periodicals. Most of these are listed in the bibliography in Packe's *Life*. The largest single collection is, of course, the *Letters of John Stuart Mill*, ed. H. S. R. Elliot, 2 vols., London, 1910; the letters contained in *John Stuart Mill and Harriet Taylor*, London, ed. F. A. Hayek, give far more information about Mill's personal life than do the letters in Elliot's volumes. For the best argued discussion of the relations between Mill and Mrs. Taylor, H. O. Pappe's recent study, *J. S. Mill and the Harriet Taylor Myth*, Melbourne, 1960, should be consulted.

I I I

GENERAL BACKGROUND.   For the history of Mill's times, Elie Halévy's great *History of the English People in the 19th Century*, 6 vols., 2nd (rev.) ed., London, 1949–52, or, more briefly, E. L. Woodward, *The Age of Reform*, Oxford, 1938, may be consulted.

Elie Halévy's *The Growth of Philosophic Radicalism*, London, 1928, is a basic study of the development of the political and economic doctrines of the Benthamites and of their philosophical views. Similar topics are covered in the first two volumes of Sir Leslie Stephen's *The English Utilitarians*, London, 1900, which deal with Bentham and James Mill; Stephen's third volume is a valuable study of J. S. Mill's life and work. E. Albee, *The History of English Utilitarianism*, traces the history of the type of ethical doctrine that Mill espoused, and relates Mill to the tradition. J. P. Plamenatz does this also, but in a much more critical manner, in a long Introduction to his edition of *Utilitarianism*, published as *The English Utilitarians*, Oxford, 1949. Mill is discussed in numerous histories of philosophy, of which one of the best is J. A. Passmore, *100 Years of Philosophy*, London, 1957.

I V

STUDIES OF MILL'S PHILOSOPHY.   The literature on Mill is quite large. The third volume of Sir Leslie Stephen's *English Utilitarians*, already mentioned; W. L. Courtney, *The Metaphysics of J. S. Mill*, London, 1879, and two studies by Charles Douglas—*J. S. Mill, A Study of His Philosophy*, Edinburgh, 1895, and *The Ethics of J. S. Mill*, Edinburgh, 1897—are among the best of the older books. More recent studies include those of R. P. Anschutz, *The*

Philosophy of J. S. Mill, Oxford, 1953, and Karl Britton, *John Stuart Mill*, London, 1953, which survey Mill's work in general. Iris W. Mueller in *John Stuart Mill and French Thought*, Urbana, 1956, gives an exhaustive analysis of French influences on Mill.

V

SPECIAL DISCUSSION OF MILL'S ETHICS.   The literature on Utilitarianism is enormous, and Mill figures largely in it. Some Victorian critics may be noted. John Grote's *Examination of the Utilitarian Philosophy*, Cambridge, 1870, is a tough-minded and difficult criticism, well worth study. The third chapter of F. H. Bradley's *Ethical Studies*, Oxford, 1876, is a famous and brilliantly written polemic. Sir James Fitz-James Stephen (older brother of Sir Leslie Stephen) delivered a virulent attack on Mill's views concerning liberty in *Liberty, Equality, Fraternity*, London, 1873. And W. S. Jevons, the logician, attacked Mill's ethics as well as his logic in a series of papers reprinted in *Pure Logic and Other Minor Works*, London, 1890. Charles Dickens's novel, *Hard Times*, attacks a version of Utilitarianism and is of considerable interest as a social document, though its connection with Mill's actual views is most unclear.

For an understanding of recent criticism of Mill, the work of G. E. Moore must be studied, especially *Principia Ethica*, Cambridge, 1903, chs. I and III. Moore's criticisms of Mill have been one of the most popular topics of discussion in the last fifteen years. I list some, but not all, of the articles published on this and closely related topics.

Atkinson, R. F. "J. S. Mill's 'Proof' of the Principle of Utility," *Philosophy*, Vol. XXXII, 1957.

Burns, J. H. "Utilitarianism and Democracy," *Philosophical Quarterly*, Vol. IX, 1959. (Comment on Kretzmann, see below).

Hall, E. W. "The 'Proof' of Utility in Bentham and Mill," *Ethics*, Vol. IX, 1949.

Kretzmann, N. "Desire as Proof of Desirability," *Philosophical Quarterly*, Vol. VIII, 1958.

Mabbott, J. D. "Interpretations of Mill's *Utilitarianism*," *Philosophical Quarterly*, Vol. VI, 1956.

McNeilly, F. S. "Pre-moral Appraisals," *Philosophical Quarterly*, Vol. VIII, 1958.

Raphael, D. D. "Fallacies in and about Mill's Utilitarianism," *Philosophy*, Vol. XXX, 1955.

Urmson, J. O. "Interpretation of the Moral Philosophy of J. S. Mill," *Philosophical Quarterly*, Vol. III, 1953.

The reader may also wish to consult J. Seth, "Alleged Fallacies in Mill's Utilitarianism," in the *Philosophical Review*, Vol. XVII, 1908, and M. Warnock, *Ethics Since 1900*, London, 1960, pp. 28–35.

The place of what Mill called "secondary principles" or "secondary rules" in moral reasoning has been the subject of much recent discussion, and some attention to this discussion is necessary for an adequate assessment of Mill's views. The most important article here is J. B. Rawls, "Two Concepts of Rules," *Philosophical Review*, Vol. LXIV, 1955, and the following discussions bear on the issues Rawls brings up and on connected topics.

Brandt, R. B. *Ethical Theory*, Englewood Cliffs, 1959, ch. 15.

Brown, S. M. Jr., "Utilitarianism and Moral Obligation," *Philosophical Review*, Vol. LXI, 1952.

Duncan-Jones, A. E. "Utilitarianism and Rules," *Philosophical Quarterly*, Vol. VII, 1957.

Harrod, R. "Utilitarianism Revised," *Mind*, Vol. LXV, 1936.

McCloskey, J. H. "Restricted Utilitarianism," *Philosophical Review*, Vol. LXVI, 1957.

Melden, A. I. "Two Comments on Utilitarianism," *Philosophical Review*, Vol. LX, 1950.

Smart, J. J. C., "Extreme and Restricted Utilitarianism," *Philosophical Quarterly*, Vol. VI, 1956.

Among a host of articles relevant to Mill's position, the following may be noted:

Britton, K. "Utilitarianism: The Appeal to a First Principle," *Proceedings of the Aristotelian Society*, New Series, Vol. LX, London, 1960.

Burns, J. H. "J. S. Mill and Democracy," *Political Studies*, Vol. V, 1957.

Harrison, J. "Utilitarianism, Universalisation, and our Duty to be Just," *Proceedings of the Aristotelian Society*, New Series, Vol. LIII, 1953.

Penelhum, T. "The Logic of Pleasure," *Philosophy and Phenomenological Research*, Vol. XVII, 1956–57.

Ryle, G. and Gallie, W. B., "Pleasure," a symposium published in the *Proceedings of the Aristotelian Society, Supplementary Volume XXVIII*, 1954.

Viner, J. "Bentham and J. S. Mill: The Utilitarian Background," in *The Long View and the Short*, Glencoe, Ill., 1953.